Anthony Hopkins

By the same author

Non-fiction
Sean Connery
Richard Harris
Julie Christie

Fiction
Lovers and Dancers
Did You Miss Me?
Best Irish Short Stories 2 (ed David Marcus)

Poetry
Fifty Fingers

For Children
Jockey School

Anthony Hopkins

A THREE ACT LIFE

Michael Feeney Callan

ROBSON BOOKS

This edition first published in Great Britain in 2005 by Robson Books,
The Chrysalis Building, Bramley Road, London, W10 6SP

An imprint of **Chrysalis** Books Group plc

British Library Cataloguing in Publication Data
A catalogue record for this title is available from the British Library.

ISBN 1 86105 761 X

Typeset by SX Composing DTP, Rayleigh, Essex
Printed in Great Britain by Creative Print & Design (Wales) Ebbw Vale

To Paris Callan,
whose creativity, strength and love
guided this book,
for always

CONTENTS

THE MYTHIC WAY:
INTRODUCTION

This is an independent biography meaning that it is neither official, co-authored or compromised in any way. I feel the need to state this at the outset, because experience in the writing of other biographies has cautioned me both to the partisan viewpoint and to the kind of generalities of definition that allow inattentive reviewers to denigrate sources or substance. The initial text at the heart of this work was published in 1993, to mark Hopkins' knighthood and the endorsement, if such is the fair summation, of 'Oscarhood' for his performance in *The Silence of the Lambs*. Then, I stated clearly the position: that Hopkins himself had been pretty much absent from the making of the book, other than by facilitating my acquisition of research material. I opined then, with consideration, that in this case I believed the arm's length approach was best. I'd read Hopkins' authorised biography, written by Quentin Falk, which was most significant for its omissions: the deal struck with Falk in the late eighties permitted no analysis of his first marriage to Petronella Barker, an actress he met in Wales and grew close to during their contract period at the National Theatre, and who shared with him the storm of his early alcoholism. It also restricted analysis of the alcoholism itself, I believe, in a subtle censorship (though Hopkins is on record admitting to fifteen years of alcohol abuse, Falk's book offered a bald graph of that illness and a one-page reference to Alcoholics Anonymous in the index).

My feeling then, as now, was that meaningful biography required disciplines that might not always be achieved by formal access to, or involvement with, the subject. In 1993, I spoke sceptically about the concept of 'authorisation'. Today, in a celebrity-obsessed culture where Everyman rushes to the imagined bliss of communal approbation in every dodgy enterprise from reality television to desktop publishing, the stamp of authorisation is soma to the media arbiters, an apparent seal of quality, like pedigree papers for a dog, that suggests the owner – the author – carries the one true bloodline. This, of course, is assumptive drivel. Unquestionably the biographical subject, or the allied authorised author, has access to the lowdown. But will he honestly and honourably utilise it, and, even if he does, will he, or they, deploy the objectivity to extrapolate the useful in the interests of illuminating work? Strict auto-biography, we acknowledge, inherently mandates the writer to hedge and exonerate. Noble character, of course, transcends. The paragon works, like the autobiographies of Bertrand Russell (where he admits to failings in love because of his dental pyorrhea) or H. G. Wells (where he confesses to what amounts to sex addiction in his seventies), are rare meat. More typical is revisionism, the whitewash or – worse – the kind of effusive self-aggrandisement most commonly seen in works by, or about, the professional mask-wearers of society, like politicians – or actors.

My interest in Hopkins' life – my way in – was always his work. What won me at the start were the dichotomies. As a young author, script editing for the BBC and writing my own plays, I was immensely impressed by Hopkins' gift. His short-of-breath performance as Pierre Bezuhov in John Davies' momentous BBC production of *War and Peace* was some kind of personal artistic epiphany. But then he spun, and before I knew it he was 'Hollywoodised' in Alistair Maclean pap (*When Eight Bells Toll*) and he was Hannibal Lecter. The chasm between types, so profound was it, intrigued me. I had written a book about Sean Connery, the first truly international British film star since Cary Grant, and one about Richard Harris, a compatriot and friend, whom I'd known for ten years and enjoyed for reasons beyond his film stardom. But I had no great desire to write about Hopkins. Bit by bit, though, the dynamism of those contradictions got me. It was the late Susan Hill, the visionary editor responsible for the *Live Aid* book and for moulding Bob Geldof's autobiography, who pushed me. She, along with publisher William Armstrong, believed I could 'crack' Hopkins – and that he was worth cracking. 'There's more than an actor's story here,' Hill would say. 'His *darkness* suggests so much more.' She was doubtless referring to the extensive media about Hopkins' 'demons' – the alcoholic mania that drove him out of the National Theatre in mid-season, crippled his success on Broadway and distorted his early work in international film. I became involved bit by bit. Over many months during the early nineties I read all the print features and transcripts of the TV interviews where Hopkins explained his work and diagnosed his troubles. Absorbed, I then spoke with people who knew him and worked with him and listened to their interpretations. What immediately presented itself from this nursery research was, as Susan Hill predicted, an astonishingly tangled skein. Every preconception assumed – mostly based on Hopkins' own accounts – was dispelled. The friendless childhood turned up many friends; the chronic apathy about living transformed into intense teen-age passions; the rampant adult indulgences uncovered paralysing insecurities. More than anything, what impacted was the abiding mystery, amplified at every turn by so many people close to him who alluded to the bigger picture. 'You could learn much about modern acting paradigms and modern cultural choices from him,' said David Scase, one of his important theatrical mentors, 'if only he would step out of his own shadow.' And, of course, by 'shadow' Scase meant not just his onion-layered nature, but the cast-iron casing that comes with celebrity.

The great James R. Mellow, chronicler of Emerson and Hemingway, wrote that biography at its best is 'a study of the whole man in the context of the time'. As I studied Hopkins' work, I became fascinated by Michael Medved's *Hollywood Vs America*, a cultural polemic that argued the issue of entertainment's influence on social values. Among its cogent arguments was the declaration that heroism in films has changed, and the days of the clean-cut, Audie Murphy-style role-modelling are over. 'Ever since the Joker walked off with a movie called *Batman*,' wrote Medved, 'evil, not love, is what the movies are all about.' As a consequence of changing entertainment ethos, implied Medved, the world has become a more parlous place. Not long before Medved's book hit the shelves, Hopkins' career peaked with his portrayal of seductive evil in *Silence of the Lambs*. Not long after that, the appallingly sadistic murder of a British child, Jamie Bulger, by other children allegedly influenced by the horror movie, *Child's Play*, sparked a media frenzy of speculative analysis. In the press Hopkins avoided head-on debate about the contributory factors of modern cinema in social pathology, but he was quick to distance himself from Hannibal Lecter. In showbiz columns he was now nicknamed 'Hannibal' as often as Connery was 007, and the kind of hysteria that today pursues J. K. Rowling for the next Harry Potter was foisted on *Silence* author Thomas Harris. When would Harris deliver his contracted follow-up to *Silence*, and would Hopkins and Jodie Foster, the original stars, sign on again? Foster stayed mum but Hopkins went on record to say he'd had enough: 'There are such terrifying films coming out that I think it might be time to say "enough is enough". As an actor, I do have some responsibility.' In *The Times*, Simon Jenkins castigated Hopkins: 'Sir Anthony has just discovered that some Cardiff children had actually seen his appalling film, and he himself is appalled. What world does he inhabit? I take it he is unconcerned at the impact the film might have on adults. What is naïve, some would say dangerously so, about filmmakers, is their double standards . . .'

But, if anything, Hopkins was expressing a single-standard, con-scientious morality. His first wife, Peta Barker, in conversation with me, expressed her undiminished admiration for his uniqueness. During their days together, she insisted, he had 'no true grasp of his own extraordinary powers'. While he was 'bedevilled' by the neuroses that drove him to drink and unleash his demons, he could never achieve orientation. In her view, ultimate self-acceptance allowed Hopkins to harness his dark side and produce work of genius. For all to see, Hopkins adventured into every area and style of acting – from Elizabethan classics to pulp TV – before Hannibal Lecter delivered him to superstardom, the Oscar and the knighthood. Such a summary might seem too facile, but it is as unavoidable for the audience as it probably was for Hopkins: out of his personal anguish came the resource to project madness on screen, and the truth of that madness won out. Realising the power in his keep – the enduring intensity of his demons – Hopkins stepped back from himself.

Or such was the situation when I embarked on the first version of this book. In my conclusions, then, I expressed pleasure in Hopkins' choice to reject Hannibal Lecter: I, too, believe in responsibility and culpability, as much in art as elsewhere. Pyro-technics, for me, are taking cinema into a dead-end as chasmic as Dadaism. Today, acting seems secondary, the province now of second league or 'independent' cinema, and too often detached from real human experience. We need to go back, it seems, to go forwards; we need to reverse past the boundaries of computer graphics to rediscover the great experiments of American Method, or the Theatre of the Angry Young Man, or the Hawksian folk heroes of the forties. We need to look upon the world as something other than a place of polarised extremes where cartoons prevail.

Studying Anthony Hopkins, in my original book, became a psycho-analytical detective story. Hannibal Lecter, in my view, was an important creation – an 'extreme', yes, but never a cartoon, and unquestionably powered by some extraordinary authenticity. To understand his resonance one had to understand Hopkins and, I learnt, in an unavoidably fused logic, one could only really understand Hopkins by examining his choices. A recently published study of autism suggests that Michelangelo suffered from Asperger's Syndrome, a mild form of the malady distinguished by sharply repetitive behaviour patterns. The conclusions were drawn largely from a study of the artist's *oeuvre*; it is unlikely that such a deduction, credible and important as it may be in our understanding of human creativity, could have been drawn from a formal social biography. I, too, took this viewpoint, and set out to uncover the source of Hopkins' inspiration – his darkness and his drive – through the pathways of his work.

When I 'found' Hopkins, I felt the exhilaration a therapist must feel when he has breached the emotional firewall. With the help of so many who knew him well, I learnt the deep background of his motivations in choosing roles and tackling certain subjects and directors. I learnt of great personal violations that downed his spirit and distorted him, and against which he heroically fought for redemptive balance. I saw what, I believe, he himself finally saw in the dark self he christened 'His Majesty the Monstrous Baby', and I saw why he turned away from that sinister outflow for the higher ground.

And so I published my book, with the serene belief that I had explained the actor's incubation and the personal crisis that fuelled his achievements. But I neglected to take into account the great dilemma of contemporary analysis. Individuation, the personality integration the Jungian aspires to, requires the admission of the dark side. Such analysis offers not cure, but resolution. But the resolution beggars the big question: armed with the resolve, what does the subject do next?

In the first version of this book I wrote about the stubbornness of Hopkins' contradictions:

> The stagecraft, the voice quality, the genius for mimicry, the mystical presence, the popular appeal . . . and yet every triumph, cliché as it sounds, throws a shadow. For Hopkins, no moment seemed true enough, no peak high enough. All his friends, co-workers, actors and directors, from his first days at the YMCA in Port Talbot to his Hollywood heyday, speak of him as 'an actor of instinct'. Yet, even out of alcoholism, his best instincts were frequently counter-balanced by major professional misjudgements: *Victory at Entebbe, A Change of Seasons, Hollywood Wives* . . . effusions of vapid nonsense every bit as careless as the trash for which he privately castigated lesser actors. What was this self-checking mechanism that operated too in his private life, unbalancing him at moments of great domestic peace, precipitating crisis after crisis? . . .

Sure enough, despite his initial rejection of a reprised Hannibal Lecter, despite the remedial speculations of my book, within a few years Hopkins was back into darkness, divesting himself of all promises and contracts, abandoning his seemingly perfect second marriage, rescinding his UK citizenship to become a fully fledged resident American – resuming even Hannibal Lecter.

It was tempting, for a moment, to give up on him: to call him another 'sell-out' who traded ethics for lucre. And, certainly judging by the simple criteria of returns, the trade-off worked: the two Hannibal Lecter movies made in the decade after *Silence* – *Hannibal* and *Red Dragon* – earned more than $440 million at the box office, from which Hopkins took home more than $30 million. But 'sell-out' is a cop-out. In the course of biographical analysis of other actors, I learnt to acknowledge, if not respect, the deep mystery of stardom. The pact we, the audience, makes with the star treads the path of myth. There is a dimension to the psychic and spiritual travel of the vaunted star that is just beyond us and yet reflects on the profoundest level the breadth and capacity of our existence. Hopkins himself acknowledges the deal. Evaluating Lecter after *Hannibal*'s success, he told an interviewer, 'Maybe I could offer some pseudo Jungian interpretation. But maybe it's just that Lecter reflects a little bit of who we all are anyway.' For him, Hannibal was the equivalent of Shakespeare's Iago, or Goethe's Mephistopheles, or Richard III, endlessly challenging representational giants of our collective imagination. Not taking up producer Dino De Laurentiis' offer to reprise him, said Hopkins, would render him 'just a party pooper'.

Ten years ago, I wrote about Hopkins that his demons were uncovered but his essence was unknowable: 'Even as I conclude this work . . . he moves with the coruscation of a jewel. [He] is truly what a star should be: dazzling, beguiling, comprehensible, yet abidingly remote.' His choices since I wrote those lines – not just the renewed *Hannibal*, but more than twenty astonishingly varied films in ten years – compel me back into his mystery, and this revised work attempts to chart his expanding universe and breach the remoteness anew. This time – because of the strange, contradictory energy of those choices – I've been obliged to travel farther than before. The first time, I was dealing with neurosis and ambition; this time feels like closure. For that reason I subtitled this new work, *A Three Act Life*, for Hopkins has surely taken us beyond the laboratory of his personal struggle into fantasies which, if only in their volume and diversity, truly illuminate our grey unstoppable appetite for the Mythic Way.

ACKNOWLEDGEMENTS

I must acknowledge as a priority the generous people who assisted this work through personal interviews, document donation, archive research, transcribing and collating. One esteemed reviewer of the original book – *Kirkus* – deemed it largely based on previously published work: an accusation that insults the many, many participants who contributed with meticulous dedication. Without the input of the following, the independent originality of this work would have been impossible: Brian Evans, Russell Johns, Douglas Rees, Les Evans, Jean Lody, Elved Lody, Peter Bray, Keith Brown, Evelyn Mainwaring, Harry Davies, Jeff Bowen, Sally Roberts Jones, The Reverend Peter Cobb, Douglas Watkins, Douglas Cook, Grafton Radcliffe, Dr Raymond Edwards, Connie Say, Brew Miller, Max Horton, Mrs Frances Williams, Mrs Dorothy Morgan, Bill Watkins, Dr Hugh Cormack, Amanda Cornish, Helen Williams (HTV Wales), Mansell Jones (HTV Wales), Mrs Jean Lovell, Steve Jones (Port Talbot Borough Council), Michael Prosser (*Port Talbot and East Guardian*), Mr Peter Phillips (West Monmouth School), Frank Witty, Graham Harris, Don Touhig, Eve Williams, John Elliott (*Soldier Magazine*), John Anderson (Columbia Pictures Distribution), David Cox (BskyB), Allen Eaton (Orion), Major Arber (Membership Secretary, National Service), John Hughes (Taibach Library), Pamela Piggott-

Smith, Peter Gill, Stanley Forbes, Bill 'Harvey' Thomas, Lionel Wheble, Colonel W. F. Cubitt, David Scase, Michael Darlow, Rosalie Scase, Jean Boht, Clive Perry, Roy Marsden, Peter Barkworth, Simon Ward, Adrian Reynolds, Roger Hammond, Martin Jarvis, Harold Innocent, John Moffatt, Ronald Pickup, Alan Dobie, Gawn Grainger, David Cunliffe, James Cellan Jones, Ed Lauter, Bryan Forbes, Elliott Kastner, Ferdy Mayne, Anthony Harvey, David White, Jim Dale, Dame Judi Dench, James A. Doolittle, Innes Lloyd, Marion Rosenberg, Michael Winner, Philip Hinchcliffe, Lee Gregg, Judith Searle, James Coburn, Simon Matthews, John Dexter, Signe in Jonathan Demme's office, Janet Glass, Robert Wise, Hume Cronyn, Kevan Barker, Lawrence Grobel, Nick Carter (*South Wales Evening Post*), Ivan Waterman, Philip L. Sebury (*South Wales Evening Post*), Mark Bloom (*Western Mail*), Lindsay Anderson, Petronella Barker Hopkins and Michael Cimino. A number of people requested anonymity in their contributions, and of course I have honoured their choice. In the case of Petronella Barker Hopkins, the request was made not to publish direct quotations from our conversations: again, the author has complied.

I owe overdue thanks to great friends: Moya Doherty (without whose support this revised work would never have been written), John McColgan, Dr Eamonn Callan, Michael Callan, Jeannette Kearney, Jim Kearney, Jay and Antony Worrall Thompson, Olivier and Alma Capt, Dr John Kelly, Dermot Byrne, Ian and Bernie Condy, Tommy and Jane Bracken, David and Lisa Strassman, Shay Hennessy, Larry Masterson, Peter Charlesworth, Sean Simon, Ian Hennessy, Della Kilroy, Susan Kinsella, Susan O'Neill, Trisha Hayes, Patricia Mooney, Karin O'Reilly, Susan Dickson, Donna Walsh, Audrey Hanlon, Carolann Manahan, Caroline Dunne, Karen Hodge, Susan Deegan, Renée Glennon, Anne Marie Glennon, Natasha Petali, Chiola Swanepoele, Meg McSweeney, Andrea Walsh and Trina Stalley. All have opened doors, assisted my determined enquiries or kept me stimulated in their friendship.

Fond appreciation to my diligent secretarial team: Samantha Finneran, Catherine Barry, Karen Cook and Mary Rees. Also to Bobby Mitchell at BBC Photo Archives, Jacqui Roberts and Phil Wickham at the British Film Institute, Barry Norman at the Theatre Museum, and the patient library staff of the National Theatre and the American Academy of Motion Picture Arts and Sciences; also staff at *Spotlight* (especially Dave), *Screen International* and British Actors' Equity. The late Francis Xavier Feighan, a wonderful writer and friend, was the indispensable key to much of the American research.

Thanks, too, to my inspirational editor and muse, Susan Hill (whom I miss every day), William Armstrong, Helen Gummer, Bill Goldstein, Robert Stewart and Mark LaFaur at Scribner's. And to the supportive, creative team at the Blue Leaf Art Gallery – especially Ciara Gibbons and Cathy Boyle. Also thanks to Barry Noonan and Alan Williams for legal guidance, and to Susan Malvern, Beverley Cousins and Bernie Verdon for their conscientious combing of the early drafts of the manuscript. At Robson Books, the imaginative backup of Vanessa Daubney, Chris Turner, Clive Hebard and Richard Mason was indispensable. Without the trust and dedication of Jeremy Robson and my new editor Barbara Phelan, needless to say, this new work would not be in your hands. I owe the greatest debt to my loving mother, Margaret Feeney Callan, whose devotion to movies – and tall tales – inspired my lifelong interest. I miss her.

Finally, deepest love and gratitude to Corey, Paris and Ree Callan, who are the heart of it.

THE TYRANNY OF MYTH

I

*'I must become a borrower of the night,
For a dark hour; or twain.'*

Macbeth Act III, Scene I

He stood Welsh and wide, overweight and under height, his hands knuckled deep in his pockets in a way that Old Dick or the masters at West Mon or Cowbridge would disdain ('Upright, Hopkins, and with us! Wake up, boyo, and rage, rage!'), pasty, soft and sanguine. Outside was Turtle Creek, Pennsylvania, in the steel-skied chill of winter, an unexceptional part of town, hosting just another movie unit. Some kids hung fast with their autograph books, held at bay by runners chewing Twinkies from the catering tables.

He saw the mirror of himself through bars and laughed with his British facility at the jibes. Even now, after 25 years of it, after fifty-something start dates and two thousand call sheets, he could still parry. 'Scary? You haven't seen scary! Fava beans or kidneys? What's good for a finger-lickin' cannibal?' And smile.

When make-up was gone – for a piss or a Twinky – when the fellowship passed, he was alone in the cold, comfortless trailer in the violet hour, in his favourite place and time – between takes. *A movie actor! An American movie actor like Bogie or Jimmy Dean or . . .*

He could flash, in those moments, through the panorama of the poverty-smelling stalls of the *cach* – the shit – which was the Taibach Picturedome, through the wet Saturdays of his only-child despair, through the loneliness of Margam's mountain, through the mystery of parents, of home, of learning, through the finding of music and drama, the marshalling of instinct, emigration, the waxwork faces of fame that flanked the course – Olivier, O'Toole, Hepburn – the recovery of ego, the discovery of Id, the grasped nettle of trust, the pricking rose of hope, failed marriage, failed ambition, failed endeavour, failed theatre, failed films. And, worse, the hollowness of success. Setting forth with arsehole directors whose 'vision' stank, and fulfilling that vision. That fucker in LA with *The Tempest*, who could talk but knew nothing. And Dexter, always scratching away at comfort: Dexter. Dexter doing Shaffer this way and that till it was his *Equus*, his way, and who gave a fuck anyway, because all that Broadway run – that fucking meaningless 'breakthrough' – was in an alcoholic haze of vino and tequila and . . . His bones tautened and his mouth dried because these memories punctuated all memory and ran rampant through him – even after the years of counselling, of summoning heroes – and poured forth bursting, toxic effusions.

He breathed deep and slipped on the easy mantle of mimicry. Today he was Truman Capote and HAL in *2001*. Ha! And he recalled: 'Do Cary Grant!' 'Do Gielgud!' 'Do Larry . . .' It was a party piece, honed on Sergeant Rawlings at Woolwich, bless his hide. *'C'mon, ye miserable buggers. Hop to it! Bit o' square bashin'!'* It was a giggle. No, it was more than that. Sometimes confoundingly more. For commerce, it was easy. They phoned you, or the agent, and said, 'We need Tony to dub Larry. Remember *Spartacus*? Well, we're updating it. Yeah, *Spartacus*, the classic, that piece of shit Dalton Trumbo wrote but they didn't want to give him the credit for because McCarthy nailed him and all that. The one Kubrick told Kirk Douglas he'd be happy to steal the credit on, but Kirk thought, what a bastard, even to suggest stealing a credit . . . that one, that piece of art. We want to put back in the homosexual scenes we cut. Yeah, Larry propositioning Tony Curtis. You know the famous omission: "Do you eat snails, Antoninus? Do you eat oysters? It's all a question of taste . . ." It's going back in because it's relevant today, with half of Hollywood dying from AIDS. So let Hollywood stand up and be counted. We have nothing to be ashamed of, do we? And Tony can do truth like no one else. So let's have Tony fake Olivier in *Spartacus 2*, yeah?'

That simple.

And after the party games of squashing the gullet and making them applaud and admire – even now, with the demons settled – there remained that terrible void. That sense of cheat and perfidy that Scriabin études and preludes used to calm, but often didn't. A rush that still made him wake in the night in the Miramar Hotel, or the house in Chelsea, and pushed him into Room 101 to face again that ultimate demon, that damned fuckingly human face, that roly face, in the mirror. Well read, if not well educated, he might hear T. S. Eliot:

> *Who is the third who walks always beside you?*
> *When I count, there are only you and I together*
> *But when I look ahead up the white road*
> *There is always another one walking beside you.*

'Couple of minutes,' the kid with the water said when he knocked at the trailer door. So he said fine and gargled the water and adjusted the straps of the dog face mask and looked back into the grilled eyes. It was hot in the chill. The heat he was well familiar with: it was the heat of creation. Demme, this new director, was mad, too, and generous in his insanity. His eyes were reptilian, never ever flickered. But he believed eternally in him for Lecter – from the start – even when doddering Orion, the producers, were whispering, 'What the fuck? He's a Brit. We need someone genuinely dark. Like Karloff or Tony Perkins. Dark and suffering, with a hint of an underside . . .' But Demme took him to New York for the readings with Jodie and of course he did it massively, winning half of it with his BBC charm and the voice, the voice that was a baritone in a universe of Hollywood tenors.

And today, Demme had generously asked him how they might introduce Lecter the cannibal on the screen. Close-cut montage? Overhead zoom? Crash cuts? Reverse subjective . . . ? His reply was modest. Let the camera simply find the cannibal's cell, do it in a natural movement, from Jodie's point of view. He would smell her and she would walk to the cell and there he would be, waiting. Contained, hidden, but bursting to be free.

In the long silent interlude, through the bars, he glimpsed again a consummate truth. He had glimpsed it before, when he'd first read the Ted Tally script.

'Stand by, Tony.'

At the National, in the smouldering past, Larry said, 'I know you do a devilish take-off.' In the trials and travails that followed which gave him a fortune and gave him great unWelsh privilege, the trick had been the roller-bearing on which all the machinery turned. It really fucked him off when they likened him to Burton because his voice was similar, or his history. It fucked him off because the roller-bearing was distracting and untrue. Other forces were at work, with their burden of price – and why had it taken Larry and all the rest of them so long to notice?

Who was the third, though? The answers he held were partial answers. But maybe that was all there ever would be, or maybe it was enough?

Kafka, Pinter, Shakespeare, Chekhov, O'Casey, Shaw, Shaffer . . . They sketched and winged and he grabbed those words and put them into full-ranged flight. Sometimes, true – as Larry, sometimes as Burton. But sometimes as Anthony Hopkins. He had been Coriolanus, Macbeth, Prospero, Petruchio, Lear, Le Roux, Bligh and Hitler. He had delivered them all into our skies with a muddled skill – part game, part instinct – which wasn't to say that he hadn't been formally trained, but that just gave him the tricks of containment and despatch. No, the magic worked in a different way – yes, magic! – fired by a private darkness.

Who was the third?

Hopkins grasped the nettle and plunged. In the mirror, in this moment, he was trusting the pit again. Speeding into darkness and carrying with him just the rose of hope, of renewal. In his memories, through the dubious effusions of 'making it' was always this mystery, this pain.

He looked into mirror eyes, into the terrifying vacuum of truth. Here was Lecter, a monster smiling behind a mask.

Here was the soul of it.

'Ready to do it,' the kid said, and Anthony Hopkins walked backwards into his memories.

It was a moment of truth, between liquor and death.

2

'The angst of people in Westwood is just not troubling or deep'

Steve Nicolaides, producer of *A Few Good Men*

In Westwood, where the world is Hockney sunlight and chausan palms and Brentwood kids in convertible GTIs making their way to the nearby UCLA campus, Anthony Hopkins ended a fifteen-year alcoholic binge by hearing the voice of God in the street. It was 29 December 1975, two days before his 38th birthday, a time of stodgy career achievement. He had been on a bender for days – at one point waking up in a Phoenix, Arizona, motel that had shit on the floor and blood on the pavement outside, not knowing how he'd got there – and as he left the umpteenth trendy bar, very clearly and sensible, he believes, he heard a voice say in his ear: 'It is all over. You can start living.'

In 1988, he told religious TV programme-maker Eric Robson that 'This was the turning point.' The sanctity of the experience gave him an instant 'sense of belonging', which had eluded him, despite a childhood 'bursting with parental love', inherent musical skill, scholarships, a silver medal at RADA, diverse and celebrated leading theatrical performances, the friendship and respect of some of the greatest living actors (Katharine Hepburn, Laurence Olivier, Peter O'Toole), wealth in films, the achievement of his great goal of transferring his life to America, fatherhood and marriage. Immediately after this 'humbling experience' he joined Alcoholics Anonymous. He has not touched alcohol since.

It is tempting to concede to the preceding quotation from Hollywood resident Steve Nicolaides and interpret Hopkins' mid-life road to Damascus as the fizzling of actor vanity. Hopkins himself, in many interviews, had done much to promote the deduction. From the start, he says, he wanted Hollywood, and colossal fame. The best, no less. Like others who sought that Olympus, he paid a hefty price from early on. David Scase, who gave him his first important theatre break, is in no doubt that that frantic, risky ambition drove him from the outset. When he met Scase, who was then artistic director of the Library Theatre in Manchester, he was 22, just out of National Service and chronically shy. Nonetheless, Scase observed a 'young man with a vivid sense of direction . . . there were no 'ifs'. He wanted to go on to great things and I helped him where I could, although he didn't always listen to me. One was left in no doubt that he would do whatever it took to succeed.' Clive Perry, artistic director of the Phoenix in Leicester, inherited Hopkins after RADA and found 'definite talent and a yearning beyond what [rep theatre] could offer'.

The gypsy friendships of rep were early casualties – but they left their mark. In fact, the early relationships, hungrily clawed at by a lonely boy desperate to understand the artistic murmurings within him, unstrung him and contributed greatly to the miseries to come. Hellbent on career achievement, he was suddenly burning up double the energy running from himself and the past. Gulfs of confusion opened. He enjoyed RADA camaraderie but, addictively, he buried such friendships as soon as they formed. A quarter of a century later, the evidence of the damage was still there when he told Tony Crawley in an interview: 'I'm always surprised to meet anyone from RADA. They are still seeing the friends they knew then, not just for friendship but to [stay close] to their roots. I don't like being around actors at all.'

'He seemed in such a crazy hurry then,' says actress Jean Boht, one of the many women at the Liverpool Playhouse who idolised him. 'But ill at ease in his skin.' After the briefest limbering up in the provinces,

Hopkins won his place at the National under Olivier, a crowning honour that hardly impressed him. Within a season he was bickering with the greats, contesting direction. Five years out of RADA, he was on the silver screen opposite Katharine Hepburn, then Broadway fell, then came the rapid inroads on Hollywood proper. During the first few films came the fall of his marriage and the separation from his daughter Abigail, a period of fury of which Hopkins rejected all analysis. Author Larry Grobel spent thirty hours with the actor in a succession of intimate interviews for *Playboy* magazine in 1992 and 1993. The initial candour didn't last:

> He came to the *Playboy* offices in LA with his friend and publicist Bob Palmer and we commenced. We did four hours, then resumed at the Hotel Miramar [his favourite LA stopover]. He seemed very much the guy you'd like to hang out with – informal, concerned about me and my life. The conclusions about acting were straightforward, a bit jaded – 'Everything's fucked up, I don't know where acting is at.' Then, the minute I touched on the daughter and the disastrous first marriage – a wave of the hand and 'No, no, no, we don't want to go into that!' And it wasn't negotiable. It was: Bury the past, all right? A touch belligerently. But I got the impression that the key to him was there, in the failed marriage, in the daughter. But that is a key he doesn't particularly want to turn. Not in public, anyway.

Anthony Hopkins, the 'spoilt child from Taibach' in the words of a Margam neighbour, strove to maintain balance. Even sanity. In common with other notorious actor-drinkers of his generation, the press file of his development is mind-numbingly full of hairpin paradoxes that reflect the madness. Here, acting is 'just a bag of tricks'; elsewhere, it merits hours of intellectual gobbledegook. Here, Shakespeare is the summit; later, he's a complete waste of time. Sometimes he doesn't care whether posterity remembers him or not; then he wants 'to be around a long, long time, as long as Olivier and Gielgud'. All of it hurt. In the late sixties he first visited a shrink in Harley Street. He regretted it. 'It cost £20 for half an hour. A waste of time and money. I wandered over to a pub and got drunk for several days . . .' Then there was the frantic chase, devouring Jung, Freud, Gurdjieff . . . None of it worked, none of it. The peaks still came, and the inexplicable, horrifying dells. There was no respite.

After the anguished first marriage came remarriage to Jenni Lynton, a film-worker from his first big try-out, *When Eight Bells Toll*. It offered no immediate answers and withstood many fragile years of trauma which one friend calls 'a continuing emotional tornado'. Nineteen seventy-five, in his prime, was the worst of times, a year he hardly remembers despite its patina of theatrical and TV successes. Jenni drove him everywhere that year because he was rarely sober. He smoked pot, tried to drive, but often didn't know what day of the week it was. In company, he was obnoxious and unreliable. He verbally assaulted co-workers and friends. He was sometimes physically violent, often physically ill. There were many who thought he would beat Richard Burton, his subtle *bête noire*, to an early grave.

Hopkins speaks volubly in terms of redemption and near-miss survival. He admits to the horrors cheerfully but has drawn a veil across the battlefield. He prefers not to discuss the fact that the battle smouldered on, that true redemption took another fifteen years. It is past. He can breathe. And, as he has grown in emotional strength, so he and the few friends he has drawn to him at last have dug deep into the hidey-hole safehouse of silence. 'He was never gregarious,' says David Scase. 'It's hard to say what friendship is to him.' Today – still – Hopkins admits to 'just two or three' close friends. For a long time Jenni, his pragmatic alter ego, was closest. She remains, but has been displaced by Stella Arroyave, his third wife. Bob Palmer, now de facto manager, still ranks in the top three. Also an alcoholic, Palmer was the one who guided Hopkins through the life-saving counselling in LA after the Westwood experience and, along with ICM agent Ed Limato and CAA's Rick Nicita, moulded his matured career. The secrets they share are divided between a hillside 'married home' at Point Dume in Malibu, the elegant four-storey house in Alexander Place, London, where Jenni still lives, and the various expensive hotels around the world that accommodate his unquenched wanderlust.

Hopkins will talk most now on neutral territory, with Stella or Rick Nicita never too far away, and, as with Larry Grobel, jauntily discuss the furniture of his life and the theory of celebrity.

The interview offerings, though, seem more like a smokescreen that diverts from the real Anthony Hopkins. Detached from the hazy past, he has become comfortably enough, a tabloid cartoon called Hannibal the Cannibal, an overnight Hollywood hit. It suits because it is buried in hyperbole. It has set his star on the Hollywood Boulevard Walk of Fame and invites the world to trample onwards. It takes us away from him.

The truth is that Anthony Hopkins still walks, gingerly and undetected, in the shadows and light of his past and his moments of redemption. He revisits for sustenance, for inspiration, but then he runs to ground, to the hills of Malibu or the mountains of his childhood Wales, or the wild open spaces of Nevada and Montana. After the Westwood experience, he says, he found comfort in the wilderness. 'I'd go up to the mountains around Los Angeles, or I'd head out through the California desert towards Bakersfield . . .' The Grand Canyon became a place of frequent sanctuary, reminding him of the vast, unmanageable geography of Wales.

In 1990, Hopkins contributed a foreword to a book about alcoholism*. Many who know him say it is the closest he has come to opening the wounds of his childhood and showing the soul of the consummate actor.

He wrote:

> Although raised as an only child in an ordinary family, I felt from early days an overwhelming anxiety that I would be deprived of something that was rightly mine. Just what that 'something' was is hard to define, but fear became the driving force of my life for the next thirty years . . . And when professional success came, I lived in fear that someone else would be more successful than me. I spent those years constantly looking over my shoulder. It all seems pretty laughable and pathetic now, looking back, but at the time I felt I was in hell. His Majesty the Monstrous Baby now reigned supreme inside me, waving his rattle and banging his spoon,

Freedom from the Bottle by Liz Cutland (Gateway, 1990)

demanding yet more gratification and, in turn, more alcohol to dampen the fire . . . I was a squirrel in a cage, chasing my own tail.

In chasing himself, and all the bewildering mythology of the past and of Hollywood, Anthony Hopkins found a future, but almost lost his life.

Part One

GRASPING THE FAIRY'S WING

'For a while these reveries provided an outlet for his imagination;
they were a satisfactory hint of the unreality of reality,
a promise that the rock of the world was founded securely
on a fairy's wing . . .'

The Great Gatsby
F. Scott Fitzgerald

Chapter 1

THE CORNISH
GABBRO AXE

'There are two public houses here at present, namely, the Miner's Arms and the Somersetshire House. We regret that the latter inn sells intoxicating drinks on Sunday until the latest hours allowed by the law. It is not unusual to see workers emerging therefrom with pitchers of beer on their shoulders, even when people are passing by on their way to worship God in their respective chapels. If the publican had any respect for God's commandments, and the people's wish to better the place, he would keep his mouth shut. Because of his terrible presumptuousness in making God's day a day of business, he is jeopardising his chances in the next world . . .'

A History of Tai Bach, 1872
The Reverend Richard Morgan

It was, then, the last great gasp of Arthurian Wales, a proud place descended from the Silures and the Romans, who laid the ground plan that lasted till the twentieth century. Antiquity made it noble: an axe of Cornish gabbro found on Aberfan beach – a beach of Hopkins' boyhood – has been dated to around 4000 BC, twice as old as Stonehenge. The Talbots of Margam Castle, just down the road from Hopkins' birthplace at 77 Wern Road, Margam, recorded for posterity: 'Yesterday, found at the harbour, Port Talbot, about 25 feet below high water mark, a brass spear head about nine inches long, many stags' antlers, a large brass coin of Commodus, several pairs of old-fashioned leather shoes, foundations of buildings . . .'

The Romans landed in Britain in AD 43 and set about designing the modern infrastructure. Along the via Julia Maritima – the seaside road of Julius Frontinus – they built the forts that became Cardiff, Neath, Loughor and Margam. They put the women to work in the bath houses and homes and set about mining for gold. They conquered everything but the native spirit and the native spirit gods. The locals embraced the wisdom of Latin and the toga-clad priests, they enjoyed the settlements and docks, but they still cherished their arcane, secret tongue and paid homage to Cernunnos, the horned god of the forest, and Rhiannon, the mother goddess. The Britons of South Wales were cunning but unconquerable. They took, in their obstinate way, only what they wanted.

In the early twentieth century, Wales was not much changed. The gold mining had been replaced by the Port Talbot Steelworks, the dockland boomed, Taibach and Cwmafan were administrative and industrial centres, and Margam Moors was still the home of terns and geese and sea holly. Sixty per cent of the natives spoke Welsh and, under the smoky pall of the collieries, exercised their true spirit in the twin pursuits of church and pub. The chapels were everywhere, and of varied and odd persuasion – Bible Christians, Primitive Methodists, Independents, Baptists, Presbyterians, Catholics; the pubs innumerable and in staunch attendance.

Then came the First World War, the Depression and the great stalling of growth and prosperity, which drove the natives into a greater insularity and, for many, enforced idleness. In the twenties and thirties, social and cultural life boomed and threw up some unforgettable 'characters'. Even today the folks of Port Talbot recall with pride the achievements of the boxer Billy Beynon, the 'Great Marvello' Percy Hunt, Leon Vint's Palace of Varieties in Water Street, and the great rash of music halls, social societies and cinemas that sprang up almost as one. The recollections of the Port Talbot Operatic Society, the Cymric Glee and the YMCA drama group of Leo Lloyd are as cherished today as Talbot's Roman antiquities were in his day. They are the proud memory of a recent 'finest hour', a moment of undiluted Welsh regality before the steelworks expanded and raped the countryside and the emigrant workers took the spoils and left in their wake a Meccano graveyard and a generation of unemployed immigrants. Les Evans, a neighbour of the Hopkinses from Caradoc Street and a teacher at one of Tony's first schools, the Central in Port Talbot says.

> Don't get it wrong. They were stiff times, with a lot of poverty and hardship in Taibach. For example, from the miners' strike in 1921 till the strike of 1926, the soup kitchens set up in Bethany Chapel fed about half the Taibach population. There was quite a division between the gentry – the Talbots of Margam Castle – and the ordinary folk who worked the collieries and the copper, later the tin, mines. My father was a stonemason running a small business, sometimes employing five men, so I suppose we were the lucky ones. As were the Hopkinses who ran their bakery in Taibach in the late twenties. But it was still an era when lucky men brought home two halfpennies for a day's work.

Arthur Richard Hopkins, the actor's grandfather, known to all and sundry as Old Dick, was the clan patriarch, who took the distress of the impoverished very seriously and helped where he could. Self-educated, he was a Fabian and a follower of broad Socialist principles. Some said he would end up in politics but he made his fortune in London, working for Peak Frean the biscuit makers, then spotted his golden moment when Huxtables, the long-established bakers of Taibach, ceased trading. He packed his five-strong family, headed back to the pastures of his childhood and set up shop in 151 Tanygroes Street, amid the blackened workers' cottages, just a spit from the Ffrwdwyllt, the 'wild river' whose tendency to flood yearly added to the troubles of the harassed masses. 'My mother knew him in London, at Catwood, where he was a baker,' says Evans, 'and they often shared memories when he called to her doorstep delivering bread.'

Old Dick had been born in Neath, 'but he wasn't madly Welsh. The overwhelming impression he gave was of political awareness and generosity for his fellow man. He was a hard worker, very solid and dumpy, and ready to work till he dropped.' A. R. Hopkins & Son (the son being Young Dick, Tony's father) needed all the energy they could muster because the contemporary competition was thick and fast. 'I think Old Dick turned away from his Fabian concerns to make his business and his family secure,' recalls Evans. 'At that time, people did their baking at home and got their ingredients where they could, as cheaply as possible. Old Dick had to confront that to make his place succeed.' At first, says Evans, Hopkins concentrated on manufacture and delivery on a wholesale basis. The dainty green vans of A. R. Hopkins were a regular sight around Taibach at all hours. Then Old Dick tilted at expansion into over-the-counter retail. 'There was talk that his father was an alcoholic,' says Evelyn Mainwaring, another Taibach neighbour who still resides in the now diminished smog. 'But Old Dick was the opposite. He was a teetotaller, very correct and quite a bossy man – bossy perhaps in a compensating way.' Les Evans says, 'I certainly never saw him around the pubs or tipsy in the street. There was no gossip at all about Old Dick, and that speaks volumes in an area where gossip flowed easy and people liked the pubs.'

Taibach itself lived a curious schizophrenia in its attitude to the demon drink. The district of Taibach started life as five small farms (Taibach means 'small houses') which underwent dramatic transform-ation when copper mining was introduced to the area in 1770. The men responsible for this were John Cartwright and one Isaac Newton (a likely relative of the immortal astronomer), who leased a slice of Margam Estate from the Reverend Thomas Talbot in July 1757 for an annual rent of £89 15s 0d, developed a colliery, then merged with the English Copper Miners' Company to broaden their profits. The Talbots benefited considerably: in their original agreement with the developers, the landowning family received their coal indefinitely at a knockdown 3s 6d per ton, and also took 5 per cent of all sales.

Taibach bloomed like a black flower, and the spiritual saviours came hurrying in. The Calvinistic Methodists established the first Nonconformist church, Dyffryn, in a farmyard in about 1772, and the Independents and Baptists followed. As religious wars were fought for the souls of the miners, Taibach stumbled through a dark age of social growth. Though by the late eighteenth century there were, according to public records, 282 homes and 2,000 residents in the district, its very first doctor had only recently joined the community and no hostelry or restaurant existed. By the turn of the century, all this had changed and the flagship pubs – the Somersetshire House, the Miner's Arms and, later, the Talbot Hotel pub – became the great focal points of social gathering. 'I'm sure it had much to do with the mining conditions, the taste of coal dust, the oppressive atmosphere in the pits,' says Sally Roberts Jones, historian and author of *The History of Port Talbot*. 'There is, too, that pursuit of the Celtic muse, the poetry of an ancient tribal society whose rituals transcend those of organised religion. It's easy to say: Witness Dylan Thomas, Richard Burton, all that. But clichés often conceal truth.'

Les Evans remembers in the late twenties, around the time that Young Dick took the bakery reins from his ageing father, that 'most of the excitement in the town concerned the goings-on at the Talbot Hotel, which is now the Taibach Rugby Football Club, and the Sker, which was the local name for the Somersetshire House. It wasn't unusual to see fistfights spilling out on to the streets. Often very entertaining they were, too. It was a way of settling disputes in a town that often felt neglected by the powers that be. It was also a direct end product of the tough times, a kind of escapism.' He elaborates: 'I don't think that rough and tumble affected the Hopkinses, really. They were kind of above it all, not really the miners' types.'

The Hopkins family was, in fact, much respected and perceived, even in depressed times, as distinctly upwardly mobile – all credit to bull-headed, non-stop Old Dick. Relatives, of course, were scattered through-out the country, though the baker Hopkinses remained, says Evelyn Mainwaring, 'very close and private'. A branch of the family had been noted masons and three Hopkins brothers were builders of Margam Castle, no less, according to local diarist Douglas Watkins. Until quite recently, distantly related Hopkinses lived on the castle estate. Sally Roberts Jones notes the preponderance of Hopkins graves in the nearby St Mary's graveyard. Conspicuous, she says, are the side-by-side Jenkins and Hopkins headstones, dating back to the middle of the nineteenth century. The actor Richard Burton – originally Richard Walter Jenkins – was born in nearby Pontrhydyfen (on 10 November 1925, twelve years before Anthony Hopkins) and his sister Cis lived in Caradoc Street, at the top end beside 'the Side', a slurry tip that was, after the pubs, the forum for many fights. Various Jenkinses knew assorted Hopkins family branches, though neither Anthony Hopkins nor his parents claimed any kinship with the 'Burton' Jenkinses. 'Then again,' says Jones, 'the Jenkinses were coal-mining people and the Hopkinses were very much middle-class businessmen, so there was a natural distance.'

Young Dick Hopkins was quite unlike his father in temperament and in looks. The only son, he was tacitly expected to help out at the bakery and ultimately assume control. He did this dutifully and was a competent bakery manager, though not, most will tell you, the powerhouse that his father was. 'He was strikingly handsome,' says Les Evans, 'a good three to four inches taller than Old Dick, which made him near six foot.'

Anthony Hopkins today reflects on the influence of Old Dick and Young Dick on his actor personae. Old Dick was 'the dynamo', but Young Dick a man of equal effort, a man Hopkins remembers for his sweating, straining energy, who influenced a variety of stage and film creations, from a personal breakthrough – Undershaft in an early *Major Barbara* – to the role of Dafydd Ap Llewelyn in Michael Winner's *A Chorus of Disapproval*.

As Hopkins describes his father today, he winces, painting a man of purpose and practicality, not overwordy, perhaps not over-talented, but humorous and physically strong. More than anything, a man whose personal role model – Old Dick – pushed him beyond himself.

The image of fortitude lingers, indeed was all-pervasive in Hopkins' vision of his father throughout his life. Dick may not have had his father's ingenuity but he was a courageous man, a man who tried, and that is what scored deep and formed the rock on which Hopkins built his vague but solid father-worship. Throughout Dick's life, Hopkins held him in a distant, fervent respect. Even in his mid-twenties the actor was seeking his counsel, looking for the combined comfort of strength and erudition that was just beyond his mother, Muriel. Then, Hopkins says, his insecurities manifested themselves in a temporary obsession with the Cuban Missile Crisis and its implications. Living in London, man enough to provide for himself and his career, he craved reassurance. 'Just get on with your life,' Dick told him. 'Don't worry about it. If they drop a bomb in London, you're in a good place because it'll all be over in a couple of minutes. We're all going to die one day anyway.' When the actor objected to this robust fatalism, Dick replied, 'Well, there's nothing you or I can do about it.'

A neighbour from Tanygroes Street says, 'Young Dick was hot and cold. I believe he slapped the boy a bit. Not because he was hard, but because he couldn't understand him. Anthony Hopkins was a difficult, obsessive kind of boy, but then Young Dick was a frustrated, obsessive kind of man.'

Dick Hopkins' only child, Philip Anthony, was the product of a sound marriage to Muriel Yeats, the daughter of Fred Yeats, a steelworker from Wiltshire, and Sophia, a Port Talbot Welsh-speaker. Muriel was raised in Ford Road, in Velindre, where she met the young baker of Taibach, who liked a jar, smiled freely and could be quite companionable, and, after a short courtship, married him on 2 August 1936 at the Church of the Holy Cross, Taibach. Their first home was a pebble-dashed semi at Wern Road in modern Margam, the other side of Taibach from Port Talbot, and it was here that baby Tony Hopkins first opened his eyes to the paradoxes of wilderness Wales. He was born on a freezing New Year's Eve, in 1937, after a labour which, says a neighbour, 'almost killed Muriel. It was touch and go whether she'd pull through and it stopped her having other kids.'

Muriel stayed at home to tend to the baby as Young Dick concentrated on building up the bakery towards the eventual post-war expansion that would give them bigger premises with a delicatessen shop in Commercial Road, Taibach. The conflicts and contrasts were vivid in those days, had Muriel had the time or focus to see them. Margam was, relatively, well off. The family house was a three-bedroom, two-storey place in an area that was leafy and open, on the fringe of acres of parkland at the foot of Mynydd Margam. Taibach, by contrast, cowered under its industrial pall and was serenaded to sleep each night by the alehouse wars. 'What kept it all together was a strange community spirit,' says Les Evans. 'We were a close community, all in one boat. Most people were beholden to Joseph the Jew and the Friendly Societies. But people helped people, and that was the glue.' Arthur Bowen, a bakery supplies rep for Cheverton & Leidlers of Bucks, who sold cake tins and platters around South Wales, supplied Young Dick and grew friendly with him. Arthur's son Jeff, soon to attend school with Tony Hopkins, recalls, 'The freemasons ruled the business community and to do well you stayed in the system.' But Evelyn Mainwaring says, 'Dick stayed remote from all that. He was unmistakably a self-reliant, self-made man – like his father. And very proud, too.'

Anthony Hopkins' first exercise in discernment in this strangely theatrical setting – with its stately castle, colliery skyline, wide fields and black-faced men – was to display a distinct preference for Grandfather Yeats' elegant Port Talbot garden. 'My parents used to take me there and leave me for weekends . . . My grandfather doted on me. His name was Yeats and I have [come to] love Yeats' poetry. It reminds me of sitting on that bench in my grandfather's garden, among the hollyhocks and lupins and a trellis of tree roses . . . and those depressing flowers, begonias.'

There are other blotched memories of those infant years – some horrifying vibrant visions of demons (he believed he saw the devil's face in Mr Hodges, the postmaster from Tolgeen Road), some perhaps subliminally moulded by Hitler's bombing attacks on Swansea and Port Talbot during 1941. Young Dick had joined the Observer Corps as soon as hostilities broke out and his wide-eyed son took great joy in the crisp, dashing uniform, the field glasses for watching the night sky, and the bunker half-buried amid the crab grass at the bottom of the garden. Understanding nothing, observing everything, four-year-old Tony Hopkins would forever remember his patrols with his father in the long summer twilights, watching the sky for German aircraft but picking out instead the evening stars – and Venus, and Mercury and the changing moon. It was here Dick gave him his first education – about the universe, the planets, the mysteries of Creation.

The district, far as it was from the frontline south coast of England, was no stranger to the effects of war. During the First World War, a local man, Rupert Price Hollowes, assistant manager of the Mansel Tinplate Works, was killed in action with the Middlesex Regiment in France. His courage won him the Victoria Cross and began the tradition of local military volunteers. Harry Davies, an octogenarian, remembers that 'the area was immersed in the officer spirit, seeing itself very much part of the war'. Soldiers were billeted at the Grand Hotel and Belgian refugees housed in Springfield Terrace and at Bethany Chapel. Davies says, 'The Port Talbot Steelworks, which was the biggest local employer after the coal mines, had a huge upsurge in demand in the First War, and in the Second. So we were in the conflict whether we liked it or not.' Throughout 1940 and 1941, the sense of threat and danger was widely felt. 'There were barrage balloons over Port Talbot and uniforms every-where. Nobody felt safe. There wasn't the remoteness [of the action] of the First War. It felt like it was on our doorstep.'

Swansea was repeatedly bombed but Port Talbot, because of its proximity to high mountains, remained relatively safe. None the less, the German bombloads did get through. On 14 February 1941, six civilians were killed at Sandfields, within earshot of the Hopkins home in Wern Road, and three months later four people died in a raid on Pontrhydyfen, among them the family of the popular singing star Ivor Emmanuel.

Anthony Hopkins was too young to absorb the moral horror of what was happening, but old enough to register the novelty. For him, those anguished years meant star-gazing with Da, spooky mid-evening black-outs, the absence of chocolate and the arrival in his narrow world of an army of grinning, louche, gum-chewing alien saviours called Americans.

In 1941, when Tony Hopkins was three and a half, one of his soon-to-be idols John Fitzgerald Kennedy was 24 and fully fuelled on his ambitions for the American presidency. He was already a senator and well versed in the social and sexual advantages of power. Thirty years later, Jack

Anderson, among many, revealed the true character of America's New Frontier pioneer, when he disclosed details of the raw FBI files compiled by J. Edgar Hoover on the rising senator's private life. 'One report,' wrote Anderson, 'claims that in 1941 young John F. Kennedy romanced a woman suspected of espionage. His exploits with the lady occurred in Charleston, South Carolina, where he was working for the Navy to protect defence factories against bombing.' The woman cited was Inga Arvad, the former wife of Egypt's ambassador to Paris and a friend of Josef Goebbels. Jack Kennedy called her Inga-Binga. She was not a spy, and Hoover well knew this, but he taunted Kennedy with the hint of compromise and this incident, allegedly, was the first building block of a dossier of indiscretion that blackened Kennedy and allowed Hoover to blackmail him not only into extending Hoover's extraordinary tenure as Director of the FBI (he remained in situ for more than forty years), but also making his friend Lyndon Johnson – a man Kennedy distrusted and disliked – Vice-President.

Nineteen forty-one was for Kennedy, as for all America, a time of unchecked opportunism and naivety. It was the Honeymoon of Hope at the tail of the Great Depression, the lull before Pearl Harbor.

The Americans who arrived in Margam in the spring of 1942 came from a nation less than two hundred years old, a polyglot place where individuality was cherished, and religion obsessed about, where the Second Amendment gave to all citizens the right to carry firearms, thereby acknowledging, if not sanctifying, the essential darkness in man. They came from a country which had defied the Crash and burst through the Great Depression led by Franklin D. Roosevelt, the three-term president who beefed up the trade unions, repealed Prohibition, opened the first publicly owned electricity service and created six million jobs in four years. They came wealthy and sanguine and motivated by optimism and success – and by their celluloid conquering heroes.

By the late thirties, the colonising influence of Hollywood was sensed and American films were flooding out into the flea-pits of Bangkok, Berlin and Britain, inciting a subculture of bastardised English, starchy morals and dubious ethics. The icons were already world renowned:

Clark Gable, Gary Cooper, Errol Flynn and, among the women – who were most often marginalised as fluffy but marriageable sex objects – Ginger Rogers, Joan Crawford and Betty Grable. During the thirties, the craft of cinema had grown into an art and the years 1939 and 1940 produced a high yield of films that transcended pop diversion and created a watershed. Among them were Lubitsch's *Ninotchka*, John Ford's *Stagecoach*, Victor Fleming's *Gone with the Wind*, Hitchcock's *Rebecca* (starring the obstinately English Laurence Olivier), Chaplin's *The Great Dictator* and Disney's *Fantasia*. Though 1941 brought a smaller crop there was magic just the same in films like *The Maltese Falcon*, featuring that enduring role model for American tough guys, Humphrey Bogart.

Many of the Americans who came to Margam in the wake of Pearl Harbor and America's entry to the fray, came imitating their idols, swaggering like Gable and Bogie, dispensing Hollywood street lingo and, says Harry Davies, 'unquestionably performing for us wee Welsh folk'.

Major changes were afoot throughout the area. Margam Castle was – unthinkably – sold in the summer of 1942, marking an end to the Talbot dynasty. Its elegant halls were offered for the billeting of American troops and for the use of the Home Guard and the ARP units. Margam, Taibach and Port Talbot were immediately saturated with crew-cut Americans whose principal entertainments were chasing the local girls and replenishing their charm kits at the Plaza, the Grand, the Capitol, the Electric and the brand new Majestic Cinema (opened in 1939) in Forge Road. Such bracing homespun fare as *The Foreman went to France* perked up the locals, but the Americans preferred watching Betty Grable's legs.

'They certainly added colour to the district,' says Les Evans. 'The uniforms were everywhere, very bright and eye-catching, and a source of obvious competition for the local lads. They had confidence, too, see. They brought with them the impression that the world was their oyster, that it was all a game more than anything else.'

Everyone who knew the Hopkinses of Wern Road remembers young Tony as an insulated, withdrawn child. Evelyn Mainwaring says, 'I had three boys, all of whom became friendly with Tony. But he was an only child and I think the loneliness of a small family, with his dad out to work most of the time, had an effect. Muriel was really his best friend, his idol, I suppose, and she fawned on him like he was the only child in existence . . . But he remained a kind of dreamer, in a world of his own.' The Americans, of course, were the stuff of dreams and made relaxed friendships around Margam by the easy expedient of dishing out chocolate and comic books. Muriel Hopkins – more outgoing than Dick and an easier conversationalist – liked them, their sunniness, which matched her own disposition, and their generosity. 'Muriel was a very giving person,' says Evelyn Mainwaring. 'Not a touch bad about her. A caring, sharing person. A neighbour who you could call on in trouble.' In their second and third years at Margam, the Americans found good friendship – and excellent trade-offs – with the Hopkinses of Wern Road.

Hopkins later recalled in conversation with Tony Crawley:

> It was part of the national hospitality thing. I don't know if it was official, but I guess people were told to encourage their allies and be friendly – and a lot of us did just that. My mother used to bring these guys home. She'd take pity on them, so far from home. My father and I had a lovely time. I remember two guys in particular: Lieutenant Cooney and Captain Dirk, both later killed at the Ardennes by von Rundstedt's troops. I remember them bringing me marbles and cookies and gum. They made quite an impression on me.

Eisenhower's visit as the tank regiments and Free French prepared for D-Day provided additional excitement and Hopkins relished the drama even if, at that time, he hardly understood it. Here, too, he made his first real friend, a sergeant from New York who had a lazy, jocose manner and who took him for walks to the mountain beyond the castle, filling him with tales of the Bronx, of cowboys and Indians, of the wild, distant west. 'I remember when he was leaving for D-Day and I was in bed with the flu and couldn't go to see him off. I was crying – but I couldn't show it because I was a boy and he was a man.'

This American friendship was deeply inspirational – and not a little disturbing – for the insular child, Tony Hopkins. It gave him his first inklings of an exotic foreign culture, an alternative way of being, and it threw him into a youthful quandary about the uncertainty of kinship in an unstable world. Russell Johns, who would shortly be his close friend, recalls that 'Anthony always felt things very deeply and thought deeply about things and that set him apart from the rest of us even when he was a very small boy. Nothing just washed off him. He was too sensitive for that'.

The departure of the Americans foreshadowed D-Day. Then before Margam knew it the bonfires of VJ Day – 15 August 1945 – were roaring up the coast, signalling a new era of even greater change. 'So many things changed immediately after the war,' says Douglas Rees, who grew up down the road from Hopkins and became friends with him in his teens. 'The new steel industry came to town and altered forever the landscape and the character of Margam and Taibach and all the rest.'

It was a period of colossal upheaval that affected all aspects of Tony Hopkins' world. Locally the landscape changed. Port Talbot district had always been, in the words of Sally Roberts Jones, 'at the forefront of advances in steel technology'; now it was selected as the site for the first integrated steelworks in Britain, based at Margam Moors, the 'back garden' of Hopkins' infancy, and vast redevelopment of the area began. Newcomers filled the pubs and hotels – immigrant workers from Ireland, London, Scotland – and the daily rhythms of Muriel and Dick's life were altered for ever. During this period Dick eventually negotiated the lease on a bigger bakery premises, at Commercial Road in Taibach, not many yards from the old base. Wern Road was sold and the family moved to rooms above the bakery.

Tony Hopkins' arrival at school marked his first serious life crisis. The war had not delayed his education and when he started – at the primary school in Groes village, a short bus journey from Margam (and now buried under the serpentine M4 motorway) – it was immediately obvious that he had no academic aptitude, at least not in the classroom. One neighbour believes this was a result of Muriel 'spoiling him'; according to the neighbour, Muriel had a tendency to allow the boy to make his own way, which was contrary to Dick's more disciplined, organised nature.

Another counters this by remembering that it was Dick who indulged the whim of his son when he craved a piano. Dick went out and bought a baby grand, which cramped the parlour – but he was rewarded by his son's rapid ease with it. In a month, Anthony had a dozen tunes down, copying ditties from the radio and giving his first indication of an extraordinary flair for mimicry.

The general consensus is that Dick supported Anthony's piano playing to start with, but grew tired of his son's obsessive introversion. 'I know it was a worry for both parents,' says Evelyn Mainwaring. 'I recall seeing the lad ambling round, carrying his books. He liked to go to the valley, alone, with those books. It seemed a little sad.' It was Dick who first objected to the insularity and the non-stop music, and it was Dick who eventually pushed the boy out into the street to play. In this way Hopkins finally made his first solid friendships since the Americans – with Brian Evans, Havard Hopkins (no relation), David Hayes and Russell Johns. All of them perceived a quiet boy with an unusually complicated personality who, like Muriel, wished to dominate his environment. Brian Evans, who has retained a lifelong friendship with Hopkins recalls:

> He was about eight when I met him. A loner who had a fascinating and strange variety of interests. He loved *Dick Barton* on the radio. He loved astronomy and waxed eloquent about the Great Bear and the various galaxies – in fact, he taught me all I know about the stars. He loved Russian history, Russian legends. And he loved mimicking the stars of the day, the stars of radio and theatre. He could do Jimmy Jewell, or Tommy Handley or Ben Warris . . . with a kind of unnatural skill. It was something that made him stand out.

Evans saw two sides to the boy: a vast sensitivity, and a swaggering daring that often raised his father's ire.

> He earned himself the nickname of Jamtart Hopkins by pocketing all the pastries from the bakery in Tanygroes Street, where I first met him. It didn't please his father – but his mother turned the blind eye, as she

always did, for everything. [In front of Evans, Dick was often verbally tough with his son.] The father was hard on him. I don't know whether he did it for my benefit, but I often felt sorry for Anthony. He was loved, I'm sure, considering. But Dick could be quite aggressive in chastising him, and was always criticising him. We later learnt he'd damaged his back – I think it was lifting all those weights in the bakery – so maybe his pain was the cause of the upset and the abuse.

Another neighbour believes, 'Dick would explode at Anthony because he would get frustrated that Anthony only ever listened to his mother. Muriel overdid the pampering and that drove Dick crazy. He used to say, "He should be more a boy!"' 'We all came together because we were loners,' says Russell Johns, whose home was half an hour's walk from Commercial Road. 'Havard loved to talk. But not boisterously, in the style of the boys in the street, the usual gangs. Havard lived close by so we all met up, usually in his house, and regularly in the primary school years.' The meetings took place in late afternoons and at weekends, and school was never discussed because the other boys attended Dyffryn Primary and knew nothing about faraway Groes. The shared time was spent drawing, writing and chewing over yarns.

'Tony liked love stories,' says Johns, 'but his big thing was astronomy, the heavens, how it all worked. It completely engrossed him.' Despite his outward quietness, Hopkins' personality easily overshone the others. '*He* was the one who decided what we talked about. Havard could talk, but Anthony dominated. He was full of odd ideas and imaginings. I believe his father saw that in him and wanted to develop it, but it must have been annoying because Anthony disliked even the notion of school . . . and he did poorly at school, though I don't think his mum minded.' Russell Johns knew nothing of the home tensions Brian Evans saw. 'But then Anthony was a very private person, as was I, so I knew no more about his troubles with his father than he knew of mine.'

As Hopkins' term results at Groes indicated, little academic progress was made. In desperation – and anger, according to some neighbours – Young Dick moved his son to Port Talbot's Central School, much nearer to home, where Les Evans taught. 'I was in charge of cricket, as well as everything else,' says Evans, 'so I can testify first-hand that Anthony was not a sporty type. He was also poor academically. One wondered what would become of him.'

As a reflex gesture of defiance – against Dick and the Central – Hopkins was briefly rebellious. On the late afternoon walks that Evelyn Mainwaring witnessed from her front window, he would now often meet up with Peter Bray, another local loner, and together they would drift up to the steelworks site, or through the ruins of the derelict abbey nearby. Bray emphasises that Hopkins liked space and isolation – and spinning yarns. 'There were no girls involved, ever. Just me and Anthony and another pal called John Chitsoy who shared the same interests, which involved mostly just getting away from home.' Jamtart Hopkins often shared the spoils of his petty theft on the hillside with Bray and Chitsoy and, as with Evans and Johns, prohibited conversation about the analysis of home tensions.

'What I do remember best is the scrumping for apples,' says Bray. 'Anthony was a ringleader, and very good at it, very good at taking chances and not much caring whether he got caught.' This marauding friendship, like the friendships with Evans and, separately, with Johns and Hopkins and Hayes, was kept compartmentalised and private, barely discussed even with Muriel. All the boys, with the exception of Evans, speak of their unfamiliarity with Muriel and Dick and the bakery and suggest a need on Anthony's part to put some distance between himself and the stifling home atmosphere.

One former friend is explicit:

> I think once Anthony broke the spell of Muriel's domination and was pushed out into some kind of extrovert life he wanted to get away . . . He really loved the open spaces of the Valley and the beach, he loved the escape. But there was a lot of internal pain because he had been for so long a home boy, a mummy's boy, fawned on by Muriel's parents and very much spoiled with nice holidays in the countryside and ice-cream treats every day and all that. He was insecure and he was bad at expressing

himself. He felt his father misunderstood him, or was too impatient with him, and it was all too much having the father there in the bakery, just a room away, all day long. He wanted to break away, but he was afraid of breaking away and in that respect there was a terrible confusion about him. All our fathers worked at the steelworks or in the mines or somewhere, and we hardly ever saw them from one end of the week to the next. Anthony's life was different. Outwardly, it looked nice. Inside, he was a mess. A lot of it, I thought, was Muriel's fault.

At the Central, as a manifestation of his confusion, Hopkins stumbled from failure to failure. His maths was so bad that Muriel asked Brian Evans to allow him to join the afternoon private grind, where Evans studied twice a week. 'I asked the lady [teacher] if that would be OK,' says Evans, 'and she agreed. So Anthony came with me for a few weeks and kind of . . . sat there. But after five or six sessions the woman said, "You'll have to tell his mother to forget it. He's just useless."'

No records exist of Hopkins' examination results but Russell Johns believes,

> He must have failed the graduation because he didn't automatically move on to the Sec [Port Talbot Secondary School] or the County School, which would have been the way. Instead, his father took him immediately out of town and put him into boarding school. I know Havard went too, since the fathers were friends and the boys sought each other's company, and I suppose the comfort of contact. But Havard just boarded overnight and came home. He didn't like it at all. So Anthony was cut off pretty abruptly.

Johns recalls that in the days before Hopkins' exile their gang often went to the Taibach Picturedome, which the locals called 'the *cach*'. It was an illustration of the individuality and isolation of these boys that they never went in organised groups. 'We would just meet up there every so often, very informal, in the foyer maybe, and go in. It appealed to us all but it especially took Anthony because he had this imagination, see, and he

loved the stories.' It also suited Anthony because Brian Evans' grandfather, Charles Roberts, owned the *cach*, and Evans regularly manoeuvred
free passes for both of them, here and elsewhere in town. Apart from the
cach, Hopkins' other favourite cinema was the Plaza in Port Talbot, which
he frequented when staying with Grandfather Yeats.

'The first film I ever saw was *Pinocchio*,' Hopkins recalled years later.
'And one of the first I ever saw was *Sahara*, starring Humphrey Bogart. I
was just a little kid . . . I remember sitting in the dark of the Plaza, watching
this tank getting lost in the desert and taking on the Germans single-
handed. I remember I'd never seen anything like it. And I remember I
never saw anyone like Bogart. I don't know if it was the 'star' business that
appealed to me . . . but I developed this obsession. I wrote him a little letter,
even, a fan letter, and he sent me a photograph with his signature on it.'

Undeniably this attraction to the louche Bogart was an echo of his
banished hero friends – the New York sergeant and his generous cronies
– combined with a vision of escape from school, from Dick and his
expectations, and from an ever-dirtier, ever-noisier Wales. The deserts of
Africa seemed instantly inviting in their openness, their simplicity and
their mortal challenge. They were where Anthony Hopkins wanted to be.
On the big screen he saw the resilience and courage of Cagney and Bogie
and Edward G. Robinson – loners all – as they triumphed over adversity
and failure and won the unmoving sunshine of the promised land,
America, the home of the free. Hopkins saw it, and he wanted it. It was
unreal, but it was just what he wanted.

'He just wasn't happy as a school boy,' says Evelyn Mainwaring. 'There
was no joy in him at all.' Russell Johns doesn't remember saying goodbye
to his friend – emotion of any sort was rarely expressed between them –
but he does recall that Hopkins was 'deeply, deeply, deeply unhappy' at
the idea of more compulsory schooling. The boy may have wanted
permanent escape – to Fred Yeats' haven in Port Talbot or to the exotic,
promising foreign deserts – but he didn't want this escape. 'The choice
wasn't his, though,' recalls Johns. 'It was his father's.'

Dick Hopkins sounded out his customers and his friends at the bakery.
'He was so work-obsessed,' says one man, 'that these were the only

friends he had.' He became convinced that West Monmouth School in Pontypool, all of thirty miles away, would shake Anthony's complacency and put him right. The daydreaming and the astronomy and the fondness for cinema had to be filed away. It was time to grow up. In a few strict years Anthony would be back, focused and trained and ready to assume career responsibilities as befitting the proud tradition of two generations of Taibach bakers.

'Dick wasn't enamoured of the idea of the boy entering the bakery full-time,' says a neighbour from Commercial Road. 'It was successful, but it was dog work and I believe the marriage was under some pressure, that Muriel wished he would slow down and sell out – which of course happened soon after.' But for the moment, the bakery represented some kind of model of rarefied excellence that Anthony should, in Dick's eyes, be reaching for. It was a source of great pride to him that the bakery was considered the best business on Commercial Road, that it employed eleven people and that he, and now Muriel in Anthony's absence, worked all the hours God sent.

Chapter **2**

THE INVISIBLE BOY

'There is always one moment in childhood
when the door opens and lets the future in.'

The Power and the Glory
Graham Greene

Anthony Hopkins left no impression on anybody at West Monmouth, a school celebrated for its academic successes. He arrived in the Christmas term of 1949 and was gone within five terms. Twenty-five years later, on one of his many obsessive return pilgrimages, he visited West Mon and was shown around by Frank Witty, who taught chemistry and maths in the late forties and early fifties.

'I had no memory of him,' says Witty, 'and when he visited I thought nothing much of him other than that he was a cheerful chap. He was unassuming, that was it. And retiring. When I got home and told my wife I'd been showing around an old boy called Anthony Hopkins she tore a strip off me! She said, "Don't you know who that is? That's Hopkins the Hollywood star!"'

Years later, when school governor and county councillor Don Touhig asked Hopkins to open the new Pontypool offices of the Free Press the actor blithely obliged and told Touhig to send fond greetings to Max Horton, the physical education teacher of Hopkins' day. Horton expressed surprise because, 'I didn't come into much contact with the boy, although I was one of the two boarding housemasters. All I recall is that he was a very, very quiet boy.'

Graham Harris, the classics teacher, also has no memory of Hopkins. Neither has Fred Hagger, who taught French. By all accounts, Anthony Hopkins arrived, toed the line, kept his head down. He was one of the few boarders there – they numbered just one in a hundred boys – and is remarked upon only for his studious avoidance of the sports field. Bryn Meredith played daily rugby at West Mon and stresses that Hopkins never showed his face. 'I was a day boy and he was a boarder, so our meetings would have been limited anyway. But I take it he had no interest in physical activities. He had a reputation for quietness.'

Dick Hopkins' monitoring of his son's progress – or lack of it – was a talking point around the bakery and among its customers. Evelyn Mainwaring makes it clear that Young Dick hadn't exiled or abandoned the lad; on the contrary, he was in close touch with the school's head-master and was, accordingly, utterly dismayed by the boy's inability to come out of his shell. 'Dick was an intelligent man,' says one neighbour who visited the cake shop for weekend treats and who knew Muriel well. 'He was good at bandying chat and was friendly and open with a lot of people, like the local poet Gwyn Thomas, who was regularly in the shop. He lamented the failure of the boy. He thought, the boy is just stubborn. He's been pampered and he doesn't want to grow up. He only wants to spend his time rambling on the beach.' She points out that Anthony never helped out in the bakery in those days, although it was customary for young children to assist in their parents' businesses.

A conversation with a customer persuaded Dick Hopkins to move Anthony from West Mon to Cowbridge Grammar School, which was somewhat nearer to home, not far from Cardiff. According to local lore, Cowbridge, which had a reputation for the strictest discipline and a rather unique 'classical education' system, rarely failed a boy. Among its 350-strong pupil complement there were about sixty boarders, many 'difficult' boys from far and wide, directed there for salvation. They, like Hopkins, learnt that knowledge began with the word – and the word was Latin.

Anthony Hopkins made some progress here because, within the first year, his father was boasting of a transformation and congratulating the Cherverton's bakery rep Arthur Bowen, who visited weekly, on his choice of Cowbridge for his son Jeff. Bowen asked Dick if his son could 'look after and keep an eye on' Jeff. Today, Jeff Bowen – who was himself a rep in the Taibach area but now lives in Essex – recalls Cowbridge vividly, for its discipline and precision and care in education . . . but not much for the companionship of Anthony Hopkins.

Founded in the early 1600s, Cowbridge Grammar's concept of education was developed by Sir Leoline Jenkins, a luminary of Jesus College, Oxford. It was one of the first schools in Wales and was built next door to St Mary's Holy Cross chapel, but it was not strictly Church of England. Many Catholics attended the school and, since its early days, the pupils represented a broad cross-section of Welsh life: there were grant-aided pupils and fee-payers, sons of military and clergymen, all walks. Parents of Cowbridgers valued the school as an innovative semi-public school whose masters were mainly English – 'not from redbricks,' says one present-day teacher, 'but mostly Oxbridge types trained in the classics.' Idwal Rees, a once-famous rugby player who had been centre three-quarter on the Welsh team that beat the invincible New Zealand All Blacks in 1935, was headmaster during Hopkins' stay and was, says Bowen, 'a tough cookie'.

Jeff Bowen arrived when Hopkins was in his second year and found 'a huge old greystone building with desks carved and dated a hundred or more years ago. It hadn't been updated at all except, surprisingly, it did have a central heating system – big iron pipes in all classrooms – which was needed during those freezing winters'. Bowen remembers first and foremost the mood of discipline which, he insists was honest and fair.

There were chapel services each morning, though the Catholics and other denominations were excused. When the teacher came in we stood up and saluted – in Latin, of course – 'Salute Magister'. And when we said goodbye to people we said, 'Valete.' The corporal punishment was routine – usually six from the cane in Idwal Rees' office, in private. We were, at least, spared the humiliation of public beatings. It was a school where you succeeded if you had a fondness for the classical values, or for sport. I don't believe Anthony had either – at least not in those early fifties, when I knew him.

Bowen remembers Hopkins dutifully carrying out his father's request and approaching him just a few days after the new lad had arrived at the school. They met in the open garden, resplendent with its almond blossom and birch trees, and Hopkins gave Bowen a quick summary of what the school was about, where everything was, and what to expect. 'He was pretty abrupt. Helpful, but abrupt. He didn't really have much to say for himself and one got the immediate impression that he didn't want to be there, that he was deeply unhappy.' Hopkins himself has described the Cowbridge days as 'very uncomfortable; I was away from home, in a place that operated like a tight ship . . . I was really in a daze'.

'I think his resistance to and resentment of Cowbridge was unfounded and unfair,' says the Reverend Peter Cobb, who taught geography and scriptures and was one of the boarding masters, along with Iolo Davies and Idwal Rees. 'In my eyes we had an outstanding school, with a very fine atmosphere for boarders. Anthony withdrew, is what I'd say. He held himself back and refused association with a lot of what we were doing. For example, he point-blank refused to continue with School Certificate [the equivalent of today's "O" level] geography on the basis that he'd decided he just wouldn't bother with it – though he did, I'm delighted to say, pass scriptures.'

The Reverend Cobb recalls that dormitory life was chaotic, but stresses that Hopkins 'wasn't one who fell by the wayside, he never went missing, as it were'. There were three dormitories – Little Nine (nine beds), Top Dorm (where the juniors resided at the top of the house) and Long Dorm, housing 25 beds, among them Hopkins', which was two down from the sink alongside John Barnard, another quiet boy. 'It was actually a lovely life,' insists the Reverend Cobb. 'By the standards of the day, we were not a terribly strict school. But a school is what you make it and it is a matter of regret that Anthony has been in the past, well, contentious about Cowbridge.'

Dick and Muriel visited at weekends and one teacher hints that Hopkins was rallying to get out from early on. He recalls the family strolling on the green, locked in animated conversation 'that wasn't reassuringly peaceful'. But Dick wouldn't budge. The only 'out' permitted was a continuation of piano lessons during the weekend trips home to Taibach. Hopkins' first music teacher had been a Miss Llewelyn, but the Reverend Cobb remembers that Hopkins was proudest of 'some gentleman involved, I believe, in variety, who continued the tuition'.

Jeff Bowen contends that Hopkins withdrew into his piano music as a way of shutting off the oppressive world of Cowbridge. 'The school room [assembly hall] had an old piano. I frequently saw Anthony there, at all hours, always alone, playing the damn thing. It seemed to transport him, to take him away from the drudgery that he saw himself bogged down in.'

The Reverend Cobb agrees:

> He wasn't a boy who smiled a lot and his dress sense left something to be desired, but there was a definite aptitude for music. We had no music department as such and as I was the only teacher who could play the piano, I became a kind of music instructor. Anthony finally seemed in his element there, in the school room. There were other boys who could play the piano too, many with a greater technique. But Anthony had a better feel than the others. He was, if it doesn't sound so absurd, the most musical pianist we had.

Hopkins' playlist was revealing, Cobb thought: in an atmosphere of macho-posturing pubescent boys, he favoured frothy, whimsical tunes – 'quasi-classical things with a leaning towards the romantic'. Cobb also found it revealing that Hopkins' handwriting was unusually confident and mature, a signal, he believed, towards untapped inner strength. 'He had a most adult hand . . . and for a young fellow he could be disarmingly resolute.

There was, I suppose, more to him than immediately met the eye. In later years, in my church life, I have studied people and their troubles and their lives, and expressed surprise that this person or that achieved so much, or won recognition in the Church, or won a knighthood. In Anthony's case it was somehow not all that surprising. Quite apart from anything we attempted to do for him educationally, he kind of took off on a course of ambition he set for himself. He was, even then, very single-minded.'

In study terms, Hopkins did what he had to do to satisfy Rees and Cobb and get out unscathed. 'He just wasn't committed,' says Cobb with a grunt of irritation. 'We tried to get the boys to read in prep, if only to keep them quiet. But he showed no fondness for it.' Hopkins' recollections are slightly at odds with this. He was, he insists, no prodigious reader, but he enjoyed certain books – especially the Russian tomes to which his Grandfather Hopkins had introduced him. In one instance he remembers reading a library book that wasn't, admittedly, part of the curriculum. It absorbed him, but didn't impress the masters. It was immediately confiscated, which infuriated him. 'I didn't speak to anybody – teachers or pupils – for nine days. As I recall, I had been reading Trotsky's *Russian Revolution*. I sent myself to Coventry. It was the most cleansing thing . . . but I was severely punished for it.'

The smouldering one-man-war that Hopkins quietly waged against Cowbridge frustrated all his teachers and not just a few of his classmates. On the one hand, he was withdrawn, almost timid; on the other, maddeningly sardonic. Even after 35 years there is grief in the Reverend Cobb's voice when he talks about Hopkins' rejection of even the simple pleasures of school life.

> For example, he could not bring himself to express any interest in our little drama efforts. Every year we put on a production in the school room. We did *Twelfth Night*, things like that. We encouraged everyone who showed the slightest interest or aptitude – but of course Hopkins would have none of it. Maybe he thought he would be revealing too much of himself to us by getting up there on stage, or maybe it was just his way of saying that he didn't want to conform to our ways.

Hopkins told Tony Crawley that nothing other than innocent honesty lay behind his rejection of Cowbridge's drama productions: 'I remember the headmaster [Rees] one morning saying, "The school play is on tonight. Hands up everyone who wants tickets" . . . and I didn't put my hand up. "What about Monday night, then?" And I didn't put my hand up . . .'

Rees was furious, but contained himself. Hopkins was sitting directly across the breakfast table from him, spooning cereal, impassive and untroubled. Very evenly, through his teeth, Rees asked, 'What's the trouble? Why aren't you going?'

Hopkins didn't flinch. 'I don't think the standard is very good,' he offered.

'I was very likeable,' Hopkins told Crawley, 'but [Rees] didn't like me at all.'

During his second year at Cowbridge, Hopkins thawed in the enjoyment of his first ever foreign holiday. Iolo Davies and the Reverend Cobb took a group of several dozen boys to the shores of Lake Lucerne in Switzerland – 'Not for educational edification,' says Cobb, 'but for some laughs.' Muriel's usual choice of summer escape was an outing to her beloved Cotswolds, in the company of the Yeatses. Hopkins liked those sylvan rambles but he positively enthused about the chance to tread foreign fields. For once he joined in the spirit, and for the first time Cobb remembers him laughing, relishing the locale – putting paid to the suspicion that he suffered a basic displacement neurosis. 'There was gossip that Hopkins was maladjusted and incapable of leaving his mother's apron strings and facing the responsibilities of growing up,' says a Cowbridge resident. 'But one was always jolted by the other side of him. He was not passive. He could be excessively arrogant. Not really aggressive, but big-headed.'

The Reverend Cobb says, 'I have a photograph from Switzerland that shows Anthony looking very content, very much smiling and coming out of himself. Which is what he did. He behaved quite independently, which was his way, but when he was abroad he let his hair down.'

Cobb wonders whether Hopkins' unease wasn't exacerbated by playground bullying.

'It is part of boarding school legend everywhere that homosexuality is rampant and weak boys are pounced on,' says Keith Brown, a contemporary of Hopkins who was a day pupil by grace of the fact that he lived in Cowbridge village, just a walk away. 'There's a grain of truth there, for sure, and Cowbridge had its measure of gays, as everywhere else, I've no doubt. But there was nothing that told me that Hopkins was anything other than sexually straight – though he may well have suffered, as many of us did, at the hands of the seniors.'

Another contemporary points out that Hopkins was quiet, but 'normal and average in every way'. He smoked on the rugby pitch, enjoyed 'window-shopping with the girls from the next-door girls' school', did all the usual boyish things, 'except play rugby or cricket or put his back into studying'. Cobb believes that Hopkins' 'kind of arrogance' kept him away from the games field and from ever allowing himself to settle in. 'I was often suspicious of whether he suffered as a consequence of that self-sufficiency and retiring nature. It is difficult for teachers to reach into and comprehend the codes of boys among themselves. How do they punish each other for not conforming?'

Keith Brown says,

> The prefects gave us all a hard time. They had their own standards of trial and punishment, with punishment issued by the 'dap', which was the local term for plimsoll shoes. If you did wrong – say you were caught speaking when you shouldn't during assembly with the prefects – you were measured for the dap. They took a look at your behind and said, This lad looks like a size eight, or whatever. And they let you have it. There was also the division between the day pupils and the boarders. And the division between the local lads and the others from outside the area, from North Wales and beyond. These groups tended to band together and form their codes and take spite on each other. Petty stuff, but that can hurt too.

Brown walked to and from school each day and rather pitied the boarders like Hopkins, who was a few years senior to him. 'They hadn't got it easy, no matter what Peter Cobb says, locked in there day and night.' The compensations, he believes, were few. The boarding masters who lived in with the boys, at least, were decent sorts: 'Rees, Davies and Cobb were fair men. Cobb particularly was easy-going and a joy for us lads. We all knew him as an affable chap, a chap you could laugh in front of without fear.' Another compensation for the suffering boarders – lights out at 9.30 p.m., first bell at 7 a.m. – was the weekend allowance for cinema outings to Cowbridge, where Ealing fodder played continually in the main street cinema, a rickety, converted ballroom that was often the setting for schoolboy wars. Hopkins took advantage of this, but preferred weekends at home in Commercial Road, where he would lie in bed and read his comics, or meet up with Brian Evans for walks along the beach.

Hopkins' salvation, the trick of regular relief from depression, came from his easy facility with mimicry. 'I was aware of it,' says Cobb. 'Within Long Dorm it was legendary. When it was time for lights out Hopkins was often up and parading and taking off the various masters, which offered him good scope since they came from far and wide.' Hopkins could do them all: the disciplinarian French teacher Lloyd Davies, with his loud bombastic style; Don Pugh, the physics man who much preferred a Friday afternoon jar than a Friday class; Arthur Codling, the eminently 'English' English teacher who introduced him to Shakespeare; Taffy Hughes, the gentle Welsh giant; Velon, the Frenchman on a year's exchange; H. E. P. Davies, the teddy bear . . . To some of the dormitory boys Hopkins became 'Mad Hopkins' – as much for his manic performances as for his depressions. It was a nickname that shadowed him and, according to one pupil, irritated him: 'He expressed no fear of anyone, except perhaps Mr White, the rather ferocious history teacher, whom he was very, very careful of mimicking.'

Keith Brown says, 'Pinky White was a madman – there's no other word for it – but he had a sad background. He was a big man, and rather stooped, rather unhealthy looking. I believe he'd had a bad time in the war. But we boys got the rough end of it. He could certainly control a classroom. You didn't dare move when he entered. He was so dangerous. So you just sat there – petrified – following orders.'

Hopkins was terrified of James White – and adored him. Later he spoke of his respect for White, the only teacher at Cowbridge who left an impression on him. Some believe that White reminded him of his own father in his forthright, unapologetic commanding manner. Certainly, White was the 'gloves off' version of classical schooling. He was immensely well read and knowledgeable but he wasn't strictly a bookish type. He was physical – animated – emotional – unstable . . . and Hopkins found his performances at the head of the class riveting. History came to life when White taught it: he himself had witnessed the front lines of war and the deprivations of a POW camp. He knew starvation and mortal fear and the naked knuckles of fate. And when he mixed this with Euclid, Aristotle, Wellington and Hitler, the brew intoxicated Hopkins and excited his imagination as nothing else at Cowbridge did.

In the evenings, when Rees and Cobb were out of sight and the boarders bored, Hopkins paraded his catalogue of clowns but reverentially honed his Pinky White. He rarely offered a parody of White, even when Barnard and the others begged him. Instead the observations and images went deep into the machine, to be recalled in a distant future when, in David Hare's *Pravda* at the National Theatre, he created a liberating character called Lambert Le Roux.

'I believe the years in Cowbridge were a waste of time for him,' says Jeff Bowen. Another pupil agrees: 'All he took out of it was a bad English "O" level, the certainty he was a misfit . . . and the memory of a few oddball characters.'

Anthony Hopkins himself says, 'When I left I didn't bother to say goodbye to anyone. I made no friends there. Simply, I hated it.'

Russell Johns, Havard Hopkins and David Hayes all lost touch with Hopkins through the Cowbridge years, but when he returned to Taibach, a boarding veteran aged seventeen, they found him little changed. 'He was exactly the same boy,' Johns insists. 'A little quieter, if anything.' When Johns and the others called at Commercial Road they found a brooding, gawky teenager, hellbent on resuming the old ways – the idling, the book browsing, the valley walks, the avoidance of Dick at all costs.

He was still vague about the opposite sex, but there was one perceptible burning passion brewing: the cinema. He didn't articulate or share it. He just went. Sometimes twice a week. Sometimes daily. Almost always alone. Johns and the others shrugged and resumed their individual teenage pursuits, but Muriel put her foot down. After the years of absence, Anthony was worse than ever. He was argumentatively restless and unreliable and rude. Had Cowbridge helped him at all? Where was the reformed, disciplined, young man Dick had promised? For a time she persuaded him to join the bakery delivery run, but that didn't last. As the piano lessons didn't last. Miss Richards, the newly appointed, advanced tuition lady, he found too impatient and intense. He complained to Muriel that she didn't listen to him, that she hurried him through his exercises and had no interest in the classical pieces he favoured, or the pop tunes he had grown to love – Bing Crosby and the London stage hits. With greater obstinacy than ever, it seemed, he refused further tuition. Instead, he went to the pictures.

Brian Evans had now embarked on his career as a carpenter but met up with Hopkins immediately on his return. 'I'd seen him on the various weekends, during his leaves from Cowbridge, but we became very close again when he came home. Nothing much had changed except that every time I approached the house I'd hear the piano – Beethoven's *Moonlight Sonata* or something by Chopin or Mozart.' Evans believed that Hopkins was 'deeply muddled and unstable' at this time, and blames it squarely on Dick Hopkins' aggression with the boy. Hopkins himself is on record confessing to his father's relentless career pressurising on his return. As Hopkins tells it, Dick would berate him for indecision and laziness and Fred Yeats would retaliate, urging Dick to ease off and allow the boy space to find his feet. Muriel stayed neutral, avoiding the fray in the open rows that Brian Evans witnessed.

'He was an oddball,' says Evans with fondness.

He'd be playing with you in the street and suddenly, very abrupt, he'd say, I have to go to see a relation – maybe his cousin Bobby Hayes or someone. No explanations, he'd just suddenly go and you'd be left there saying, Oh, right, I may as well go home. He never changed in this regard. The quick changes and the lack of expression or emotion one way or the other. I remember meeting up with him later, about 1962, and we had a great chat and then he just said, 'I'm off, back to London, I'm spending the weekend with Dirk Bogarde.' And it wasn't said to impress you. He wasn't impressed. To us Bogarde was a giant. To him, it was just . . . 'I'm off to see another friend. 'Bye.'

The tension of continuing insecurity was easily visible to the likes of Evans but Hopkins held it at bay, deeply within himself. 'He didn't drink then,' says Evans. 'We didn't go to places like the Somerset, or the other pubs. I had an aversion to booze, but Anthony wasn't like that then. I think maybe he would have felt embarrassed going into a pub, because he was terribly insecure around the social scene in Taibach. Cowbridge did nothing for him in that regard.'

Evans was further amused by Hopkins' narrow and naïve sexuality. 'He was hopeless, hopeless around girls. That was a laugh, actually. We used to chase girls on the street – but he never took girls seriously. It was a fleeting thing. He couldn't understand them – maybe he was too busy trying to understand himself and his home life . . . He wasn't gay, there was nothing remotely like that about him, but the idea of kissing a girl – Uuugh! I think he'd rather have kissed a handful of dirt!'

Despite his success with the scriptures, the 'educated' Hopkins was anything but religious. 'There was no chapel routine,' recalls Evans, 'no choir practice. He was an agnostic, very set in his opinions, but not imposing them on anyone, which was the gentleness of his way. Russia still intrigued him and I think he was a believer of that whole way of Communist life – the lack of church intrusion in affairs of the state, all that. He was interested in current affairs, impressed by the news – but, again, it was all inward, all inward.'

In the autumn and winter of 1954, Hopkins moved through a variety of casual paid jobs, mostly driven on by Dick. These were all so short-lived that Brian Evans holds no memory of them. For a time he was a stores assistant at the steelworks, a little later a helper at the bakery ovens. Evans saw the rising panic in his friend and, concurrently, a sullen reconciliation with the smothering, inescapable demands of his father.

Dick's requirement for the boy to act responsibly and make a move on a career was reasonable, everyone knew, 'but Tony was crucified with insecurity'. The time was ripe for some soul-saving, daring move, but Hopkins had no idea what that move might be. Evans, however, did.

> I had always been interested in drama – indeed, long after Anthony left Port Talbot I was pursuing my own acting, though it sadly came to nought. At that time, I had been involved with a small church drama group and was cast in a play called *The Butterfly Queen*. I was the ogre, and I wanted Anthony to come and see it. I don't know why – probably because of his fondness for mimicry and liking stories as much as he did. I just felt it might hold some interest for him, that he might enjoy it and it might stimulate him.

Hopkins eventually went to the church hall, saw the play and was politely impressed. He would not, however, agree to join the church drama group. Evans knew better than to try to twist his arm. 'It sounds ridiculous in light of what he has done since, but his reason for refusing was that he didn't wish to wear those ridiculous costumes. I told him it was drama, that that was what it was about. But he would have none of it. He said it would make him feel silly, so he didn't want to do it. When he made up his mind about something you just had to let it go. So I left him to his options.'

In truth, Hopkins' options in Wales, professionally speaking, were limited. His educational standard was appalling and his best qualification was undeniably that he was the son of a prominent baker. According to friends of Muriel she particularly did not want him to join the bakery, but equally she didn't want him to leave Taibach, least of all so soon after his return from exile. Real job choices centred on the burgeoning, unstoppable Steel Company of Wales, now employing 19,000 and attracting immigrant workers by the cart-load monthly; otherwise it was coal mining or the limited access public services. None of this appealed in any way to Hopkins: after his steel workshop experience he swore he would never work in a factory again. Coal mining horrified him and he was plainly not eligible for accountancy and public record-keeping. *'What can I be? What can I do? I'm utterly useless* . . . This is the way he thought,' says Brian Evans, who lamented for his friend but felt powerless to help in any practical way. 'There are limitations to what young boys can say or do to help each other, even express understanding of each other. I was his friend, which was the best I could do.'

Though Hopkins hated the formality of organised social groups, inevitably, to discharge his pent-up, directionless energies, he was drawn to Brian Evans' wider social scene and the snooker hall of the YMCA building in particular, which his cousin Bobby Hayes also frequented. Here the boys played, and here, with a grudging curiosity, Hopkins turned his eye to the drama players of the YMCA group who rehearsed nightly, from eight o'clock upstairs above the billiards and snooker room.

Douglas Rees, recently retired chairman of the National Union of Journalists, was then, in the fifties, chairman of the YMCA Players and ever open to the possibilities of new entertainments and new talent. The Port Talbot of that era, he describes, stood at a floodtide of cultural promise.

It was a brilliant time, a moment in space. There were the operatic societies, the music groups. There were six major cinemas, twelve working men's clubs, three drama societies. People had money in their pockets as a result of the success of the Abbey Steelworks. The pubs were full every night, the queues to the cinemas started at six o'clock or earlier. If the concert scene was your thing, the working men's clubs absorbed you. I was an entertainment secretary at the Trevelyan Club and we very quickly exhausted the local Welsh acts. So we imported the best performers from all over Scotland, the Midlands, London. There was nothing parochial about that time. The accent was on live performing and new experiences. In that sense, the steel boom helped Wales culturally. It put money in people's pockets and, as it did, it increased the demand for evening entertainments and that is why such groups as the Port Talbot YMCA thrived.

Evans himself takes no credit for Hopkins' fateful volte-face at the YMCA hall one night in February 1955. As with everything else in his young life – and in most of his adult life – Hopkins adamantly made his mind up, alone. Evans is unclear about what that final impulse was, as are all Hopkins' earlier friends. Perhaps it was the memory of the laughter and of Evans' fulfilment in *The Butterfly Queen*. Perhaps it was the twinkle of Bogart in the eye of an elderly player, strutting up the stairs, unfettered by the weight of the real world, to live out a fantasy in some wistful play. Douglas rees remembers:

> We were in rehearsals that evening, and Ray Storey, the YM secretary, came up and told me there was a lad downstairs who was interested in our group. So I went down and found Anthony seated on a bench, watching some boys playing snooker. I asked, was he the lad who was interested and he said, 'Yes I am.' So I said, 'Come upstairs and watch the rehearsals. You're welcome.' We had an excellent producer called Cyril Jenkins who strongly believed in encouraging any boys who showed a scrap of interest. And Cyril was upstairs that night, so I brought Anthony up.

Jenkins was at that time rehearsing two pieces: a fragment of the upcoming YMCA Easter show called *Emmanuel*, which was a conventional biblical epic, and a section from *Othello*. Elved Lody was the young actor taking Jenkins' direction and Hopkins entered shyly, white-faced, unsmiling, 'with the look of a lad who has just been convinced to walk the plank. Would he live? Would he die?'

Lody recalls that it was early in the evening, before the main rehearsal was due to commence, so Jenkins' attention was very narrow and fixed. It was one-to-one. 'The piece we were doing from *Othello* was compelling stuff, aimed at the Glamorgan Youth Drama Festival that was coming up. This young lad came in very, very quietly and sat down and watched from a corner and when it was over Cyril sat beside him and said, "What do you think? Do you want to join us?" And Anthony nodded and said a simple, "Yes". From that moment of *Othello* he had made his mind up. That was his turning point.'

It was a muted, casual turning point but its cathartic effect was undeniable. Hopkins returned to the YMCA the next night, and the next. Within a few days, Jenkins had cast him in a walk-on part that was of little or no consequence to the group players, most of whom hardly noticed the baker's son, but which upended Hopkins' embattled world. 'He came every single night after that,' says Rees, still with a sigh of awe, 'quite obsessively really. He was obviously a quiet boy, a shy person with no desire to socialise. But he was at the Y every night before rehearsal time and he was the last one to leave as we locked up at midnight. I believe we were a kind of family to him, that he found another home at the Y.'

Within five weeks Hopkins was to face his first stage appearance in front of an audience. He was a Roman centurion at the tomb of Christ, restraining Jean Lody – Elved's wife – who was playing Mary Magdalene. The notion set him on fire, though, not unexpectedly, he kept it quiet from most of his cronies. Brian Evans was bewildered by the sudden conversion to costume playing, but, on reflection, was not really surprised. All along he had guessed that Anthony had a theatrical spirit, that he craved an unprejudiced audience, that he wanted stories and laughter – and any convenient cover-all for his paralysing insecurity. All in all, the conversion seemed somehow inevitable – and it was surely hurried by desperation. Everyone saw that Hopkins' idle time was running out. He was too big, too ready, to get away with it. He had to commit to some activity, some target. The alternative was another short summer of indolence inspiring yet more brutal unilateral action from Dick. What would it be next time? More enforced schooling? Or an arrangement in some Taibach businessman's failing factory?

Easter 1955 is vibrant in Anthony Hopkins' mind as his moment of baptism, the magic hour when, for the first time since infancy, life assumed some comforting shape and he felt, in his definition, 'useful at last'. Douglas Rees, Elved Lody, Jean Lody and the friends at the YMCA bear witness. Rees says,

> He was blissfully happy in all the preparations and rehearsals, and he had a sense of humour about the costuming. Which is just as well, because

he needed it. We made up our own costumes, so we gladly made up something for him – a shift sort of thing. But we had trouble with his feet. I had never seen feet so big on a young lad. They were size twelve or thirteen and we simply could not find sandals to fit him. Finally, we located some huge size, but still they were too small. So we cut out the toes – and Anthony went around rather proudly with his bare toes poking over the edges. We ragged him mercilessly about it, and he took it all in good part. There were no upsets. He was part of the team, a blood brother.

The actual performance is memorable for Jean Lody because of Hopkins' positively dangerous presence, which somewhat hindered her own playing. From the start, says Jean, she found Hopkins 'devilishly attractive, though I was committed to my husband by then . . . but a bit scruffy.' As his role was so small, she hardly noticed him in rehearsals and did not engage him in conversation at all. This might have been a mistake because Hopkins was completely untrained and prone to stage fright. 'He was rather clumsy from the moment he walked on stage and, at the crucial part, he stepped on my feet and fell and grabbed me . . . in a very embarrassing place. I don't know whether I was supposed to faint or trip at the sight of Christ risen, but to be honest Anthony had kind of eliminated the meaning of the scene anyway.'

In another role, Hopkins was a disciple attending the birth in the manger. The brief appearance allowed him his first stage words: 'Blessed are the meek, for they shall inherit the earth.' Hopkins later remarked to Tony Crawley that this was certainly 'ironic and appropriate', since he was nothing then if not meek, and certainly poised on the brink of 'a career that gave me everything . . . including the agonies'. He told a Welsh newspaper years later: 'I have never forgotten that night. The scratchy record player playing Wagner's *Lohengrin*, the lights in front of the stage, the excitement of the audience. It marked me. After it I decided I would either be an actor . . . or a vicar.'

The Easter show, garbled and informal as it was, was a revelation of self-worth for Hopkins. People back-slapped and applauded him for doing nothing much more than pretending to be someone else. There was laughter, music, festive bunting, sparkling social intercourse – albeit with a curious anonymity. When this play was over, who would be cast in the next one, or the one after that? Would he work with, even see, half of these people again? Did it matter?

He nurtured this breakthrough in a secretive way. He spoke to Muriel of his great new pastime – far more rewarding than the snooker cousin Bobby and Brian Evans wallowed in – but he didn't bother Dick. No one took the Easter outing seriously but someone said, 'Tony, you could be the next Dickie Burton. He did the Old Vic and all. He did a film with Edith Evans and Emlyn Williams and now he's in Hollywood doing these great epics. He's worth a fortune, is he.' Muriel told Anthony the background, how Burton, then Jenkins, had worked in the Co-op not far away on Commercial Road. How it all began with a whisper there. Hopkins just said, 'Um'. Brian Evans accompanied him to the *cach* where, on his grandfather Charles' free passes, they watched the wide-screen splendour of *The Robe*, drippingly Hollywood, with wide open deserts and a Welshman being Bogart. 'He didn't say much,' says Evans. 'He just laughed and said, "Eh, he did all right."'

Chapter **3**

BLOOD ISLAND

He learnt nothing till he learnt the deathbed *Othello*:

> *It is the cause, it is the cause, my soul,*
> *Let me not name it to you, you chaste stars! —*
> *It is the cause, yet I'll not shed blood,*
> *Nor scar that whiter skin of hers than snow,*
> *And smooth as monumental alabaster;*
> *Yet she must die, else she'll betray more men . . .*

It was Cyril Jenkins who helped him digest it, meeting with him at the hall nightly, colouring, coaching, explaining the dynamics of Shakespeare, the qualities of verse, the value of voice. It was Cyril Jenkins who first spoke about the divinity of acting, about Stanislavsky and his code: that an actor is born with certain qualities of his own and that it is a mistake not to use them. It was here he heard the Stanislavsky quote from Tommaso Salvini which declared that what made a model actor was 'Voice, voice and then voice.'

'There were two remarkable things about Anthony,' says Brian Evans. 'His hands, which were huge. And his nut-brown voice.' Everyone, from David Scase to Lindsay Anderson to Michael Cimino, speaks of the

38

voice, with its Welshness apart from Burton's – who cherished the native tongue while Hopkins did not. For Hopkins, *Othello*, his 'Rolls-Royce of a part', was a liberation, though no one at the YMCA much noticed the explosion in his eyes. Until then, he says, all learning was a burden. Miss Richards, the piano lady, who wanted results overnight; Cobb and Rees and Davies, who expected formulae; Dick, who judged things by old, tired yardsticks. Now, in the *Othello* fragments he relished, he had discovered another learning, a connection of spirit and expression that had eluded him all his life. The voice, it appeared, was the price of admission. It fitted and gave life to the inciteful, brilliant words on the page. He liked to speak them, quite suddenly. He liked to cannon it out and hear the syllables boom back from the wooden YMCA walls, to see Jenkins' joy at the perfectly enunciated verbs, to feel the vibration of the golden rhythms on his skin. Suddenly his books had meaning. The comics faded, though he never lost the warmth for Dick Barton and Sherlock Holmes, or those cartoon heroes who challenged the fates with more brawn than brain. It was just that he suddenly felt a purpose to his existence: if only to articulate words that resonated. 'I felt whole for the first time,' he said, 'when I learnt a full play text. I felt at last that I could finish something.'

Late in the summer, Douglas Rees was strolling with his wife Elizabeth and decided to call in on Cyril Jenkins who lived not far from the YMCA in an austere bedsit. They were welcomed by Jenkins' wife and the foursome sat and enjoyed a cup of tea and a rolling chat. The doorbell went and Jenkins opened it to find Hopkins 'Just stopping by to say hello.' The youth joined the group and the chat, then suddenly said, very casually, 'I have some good news.' 'We all said, "Well, come on and tell us," ' says Rees. 'And he sat there, not at all impressed, and said, "It's just, I won a scholarship to the Welsh College of Music and Drama." We were utterly fazed and absolutely delighted! But he had told no one. All along he was learning this *Othello* and studying Cyril and he said nothing at all about his intentions. It was obviously carefully thought out. But he told no one.'

Brian Evans knew nothing about it, which was particularly surprising since he loved drama and Hopkins well knew of his local ambitions. 'We were out walking and, totally casually, he said to me, "I've just been to Cardiff to meet Flora Robson." Flora Robson! – I wondered, was he joking? And then he said, "I'm going to be studying acting at Cardiff Castle. I'm going to be an actor, Brian."'

Hopkins' quiet choice of the Cardiff college was partly a result of conversations with Lody and Jenkins and other part-timers at the YMCA. But it was primarily prompted by an ad in the *Western Mail* promoting the two-year scholarships, worth £200. Hopkins was realistic about his new interest: first, Taibach had no tradition of professional actors, though Burton's newfound success had them chattering in the streets; second, to expect Dick to fund him after the disaster of Cowbridge was a joke. He would have to go it alone, and do or die in a bid for a scholarship. RADA or the Central School of Speech and Drama in London seemed like surer bets, but many who knew him believe that Hopkins gave himself the litmus test of immediate scholarship: Cardiff suited because it was on his doorstep.

Hopkins applied in June, and in July was summoned to an audition at Cardiff City Hall – not before Flora Robson (who was a frequent visitor to the Prince of Wales Theatre in Cardiff, though not involved with the college), but before Dr Raymond Edwards. The stipulation was for a piece of Shakespeare; Hopkins prepared *Othello*.

Raymond Edwards, like Hopkins, was an only child and had much in common with Hopkins, though he was a decade older. Edwards had pulled himself to the culturally influential ranks by dint of unsupported hard work. But his rise had been shaky. He had planned an acting career but didn't have the courage, he says, to see it through. Instead, having earned his English degree at Bangor, he made tracks for Liverpool rep. From here he applied for and won the post of Drama Advisor to Cardiff City and head of the drama department newly set up at the college situated in Cardiff Castle, 'bang slap in the middle of a very uncultured town'.

Cardiff Castle had been given to the city Corporation by the Lords Bute, two of whom, both haemophiliacs, had died within a short time of each other, leaving crippled estates unable to pay death duties. The

Castle was given in lieu of these taxes and the Corporation put it to good use serving the educational needs of the city. In 1949, the music department was founded and, in 1951, Edwards arrived to 'bring drama to the city'. The task, he says, was a daunting one.

Cardiff at the time was a city of philistines who had no appreciation for or awareness of its drama talent. There was quite a bit of it around, but it needed to be organised and encouraged. We started with our hands tied. Glamorgan Council refused us grants but we were saved by the impresario Prince Littler, whose family had been very supportive of the theatre in general, and who funded the student scholarships. When we started we had nothing, not even a theatre in the building – that didn't come until 1972. We worked from very inadequate, cramped rooms. But the situation was made exciting by the students we found – like Hopkins.

Two aspects of Hopkins' audition performance impressed Edwards, who was not, by reputation, someone easily impressed: the coiled fury of the youth, and the power of his voice. 'He moved with a very animal energy. He also had the voice of Burton.' Edwards is emphatic about the uniqueness of a particular inherent Welsh strength:

The South Wales actor has an advantage in the voice. I have come to believe that it is an inherited quality derived from the mines. Generations of coal workers have lived in cramped, acrid environments where they cannot stand up properly in the mine shafts and are breathing appalling air. The consequence of this oxygen deprivation is that they breathe very deeply into their lungs and use dilated nostrils and a stretched and open air passage. These are the specific requirements of voice projection, as taught to aspirant actors. So the South Wales actor comes with the voice technique down pat. It is natural to him. And it was something Hopkins had, before I taught him anything.

After the ten-minute audition, Edwards told Hopkins on the spot that he was in, advised him to go home, pack a kit and prepare for two years under the Castle roof. Accommodation would be, and was, arranged with the caretaker Edward Donne and his wife, in furnished rooms on the premises. For 24 months, then, Hopkins would eat, sleep and breathe the world of acting in hallowed halls that hummed to the musical accompaniment of Cardiff's hopefuls. It was, after Cowbridge's costive mood, an intoxicative delight.

Hopkins displayed his pleasure by relaxing and revealing himself in a manner that would have surprised Dick and the masters of Cowbridge, and probably annoyed Muriel. According to one close friend, Muriel had 'the gravest doubts' about allowing her boy to leave home again, especially for the world of acting, but 'the notion of a castle and a college impressed her – she was a bit of a social climber in her heart'.

Edwards' affection for Hopkins grew fast and he found the youth 'manifestly content' while 'self-effacing, but not shy' in the tiny, linoed studio in the bowels of the Castle where twenty students – mostly girls – gathered for lessons given by a variety of specialist teachers. Edwards knew nothing of the strife of Commercial Road, but he had his suspicions. 'His school record was so bad, it must have been heartbreaking for his father. A pupil with his one O level would not get into the Cardiff College today. And his father had splashed all his money getting him educated – for this! What must it have been like for his father, this failure? Maybe for one moment I thought: Will this boy have the tenacity to stay the course? I mean, his record was not good.'

Assisted by his wife, June Griffiths, and actor-directors like Rudy Shelley from Bristol, Edwards plunged his students into a comprehensive technique course. 'It was pretty harrowing, sometimes fourteen hours a day for me, but we didn't overtax the students. They had a good time and a broad curriculum. We studied Greek drama, Pre-Shakespeare, Restoration Comedy and Tragedy, Modern and Anglo-Welsh drama. Along with these were the various departments of technique: movement, voice, et cetera. We reviewed Stanislavsky, the Method, the applications of the visual media.' Through it all, Edwards recollects:

Hopkins was a shining pupil – apart from a lack of physical control. He was quite manic, with props and what have you. The damage count on chairs, I recall, was high. He broke things. But . . . there *was* something. He was Chekhovian. Much of his developing technique wasn't really taught to him. For example, people today point out to me his perpetual gesturing – the finger twiddling the ear, the twitching nose. I say to them: 'It is *him*'. His own characteristic way.

Edwards assiduously worked the requisite drama texts but Hopkins, as at Cowbridge, 'was inclined to go off on his own things. Chekhov, the Russians, he loved all that. It was precocious, and I let him do it because he seemed very happy. There was an aura of happiness about him, and it grew while he was with us . . .'

The aura of happiness owed its origins to a mousey-haired girl called Pamela Miles. Welsh-born but raised 'all over the place – my father was in the RAF', she took Hopkins' eye immediately he joined the class. The instant attraction was reciprocated. Pam Miles (now Piggott-Smith) says,

I'd got a grant, though not a maintenance allowance because I was so young – just seventeen when I joined the college. My parents had been living in Cardiff and I thought the time was right to pursue my dream of being an actress, so I applied for the new drama at the college. But then, just as I got in, my parents moved on, so I was obliged to stay with an aunt, about a half-hour away from the college. I bussed there every day – and cycled later, when I moved into the YWCA, which was a lot nearer the college – and was very content with my 'mature' new life. I was there for a few weeks when this handsome Port Talbot boy arrived – Tony – and I was pretty immediately smitten. He became my first great love.

The central attraction, physical chemistry apart, says Pam, was their similar childhood experiences. Like Hopkins, she was an only child, used to isolation and the intermittent removal from family on the dictates of her father's work. 'Tony told me he had never had a girlfriend and I had never really had a boyfriend so it was quite the magical thing. There was a lot to share, and over the next two years our closeness grew as our acting grew. I suppose there was an undercurrent of competitiveness but, honestly, at that age you are blinded by love and, in our childish way, in a very short time we were talking about marriage . . . but not until I was 25 . . .'

Hopkins bloomed in the relationship, finding a confidence and open humour he had never known. Edwards affirms:

> He wasn't a show-off, but he was domineering in a very strange way. And that part of him – the charisma, I suppose you'd have to call it – was growing all the time. I remember, for instance, the keenness of his wit, doing an improvisational piece [with Pamela] and asking where she was from. She was from the town nearby which, in turn, was near the town of Pyle. When she said 'nearby', he reciprocated so fast with, 'Oh really, a *mile* from Pyle, would you say?' It was a deadpan, cutting delivery that had everyone laughing.

As Pam tells it, she and Hopkins lived a chocolate-box romance in the coffee houses of Cardiff, rarely venturing further afield. In their two years together they only once went to London, for the LLAM drama exams, and only a few times back to Taibach. Mostly they drifted with groups of students, avoided pubs, kept out of trouble. It was the era of the Teddy boy, the barb at the tail of the post-war honeymoon, but Hopkins was too much the individualist – and romantic, Pam insists – to conform. 'He was more like a Left Bank beatnik than anything,' one friend of the era opines, and Pam concurs: 'It was desperately innocent, childhood posturing. He didn't go deep into his problems, or his dreams. But he was restless and I learnt a little as we went along.'

Back in Wales, Pam was introduced to Muriel, who was wary of her. A friend says: 'Muriel hated anyone who was likely to take her son from her. He was her shining joy, her boy, and he was only a teenager himself.' 'I suppose Muriel wasn't mad about me,' Pam admits, 'but Dick was terribly kind and I really liked him.'

By the start of the second year at Cardiff, Hopkins was wrestling with his opportunities and his weaknesses. Edwards had already tested him with a prominent role in the college's *Insect Play*, by the Czech Karel Capek. 'In it,' says Edwards, 'he just shone.' Acting thrilled him more than ever but now, with sharpening objectivity, he recognised his problems. For starters, he was bad at learning lines. Secondly, his physical grace left something to be desired. Pam, on the other hand, while often hounded by June Griffiths (who seemed to take a special interest in criticising her), had the grace of a ballerina. 'He was jealous of it,' says Pam. 'There's no polite way of saying it. But we were in love, we were children, we kept it under control.' However, Hopkins did have a tendency to brood and pick privately at his worries. His progress was not what it should be, he felt, and this experiment would be over in another year or so. Where could he go next? What if he failed, as he had failed in all his academic endeavours, and won no certificate? How would he then persuade Dick, or Muriel, to allow him to stay in an acting life? And, anyway, how could he overcome Muriel's dislike of Pam?

Riddled with doubts again, Hopkins entered his second year at Cardiff bound up in his love for Pam, but at the edge of his nerves. Into his life at this doubting moment came Peter Gill, a seventeen-year-old Catholic boy from Cardiff whose father was a manual worker and whose academic life had been as half-baked as Hopkins'.

Gill joined Edwards' class with the same wide-eyed enthusiasm 'to be an actor at all costs' and, like Hopkins, quickly rose to the top of the troupe. Gill says,

> To understand what happened next, you will have to picture it as it was then. This baroque, wondrous castle in this philistine, awful town. The Cardiffians were barbarians. And here were we, trying on the classic mantle. Instantly Tony and I clicked. Instantly, and deeply. It sounds immodest to say, but we became the luminaries. We were both great actors – I probably better than he – and we dominated the proceedings. We were the only two talents there, as I recall, and there was a piece of history in the making.

Others attest to Gill's qualities, and his undeniable, flattening impact on Hopkins. 'Peter was small, stocky, swarthy,' says Pam Miles, whose flickering love was about to be doused. 'He had a fascinating face and was extraordinarily well read. He was something fresh at the college and, yes, he was a dynamic natural actor. Tony took to him. But I think, really, the energy was mostly the other way. Peter developed an obsession with Tony, and it left me very confused.'

Gill says,

Tony was the oddest, most remarkable and most lovable boy I had ever met. He was one year ahead of me, and older than me, and these were big things in a student's life. But he entranced me, as he enchanted many people. He was bullocky, tough in ways, but very sensitive, with these pale, pale Welsh blue eyes that are unlike the Irish or anywhere else. We looned around on the coffee-house scene, never went into bars, but I was captivated by his spell. And I am not a weak person. The opposite. I am manipulative and strong. But Tony took me in. Part of his hold over people was his difficult, tantrumy thing. He broke furniture and told us all he wanted to be great. But I believe there was the other side, the feminine side, if you will, and I think that ultimately his enthralling of people was mysterious to him, too. I don't think he could make out the meaning of so many things happening in his life. In my mind, with the benefit of hindsight, it was the strain of adolescence, mostly. I suffered it too. But the pain of it, or the anxieties or whatever, drew us very tightly together.

Pam Miles saw the emergence of a curious triangular relationship in which, quietly, she vied for Hopkins' attention. 'We still dated and held hands and went walking, but Peter often got in the way. I was, I felt, the outcast in that relationship, and I knew that Peter would have liked to destroy us as a couple. It became very confusing. I didn't discuss it with Tony, at that age I don't believe one would know how to start.'

Though Gill was less close to and less fond of Edwards, both boys found themselves cast in leading roles, alongside Pam Miles, in Lorca's

Blood Wedding. 'I was the Moon,' says Gill, 'and Tony was the lead. He was exceptional, and we were good together. I thought, here is a special moment. Two important talents emerging – and how strange it all seems in this quaint, downtrodden place.'

Gill and Hopkins continued to benefit from Edwards' ambitious determination to spread the cultural word round West Wales. Edwards says,

> I developed a plan to exercise our young actors and bring the drama to the homes of Wales. It was very simple: when we had a play assembled and ready we loaded on to a bus and drove around the West, to the various towns like Caernarvon and Pwllheli and Bangor and Ffestiniog, where we put that play on at church halls or theatre clubs. It was a tremendous practical education for the students who had their hearts set on acting, because it showed the other side of the acting world: life on the road.

Edwards saw Hopkins especially rise to the delight of it. Gill says, 'I think that said something about him, that perhaps instinctively he felt he had to get away from Wales – from Muriel, I would say – so the life on the road seemed an answer perhaps. Like, maybe this will be my future, and it's not such a bad life . . . though I'm not sure where Pam fitted in this, because I was aware that he loved her, and I was afraid of what that might become.'

Raymond Edwards remembers: 'Each trip was a new town, new people, a new life. We were housed in the various clubs and theatres, and we usually overnighted in people's homes.' When the bus took the group through Taibach, Edwards was amused by Hopkins' cheek in stealing scones from the bakery.

> He filled his pockets and brought them back to the bus, which made him a few new friends. He was mischievous and very kind, and I feel the acting had quietened something in him, so a lot of the early tension went. [Edwards believed that] whatever tension existed between father and son was on its way to resolution. Acting is not seen as a stable

occupation. It takes courage and determination to make it work. This often causes trouble . . . But I'd say the father reconciled himself quickly, once he saw the earnestness of Anthony's conviction. I remember I gave a dinner lecture at Neath a few years later. And I recall that Anthony came, with his father. They were really close, I thought, and they had an understanding. A definite affection. I know his father came to admire his chosen direction, and there was a deep love, an empathy, there.

Peter Gill met both Dick and Muriel and perceived two very different people whose impact on Hopkins was equally dramatic.

'Dick was essentially kindly and warm. But Muriel was the boss. A working-class, portly, rather large, I'd say Tory-voting woman, who had a great hold on Tony, who really ruled his life. I can imagine that Pamela feared her – I am certain she could be quite frightening. I think she was the kind of woman who would have found it equally hard to love and to hate. But, for any prospective girlfriends of Tony, she must have cut a daunting figure. She didn't like me, which was very unusual, since that kind of woman tended to be very fond of me, then. But she saw that Tony and I were very, very close and – maybe it was the competition element – but she couldn't wait to see the back of me, really.

On their return to Cardiff Hopkins and Gill grew closer, though Hopkins continued to date Pam and pledge his devotion. Gill recollects:

We spent all our free time together. Tony was the one with the money – never me or Pamela. Tony and I began the movie circuit. It ran our lives. Three movies in particular occupied our fantasies – and it was a fantasy world we inhabited, as though we had been bashed about by adolescence and now clung to each other for the affirmation of happiness and freedom. The three movies were *Rebel Without a Cause*, *On the Waterfront* and *Richard III*. We went to them again and again and looned around Cardiff mimicking Olivier and Brando and Dean. Tony did Dean a lot, and it was all great fun. Raymond Edwards became the butt of all kinds of jokes, as he was the authority figure. We would take him off, telling the younger girl musical students that he beat us, or that June did. The running joke was that Raymond did everything. So, when the first satellites were shot into space we'd say, 'Raymond did that.' Tony really gave vent to his suppressed sense of fun. It was a great time for both of us, though I think a hard time for Pam.

As the sands of time at Cardiff Castle were running out for Hopkins, Gill and he invested as much as they could in widening their experience of acting life and debated future possibilities. Gill says,

In truth, we were wet behind the ears, we were innocents. But it was clear that we stood out as talents. If it happened for anyone, it would happen for us. Plus, of course, we loved theatre. I remember we hitched to Stratford, to see Alan Badel's *Hamlet*. We shared a tent at Stratford or slept in the doorway of the theatre. Both of us were enchanted by the play. It had Harry Andrews as Claudius and Tony enjoyed the performance, and of course went on himself to play a very interesting Claudius [in Tony Richardson's 1969 film]. At the time I felt we would go on to work in theatre together as some kind of endless double act, but of course that's nonsense, but it's how you are when you're young and you have developed a great passion.

The intensity of the relationship between Hopkins and Gill augured bad. Pamela Miles, among many, was bewildered by the complex emotional tussle, without fully comprehending its implications. It maddened her and deeply unsettled her peace with Hopkins. 'But whatever it was, it was private to them,' she says, emphasising that Hopkins' gender was pure and his love for her typically 'one of teenage heterosexuality'. Gill wasn't so sure. For him, Hopkins was 'not a bloke for women at all', though emphatically not homosexual.

'Our experience in psycho-analytical terms was oceanic, and it had a very great effect on my life, though Tony has curiously denied it. I have always thought he came very close to showing me a very adult affection . . . but it all became terrible. Looking back, yes, we were caught in a classic triangle of affection and choices, and perhaps I was more sensitive, and manipulative and super-egotistical in the workings of my brain and my talent to control it. But we were all going through such changes and we were all casualties of our teens. I had pain, so did Pamela.'

As graduation approached, and the inevitability of goodbyes, the three-part union came unstuck. Gill maintains:

> None of us wanted to let it go, but Tony was about to leave and that made the crisis. He really had this power. Raymond's college was no good for me, because I was too unformed and I needed more discipline. But it was good for the kind of blundering talent Tony had. For me, I was too full of insights and I was writing poetry and plays then and starting a direction that would create my eventual career as a playwright. But Tony's departure brought about a turning point, because, just as he left – and I was desperately unhappy – I ended up before the chief education officer in Cardiff having to give an account for myself as to why I wanted to get out of the college and how it was educationally no good for me.

In Pam Miles' view Gill was 'too scared of acting' but 'too talented not to go on to something extraordinary'. But he was also still clinging to Hopkins' side and obstructing her faltering love affair.

> The writing was on the wall. We had been together for about two years and Tony's jealousy of my particular skills, modest as they were, had positively got in the way too. He hated it that I had no Welsh accent, and that I was considered a very graceful stage presence, someone who moved well where he was so awkward physically. So, as soon as our exams came, I got a job touring with the children's theatre group and our relationship was fractured for the first time. Very shortly after that I got a letter from Tony breaking it off. He said he didn't want us to be lovers

any more, that it was dead. I was heartbroken. But I was young. You forget it very quickly.

From Hopkins' point of view, graduation from Cardiff College was a piece of cake. For the first time in his life, qualifying was no strain. 'His diploma was a foregone conclusion,' says Raymond Edwards. 'But God knew where he would go. Despite the success of Richard Burton, Wales wasn't a hotbed of rising stars, and stage opportunities were still very scarce. I remember thinking, he'll have to go to London, but I also remember thinking, he'll succeed.'

The boarding experiences at Cowbridge and Cardiff Castle profoundly strengthened Hopkins' sense of independence and, despite his closeness to Gill and Pam Miles, in some way strengthened his capacity for solitude. Though Gill and he were 'closer than brothers', a physical distance was maintained. Gill poignantly recalls 'the gap', pointing out that he never once visited Hopkins' upstairs rooms at the Castle: 'I had just the vague idea of his haven out there, away, past the kitchens. In that sense, he was private, and had the ability to hold things in compartments.'

When Cardiff ended, in the summer of 1957, Brian Evans expected his friend to return to Commercial Road and the baby grand piano: 'I thought maybe he'd pick up a local job, keep up the amateur acting and settle down – though I must admit I could never ever imagine him getting married . . . so much so that when I heard years later, after we had drifted apart for a spell and he was about 28, that he had gotten himself married, I refused to believe it.' Hopkins joined Evans for the odd walk and chat but, in his usual way, kept the secrets of other friendships apart from him. 'To me,' said Evans, 'he was still a loner, still into himself.'

Meanwhile in Cardiff, Peter Gill had left the college prematurely, determined to pursue an acting – or at least a theatrical – career by other means. 'I was so terribly unhappy. All the fun of the last year was gone and I missed Tony, and Pamela. The college had not been a bad experience, though I was not impressed by its educational value. But we had had the chance to appear on stage, and in a few little local TV things, so in that education it helped. But I knew Tony was back in Port Talbot and I wanted to bridge that distance.' Gill went to the Arts Council offices in Park Place and was advised to contact the director Frank Dunlop, based in London, who was planning a tour of theatreless areas, much in the style of Edwards' ground-breaking scheme.

'I wrote away – my first ever job application – and in a few days got a reply. My mother woke me with this letter from Frank Dunlop that said I had to be in London at eleven o'clock the next day. So I begged the train fare and charged at it.' Dunlop, says Gill, took pity on 'this kid who looked like he was fourteen and had come all that distance' and gave him his first paid job, as an assistant stage manager for the upcoming tour of South Wales and the north-east. The play was to be the first ever version of *Look Back in Anger* outside the Royal Court, and it was followed by *She Stoops to Conquer*. 'I was beside myself with delight, and then the best thing happened. Another of the ASMs got married, so there was an opening in the group. I rang Tony in Wales and said, "Come to London, quickly. There's the chance of a great job."'

Hopkins took the morning train, defiant in the face of Muriel's spoken doubts, insistent on pursuing his acting. But something had changed in the period of separation, short as it was, from Gill. Hopkins had had time to review their friendship, undistracted by the rhythms of Cardiff life. He had privately dissected his life, his feelings, his future. The line was drawn with Pam – and now he was reconsidering the closeness with Gill.

Gill recalls, 'I went to Paddington to meet him from the train. Suddenly, in an instant, this curious dislocation happened. I had been enthralled by him, dying to see him and be with him again – and then this, this let-down. I thought: What is this, with this perfectly normal bloke! What is this spell I am under?'

As Hopkins met Dunlop, clinched the job and the tour began, Gill felt the need to force some consummation in the relationship, a kind of do-or-die intimate Waterloo.

It all went awfully wrong. I forced something, and I should not have. But, really, neither of us was to blame. Yes, I was manipulative and in that sense predatory. I had come between Pamela and Tony and I had won.

But I was also under his spell. I don't think, then, he knew what that spell was – though later he did, when he studied its practical application at RADA with Yat Malmgeren . . . which was something I contend ruined his acting. But, there and then, I wanted to push our relationship forward, and Tony balked at it. He wouldn't follow it through. I believed that what we had had was minutely sexual, but I think he would say that that was untrue. In his mind it was not sexual, nor romantic. He could live with what it had been, in its innocent, circumspect way. But he could not accept what was now happening. So denial came into it. A positive tempest was going on there. Had we been New York children, I believe, we probably would have become junkies. But we were South Wales children, lost in our sexual hunger and confused. We went out on the road on that first tour, the first job in theatre that I had landed for him, and it was hell. We were caught in an irrevocable breakdown.

'I am a cold fish,' Hopkins later told an interviewer. 'I think I am not great friends with people. I am not interested if other people want to make a hash of their lives, for instance. I am a bit pitiless in that way. I don't mourn much. Perhaps it's a defence mechanism. But my philosophy has basically been: Fuck 'em . . .' Through the winter of 1957, recoiling from Gill, he metamorphosed into James Dean, his recent hero, and ascribed to himself all Dean's attributes. Though he would later tell his first wife Peta Barker that he had been a boozer since he was fourteen, only now did the neighbours of Taibach see him hit the Sker. 'He was a bit thuggish,' says one. 'The collar turned up, all that man-of-the-world spiv thing. And he didn't talk about acting. We knew he was into it, so we called him Young Dick Burton – but he hated it.'

He hated most, perhaps, because he envied. He envied Burton the unWelsh wealth, the independence, the confidence, the distance. Once, struggling away from Muriel's cosy grip, he took it on himself to visit Burton's sister, Cis, in Caradoc Street. As soon as he approached the house, he knew Burton was there. Outside was a sparkling new Jaguar car, a symbol he craved. He knocked, was taken inside by Cis and found Burton shaving at the sink.

'Where you from, then?' Burton asked.

'Commercial Road.'

'Oh, I worked in the Co-op there.'

'I know.'

Intimidated, he took an autograph, and left. Later, ambling down the Side, Burton passed in his slinky limousine and waved from the window. It irritated him in a way that confused him. Occasionally, he spoke cynically about Burton who, inevitably, 'sold out'. Always, immediately, he regretted it. Because always, immediately, he knew he wanted the richness and remoteness of Rich Burton. Very early in his career he was telling journalists how all he wished for from an acting life was 'fame and wealth – all the rest is crap'.

The Taibach of the late fifties that Hopkins hesitated in was vastly changed from his childhood days. Drunk on steel as opposed to the coal of former times, it was a cleaner, colder, less characterful place hedged in by ever-growing machine plants. People came and went without obvious reason. Strangers' faces filled the Sker. Businesses opened and closed. The grocer's. The tea shop. The bicycle repairs. Money moved fast, meant much, did little. It was a rut of prosperity in a time of gas fires and cabbage-and-potatoes and no refrigeration and Woodbines and fireside radio. An era of non-hygiene, in the words of the writer Gillian Tindall, when the prevailing smell in the street was that of unwashed clothes – and, always, tobacco. But monumental, enduring change was at hand. The soul of society was in flux and with the prosperity here, as across the land, came the rebellions: against austerity, against regiment-ation, against spiritual inertia. In London, the heart of an empire, the Bulldog Breed was dying and its death rattle was loud in the Theatre of the Angry Young Man, and in rock-and-roll, and on TV. Television was the arch proselytiser, spreading the message daily, reporting the techni-color, bountiful world beyond the Valleys.

Almost immediately, whether he liked it or not, Hopkins found himself confronted by yet another exile. He had become eligible for National Service in 1956, but dodged it on the basis of commitment to academic scholarship. Now the writing was unavoidably on the wall. He resented the duty, says a friend, because more than anything else he perceived the concept as anachronistic. He had great respect for soldiers, for the uniform, for the emblems of his American friends and Dick's enthusiastic wartime comrades. But the war was over and few were prophesying the likelihood of another one. Still, the world was anything but stable. Between 1957 and the early sixties, the potentially apocalyptic build-up of antagonism between East and West was growing. While the optimists clouded the risks as a non-war Cold War, the Soviet union was threatening the freedom of West Berlin and boasting the backup of medium-range ballistic missiles targeted on Western Europe; it was also consolidating its foothold in the Western world in Castro's Cuba and articulating brazen expansionism in billion-dollar investments in the developing nations, helping Egypt's Aswan Dam, giving arms to Indonesia and the Algerian rebels and building steel mills in India. In the wings, the Hanoi Communists prepared an onslaught on South Vietnam while China concentrated on beefing up its own client states and planning its own nuclear bomb.

Hopkins' response to this tangle of political signals was understandable confusion. Not politically widely read, he was torn between loyalty to his American idealism and the legacy of grandfather Hopkins' Socialist beliefs. To many acquaintances, he was distinctly pro-Western, hellbent on America and seeing the accelerating space race as a sign of healthy competitiveness between East and West. Others perceived a contradictory rallying for Russia at this time, and recall regular averring to his proud grandfather – 'one of the first British Communists' – and an obsessive, romantic interest in Russian literature. In fact, though Old Dick had been involved in setting up the railwaymen strike of 1912, his active political days were few and long behind him by the time he settled into the Taibach bakery. Nonetheless, Hopkins was undoubtedly touched by his grandfather's ideals, though the nearest he got to a coherent statement of support was his participation – briefly – in Ban the Bomb marches that railed as much against the Americans as anyone else.

Anthony Hopkins tried energetically to avoid National Service. During his Swansea medical he feigned deafness, but his acting fell short of persuasive. In February 1958, he was enlisted in the Royal Artillery at Oswestry, in Shropshire. Six weeks later, he was posted to the Clerks' School at Woolwich, in London, and from there shunted to Bulford Camp on Salisbury Plain. Dick was proud, Muriel concerned in her mother-hen, possessive way. Hopkins himself was plain agitated. Having essentially proved the rightness of his choice of an acting career by funding himself for two and a half years, he bitterly resented being derailed. 'I didn't know if I could be an actor. I just suspected it, and hoped for it. So I didn't welcome anything that slowed me down in getting on with it.' Upsetting, too, was the echo of Cowbridge, with dull conventional minds imposing unwanted disciplines and detention.

As Hopkins tells it, he arrived off the London train with three other clerically trained soldiers enthusiastic only for the hope of a quick transfer to Cyprus. Staff Sergeant Little decided Hopkins' fate: he would work under Little as a Clerk at Regimental Headquarters, serving the organisational needs of three batteries – 26 Battery, 32 (Minden) Battery and 30 (Rogers' Company) – that made up the 16 Light AcAc Regiment RA, under Colonel Willoughby Cubitt. The job detail itself didn't bother Hopkins: at Woolwich he had adapted fast to the lonely comforts of the typewriter keyboard and had made the firm decision to play whatever games of obeisance were required to get on and get out fast. Cyprus was a mild disappointment, but he did consider himself fortunate to find the friendship of the easy-going Ernie Little, and Ernie's wife Cynthia, who quickly took a liking to him and booked him as their semi-resident babysitter (in exchange for contraband sausages from the Sergeants' Mess) at the married quarters across the camp. Hopkins was depressed by the pay – 28 shillings for, in Provost Sergeant Lionel Wheble's words, 'dog work' – but at least it afforded him treats at the army stores and weekends at the pub.

His luck with new companions continued when, following the unavoidable patterns of tribal kinship, he was introduced to veteran soldier Sergeant Bill 'Toma' Thomas. Toma Thomas was an affable, much respected son of the Valleys who would go on to become Rogers' Company's longest-serving soldier. Thomas loved to speak Welsh and actively hunted out fellow Welshmen who would parry with him – much to the annoyance of his best and lifelong friend, Sergeant Stan Forbes from Aberdeen. Forbes, too, was destined to become Hopkins' friend for the duration.

'We met on the milk run,' says Forbes. 'This was a bus that the army, in its generosity, laid on to ship the troops home for weekend leaves. "Home" was a magical word. But home for me meant the tip of bloody Scotland – so it wasn't practical. Accordingly, on the occasional 48- and 72-hour leaves, Toma would invite me to his own Welsh home. It was there, on the bus to Swansea, I met Tony and this great relationship developed.' Forbes points out that the separation of rank was a negligible hindrance:

> Within the camp, of course, it was Sergeant this and Bombadier that. But I had great sympathy for the National Service men. They were brought to us in their hundreds and paid a measly 28 shillings when the equivalent regular soldier got eight quid. It was really cheap labour – and those lads worked bloody hard for it. Tony was no shirker. He was known as a fine clerk – and his voice, his enunciation when he lifted up the telephone, that was especially exemplary – but he didn't want to be there doing National Service, so he was sometimes a bit glum.

Hopkins hid his gloom effectively, though – aware, perhaps, that a 'mope' in the military is one of the main targets of ridicule. Instead, he wallowed in this new friendship, founded on shared Welshness with Thomas and all three men's love for the arts.

'Bulford was a fairly remote place, full of wooden huts and an irregular heating system put in' – Forbes chuckles – 'by an Intelligence officer working for the Gestapo. Bulford village was tiny, just a chapel, some shops, a post office and a cinema. But at least it was within walking distance. And Salisbury was only a half-hour or so away.'

On their regular evenings off the three men usually enacted the same routine:

Our favourite place was the Salisbury Arts Theatre which had its own rep company. It was a very small, cramped setting but they entertained us with as many as five or six plays a week. Anything from *Journey's End* to farce. There was no room for Shakespeare, no time I'm sure to learn all those damn lines. Anyway, we started our evening by taking high tea at the Bluebird Café, where the girl there, Anna from Austria, made the most succulent omlettes. Tony wolfed them down – he loved his grub. Then, with the five o'clock feed out of the way, we made for the theatre and a night with our boots up.

Forbes noticed that Hopkins was the least committed theatre-goer, the one among them most likely to skip an evening play. 'But when he went he relished it and irritated the hell out of me by babbling in semi-Welsh to Bill Thomas. The two of 'em loved it.' He remembers that the three men took their theatre evenings very seriously. 'There was not much cavorting with the girls or anything like that. A few beers, a few smokes, that was it.'

Hopkins' military experience, which stretched over a monotonous two years, was enriched by the kind-spirited 'hard men' he met, men of education and wit and irony like Stan Forbes and Bill Thomas and Ernie Little; men of greater experience and accomplishment who treated him as an equal. The warmth he found in them encouraged his respect; and, accordingly, he let the barriers down. 'Tony wasn't a James Dean at Bulford,' Stan Forbes insists. 'There was nothing of the rebel in him.' 'Then again,' says Brian Evans, '*anything* was probably an improvement on the imprisonment of boarding school, where there was really no chance to express yourself. Tony always needed to express himself, even through all that shyness.'

The one incident of battle stress that Hopkins did suffer during National Service occurred, appropriately, at the cinema. Forbes, Thomas and Hopkins had trekked to 'the gaff', the Bulford AKC, to see a Hammer movie billed as 'powerful' and 'exciting'. 'It was that horrific film *The Camp on Blood Island*,' Forbes says. 'The outing remains with me vividly because it upset Tony so much. It was life in a Japanese POW camp, very grisly and melodramatic, with beheadings and crucifixions. All of us who had friends who suffered at the hands of the Japanese knew it to be basically true and we were upset by it. But Tony was inconsolable. He was utterly shaken by man's inhumanity. Ironic, isn't it? When you see him as Hannibal the Cannibal today . . .'

Throughout their friendship and the few milk runs back to Wales, Hopkins rarely spoke of his intimate home life, or of his ambitions as an actor. Provost Sergeant Lionel Wheble's job was one of overall supervision and, to him, Clerk Hopkins was just another face at Carter Camp, the section of Bulford that housed Rogers' Company. 'He wasn't given to vanity,' says Wheble. 'He was slightly unruly looking, and not inclined to call attention to himself. He wasn't your "starry" type at all. I knew his work, and it was competent. I also knew that he wasn't really happy there, but I sensed no particular future for him. Really, I suppose, he could have ended up doing anything.'

In the spring of 1960 – the beginning of the decade that would liberate youth and pour forth so many working-class heroes – Hopkins faced his demob with relief and apprehension. He had achieved the distinction of Bombardier, the equivalent of the NCO rank of Corporal, and appeared to have calmed his demons. He was proud of having survived the army and, says Evans, 'eager for a pat on the back from his father'.

The train home did not take him to Taibach, however. In the autumn of 1958, Lovell's, the toffee manufacturers, had made a bid to acquire the bakery premises on Commercial Road that Dick, now in his late fifties, decided was too good to let pass. He sold out, ending forty years of Hopkins enterprise in the bread and pastry business, and moved with Muriel to a large, semi-detached house faraway in Laleston, near Bridgend. 'We were surprised they left,' says Evelyn Mainwaring, 'because they were part of the scenery in Taibach. But they were quite well off by that time, and Muriel had the idea of early retirement in her head.' Few believed that dynamo Dick Hopkins would last long in retirement. And they were right. After not too many months he had acquired a new property and a new business. He and Muriel became landlords of the Ship Inn at Caerleon, near Newport.

*

The baby grand piano that was still Hopkins' truest soulmate was destined to find its way into the lounge of the Ship Inn, but Hopkins had no intention of joining it. The fact that the furniture of Taibach was upended, that domestic life looked not at all like the life he had left, suited him. A line had been drawn. The friendships of Taibach – Evans, Johns, Hayes, Havard Hopkins – were filed away, never fully to be returned to. He didn't stop for more than a gathering of breath. Unlike other returning servicemen he didn't flaunt his uniform. He filed it, with the friends, in the black angry past.

His first calls were to the contacts at Cardiff Castle and the Arts Council: he wanted to get back into theatre quickly. Unknown to him, Raymond Edwards was already paving the way, recommending him to Thomas Taig, the esteemed academic who was Britain's first ever Professor of Drama, based at Bristol University. Edwards says, 'Taig was a genius in his way, but he had fallen out of favour with the Vice Chancellor of his university and his ambitions for drama tuition were not quite being fulfilled. So I invited him to Cardiff to join our group.'

Shortly afterwards, while Hopkins was typing up Colonel Cubitt's latest circular commands, Taig was forming his own ex-Bristol drama group with the intention of reviving modern provincial rep. As Edwards describes it, 'His idea basically was to bring indigenous drama of the highest standard to every corner of Wales. He wanted to use Welsh authors and, where possible, Welsh actors. He was, typically for Taig, passionately committed.' Hopkins was advised to call Taig and was immediately cast by him as Mark, the lead in a little-seen but much-admired play called *Will You Have a Cigarette?* by Welsh dramatist Saunders Lewis. This was to be followed by another, similar play based on a true incident (as Lewis' play was) about Adolf Hitler. In *Will You Have a Cigarette?*, Hopkins was an ardent Communist subversive getting ready to assassinate a Western diplomat. As he fudges his assassination attempt – mixing up a poison dart cigarette with a crucifix – he is suddenly converted to Christianity.

Hopkins relished the responsibility of the role, but those who saw the play as it wove through the towns of South Wales, recall a wooden and oversized performance. Hopkins concurs: to his thinking he was still ignorant of acting technique, still reliant on aping James Dean. Revealingly, Taig was comfortable enough with Hopkins' performance, despite the doubters. Stimulated anew, Hopkins decided – without consulting Edwards, with whom he'd resumed a surrogate father-son relationship – to seek wider tuition and experience. He didn't want more Welsh drama and had already, Edwards suspects, designs on the London stage, despite never having personally seen anything of theatrical significance in London.

Hopkins asked questions among his fellow quasi 'professionals' on Taig's tour and found out that David Scase's Library Company in Manchester was among the most adventurous and accessible. He wrote immediately to Scase, seeking an audition. Scase summoned him to London where, that summer, he was conducting auditions for new recruits at the Arts Theatre. Hopkins prepared two pieces: the deathbed soliloquy from *Othello* and a piece from Maeterlinck's *Monna Vanna*. Scase was impressed by the Maeterlinck choice and, exactly as Edwards had been, by the energy Hopkins unleashed. He offered Hopkins a job – as assistant stage manager, with the probability of tuition and small stage roles thrown in. Hopkins thanked Taig, bade adieu before the Hitler play, and headed to Manchester.

It is easy to see how Hopkins perceived his break with Scase as the first career breakthrough. Scase's reputation as a theatrical innovator was exceptional, almost as exceptional as the swift, swerving course of his early life. Born in London, the son of a bricklayer who liked to buy a shilling seat for the balcony of the Old Vic, he joined the BBC in recorded programmes where he met Joan Littlewood, a scriptwriter in the department, and a great friendship began. When Littlewood transferred to Manchester, Scase did too. She then asked him to join her revolutionary Theatre Workshop. Scase married the actress Littlewood introduced him to – Rosalie Williams – and together the three founded the Workshop in 1945.

Scase's departure from Littlewood came when the Library in Manchester invited him to direct one of his favourite plays, *Volpone*. The finding of new talent became first priority. Always cognisant of the vagaries of commercial theatre and the difficulties experienced by impoverished newcomers, he took special pride in spending time on his yearly auditions, often seeing as many as 150 aspirant starters. But there was a busy commercial enterprise to run, and Scase is frank about the demands on his time and the limitations of comprehensive tuition for someone as inexperienced as Hopkins.

'I suspect he was frustrated very quickly because I didn't give him a lot to do. He did some quick walk-ons – a small part in *The Quare Fellow* – nothing much. But he made his mark. He stood out. Basically because of his anxieties, which manifested themselves in a fair deal of, well, shouting.'

For most of his three-month stint Hopkins served as ASM, utilising the experience gained with Frank Dunlop on the earlier tour with Peter Gill. Here he was an undisputed hard worker – often bragging about his father's physical stamina and keen to outdo it – but undependable on account of his volatility. Scase saw an insoluble dilemma and advised him to seek proper acting training. 'It was clear he sincerely wanted to do it, and I didn't think the Library was the right place to do it from, and I told him so. I advised him to go somewhere like the East 15 [drama school]. But of course he didn't listen to me. He did it his way.' Reluctantly, says Scase, he decided to fire him.

Eight years later, when Hopkins had made his film breakthrough and was reflecting on this first ambitious theatre opportunity, he spoke of his 'resentment' of Scase. In one of his first 'film star' newspaper features the *Evening Standard* chronicled his life since Port Talbot and reported that he 'got the sack after being involved in a punch-up in the theatre . . . David Scase told him it was bad news for a stage manager to be seen punching someone's face . . . He told him to go away for a couple of years and cool off.' Hopkins gave the *Standard* an apologetic explanation: 'I think it's the Slav element in the Welsh. Basically we are a bunch of manic depressives.' Scase today laughs at the 'mischief' of such reports and says that it is all untrue. 'I've read elsewhere that he put his fist through a door, but I can't remember it.' Peter Gill, who had now lost touch with his friend, insists: 'Yes, Tony was a bit of a fibber. But the anger and volatility were there, and it was dangerous. I have recollections of him doing damage, breaking mirrors and so forth. But that was the combustion of the time. It was an angry era. Tony was an angry, frustrated man. I'm sure there were casualties.' David Scase says, 'Were there casualties? It really wouldn't surprise me. Tony was not a usual boy. There was an element of the unexpected in everything he did.'

Chapter 4

A DAY (OR TWO)
AT THE RACES

'All he liked to drink were pints,' says actor Roy Marsden, who holds the distinction of being the first person Hopkins chose voluntarily to reside with.

> We were cripplingly poor, and could barely afford the cost of daily sustenance. So we would go to this Chinese takeaway and Tony would order this huge, huge pile of chips. And he would douse them with a quarter of a pint of Worcester sauce. And of course this would make him sweat. Sweat horribly. And so he would have to consume lager – pints and pints of lager – to wash this hideous recipe down. And of course that would make him sweat more. I worried about his well-being. I don't think I've ever seen anyone sweat as much. It was typical of him. He was quite ferocious about everything he did.

Life after Manchester, mostly in the company of Roy Marsden, who was himself struggling for a workable theatre break, was a dramatic seesaw of disaster and laughter. Destined as the relationship was to conform to the usual butterfly brevity of Hopkins' friendships, it was the most motivational since his association with Gill. Till then, Hopkins was suspicious of the conventions of formal teaching: he believed he could mostly teach himself, undoubtedly with the help of an avuncular presence like Raymond Edwards or David Scase. Hard graft – Dick's kind of energy – seemed enough. It had, after all, built Dick his empire. And yet . . . Hopkins knew his progress was sticky, and suddenly saw that the energy of his desire wasn't enough. With Marsden's laugh-loving cajoling he turned the corner.

Marsden was three years younger, but with the edge of experience on him. The previous year he had joined the dingy warehouse-based Playhouse in Nottingham, run by Val May. He was, like all apprentices, serving as ASM and cutting his teeth in secondary roles in plays directed by the rep company's chief Roy Battersby, when Hopkins knocked on the door. Hopkins had scarcely stopped to tinkle the ivories in Laleston before repacking and hitching to Nottingham with no more than a fiver in his pocket and the bush telegraph promise of jobs available. Val May took him on, offering a few quid a week and the promise of some small casting. His official role was that of student ASM, a step down, if anything, from the Manchester Library.

'I'll tell you how I remember him from that first day we met,' says Marsden. 'He was fierce. The passion pumped out of him. He was a bit of a mess – but weren't we all? – and his diction wasn't Welsh. It was English. Maybe that's something he had concluded about the requirements of casting in British theatre. It speaks volumes about the uncertainty of where he was going, what it was all about.'

The youths decided to find accommodation together and followed an ad in the newsagent's window. It led them to a closeness and a binge of adventure that was effectively the cartwheeling, libidinous teenage rampage that Hopkins had missed. 'We were students, really,' says Marsden, 'living student excitements and, in a small beer way, earning our living as we went. Tony was terrific as a friend. He was intense, he had a ferocious temper – always aimed at incompetence or bullying, never at his friends – and he loved his food and drink.' The flat they found was up the road from the Playhouse, in a rambling Victorian redbrick.

The house was owned by a Polish couple who couldn't speak one word of English. They had a daughter, aged about twelve, who lived in another Polish house on the other side of Nottingham. So she would come across every so often to translate whatever crisis was afoot. And there were plenty of them. The place was awful, like a detention camp. We weren't allowed to use the toilet after ten o'clock. And the doors were bolted, from the inside, at ten. If anyone came home late, they were locked out. Tony and I, of course, were thespians. We had to come home late. And our flat – a tiny room with a bed and a chaise-longue we shared – was at the very tiptop of this building. So we had to break in, through other people's rooms. It was some sight, the two of us tiptoeing, stumbling through the dark, always with a few more lagers on us than was absolutely desirable.

With some persuasion Roy Battersby cast Hopkins in *The Winslow Boy* – 'the stupidest casting for Tony one could imagine,' says Marsden – and the entire company watched in a kind of muted horror as Hopkins struggled with a drawing-room English performance. The play had the advantage of well-bred popularity, so the inevitable tour followed – through church halls and football field sheds in Nottingham, Newark, Grantham and further afield. Hopkins and Marsden swung with the fun. Marsden recalls:

I think he came out of any shell he might have been in. We had fun – though Tony was quite emphatic about his personal way of doing things. He was, as best he could be, expressive of his frustrations. We were inhibited, yes. With myself from a lowly East End background and Tony from Wales, we envied the performers who had had the upbringing and social opportunities to live with some urbanity. We were in the situation of having to learn the urbanities as we went along. It was our schooling – and in that sense we were students, too. We often shared irritations or frustrations about who we were and where we were. I recall, for instance, when we took the play to Cambridge and Tony and I shared rooms. After the performance, the other actors dispersed to the various cafés or appropriate restaurants. Tony would have none of that. 'Let's go to the pub,' he said. And we did. He didn't conform to the boring old bollocks in that way. He was a bit of an outsider.

Marsden found much amusement in Hopkins' very individual way of living. 'What comes to mind first were those damn shoes he always wore: big hobnailed brogue shoes, like boats on his feet. We used to call them Blakleys, with their shards of steel to make them last longer. I believe they affected his posture, even, and assisted that natural gravitas he had as an actor and a human being.'

Marsden also found his 'world-famous temper' amusing:

The memory that lingers is of the company doing a fit-up in some country hall, where this very imperious stage manageress – a lady who loved to show off in front of her director, and treated the subordinates in a very dismissive way – began to give orders left, right and centre. She spotted a gilt-framed picture that had been broken in transit and grabbed Tony and said in a very demeaning way, 'Fix it.' Tony said mildly, 'How?' And she was very rude: 'Nail it, nail it,' as if he were some imbecile. He took a fucking great hammer and a fucking great six-inch nail and smashed it right through the frame to bond it. She made the mistake of responding with some dry remark and he took off! He flung the hammer towards her and she stood there, riveted, as it crashed into a coffee table, flashed past her earhole and took a huge L-shaped chunk out of the wall behind her. He just turned and walked away. And she said . . . nothing, not one word. From then on she treated him with a kind of bemused respect.

Amused as Marsden was, he believed these outbursts reflected 'some unspoken knee-jerk response to the past, Wales, whatever. He really *loathed* bullying.' Another crony of the time comments: 'Tony had put up with so much in his childhood, not abuse in the headlines-of-the-newspaper way we hear about it today, but negative pressure from the family, especially Dick. For fifteen years he kept a rigid control of himself. He didn't let off steam with anyone, because he had no one to let it off with. Sooner or later it was bound to explode – and that is where his alcoholism, and all the demons he speaks about, began.'

During the Cambridge run of *The Winslow Boy*, Marsden saw the eruptions as a release of steam against the abuses of the theatrical pecking order. 'He was, as I say, a bit lost. But he was also a complete actor in the sense that he could do what the leads were doing. With so little real technical training, by some process of osmosis, he was capable. And that inherent skill made him impatient of others' failings. He would huff and puff a lot. "Oh, fuck, would you look at that twat! What the fuck does he think he's doing in the last act?"' Typically, the daily grind was one of work, angst, and recovery. The friends would do their nightly performance, sleep in, then go to a pub for grub and drinks. 'Then we'd hike down to the Cam and Tony would just, well, *scream*. Scream and holler till his lungs were exhausted and his brain clear. Then we'd traipse back to the theatre and do the show all over again.'

Marsden witnessed Hopkins the lover, too. Among some members of the cast an invidious gossip suggested he was gay. Marsden declares:

> Actors are famously bitchy. But Tony and I talked intimately and shared a lot of secrets as well as a lot of living. He wasn't ambiguous about his sexuality. But he was on a journey to find himself, to overcome a huge lack of self-esteem, to bury the badness – and that absorbed him. Consequently his time for girls was limited. It reminds me of a similar time in the life of another great friend of mine, Simon Callow. Simon and I become close at the Traverse and for the three years we knew each other there he expressed no interest in finding a sexual partner or building a relationship. He was comprehensively enraptured by his ambition. Tony was the same.

At Cambridge, though, there was one indulgence. As Marsden recalls it, Hopkins was in a rare state of equilibrium when they met some attractive female theatrical aficionados. Hopkins was suddenly hooked on one, and the attraction was mutual. The group split, and Hopkins took his date down by the leafy Cam. Marsden says,

I didn't expect to see him again that night. I thought, OK, he's set up for a night of open-air passion. I'll see him all flushed and delighted in the morning. But it didn't turn out like that. Tony came back in an hour looking dishevelled and ashamed of himself. I wanted to know what disaster had befallen. He said, 'It's all over, I'll never be able to show my face again. It was terrible, terrible, terrible!' Which I took to mean his performance had left something to be desired. Which I took it had something to do with the amount of lager consumed!

Back in Nottingham, in the Polish hovel, Hopkins resumed his cinema-going and spoke of trying to find theatrical work in London. 'He used his Equity card to gain free admission to the cinema almost every afternoon. But he didn't talk about a career in films or anything so highfalutin'. He just wanted to get better jobs. And it was then I told him to write to RADA, to get a proper training. To my surprise, because he was an obstinate bugger, he did.'

This change of career strategy resulted directly from the warmth of Hopkins' friendship with Marsden, a friendship described by others as brotherliness. 'If we lived close by today,' says Marsden, 'we'd see a lot of each other and we'd be friends as we were then. I know that. I valued the time I had with Tony, and his specialness. He had – and has – a hotline to the inner life. All actors search for it. Just one in a thousand, maybe in several thousands, ever get it. Tony was born with it.'

Marsden said goodbye to Hopkins in the early summer of 1961 and did not see him again until four years later, when Hopkins had finished RADA and commenced his great climb. 'We met again in Lillie Road, Fulham, where I was buried under a car, trying to repair it . . . something you wouldn't do in the middle of Lillie Road today. Tony approached but I didn't see him. I just saw these huge, thick brogues. Just the shoes. And I knew it was him. I just said, on the spot, "Ah, Tony!" – and it was exactly like four years before. He hadn't changed, except in one vital way: he was Welsh again. Very comfortably Welsh, with that marvellous Valleys voice in place. He had abandoned his efforts to be a *British* actor, thank God. I think he was just beginning to come to terms with who he truly was.'

Applying to RADA, Hopkins was first instructed to contact his local council for a grant. Glamorgan County Council complied with the necessary £7 per week. He then auditioned at RADA – twice – before being informed, in June, that he'd won a place in the term commencing in October. His audition pieces were the usual *Othello* (though this time an Iago speech) and a section of Chekhov's *The Bear*.

In the first week of October, he sat in the RADA canteen in central London and met his fellow travellers on the first stage of a journey that would bring many to theatrical eminence. Among those present were Simon Ward, Bryan Marshall, Isla Blair and Adrian Reynolds. Reynolds, later Director of the Haymarket Theatre Company, was eighteen, the youngest of the group and the son of the editor of the *Birmingham Post*. He was subsidised by a grant from the Warwickshire Council and, in his own words, 'drawn to acting in the hopes of meeting Debra Paget, whom I'd fallen in love with when my mother took me to some Birmingham fleapit to see the movie *Bird of Paradise*.'

Reynolds entered the canteen last and saw Hopkins dominating the disparate group, just as he had done so easily with Havard Hopkins, Evans, Johns, Hayes, Bray, Gill and Pamela Miles. 'I saw this unruly fellow in a yellowish trench coat that looked like it badly needed a wash, holding forth with the fellow students, discoursing left, right and centre.' Reynolds was five years younger than Hopkins and instantly, like so many, 'fell under the unique spell of the man'. Hopkins, he judged, was cheeky. 'It was a façade. I learnt that later when we became very close pals. He was in turmoil, some unspeakable pain. And he covered it with this centre stage bluster.'

In the RADA theatre room, the students were addressed by John Fernald, the controversial RADA guru whose regime upended the traditional approach to what Reynolds calls 'British drawing-room acting'. Fernald was an aggressive director, very successful in commercial theatre, who, says television actor Peter Barkworth, a contracted teacher at the time, 'wanted to break down formulaic teaching'. Reynolds remembers, 'He faced our group and told us, "From this day on you are professionals. That is the standard you will fulfil, and be judged on. If you don't measure up, you are out."' Reynolds points out that 'this was the best way because it was motivational. These were the days before RADA needed the grants to survive. It was down to talent and commitment. There was no silliness or truancy. You were there because you desperately wanted to do it and you had to bloody well work to impress Fernald and get cast in the good parts for the finals'.

Hopkins leapt in with enthusiasm, at first taking a flat with Victor 'Alex' Henry in North Finchley, a classmate whose impressive career would be cut short by a fatal traffic accident in his early thirties. Later he would move into rooms in Kilburn with Simon Ward. Ward, who had started in youth theatre, joined RADA with reverential enthusiasm, but, unlike Reynolds, mellowed to scepticism. 'Fernald sounded great,' says Ward, 'but the problem was, there was no continuum in the educational process. It was eclectic. In some ways that was exciting, but in others it was disorienting. I remember the oddest bits of wisdom being thrown at me. One teacher saying: "When you are on stage, you are wrestling with angels, and Jesus Christ is in the audience!" I thought, *What! Bugger that.*'

Peter Barkworth, who taught technique, admits to a 'disconnected' system of tuition. 'Teachers were brought in on an ad hoc basis – brilliant people like Vladek Sheybal, Robin Ray and Alec McCowen – to augment the staffers like Judith Gick, Eve Shapiro and voice coach Clifford Turner. Many had different theories of acting, it's true, but I think that gave more zest to it, and gave our students the value of choice.' Ward wasn't so sure but believed Hopkins fastened particularly on two teachers – the Swede Yat Malmgreen and the Scot Christopher Fettes – as a cohesive focus. 'Yat and Fettes promoted a spiritual awareness. *The energy cube.* Motivational impulse from spiritual vision. This all appealed to the mystical heart of Tony. He became frantic for it. It was the Holy Grail for him, but it messed him up in a way, because after a year Yat left and the people like Tony who hung on his every word were stranded with a half-education.'

Reynolds saw the obsession with Malmgreen and Fettes' concepts of 'spiritual acting', but felt they only enhanced Hopkins' raw talent. 'From the first time I saw Tony he had it. I recall seeing Victor Henry and him, very early on, in some obscure Jacobean piece and I was totally riveted. He came with that self-containment, the talent pre-packed. Fettes affected him, directed his spiritual focus, but Tony had the raw essence like none of us had.'

Peter Barkworth says he took no special notice of Hopkins, other than registering 'competence and intent', but Reynolds, who with Ward and Henry was among the closest RADA allies, insists he was 'unmissable'. 'He was fragile temperamentally, absorbed in the spell classes of Yat and wary of Barkworth's very technically precise technique work. When Barkworth did improvisation without the script, Tony would melt. I would drop my eyes to the floor and think, Please God, don't pick me! Tony did the same but, since he was a significantly competent actor, unfortunately Barkworth was fond of picking him out, and, under Barkworth, he usually wilted.'

The vying for major roles in the term finals dominated the lives of ambitious students and in this area John Fernald displayed a critical weakness. Reynolds says,

> You learned the most in the last two or three terms. Because it was then that the outside directors came in to do their pieces and you were taught by them how to behave in professional theatre, and it was an unprejudiced approach. Fernald's problem was an obsession with using his favourites. For example, Tony and I suffered because we were there while Susan Fleetwood was there and Fernald was fixated with her to the detriment of all else. She did three terms in finals and won three Gold Medals, which was unheard of. She went on to do well in theatre but she was not the shining beacon Fernald believed in. This was especially sad when one saw other great actors being overlooked. John Hurt and David Warner did their stint just before Tony. Fernald didn't much notice them either. He was distracted by Fleetwood and Inago Jackson and the ones he took a fondness to.

Hopkins was cast prominently in *Waltz of the Toreadors* by Anouilh and Shaw's *You Never Can Tell* and briefly participated in a foreign tour, but

Reynolds witnessed the frustrations of the favouritism, experienced not only by Hopkins, but by others on his behalf. 'Tony adored Chekhov, though he wasn't a great reader. It happened that *Uncle Vanya* was programmed and the whole academy believed he would be cast as Vanya. He was perfectly ready for it. But he was overlooked for a Fernald favourite and it hurt him a lot.' Ronald Pickup, who joined two terms after Hopkins, believes that 'Fernald was a bit of a madman – though in a theatrical way that is often attractive. His great contribution was in changing RADA's conventionally boring teaching approach and in giving us – me, Tony and all the others of the era – a microcosm of *the toughness* of theatre life. The fact that the casting process was often frustrating only served to show what the outside reality was, so you cannot say in that sense Fernald was bad. You learnt by him one way or the other.'

During the holidays – at Christmas and Easter – Hopkins returned to Wales and helped out in a desultory way at the Ship Inn. He had begun to drink with greater appetite but was no less introverted to the friends of Dick and Muriel whom he met and served. Back in London he moved in with Simon Ward, into two rooms in Kilburn, but continued to 'crash' on Adrian Reynolds' hospitality by taking baths at Reynolds' Marylebone digs. Absorbed in the growth of learning, he seemed placid – but then he fell in love.

Ward, Reynolds and Marsden all accepted the nomadic parameters of the acting spirit and Hopkins' reticence for committed friendships. He was affable and witty (although not a joke-teller), but his persona was pockmarked with no-go areas. Simon Ward observes: 'He had perfected the knack of instant jolly fellowship but he didn't discuss Wales, didn't discuss family, didn't discuss other friends. You hung out with him, drank with him, shared his money, but you knew you never really got that close. There was always a distance.' Roy Marsden counters: 'Tony liked a clean break [in relationships]. I think he had refined the art of living mostly alone and relying only on himself. When he went to London there was no backward glance, no letters or calls, but that shouldn't be confused with coldness. He had a warm heart. Like most of us, I believe, he was hoping for a soulmate.'

Hopkins shared his first serious intimate relationship at RADA with Mikel Lambert, a young American actress in the class a year behind him. He was instantly smitten. 'Tony liked to help other actors,' Reynolds says. 'That generosity is a measure of many inspired talents – the sharing. He helped me a lot. We were taught the Lavan theory of acting by Yat Malmgeren, which was based on dance movement, and I couldn't quite get it. One night at a party in Chalk Farm, Tony taught me in five minutes what Yat was struggling for weeks to do. It was, I suppose, the advantage of age and experience.'

With Mikel Lambert Hopkins had the same advantage of age and knowledge and he used it to fuel an instantly hot relationship. Adrian Reynolds watched the new friendship grow and saw Hopkins first flourish, then panic, in it.

> The academy was really our home, so all life, all emotions, were played out there. Tony wasn't relaxed. He was vulnerable and Mikel added to his confusion. The whole area of sexuality seemed to confuse him. I knew he was in love, but I don't believe he wished to be. It was a distraction, it addled him, he tried to escape from it. He would run for cover with the piano and play these beautiful self-written songs. He was a romantic, but a tragic romantic.

Hopkins and Lambert were close for many months, but there was never the possibility of a long-term union. 'He didn't release his sexuality,' says Reynolds. 'And that made him combustible. Being in love only brought him more frustrations, so he tried to douse it and keep away from it.'

With Ward, Henry and Reynolds, Hopkins wallowed in the students' party circuit as a kind of counter-irritant. 'He was terrific company when he was happy, with a few pints under his belt,' says Ward. 'Then all the mystical Welshness came out. Fernald did him that one big favour. The days of the RADA plum voice went out with his regime and so Tony's Welshness was promoted. And there he was, at those parties, dispensing it to all of us, being quite magical.' Hopkins' party trick was to hypnotise Reynolds. 'He had power,' says Reynolds. 'God knows where these things come from. He could flip a finger and I was out cold. Most of the boys loved him for it. Others hated him. He was a man who drew vibrant response in those around him. You loved him, or you hated him. He made a lot of enemies just by being the powerful presence that he was.' Simon Ward agrees, but points out that Hopkins' intensity sometimes made him tough going for even his most devoted friends. 'Living with him was fun, but I have to admit he drove me crazy with his obsessions. It wasn't unusual for him to sit up all night, studying text. I got so damned fed up with the light on all night that, eventually, I packed it in and moved out.'

Hopkins himself has spoken of his period at RADA as 'a difficult, exhausting time'. He had no control of his talents then, he says, and he lived on caffeine tablets. 'It was a horse race, but it taught me something I had to learn. About discipline. I never knew what discipline was until I went there. I thought it was: Don't drink beer, Don't do this or that. But it was something else entirely. RADA gave me an understanding about *direction*. What you choose at any hour or any day is what you are.'

In the summer of 1963, Reynolds won his diploma from RADA and Hopkins, predictably to all, won a silver medal. The finishing of tuition marked, immediately, another demarcation point. Once again, as he had done in abrupt movements since Groes Primary School, he closed the book on one period, one set of friends, and lurched onwards. Mikel Lambert receded into a past life, soon to return to America and fade from view. Her departure was welcome: it removed the dilemma of sex and allowed him to refocus the provincial theatre experience that he believed – instinctively – would allow him the experimentation that would eventually win him major West End theatre roles. 'The mania was always rumbling away,' says Reynolds. 'He was challenged by Burton – forget what he or others may have said to deny that. And films had a huge fascination. He dissected them. We went to [Jack Clayton's 1961 film] *The Innocents*, based on the Henry James story about the governess fighting the evil of her charges. It sparked a great debate, 25 minutes on the pavement outside the Carlton, Haymarket, analysing whether the children were really evil or whether it was all in the mind of the governess.'

The triumph of the silver medal, and the hint of a direction found at RADA, pleased Hopkins but he was still edgy and unwilling to return to the mire of Wales without landing a job in the provinces. He considered reapplying to David Scase – an ambition that indicated his unwillingness to accept defeat in theatre – but, before he could, Clive Perry, artistic director of the new Phoenix Theatre in Leicester, asked to see him among several new RADA graduates. Hopkins went to audition in Smith's Square, just days after quitting RADA in July. He offered a speech by the General from *Waltz of the Toreadors* and – winningly – a slice of Charles Condomine from Noël Coward's great RADA favourite, *Blithe Spirit*.

'The Condomine swayed me,' says Clive Perry, who had come to the first directorship of the Phoenix via Cambridge, the Marlowe Society, an ABC television scholarship and assistant directorship of the Castle Theatre, Farnham. 'I was 26, about the same age as Tony, and deeply burdened – though privileged – by the opportunities of my first theatre, which was replacing the now defunct Theatre Royal in Leicester. I knew our group had a battle ahead of us, and of course we needed all the good talent we could find.'

Perry told Hopkins on the spot that the job was his and asked him to prepare the role of Undershaft in Shaw's *Major Barbara*, which would be one of the theatre's premier pieces. Hopkins took the train back to Wales, contained his excitement, but could hardly wait to pack for Leicester. He moved in September, a few weeks before the theatre was due to open, and took digs with a casual acquaintance from RADA, David Ryall, and Victor Henry, whom Perry had also contracted. Thus began a nine-month stint that Hopkins found tense and less than fulfilling. Perry recalls,

> He has said I wasn't the nicest director to work with, but I honestly cannot say we ever fought. I had difficulty starting him, that is true. He was very much on the bottle by that stage, very much the roaring boy. He was nervous, ill at ease in company – as he is today. I think the difficulties might have arisen from the fact that I was absorbed with making this new theatre work and he was absorbed in being Tony

Hopkins. Leicester has been described, culturally speaking, as a grave-yard through which buses sometimes ran. We were the buses. We had a 274-seater theatre and a very good company. But time, and the financial demands of running the place, took their toll on me. They kept me busy. Also, we were working very, very fast and I don't think that appealed to Tony. He later went on record to say that he liked to devote time to nurturing his characters – that David Scase would eventually give him this time. But I couldn't. We opened a play on Tuesday, started rehearsals for the next on Wednesday, had just barely the week and a half to get the next one up and running. There was no time for actor tantrums, so Tony never reached full measure with us.

In truth, Hopkins' chances were few. In the opening Phoenix play, Thornton Wilder's *The Matchmaker*, he was a waiter. In Robert Storey's *Life Worth Living*, he was, he believed, completely miscast as a country squire. Finally, in the promised *Major Barbara*, he had a suitable challenge in the role of Undershaft, which he based squarely on his father. Perry 'quite liked what he did' with this, but reserved real praise for his Judge Brack in *Hedda Gabler* and his frisky Bolingbroke in *Richard II*.

It struck me strongly that these roles were keys to his talent. In Brack, you could see his need to explore the inner life, to have time to look inward and to develop that dramatically. You see this strength right through to Hannibal Lecter in *The Silence of the Lambs*. In Bolingbroke, he was at ease because he was the leader of the pack. He was forced to be extrovert. He was far happier here than he was, say, playing Marlow in *She Stoops to Conquer*. When he has time to look inward and draw out – and when he is forced into being extrovert – that was where his qualities emerged.

Hopkins' socialising was restricted by Leicester's furious pace. He caroused with Ryall and Henry late into the night, but stayed in bed all day when he could. Among the nineteen-strong company he made no new friends of note. 'He was captive to the booze, I fear,' says Perry, 'and very clear that he had no intention of putting down roots. In conversation he made it known that he wanted to work again with David Scase, who was a friend of mine. He intended to fulfil his contract with me and move on.'

The grimmest moment at Leicester occurred in November when the world rocked at the news of the assassination of President Kennedy. Hopkins was backstage, in mid-production of *Major Barbara* and preparing Behan's *The Hostage*, when word came on the radio. In love as ever with Americana in all its glittering-prize imagery, he was devastated. Adrian Reynolds opines, 'Part of the lure of Mikel Lambert had been her American passport. He was mesmerised by the notion of Hollywood and Kennedy and all that gloss.' Hopkins' response to the assassination of a man he viewed as a liberal pioneer and an emblem of vague escape was to sit down and write a heartfelt letter of condolence to Jacqueline Kennedy. 'He personalised it. It revealed the romantic in him. Conversely, he realised the fullest triumph in this career by personalising the Hannibal Lecter insanity. He related it to himself – made it mournful and sexy, which gave it romance. That's what made it genius.'

Hopkins' crowning moment during the one-season contract with the Phoenix came when the company's production of Marlowe's *Edward II* was transferred to the Arts Theatre in London. 'I was really more concerned about our growth and the final checks and balances than Tony's progress,' says Perry. 'But I felt that if he could find solo parts that suited his uniqueness – parts where he is approached by other characters, but he stands apart – then he would succeed in a profound way.' Perry hesitates to chuckle: 'That is, of course, if he could manage to keep off the bottle.'

The return to David Scase's company was an occasion of jubilation for Hopkins that would soon turn into the greatest humiliation of his young acting life. 'It was marvellous that he had persevered and had the courage to follow his convictions and manoeuvre to come back to me,' says Scase. 'In the three years since we'd known each other he had bounded forward in terms of acting capability. Before RADA he was an untamed torrent of energy. Now he had a grip on it and I foresaw great things for us.'

In the intervening years, Scase had moved from Manchester to the Liverpool Playhouse, a venue he had admired from afar and which excited him more than any challenge in his life. Here, he mixed a wild palette of plays, from the innovative freshness of Littlewood's Workshop discoveries, to Alun Owen, Bill Naughton and the Irish classics. The company numbered thirteen, all engaged, says Scase, 'first and foremost because I liked them'. The 1964–65 programme roster was a packed one and, in observing in Hopkins an immediate maturity – 'That voice had blossomed like a damned flower' – Scase saw opportunities aplenty for landmark playing.

Jean Boht, a leading female in the company, queued up to pay homage to the new Welsh Burton.

> He was unattached, no girl in his life, adamant about performing leads ... and absolutely gorgeous. Every girl in the company would have liked to get with him, but to me – to all of us – he was just wonderfully kind. He drank, but I didn't see him drunk and I remember that once when I took aboard a little too much alcohol at a party after the show I went upstairs to lie down. He came up simply to see how I was. I was in a daze and he was so, so caring. He was a good man and beyond any question among any of us a brilliant actor. Everyone in our company envied him and if there was any concern about weakness it was merely that his voice was similar to Burton's and I used to think that that might slow him down.

Hopkins was now at full flight, aglow in the confidence of Scase's trust. In play after play Scase cast him in ever more important parts. In J. B. Priestley's *The Scandal of Mr Kettle and Mrs Moon* he played the prominent Henry Moore. In Naughton's *All in Good Time* (famously filmed in 1966 as *The Family Way*), he was the villainous Leslie Piper. In Behan's *The Quare Fellow*, he was Donnelly the warder. Scase remembers:

> But he came of age in *Mandragola*, adapted from Machiavelli by Ashley Dukes. He played Callimiaco and he brought to the role something I

didn't see in it. In this regard he was special: he did his homework. When you worked with him and broke for the night he went home and went on working. Consequently, the next morning you found he had a little extra to add to what we had done. It wasn't like so many actors, where the momentum of creativity is lost overnight and you don't warm them up for an hour or so the next day. It's eleven o'clock usually before they are ready to work. Tony was like Steven Berkoff, who joined me the following season. Both had the talent of application. The results of it were to be seen in plays like *Mandragola* and, later, his Christy Mahon in *Playboy of the Western World*, which for me was his special achievement with us.

The reverberating Welshness that Hopkins had surrendered to at RADA proved a huge asset, its melody contributing to the novelty of his characterisations, much as Sean Connery's stubborn brogue worked its spell in movies. In *Sparrows Can't Sing*, a Theatre Workshop import about East End life, Scase had modified some navvy lines to account for Hopkins' 'foreign' accent, but when it came to the casting of O'Casey's *Playboy* there was no dodging the inappropriateness of it. 'I didn't really want to use him,' says Scase, 'because I thought, Hell, they'll never let us get away with it. This play is Irish Irish. It'll sound ridiculous. But Jean Boht came and pleaded for him. He was very popular, actually, and that was a reflection of it. She said, "Go on, be a sport, let him do it." And I thought, well, I suppose they're all Celts so – all right.'

The ensuing performance, says Scase, was among the Playhouse's best – offered up with unashamed Welshness. 'I'm certain there were little old ladies leaving the theatre that afternoon saying, "I wonder what part of Ireland he was from? Obviously some new part we haven't heard about."'

Unavailable to Scase, or even those closest to him domestically, was Hopkins' spin on the emerging new confidence in youth art and theatre. Even the cloth-eared recognised the vast changes unfolding in popular culture that resulted in part from the fall of traditional British Conservatism. The Labour Party's Harold Wilson was the vanguard of a neo-socialism whose effects would run rampant over the remainder of the century. The early sixties was a watershed period, the years of hefty taxes on the wealthy, a buoyant housing market and the full employment that spurred youth-led consumerism and, indeed, unprecedented youth power. The evidence was in the dominance of the Beatles: 1964 was the Beatles' year, not just as a British phenomenon, but globally. The parallel phenomenon of James Bond, launched with *Dr No* in 1962 and successful worldwide with 1964's *Goldfinger* copper-fastened the commercial viability of Britishness. The flipside of this all-conquering popism was the tail end of the 'angry' theatre culture, manifest in a tranche of brilliant new works from the likes of Pinter (*The Homecoming*) and Osborne (*Inadmissible Evdience*) and seminal breakout plays like Orton's *Entertaining Mr Sloane*. 'Peter Hall was producing the twelve-hour *War of the Roses* at the Aldwych,' says Scase, 'and there was a feeling in the air that all the barriers were coming down. On the most basic level, regional accents – the Beatles' Liverpudlian and the local Cockney – had penetrated the Oxbridge strongholds in television and PR. It was a once-in-a-lifetime confluence of opportunities and optimism. Kids had money in their pockets, Brits were welcome in America . . . It was "all change" for everyone.' This odd confluence was, Hopkins felt, the most perfect timing. 'Any insecurities arising from one's Welshness were certainly assuaged,' he later said. '[To be in London then] was to be at the centre of the universe, the only place to start out from.'

High on the atmosphere of the moment, Hopkins travelled to London with Scase's company performing at the Players Theatre and joined the cattle-call auditions for Lindsay Anderson's upcoming *Julius Caesar*, for the English Stage Company at the Royal Court. Scase was reluctant to release him but Hopkins pleaded for the opportunity to try his luck. In fact, Hopkins had one major plus working for him in approaching the Royal Court. His old friend Peter Gill was working there, commencing what was to be an illustrious career as a writer-director by understudying the likes of Peter O'Toole and hatching out his first assistant directorial assignments. Gill acknowledges:

I was the baby at the Court at a time when it was exhilarating, bursting with new ideas and new talent, a wondrous time to be there. A season was run by [director] Antony Page, with Lindsay Anderson in the background. I was an assistant, learning the ropes with these terrific people. *Inadmissible Evidence* came up, then Lindsay was slated to do *Julius Caesar*. Nicol Williamson was set to do it, but then he fell out and Ian Bannen stepped in in his place. There was no casting director, so I took on the task of setting up the casting. And, of course, Tony was one of the people I put prominently forward. I knew he was the type Lindsay would jump for and, I have to say, my instincts served well on that play because many of the people I put forward to Lindsay almost immediately earned their places at the National, perhaps partly as a consequence of their roles: There was Tony, Ron Pickup, Paul Curran . . . and Petronella Barker, of course.

Gill had not lost his fondness for Hopkins, though, he is emphatic, the quality of their relationship had altered. 'Tony was angry with me and I was kind of irritated by his manner, and by our stubborn lack of communication since that awful shared tour. But it was under the bridge, really. We were both on our ways to important careers and I was pleased to be in a position to help him at the Court.' Gill wasn't surprised to see that Hopkins had some strong new male friendships:

Victor Henry was his best buddy then. Which was good for him in some ways, and bad in others. Victor had a massive appetite for booze – indeed, in an indirect way, that's what brought about his early death. But Tony was quite entranced. Later, very briefly, I would direct Tony in one of my own plays, an adaptation of a Chekhov short story that I called *A Provincial Life*, for the Court. By then 'it' had happened – meaning the ultimate career directions had begun and our personalities seemed more moulded, less delicate than during those terrible teen years. But Tony could still rant and rage with a passion about his friends. For example, I recall once that he butted into the Court while Victor was on stage in something and he insisted – pie-eyed drunk of course – on joining him on stage. He needed to talk with his pal. I had to restrain him and reason with him . . . which says a lot about how our relationship evened out, since I could never have reached him in that way after Cardiff and that tour.

For Lindsay Anderson, Hopkins stood out:

I engaged him in one of the lesser roles in *Julius Caesar*, and he fulfilled what was required of him and impressed me beyond that. He was recognisably serious and intelligent about his work, and had very obvious ambition. He was cast as one of the conspirators [Metellus Cimber], and this is not a very fleshed out part. But he wanted to find out as much as he could about it, and wanted all the guidance I could give him in that regard.

Rehearsals – with Ian Bannen as Brutus, Paul Curran as Caesar, T. P. McKenna as Cassius and Daniel Massey as Mark Antony – took place at the Parish Hall in Sloane Square. 'It was a big cast, so my time was divided between many. It was also a challenging and unusual production that I liked, and on reflection still like. Tony and Ronald Pickup were understudying Brutus and Cassius and they grabbed my attention particularly in the rehearsal of the tent scene one day. They were quite magnificent and I remember saying, "These chaps will go far."'

The opening of *Julius Caesar* – Hopkins' most visible London appearance to date – proved less than auspicious. Pickup, as Octavius Caesar, loved the work and found Anderson 'sensitive, innovative, dazzling – a great and gentle coach for insecure actors'; but virtually all the major reviews castigated the director and his approach to the play. The accusations ranged from 'verging on banality' to 'disappointing'. *The Times* particularly savaged the 'informality' of Anderson's Shakespeare which enraged the director so much that he responded in print, a war of words he later regretted. 'You learn as you go on that the British theatre, and especially the theatre critics of our day – and that includes the sainted sixties – demand a conventionality in mounting Shakespeare. There is a sacred tradition, which I personally reject – but there it is. Engaging in media wars is a waste of time. But I thought they were unfair to us, so I hit back.' Pickup opines: 'Lindsay got hurt easily, so it didn't surprise me or anyone else that he fought back in such feisty fashion. But it didn't really matter. It drew attention to us and we played very successfully to big crowds for several weeks.'

Hopkins, said Anderson, was drunk at the wrap party in January 1965. Among the cast he made friends, but he also made enemies. Peter Gill says, 'When he had a few drinks up he blurted his ambitions. If you didn't know him you took him to be full of himself, a big ego who had yet to do anything worthwhile. Other actors resented it.' Among the friends, though, was one young actress whom Hopkins found madly attractive. She was just 22, and a former member of the BBC rep company. Hopkins had met her before, when she was eighteen and recuperating from an appendix operation, staying with a friend in a hotel in Wales. He also encountered her briefly at a dance movement class. Her father was the popular comedian Eric Barker, her mother Pearl Hackney. In *Julius Caesar*, Petronella [or Peta] Barker was just a crowd filler but Hopkins liked her dark, sexy looks, her curvaceous figure and her earthiness. She had inherited her father's rapid wit and laughed loud, and had, says Gill, 'an immediate sense of defiance about her that magnetised Tony'. They chatted, tipped a glass or two (soft drinks in Peta's case) and began then the insidious exploration of each other's lives.

Infatuated since their first meeting in Wales, Peta Barker believed Hopkins to be quite a catch; very handsome and very kind. Particularly endearing to her were his fuddled attempts at telling jokes. Their only problem was, she recalls, that both were very shy, making any sort of union unlikely.

In those early exchanges, Peta heard nothing of fanatical ambition. To her, Hopkins was just a bright young actor doing his job and grateful to be employed. To Lindsay Anderson, however, Hopkins was more forthcoming: 'At that farewell party Tony gave voice to what he wanted to do and be. He told us he would go after the big roles, and the movies. Then we shook hands and said the nice things you say and moved on in our nomadic ways, as the theatre decrees.' Anderson suspected he would see Hopkins again soon, indeed work with him again – which he did a year later when he cast him in a small part in his satirical short film, *The White Bus*, written by Shelagh Delaney. Peta Barker also hoped that she would get the chance to meet up with the young actor again.

Hopkins returned to Scase and the damp streets of Liverpool in ebullient mood. Tactically the Royal Court had been a good move: it had won him reasonable attention and earned him a deeper friendship of Peta Barker. He wanted more. He was now happier than he'd been since Nottingham, moderating his boozing in the light of his progress and the absence of wildboys like Ryall and Henry – though still enjoying the evening pints at Don Shebeen or the Shakespeare in Williamson Square. Lynda La Plante, today a highly regarded novelist and screen-writer, was a fellow player who enjoyed his company, as did actress Marjorie Yates. Yates' mother was particularly fond of him and, says Yates, frequently burst into tears when he called at their digs in Faulkner Street and rattled off sentimental pub songs on the corner piano. 'Don't make it sound that he had become some pussycat,' says Jean Boht. 'At the Playhouse he continued to give David Scase a run for his money. He was a fierce defender of what he believed in. David, of course, came very well prepared and knew precisely what he wanted. So they continued to clash. In those situations, Tony's voice took on a whole new – shocking – dimension.'

A measure of Hopkins' accelerated outward urge – withheld as it was from Peta Barker – was that he, like Jean Boht, had secured London agency representation. 'It was with Heymans, the major international actor agency,' says Boht. 'But we were very small fry. Heymans had people like Elizabeth Taylor on their books – lots of what we call megastars today. Tony, like myself, had high hopes, but I'm afraid it didn't do wonders for either of our careers.'

The tide seemed to turn when director Bill Gaskill arrived from the new National Theatre company – 'the top of the hill', in Boht's words – to hand-pick suitable people for Laurence Olivier's second Chichester season. Boht recalls:

There was tremendous excitement. The National! Olivier! It was the peak we all reached for. But really everyone [in the company] was in such awe of Tony Hopkins that all anyone really wanted to know was what parts *he* would get. There was no question among us that he was on the brink of some massive breakthrough in mainstream theatre. And he himself had come to believe it. He wasn't smug but he was proud of himself and when Gaskill arrived we felt what he felt: that this was it! So a few of us were duly informed of what parts we were being offered, but everyone kept on asking Tony: 'What about you? What did you get?'

Hopkins played to his audience, telling his fellow players, 'My agents in London are negotiating with these National people. It's not decided, but it's just about sorted out.' Boht, like the others, were further awed. 'The impression was that he was in for something gigantic. We were all dying to find out.'

As the days and weeks passed, Hopkins became glum and withdrawn. He avoided Boht, avoided all conversation in the hallways, drank harder. Finally, as suspicions smouldered, he confronted the entire company in the green room after a performance.

'He stood for a few minutes silently and we all waited to hear what these roles would be. He looked terribly sad and then he said, "Look, I'm sorry, I know I told you that my agent was negotiating with Gaskill but that wasn't the truth. The truth is that Gaskill rang and said they didn't want me. I'm so sorry I told you otherwise but I just couldn't face it myself."'

Boht speaks of Hopkins' 'utter humiliation' and suggests the seeds of cynicism that would sprout in Hopkins' later theatre years were planted then. After RADA's conversion, after the silver medal, after the conquests of Leicester and Scase and – yes – the corralling of his demons, he had assumed London was easy pickings. Now was the reality. An actress who knew him says,

His rage didn't stem from ego, it was naïvety and I think a sudden objective awareness of it all. Scase had flattered him, served him in the way he wanted. In interviews afterwards, he said that the Scase period was the most happy and constructive of his early career. His head was filled with the ease of it. He wasn't out to capture the National, bear in mind. He wasn't enamoured of classical parts, per se. What he really coveted were those West End lights and a billboard that said 'Anthony Hopkins' in huge letters.

Many in Scase's company believed the rejection from Gaskill wounded Hopkins so deeply that it revived the horrors of insecurity and set him dangerously on edge. 'The damnedest thing was,' says Boht, 'that Gaskill didn't tell him – or tell our dopey agent – that Olivier already had his eye on Tony. There wasn't a role for him at Chichester that year *because Olivier wanted to take him on and groom him*. That is the reality. Tony didn't know that then, and he left Liverpool under a cloud and went to Hornchurch to lose himself in the sticks for a while.'

Chapter 5

NOT SO
GRAND NATIONAL

When, in 1963, Laurence Olivier began the structuring of the long-awaited National Theatre, he turned his back on the company of actors who had supported his string of film hits and on the conventions of mainstream classical drama. Determined to avoid the trap of tradition, eager to embrace sixties' change, he drew instead on George Devine's English Stage Company, and on the pool of talent growing around the Royal Court. When Devine rejected his invitation to join him as second-in-command, he took instead two Devine-trained directors, Bill Gaskill and John Dexter, both prominent achievers at the Royal Court. Their appointment as associate directors of the National signalled a stage-subsidised theatre that would deviate and dare to cross new ground. Most of Olivier's old chums – celebrated talents like Esmond Knight, John Laurie and Norman Wooland – were overlooked in favour of new faces, many drawn from recent Royal Court productions. The rebellious, mean-spirited Kenneth Tynan was appointed literary manager – outrageously, the critics said, for wasn't he the severest of all Olivier's critics, wasn't he the one who had described the movie *Hamlet* as 'technically pedantic, aurally elephantine . . .'? Tynan promised that, side by side with Olivier, he would scout for new writers, new translations and act as editor-in-situ of plays in rehearsal.

Olivier's inaugural choice for the theatre, which, while it awaited its tailored residence, would abide at the Old Vic was *Hamlet*, delivering the first National Theatre star in Peter O'Toole, recruited fresh from David Lean's *Lawrence of Arabia*. It was a risky heady mix – and it failed. *Hamlet* played 27 performances, sustained only by O'Toole's film celebrity. The *Uncle Vanya* and *Saint Joan* that joined it in repertory did little to improve the situation. Only with the revival of the rather staid Restoration comedy, Farquhar's *The Recruiting Officer*, were signs of life detectable. Then, with Tynan's coaching and flattery, Olivier finally acceded to the long resisted *Othello* – a play he believed unplayable, 'a terrible study and a monstrous, monstrous burden for an actor' – and the National was truly in flight. Reporting the *Othello* breakthrough in the *Daily Express*, Herbert Kretzmer eulogised genius incarnate: 'Sir Laurence has managed by heaven knows what witchcraft to capture the very essence . . . It is a performance full of grace, terror and insolence. I shall dream of its mysteries for years to come.' The 848 seats of the Old Vic were packed to capacity each night, royalty queued in the aisles (Lord Snowdon had to stand during a matinée) and the National was suddenly the hottest ticket in town.

Anthony Hopkins received his call back from Gaskill in the midst of this wave of euphoria. Hacking away at Shakespeare in Hornchurch, glumly recovering from a ten-week period of inactivity, he immediately took a train to London, cadged a ticket to *Othello* and sat, entranced, in the miasma of September heat and sweat, watching one of the greatest per-formances he had ever seen. The next day, still electric with the memory of Olivier's *Othello*, he sat before the maestro in a palm-wet stupor. In the five months since his departure from Scase he had tried to bury the ignominy of his National failure, but all failure swelled in him like cancer – worse than ever, it seemed, since the sweet treachery of the post-RADA successes. At Hornchurch's Queen's Theatre, producer Tony Carrick had been good to him, had given him the lead in *The Devil's Disciple* which gained favourable local notices, and the role of Leontes in *A Winter's Tale*. But Hornchurch was a stop-gap. Now Hopkins was where he wanted to be, eye to eye with the man the media called the greatest actor alive.

'He asked me what I would do for him,' Hopkins told Tony Crawley. 'I told him for audition I would do Tusenbach in *The Three Sisters* and something from *Major Barbara* and, of course, the stipulated something from Shakespeare. He said, "Well, what from Shakespeare?" And, unflinching, I said, "Well, *Othello*, the deathbed scene." There was a moment of consideration, then he grinned at me and said, "You've got a bloody nerve!" Gaskill and the others said nothing.'

As Hopkins started his piece, he found himself unusually confident. Olivier, he later said, reminded him of the comedian Harry Worth, 'looking very average in his horn-rimmed glasses and three-piece suit'. Ronald Pickup also auditioned for the National at this time and laughs at the general surprise newcomers experienced on first meeting Olivier. 'He had this legendary reputation and his name was in the papers daily, so you imagined some remote and massive presence. He wasn't at all like that. He was Larry. Very polite and normal and average looking in the flesh . . . and you stood there saying, look, he's splashing his tea into the saucer, he's going to drip it all over himself. There was a definite coming-down-to-earth at those National auditions, and Larry was good about making new people at ease and allowing them to do their best.'

When Hopkins finished his *Othello*, Olivier laughed and told him, 'Well done. I don't think I'll lose any sleep tonight but I think you're awfully good. Would you like to join the company?' Jean Boht believes that this exercise of audition was academic; that Gaskill, and probably Olivier, had already seen Hopkins in *Julius Caesar* and possibly previously in Clive Perry's *Edward II* at the Arts. Boht goes further: 'I think from the very start, from before Hornchurch, that Olivier had him earmarked for star roles at the National. It wasn't coincidence that he understudied Olivier so soon and eventually stood in for him so dramatically in *Dance of Death*. It was all planned.'

In Wales, there was disbelief. 'It was hard to swallow,' says Taibach neighbour Evelyn Mainwaring. 'Only a few years before we'd seen Richard Burton go from the Co-op in Commercial Road to the Old Vic and Hollywood. And now here was our Anthony from across the street giving him a run for his money.' Many miles away in Caerleon Dick heard the news on the phone and pinched himself – in surprise and delight. He had come to accept fully his son's career choice, but it still caused him much concern. Peta Barker, who would grow quite close to Dick and look upon him as a dear friend, believed that Dick's fussing for Tony had its roots in the difficulties of his own childhood. It had become clear to Peta that the family had once been quite impoverished and that Dick Hopkins had not had a pampered existence by any means. He had worked very hard for a better life for himself and his family and his one worry was that his son shouldn't have to sweat and toil as he had done. It was, Barker believes, undoubtedly 'reassuring' for him that Tony won a place at the National alongside Olivier.

Peta Barker was already under contract to the National when Hopkins joined. The Company's base comprised three adjoining Nissen huts on a bombsite 300 yards from the Old Vic. Here, on a noticeboard, she read with delight the announcement: 'Anthony Hopkins will be joining the company, ex-Liverpool and Leicester.'

Barker was on £14 a week, living in a bedsit in Chelsea, ecstatic that she was fulfilling her personal ambition of working at the National. An only child, born and raised in Faversham, in Kent, her schooling had been fractured by long spells touring with her father, which had given her a taste for theatre, and for laughter. Her main interest, however, was classical theatre, and Shakespeare in particular.

Barker had trained at London's Central drama school, where she was a year ahead of Julie Christie, then graduated to BBC rep and spent a year at the Royal Court with George Devine before joining the National. She remembers that though the National was certainly a peak for Hopkins he was 'not the golden student'. At that time, Ronald Pickup was the great new hope, having won a gold medal at RADA. Like Hopkins, Barker started with great optimism but had been quickly frustrated by the lack of major roles and her constant assignment as understudy – at one point she understudied every part for *The Crucible*. She longed for meatier roles.

So, too, did Hopkins. His start, by all accounts, was disastrous. Olivier placed him as the Cyprus Messenger in the long-running *Othello* and watched the début moment with some excitement. Hopkins recalled: 'It was my first night. I was standing in the wings, looking out and thinking, my God, that's the Old Vic stage. They've all been here. I was scared.' To counter his nerves and ensure his efficiency he had learnt most of the other characters' lines too.

> Frank Finlay was playing Iago and I had learnt his part. I was expert in his first speech, for instance – 'Three great ones of the city, in personal suit to make me his lieutenant' – I had learnt it as an audition piece and had certain ideas about it . . . So his lines were in my head, and then my own scene was in my head, nervousness and all that – so my cue came and I ran on stage with scroll and wig and all that, and Harry Lomax was on as the Duke of Venice, facing upstage, and I was supposed to do the Old Vic thing – 'My Lord!' down on one knee, and all that crap, you know, the silly Old Vic acting. My line was to be, 'The Ottomites, reverend and gracious, steering with due course towards the isles of Rhodes . . .' But of course I launched into 'Three great ones of the city . . .' I did it all, all of Iago, and I saw Harry Lomax's eyes going like saucers. It was like a bad dream . . . and he started to shake because he was laughing so much.

In the wings, Frank Finlay and Olivier cracked up in laughter. A stage-hand nudged Finlay, rousing argument. 'Hey, d'you see? That fella's reading your lines!' Finlay just said, 'Maybe he wants my part.'

Hopkins recalls, 'The audience didn't notice, which goes to show that nobody listens anyway. Afterwards, I went to the pub with a friend who had come to see it. I said, "Did you notice anything?" And the response was, "You were very good in it." "But," I said, "I spoke Iago's lines!" "Really? No!"' Hopkins approached Olivier timidly to apologise and was greeted with smiling forgiveness. 'Oh, dear heart, my ears were flapping. I thought you were going to start the whole fucking play over again.'

The inauspicious start was followed by many, many inauspicious months of understudying and bit-part playing that antagonised Hopkins and ingrained in him a fundamental distrust of 'Old Vic playing' as well as an unease about Shakespeare. At one point, after a rather boring tour of *Othello* and having understudied Colin Blakely, Albert Finney and Robert Lang and 'held up the scenery' in Congreve's *Love for Love*, Peter Shaffer's *Royal Hunt of the Sun*, Ostrovsky's *The Storm* and *Much Ado About Nothing* he contemplated quitting, angered by the National's rigid pecking order that was, he felt, suppressing him. Peta Barker, however, believes that suppression was something to which Hopkins always responded well, something which inevitably drove him forwards.

Hopkins himself was surprised that at one point Olivier advised him to capitalise on his facility for mimicry and 'ape' leading performers. 'It was a losing battle,' Hopkins said. 'The worst thing was understudying, because you had to fit in with the rhythms and do the precise same thing [the actor] did, otherwise you upset everything else. It really was an odd feeling, a hideous thing, because you possessed no autonomy then.'

A forthright appeal to Olivier earned him slightly better billing, but he was still 'uncomfortable in those damned tights, standing round waiting for something to happen'.

The friendship with Barker had warmed, though she is at pains to point out that the development was so gradual even she hardly noticed it. Hopkins was, she explains, an intensely passionate man, though not in the area of relationships. Despite this, after a year, they were deeply in love and she had dreams of them settling down and starting a big family.

The break from the monotony of spear-carrying came in February 1967, more than a year into his National run, when Glen Byam Shaw staged Strindberg's *Dance of Death*, with Olivier playing the vulgar Captain Edgar – Olivier's favourite role after his immortal Archie Rice. In the play the foul-tongued Edgar is a marital thug, constantly at war with women and, on his silver wedding anniversary, in final corrosive combat with his wife, played by Geraldine McEwan. The previous year's Strindberg – *Miss Julie* – had scored well and Olivier threw colossal energy into this role, making clear to everyone that he intended to outdo the plaudits of *Othello*. He did, achieving what Sir John Gielgud believed was 'his greatest non-Shakespearean performance' and winning both the *Evening Standard* Best Actor Drama Award and the Gold Medallion of the Swedish Academy of Literature for 'the outstanding interpretation of Swedish drama'.

Hopkins was an onlooker in all this. Assigned, as usual, to understudy Olivier, he was more excited about his proposed casting as Andrei in Chekhov's *The Three Sisters*. Then, in June, Olivier fell ill, with stomach pains that would be diagnosed as a neoplasm – a minor cancerous growth on the prostate gland. Olivier was hospitalised in St Thomas's and Hopkins found himself on short notice confronted with the challenge of replacing a theatre legend at the height of his powers in a hit production playing to tourist season crowds. Peta recognised this great opportunity but Hopkins admits that he was 'completely terrified' as he faced a sold-out arena.

When the pre-curtain announcement of the substitution was made, cast and stage-hands waited apprehensively for audience fall-out. 'No one left,' Hopkins said. 'I would have been bitterly disappointed if they had.' He was shaking when he went on. 'Fear made me good. I was far too young to play it, but through fear and some inner drive I just . . . did it. To be honest, I don't remember much about how I was. But I was told by the other players that I was very exciting, very dynamic. But it was all through fear.'

The great advantage of Hopkins' ability to understudy and step in, many fellow actors believe, was his genius with mimicry. Everyone who saw Captain Edgar speaks of its precision in carbon-copying Olivier's attitude, mannerisms and movements. Hopkins hardly noticed – it was second nature by now and a fundamental mechanism in all his under-studying. He accepted it. But he was dismissive of the advantages of mimicry in seducing an audience. He later said:

I heard a story about when Derek Jacobi was understudying Olivier in *Love for Love*. Derek was obliged to go on for him on a few occasions – in fact they worked like that, with Derek understudying him most of the time, just as Maggie Smith understudied Dame Edith Evans. Derek, was, by that time, very celebrated and recognised in his own right. He was certainly in a higher position within the National than I. But, after the performance, an American couple came into the bar and told anyone who would listen, 'Gee, the old man is really on form tonight' . . . They didn't even see. They didn't look at the programme and no one told them any different, so they were sure they were watching Olivier.

Peta Barker recalls that there was a definite acceleration of opportunity for Hopkins after *Dance of Death*. He had made his mark and now there was no looking back. Olivier himself wrote of the 'young actor of exceptional promise called Anthony Hopkins who . . . walked away with the part of Edgar like a cat with a mouse between its teeth'.

Despite his illness and the radical hyperbaric oxygen radiotherapy prescribed at St Thomas's, Olivier determined to pursue a full workload for himself, which included the directing of *The Three Sisters*. Recovered from his initial operation, in mid-June, he convened production meetings in his private room at the hospital and even summoned his leading actors – his wife, Joan Plowright, who would be Masha, Derek Jacobi playing Lvovich, Jeanne Watts as Olga, Robert Stephens as Vershinin and Hopkins as Andrei – to his bedside for impromptu rehearsals. His confidence in Hopkins was huge and the ensuing Chekhov, which opened early in July, just days before Olivier was released from hospital, was another personal triumph, all the more because of the adversity overcome.

It was universally hailed as one of the National's best accomplishments. Hopkins was hugely visible and hugely comfortable, at last playing a substantial role in his own right and though his brief personal notices were swallowed up by the sum of praise for the production, this was no bad thing. *Punch* reserved its sole barb for him and Louise Purnell: 'Only the breakdowns of Louise Purnell's Irina and Anthony Hopkins' Andrei (both otherwise excellent) seem pitched on too shrill a note.' No one concurred. J. C. Trewin in *The Times* wrote: 'Young critics lament occasionally that they have nothing to criticise. But appreciation must come first, and it is a pleasure to applaud the most moving and exciting revival of *Three Sisters* in our day.'

Hopkins celebrated by getting drunk and prophesying a moment of imminent departure. Ronald Pickup drank with him but foresaw nothing of the abrupt career swing – a hairpin twist away from the theatre into big-time films – that lay just weeks ahead. 'He didn't reveal those things to me, but he did exude impatience. He wanted bigger roles, and the successes dashed him forward.' Pickup observed the deepening relationship with Peta Barker up close. 'Yes, Tony was drinking hard, but I don't think it was crazy drinking, not in the way dear Victor Henry got drunk, which was insanity. But he drank and became bellicose and then Petronella, who could be fiery, would rise up against it. They would argue, quite dramatically, but not, I think, lose sight of themselves.'

In Pickup's eyes, Hopkins' attraction to Peta Barker began with her quality as an actress. 'She could be quite extraordinary, which is not to say there were not other exceptional actresses in the company. But at her best, she was very special. Tony respected talent in others – he was never mean in that regard. So I think he respected her, and then the other bits, the chemistry, took their place.'

Hopkins was now living with Barker at her Chelsea flat but, say others, in a desultory way, moving with the momentum of love but pulling back in some ambivalent reflex. All around, it seemed, he was spring cleaning and reorganising his life, as though suddenly energised by the double-slam of replacing Olivier and playing his beloved Chekhov under Olivier's direction. He had acquired a new agent, in the person of Richard Page of Personal Management, a buzzing young hotfoot with good film connections, and was keen for the Wardour Street audition trail. As Peta recalls, suddenly Hopkins had 'played terrific parts and won acclaim, and now he wanted everything'. But, though she was delighted for him, she was concerned about his constant drinking. Herself a teetotaller, she objected to his behaviour but he ignored her pleas. She now believes he was in the second stage of alcoholism, the stage in which the drinker does not admit to a problem. A lethal time.

Adrian Reynolds relished his RADA friend's glorious progress and came to the National to cheer him on. He met Peta and saw first-hand a volcanic and doomed relationship. 'They were just wild with each other. They had the most outrageous fights at that time, right there in front of everyone in the company. I suppose it was Tony's boozing and I suppose

it was the basic elements of a mismatch.' Others thought Hopkins'
insouciance inappropriate. An actor says, 'It was quite churlish. Olivier
had all the time in the world for him, treated him like a surrogate son,
really. But he abused it. He treated the National like a halfway house.
Fuck it, if it didn't do the job for him. He was thirty [sic]. He wasn't going
to wait around all his life for Larry or anyone else.'

Peta Barker only partly supports this view. She believes that the
relationship with Olivier was exaggerated and 'wasn't that exceptional',
but she does agree that part of the trouble was caused by Hopkins' lack
of patience and forbearance.

As the clashes of temperament rebounded – fired by drink and
impatience directed at Richard Page, from whom he sought grander
offers and bigger cash – he and Peta Barker suddenly incurred Olivier's
wrath. After weeks of snide remarks and angry rumbles, there came a
sudden explosion of confrontation. According to Adrian Reynolds,
'Olivier just faced them both and said, "That's it! It's just too much, all
this shouting. One of you will have to go."'

The emotional rollercoaster roared on. Peta loved him, hated his
boozing, was wary of the urgency of his desire to move on. However, she
strongly believes that Hopkins was never as single-mindedly ambitious as
even he makes out. She feels that there were many people at this time –
advisers, agents – whispering in his ear, telling him now was the moment.
To her, much of what came next had more to do with that than Hopkins'
own choices.

There was discussion and analysis between them, but already Barker
was facing the reality of his obsessive emotional independence and the
rampant, crazy inner dialogue. Marriage wasn't particularly on her mind
at that moment, so she was completely fazed when a friend from the
company approached them at a party and remarked on their topsy-turvy
living arrangements. 'I'm seeing so much of you two together,' the friend
said, 'you're like husband and wife. Are you engaged, or not?' Hopkins
replied, very casually, 'Yes, I suppose so. What do you think, Peta? We
are engaged, aren't we?' The next day, without discussion, he bought Peta
the ring and a few weeks later the couple were married.

Actors who knew both believe that Hopkins' decision to wed was made in hope and not, as the vagrant voice suggests, with the intention of imposing the camouflage of stability and assuaging Olivier's fears. 'He did adore Petronella, and she was a very beautiful woman,' says one friend. 'But he couldn't control his insecurities and, despite those stage successes, he was a rather empty-shell type of person. He married her to try to fill the emptiness and he fully intended to make a go of it . . . but he was like a lost child.'

Before the hurdle of the wedding was the double showdown with Olivier and his National contract. There were many contractual months yet to fulfil and John Dexter had already cast him in the upcoming experimental all-male *As You Like It*, scheduled for production in October, but by late summer Hopkins wanted out. The main trigger, though frequently veiled, was the sudden chance of a major role in Anthony Harvey's film, *The Lion in Winter*, an adaptation of a hit Broadway play. Peter O'Toole was the main architect of the film and it was he who persuaded the recently retired Katharine Hepburn aboard, and he who chose Harvey, a largely untested features director. It was O'Toole, also, who asked to see Hopkins, auditioning him in July. Against close opposition, Hopkins won the role of Richard [soon to be Lionheart] and instantly saw [or, says Barker, was persuaded to see] an imminent new life. O'Toole intended to start his movie in November, based at Ardmore Studios in Ireland and involving location shooting in France and Wales: accordingly, he asked Hopkins to extricate himself from his National contract. It was no argument. Hopkins immediately made a formal request to dissolve the contract.

Initially, Olivier – just weeks over his cancer surgery and absorbed in preparation for a triple-production tour of Canada – demurred. The two 'halves' of the company – the one operating at the Old Vic, the other touring – were fully extended and the year had been an excessively strenuous one; he had no wish to surrender one of his new leading lights. Already, for Olivier, 1967 had seen a fall-out with John Dexter that had led to his dismissal [Clifford Williams from the Royal Shakespeare Company replaced him for *As You Like It*], the cancer trauma and the tragedy of the death of Vivien Leigh in July. To add to this he was jaded, and fighting with his longtime friend and press officer, Virginia Fairweather (who would also be fired, after *As You Like It*). Hopkins' agent turned on the pressure, but the trick was worked by O'Toole himself, who called Olivier while he was on holiday in Switzerland and personally pleaded the case. Why, O'Toole begged, delay a powerful actor's opportunities? Hopkins was special and, O'Toole judged, ripe for cinema. Could Olivier be that mean?

In September, just before his marriage to Peta Barker, Hopkins was officially released for the film, on condition that he fulfilled the schedule of *As You Like It* till Christmas. Some saw this compromise as callous on Olivier's behalf. Hopkins had never been comfortable in his casting of Audrey, the male depiction of Shakespeare's 'poor virgin' wooed by Touchstone. Indeed, few among the company were. '[The experimental play] has been reported as Olivier's baby,' says Ronald Pickup, who would be Rosalind, the star player, 'but it was really John Dexter's. John had read the essay, 'Bitter Arcadia' by Jan Kott and that started it all.'

Kott, a Polish poet and critic, had hit upon the notion of remodelling the sexuality of *As You Like It* to enact more vigorously the ambiguities of passion in Shakespeare. According to Kott, this dazzling inspiration had come as he'd watched long-haired jeans-clad hippies kissing at a corner in Stockholm. Their interchangeability recalled the boy-girl figures of Botticelli's Primavera and the vagueness of Dark Lady imagery. *As You Like It* was the obvious choice for the sexual exploration of Shakespeare. In his essay, Kott wrote, 'Rosalind plays Ganymede playing Rosalind. She plays her own self marrying Orlando . . . The astounding poetry of these scenes has never yet been fully revealed. As if the contemporary theatre did not possess an appropriate instrument . . .'

For Dexter, and later Olivier, the National company was that instrument and, after an agreement with Kott, the production was green-lighted in February 1967. Dexter started work on it; but a dispute with Olivier about timing led to his sacking. Olivier then contacted Williams, who was teaching at Yale. Williams agreed to take over, provided he could bring his designer, Ralph Koltai. Together, through the late spring and early summer, they built an eye-boggling production, set in a pseudo-psychedelic Forest of Arden, that the cast nicknamed 'Freddie and the Freak-Outs'. Apart from Pickup and Hopkins, Williams had Charles Kay as Celia, Richard Kay as Phoebe, Jeremy Brett as Orlando, Derek Jacobi as Touchstone and Robert Stephens as Jacques. None of the four 'female impersonators' was exactly ecstatic about the production, though Pickup faced it as 'a unique challenge which I decided to approach in a low-key and androgynous way'.

As Pickup tells it, the first dress rehearsal in September, attended grudgingly by Hopkins, was 'pretty catastrophic'. Olivier was still absent, undergoing hospital treatment, the set was not quite defined and everyone was clearly addled by what Kott called 'the sexual polarity of the comedies'. Pickup remembers that, 'Charlie Kay and I came in looking like the witches from Oz. It was ridiculous really, very out of control at that stage.'

Hopkins saw the mountain to climb and was sceptical of pulling it off: time was running out, and O'Toole and Harvey had made it clear that they intended to dress-rehearse *The Lion in Winter*, theatre-fashion, within the coming weeks, in anticipation of a shooting date around 20 November. To no one's surprise, Hopkins asked Williams to release him from the production. 'There's a huge wall,' he told Williams. 'I don't think I can make the sexual leap.' Williams parried, urging Hopkins to 'relax over the weekend and see what happens'. For the next rehearsal, Olivier was present and the atmosphere changed. 'He came in splashing his usual energy about the place,' says Pickup, 'and galvanising everyone. He wasn't happy with what I was doing. Larry himself always wanted to play drag, and that's what he wanted from us: high-camp elements. During the interval he came in to me and said, "Here, give me that lipstick. Let's draw a real mouth on you! Give me those eyelashes . . .!" He made me look like an absolute tart, but it was his way of saying, Give us more, more, more.'

Hopkins did it his way. Independently he had a sudden flash of brilliance and appeared for the new rehearsals wearing a stiff canvas shift that made him look, says Pickup, 'like a countrified Brunhilde, very hairy and robust'. Olivier said nothing. Clifford Williams, keen for camp but keener to keep this dodgy production on the rails, enthused, 'That's it, Tony. Perfect. You have it. That's exactly what I want. Moo-cowish.'

'He really wasn't happy about it,' says Pickup who, despite Olivier's entreaties, managed to manoeuvre his androgynous, and tamer, presentation of Rosalind. Still, Hopkins had made the commitment of creative effort and was braced to go the distance, despite the inevitable exhaustion of balancing this with his first attempt at films. Says Pickup: 'Whatever agonies he felt, he brought home. It was a very complicated venture and it would have been fiendish to make it harder than it already was. He didn't do that. He gave it professionalism.'

As You Like It opened on schedule in the first week of October, while Olivier was in Canada, to vehemently mixed reviews. Angus Easson, lecturer in English Language and Literature at Newcastle University, had predicted in the *Sunday Times* that this Shakespeare would not receive the response of Elizabethan audiences; indeed, that 'you must not call it Shakespeare at all'. Irving Wardle of *The Times* loved it, and singled out Hopkins whom, he said, 'gave the funniest of all performances . . . that seems to have grown out of embarrassment'. Ronald Bryden in the *Observer* felt otherwise. For him it was 'basic ENSA knockabout', unfit for the esteemed National. Pickup agreed that it might be construed as 'ENSA knockabout', but believed its application was ingenious.

Peta Barker saw Hopkins' first night through the glow of love, believing it to be his peak at the National. Her enthusiasm was, perhaps, prejudiced. Just four weeks before – even to her surprise – he had married her in a simple ceremony, with Leicester rep actor David Swift as his best man, at a chapel near her parents' home in Kent. Laurence Olivier's gift to them was a pair of bedsheets that, says Peta, excited them like children. No matter the heat of their current relationship, Hopkins was not beyond rhapsodies of awe regarding his mentor: 'Well, no matter what happens,' he told Peta, 'we'll be able to look back and tell our friends: These sheets were given to us by the noble Olivier!' The tabloids later reported that Muriel Hopkins had disowned her son and his new bride, enraged that he had not apprised her of their plans. Lynda Lee-

Potter in the *Daily Mail* went a step further by stating in a 1987 feature article, which Barker contests, that 'His parents never liked Peta and were so opposed to the relationship that at first his mother refused even to go to the wedding.' Barker denies the often repeated stories that she and Muriel never exchanged a civil word, that she was not welcome at the Ship Inn, that indeed she never visited the Hopkins home in Wales. She contends that she and Muriel did eventually get on, the initial coldness being caused by Hopkins' out-of-the-blue announcement that he was engaged to a woman his mother hardly knew. Dick, on the other hand, she recalls, was always very sensitive to her situation and often made things easier on her visits to Wales.

Muriel's shock at Hopkins' overnight decision to wed is reflected by pal Brian Evans, who had seen Hopkins infrequently since the Taibach farewell. 'When I heard he had married Petronella Barker my reaction was, no, it must be a mistake. Our Anthony marrying! He had kept himself so far away from women, romantically speaking, that it seemed incomprehensible. Anyone who knew him during the Welsh days wasn't surprised that he'd left it till 28 to get hitched. The surprise was that he went through with it at all.'

In spite of Muriel's reservations, both she and Dick attended the wedding and reception at Eric Barker's thatched home. On that day, in a haze of love and excitement, Peta was convinced the marriage would last forever. There were plenty of reasons for optimism – the marriage, freedom from a long-haul contract, triumph in a major Shakespeare, the imminent high-flying film with its Hollywood connections and £3,000 fee. But to the perceptive there was cause for serious concern too. Hopkins celebrated this exhilarating run by getting progressively drunker. Though Barker saw this as just an actor enjoying his moment, others saw the upward spiral of a destructive impatience – mostly with himself, but taking its toll of victims all the same. 'He misused the National,' says one actor. 'And he offended Olivier.' Another believes that Hopkins 'made enemies by his very aggressive style of communication . . . and a general recklessness in his approach. Olivier was very good to him, but he had an attitude of "To hell with everyone, I must look after myself."'

Peta Barker feels that Hopkins was not a great communicator, that while he would talk non-stop he was deficient in expressing himself. The abruptness of his departure from the National – which would happen in December, with a whimper rather than a bang as his promise to Olivier expired – she saw as an indication that Hopkins liked to end things himself, not have people end things for him. In her view, he preferred not to keep the strings of past lives going, and constantly created energy in that kind of renewal.

Chapter 6

BREAKAGES

'*The Lion in Winter* was a scary experience,' says director Anthony Harvey, 'made no easier by Olivier's unnecessary insistence on Tony Hopkins flying almost daily from Dublin to London, usually in a terrible fog, to fulfil an exhausted commitment at the National.'

Harvey was just 32, an editor who'd started as an actor at RADA, played Vivien Leigh's brother in *Caesar and Cleopatra* and graduated by cutting *I'm All Right Jack, Dr Strangelove* and *Lolita*. In 1966, with the help of actress Shirley Knight's husband, he raised $20,000 – 'on the basis of three hundred here and two hundred there' – to finance *The Dutchman*, a Broadway adaptation shot in one week at Twickenham, starring Knight and winning for her the Golden Lion at the Venice Film Festival. 'Peter O'Toole, whom I didn't know, saw it and contacted me to say he had this screenplay by James Goldman, based on his hit Broadway play, and would I do it if he could get Katharine Hepburn.' Looking back, Harvey laughs at the unlikeliness of it all. 'To be honest, I said, well, that's a bit of a longshot. But then he took *Dutchman* to LA and showed it to her and the next thing I knew I was talking to Hepburn on the phone and offering to visit her in LA. She said, "No, save your pennies and lets get on with it, I'll come to London."'

What followed for Harvey was his happiest film experience and the germination of a friendship with Hepburn that extended through three films. 'There was no jockeying, no megalomania,' he says. 'It was Peter's project, but my film. No one contested direction and since they were the old hands I had the greatest joy in each of them in turn defending my decisions and shoring me up. Consequently when I would request something that maybe Peter didn't like, Kate would say, "Oh, come on, do it the way Tony wants it!" And vice versa. There were no rows, but there was disaster – or threatened disaster – and we met it as we could.'

As Harvey recalls, his moment of approving Anthony Hopkins – one of the many newcomers proposed by O'Toole – was 'a flash of realisation'. Several theatrical bright lights were invited to readings, among them Peter Egan, Timothy Dalton, Jane Merrow and John Castle. 'From them we worked a shortlist that I decided to screen-test.' The site for the test was a tent in Battersea Park where O'Toole sat behind the camera, reading lines to the newcomers. 'In Tony's case the decision took about two seconds. He came very composed, very fixed in his approach and did a quite amazing take-off of Olivier. It was very obvious stuff – dazzling for its virtuosity, done for effect – but it worked. Peter was delighted, I was convinced . . . so we booked him.'

When Hepburn arrived in London, in early November, just weeks after *As You Like It* commenced, Harvey decided to book the Haymarket Theatre for a fortnight to rehearse in the manner of a play. 'I saw that there was an element of wobbly knees among the new chaps, in the presence of Kate especially, and I knew I must address this. But it really wasn't necessary. She was such a kind spirit, so comforting to her fellow actors, that the expected terror wasn't much in evidence after the first few hours. In fact, we didn't last the whole fortnight, because we didn't need it.'

As shooting started at Ardmore Studios in Bray, on 27 November, Harvey reorganised his schedule to accommodate Olivier. 'But it wasn't a nightmare, we shot around the absences because Tony wasn't in every scene in those studio days where we shot the interior of Chinon Castle, where much of the action takes place.' Hepburn rented a cottage in Wicklow, a mile from the studio and surrounded by exquisite parkland. O'Toole boozed in Dublin, the rest of the mostly male cast camped – with Harvey – in the Glenview Hotel in the panoramic Wicklow Hills. As Harvey saw it, 'Tony was never a drunk in my company. Peter was our boozer, our anecdote man, our life of the party. Tony was, professionally, very disciplined and keen to make a go of it. Then again, it was his big chance.'

Hopkins later described Harvey as 'a bit nervy, a bit jumpy', which is altogether not too surprising, since Harvey had responsibility for the $3-million budget and the raw cast he had given room to. Hopkins later agonised publicly about the 'rough time' he gave so many of his early directors. When Harvey heard from a friend that Hopkins had described him as 'a very prickly man who wanted to do everything himself', he wrote complainingly to Hopkins, who replied, 'abjectly apologetic, saying he had been misquoted'.

It was clear to some that the single-mindedness of the National period, ruthless as it often was, was again at play. With Katharine Hepburn, however, Hopkins was dutifully ready to eat humble pie. He later said: 'The first time before the cameras with her in my big scene I didn't have a clue. I knew my lines and I knew the part, but when we lined up for the camera rehearsal she said, "Fine, come on, kid, let's have a coffee . . ."'

Over coffee, it was clear that Hepburn intended to teach him the concept of screen acting. Hopkins sat slack-jawed as she started a rapid interrogation through cigarette puffs.

'Do you like the camera?' she asked.

'Er, I, well, suppose so . . .'

'Then why the hell do you play the entire scene with the back of your head to it, dear?'

When Hopkins mumbled, she pointed to the Arriflex camera on its tripod. 'That's the damn lens. It's on you. Part of this scene is your scene. If you don't want it, hand it to me and I'll certainly take it. I can act you off the screen.'

At first Hopkins fluffed. He said: 'I did fifteen takes of that first shot. I was scared stiff, and a pile of jelly. Hepburn kept saying, "Let him do it again . . . Go on, do another one." She taught me it all.'

The story was a tight and claustrophobic one, demanding ensemble acting, which ideally suited so many of the newer cast members who were familiar with stage technique but ignorant of Hollywood. In the film, Henry II, King of England and half of France (O'Toole), brings together at Chinon Castle his estranged wife Eleanor (Hepburn) and three sons, along with his mistress Alais (Jane Merrow) and her brother, to debate the choice of successor. Duplicity and in-fighting follow as Eleanor favours Richard (Hopkins) and attempts to outfox Henry's choice of the more irascible John (Nigel Terry) by styling a marriage between Richard and Alais.

The script was wordy, quite static and inconclusive by the standards of today's quasi-historical bio-pics – the *Monthly Film Bulletin* would describe it as 'a kind of Shavian historical burlesque' – but it could not have been a more fitting transitional vehicle from Hopkins' point of view. Pocket-sized in conception as it was, brazenly revealing its roots of theatricality, Hopkins' performance was pocket-sized Olivier, clipped and refined, occasionally lifting to a booming high emotion that distracted from the obvious mechanical moments. Its comparative 'smallness', combined with the presence and kindness of Hepburn and O'Toole, allowed Hopkins – once he relaxed into it – to experiment quietly with mannerism, movement and modulation. Shortly afterwards, he was saying,

> I think in myself I find film acting quite easy: I can gather my resources very quickly. As a film actor, I know what the situation is going to be when I do the shot. You learn this in theatre. But in theatre you make a broad line, you make a ground plan for a part in, say, *Three Sisters* or *Cherry Orchard* or *Hamlet* or whatever, and if that ground plan is wrong it's bad luck, you get bad notices and it's a bad performance and you are stuck with it for ten weeks. But in film you can always readjust. So you do shot 139, scene 12 and by that time you can consider what has gone

before and estimate what is to come, and readjust. With the help of a director . . . But it worries me that perhaps I am too facile, maybe it's a little too easy for me. Any fool can scratch his backside or have a cup of coffee during 'To be or not to be . . .' and that worries me a lot.

The great worry in January 1968 was whether the film would get finished at all. Late in the month Hepburn completed her scenes and returned to the States, granting gifts of glasses containing crystal 'tears' to each of the cast members, including Hopkins. The inscriptions read, 'From Eleanor of Aquitaine'. Cast and crew then moved to Southern France and the Camargue on the Rhône delta for a succession of exteriors at the restored Montmajour Abbey in Arles, at Tarascon, at the walled city of Carcassonne and at the Tour Philippe le Bel at Avignon. According to Hopkins, the mood on set now was grim, reflecting perhaps the exhaustion of intensely packed days stretching into months on a film of strongly drawn characters depicted by strongly opinionated personalities. Nigel Stock physically fought with O'Toole, while Hopkins himself was, said actress Jane Merrow, at obvious war with Peta Barker. Merrow recalled Hopkins on the telephone nightly 'trying to deal with a person who was obviously his wife'. She perceived him as a man under strain, ready to 'pop' at any moment.

Anthony Harvey kept his blind side to the squabbles and focused on bringing in his film in the prescribed three months. But then disaster struck while filming a jousting scene with Hopkins in the Camargue. Harvey remembers:

> He wasn't exactly comfortable with the idea of himself as a horseman, but he got up in full armour and trotted off. We were getting ready to shoot and the Arriflex unfortunately is a camera that makes a noise. The horse heard it and startled and took off. I shouted to Tony not to panic but of course he did – he couldn't hold it. We saw him drop in a pile and lie still and I remember thinking, my God, that's done it, he's a gonner. I honestly thought he had broken his back! His first movie and he ends up breaking his damn back! We ran up to him and he was motionless, white as a ghost . . . and he said, 'My arm's gone, it's broken.'

As Hopkins was moved to hospital, with Nigel Stock electing to keep him company as the production moved on, more disaster fell. 'I was keeping my head down, just trying to finish the thing with everyone alive,' Harvey laughs. 'Then we all went out for a seafood dinner in the Camargue. Everyone got food poisoning and proceeded to throw up. I didn't, which is the worst possible outcome. A few days later, I skipped behind a bush to take a pee and out comes a stream of bright canary-yellow urine. I had contracted hepatitis.'

Harvey put his cast and crew on a train and hobbled back to England, where he was hospitalised and the production temporarily shut down. 'I lost a couple of weeks – but the worst part was when I was lying there incapacitated and Joe Levine, the executive producer, decided to take the footage, which we all felt was stupendous, and cut it himself. I was devastated by the very idea of it. But Kate Hepburn stepped in. She told Joe, "Don't you know who your director is? Don't you know what he cut? All those brilliant classic movies." She stood in the way and made Joe Levine wait until I was well enough to finish the film.'

As Hopkins returned to the new scenario of suburban married life with Barker, Harvey took his footage to Hollywood where, for the first time, the executive viewing suites of 'the Coast' had their chance to inspect the newest 'star' National fugitive. The response was unanimously good. Levine, among many, thought him 'an exceptional screen presence' and the *Evening Standard* in London carried gossip of an Oscar nomination. 'It worked magic for him,' says Harvey. 'But deservedly. He brought a quality to his Richard that enhanced the movie, was a central part of its success.' As it turned out, *The Lion in Winter* would achieve the double-hit status that guaranteed wider opportunities for all its principals: the reviews were good, the box office sublime. Harvey won the New York Critics Award and went on to receive an Oscar nomination. The film garnered three Oscars – for Best Screenplay (Goldman), Best Musical Score (John Barry) and Best Actress (Hepburn, who shared the award with Barbra Streisand for *Funny Girl*). 'It was beyond our expectation,' says Harvey, 'and it went on winning.' Today, it has grossed about $80 million – against its modest

$3-million investment – making it one of the most profitable historical epics ever.

The pay-off for Hopkins was immediate. Not yet a month back in London, Richard Page was already talking of American inquiries and the likelihood of LA auditions. Hopkins lapped it up, once again doggedly rejecting backward glances to Olivier and the National and instead settling himself into a strained routine of domesticity. Strained, because every step of the way into marital conformity brought niggly – and sometimes not so petty – problems. For starters, Peta's hope for a secure home base in which to build her family of several children ran aground. The house the couple chose, in Lifford Street, in Putney, had all the attributes of easy access to open common, the nearby BBC, and theatreland, but the Halifax Building Society turned down their loan application. Though Hopkins had put aside the money from *Lion in Winter* for the purpose of setting up home, the building society considered his profession insecure and his earnings unreliable. It was not until Peta's parents agreed to act as guarantors that a workable arrangement was reached. This was not a moment too soon because just before Christmas Peta had become pregnant and, as she tells it, wasn't having the easiest of first pregnancies. Hopkins was, she recalls, delighted about becoming a father, and took a keen interest, actively helping her with the ante-natal exercises.

Nevertheless, the boozing and arguments went on, sparked not so much by the fears of fatherhood and responsibility as by a seething, inarticulate and inward-turned rage, the return of chronic self-criticism. A colleague of the time opines:

> Nothing he did satisfied him. There was no smugness. He fell out with directors and actors because he gave voice to anger and it was misconstrued. In drink, he was an ignorant loudmouth, but it was pathologic, I believe, the side-effect of the illness of alcoholism. And where did that have its origins? In his utter inability to comprehend himself and his purpose in being alive. Tony was a deep thinker. Many of the people he had around him simply were not.

Peta Barker recalls the rows with an audibly plaintive ambiguity. Their love seemed rock solid, yet they tore at each other like lions. Hopkins was versed in argument and in his early life, as in his early acting, believed he expressed best at stentorian full belt. Time taught him otherwise but for now his standard response to the rhythms of life that distressed him – to boredom, insolence, bullying, incompetence, inefficiency – was a high-decibel, tip-of-the-toes onslaught to which Peta, in her proximity, most frequently fell victim.

Still, they held the course, clinging to the escalating good news, to their friendship, to the twinkles of the future. In the spring, noticeably pregnant, Peta retired from the National and accompanied her husband and Richard Page to LA, by invitation of David Wolper Productions, who were casting a war film called *The Bridge at Remagen*. Hopkins had been summoned on the basis of Harvey's as yet unreleased film. Since its shooting, however, he had put on quite a lot of weight, the result of booze and long lazy evenings gazing endlessly at whatever the TV had to offer. Instinctively, on his way to LA, he knew the futility of the trip. Accordingly, he adjusted himself to a touristy mentality and resolved to enjoy every blink on his expenses-paid vacation.

Barker wistfully describes the LA and New York days as among the most fun-filled of her memories. Aware as she was of Hopkins' childhood mania for Americans and American movies, she relished the joy that pumped out of him – a boy again – as he surveyed the riddled Atlantic beneath the plane, the coastline of his fabled nation, touchdown, immersion. Immediately, subliminally, he loved it – and when his brain clicked in and his eyes scoured, he loved it more. All of it. The balm of the Pacific air. The short sleeves. Convertible cars with mirror bodywork. Mimosa on the roadside. Burgers. Bud beer. Palmtrees and highways. Peta knew that Hopkins wanted to live in Hollywood and, she says, she was prepared to leave England, though she knew she would long for the countryside she had grown to love from her childhood in Kent.

A bus took them from LAX north to Santa Barbara where they stayed but, Peta recalls with laughter, a big air-conditioned limo was laid on for the long southward trip to Disneyland at Anaheim. Like excited children they played with the electric windows on their way to meet Mickey Mouse. Later, Hopkins made a lone journey to Sid Grauman's Chinese Theater and the Walk of Fame along Hollywood Boulevard and Vine Street where he inspected the stone-carved signatures and hand-and-hoof impressions of his heroes – of Bogie, Bing Crosby, Wallace Beery, Roy Rogers, Trigger and Donald Duck.

The sightseeing compensations were the best Hopkins would get from Hollywood on this first venture into Tinseltown because his screen-test proved a let-down and he was passed over for the part in favour of Robert Vaughan. In Hopkins' account of his failure, he attended a party at director John Guillermin's house in Benedict Canyon the night before the test, got drunk and appeared hung over the next day. Added to that was the producers' disappointment at his out-of-condition, overweight appearance. Whatever the reasons, he returned home via New York, deflated by his failure but not depressed: the word around town regarding *The Lion in Winter*, still locked in the cutting rooms, was superb and the agents and directors who met him, to a man, promised a Hollywood life.

Back in the grey reality of a miserable London summer, with the several-hundred-and-umpteenth *Z Cars* on the TV and the telephone not ringing, Hopkins slumped into depression. He later said:

> I ate too much and drank too much. I was lazy and I was married and I used to sit around in a big lump watching television every night. I didn't care a damn. I was very unhappy, actually. If you are unhappy you overcompensate, don't you? You eat and eat and slip lower and lower into depths of lethargy and this is what I was doing. I didn't give a fuck about my career, about anything. I was financially comfortable and that sort of business . . . I said to myself, I'll paint the house and dig the garden every summer and that's going to be my life . . .

Of course, it never could be, though Peta was still hopeful of tranquillity, despite the tantrums – and the silences. More and more she recognised the cause of incompatibility: a combination of the growing alcoholic illness and his restless need to test himself, and find himself. He knew he was making headway, by any conventional standards – in his career, in his finances, in the celebrity he confusedly craved; but the rest was a sham. He hadn't, he felt, matured or got to grips with who he was. Was he a theatre actor, or a film actor? An intellectual, or a con artist? Did he trust himself, or his judgements? Surely not – for how did he land himself in a marriage for which he was ill-suited, with a child on the way for whom he had no answers? When he fought with Peta, or his friends, it was usually through a haze of drink, aimlessly, his one focus and passion being – always – that had the last word. 'Hold on a minute,' he would shout. 'I'll get my word in, I'll get my word in last!' Three years later, looking back, he would tell *Radio Times* journalist Deirdre Macdonald, 'I'm an easy person to work with, but I'm not an easy person to live with. I'm neurotic. That sounds like self-flagellation. I don't mean highly strung in a cuddly way. I'm just nervous – even sitting here talking with you. Look at the ashtray: I've been chain smoking. I lack direction when I'm not working.'

The work came at last: another film offer, limp as tissue this time – a Columbia adaptation of John le Carré's *The Looking Glass War*, directed by wunderkind Frank Pierson, the writer-director of *Cat Ballou* – but at least it was alongside an actor he hugely admired, Ralph Richardson. The fee was good – ten times anything Olivier's National could pay – but the work was not taxing. The script was muddled and all his rather po-faced scenes were shot in dreary, wintry-damp Shepperton Studios.

Just before he commenced shooting, in August, Peta gave birth to their daughter Abigail. Hopkins attended the birth and was, says Peta, a doting father. But the euphoria was momentary, and quickly drowned in the monotony of Shepperton and in his chronic anxieties.

Pierson's approach to one of le Carré's least effectively realised psychological thrillers was to rewrite half the story, substituting the leisurely study of character disintegration in the novel with nail-biting, but dead-end, red-herrings. Dominated by two mismatched per-formances that spoke volumes for the gulf between theatre training and the thumbnail 'Method' of the Hollywood school – with Richardson as the spymaster Leclerc and twitchy Christopher Jones as his pawn – the film describes the frustrated attempts of MI6 to locate and identify a Russian missile base in Eastern Germany that had apparently been revealed on a secret roll of film. Hopkins played Leclerc's gofer, John Avery, featuring mostly in the first scenes when he journeys to Finland to investigate the death of the agent who had possession of the roll of film. Avery then fades from the film as Polish refugee Leiser (Jones) is selected to breach the barbed-wire frontier and find the base. The story follows his gruelling training under Haldane (Paul Rogers) and the mission itself.

Hopkins missed the opportunity to travel to Spain – doubling as Finland and Germany – but had no regrets on that score. He was, he told Tony Crawley, deeply unhappy during the shooting and had little comfort from the cast. Richardson was fine – humorous, wily, keen to brag about his Harley Davidson motorbike and prick the prickly Christopher Jones at every turn. But Jones, whose career was never more than fragile with only one moment of note to come (*Ryan's Daughter* in 1970), was the walking embodiment of the Hollywood sourpuss. When he could, he avoided social drinking and meals with the crew or cast, was mono-syllabic to the point of stupor and, says a technician, 'given to catatonia when everyone else was busy making sense of a non-action action movie'. In fact, according to Hopkins, Jones stumbled through the movie doing a religious impersonation of James Dean that sickened Hopkins.

The Looking Glass War proved an informative, first-hand view of sub-Hollywood film-making that unsettled Hopkins. Pledged as he was to studying the geography of the film set and the grammar of film-makers, this film seemed an exercise in tawdry improvisation and indulgence. It would, he knew, win him no progress and he was, say colleagues, momentarily confused about the direction of his work.

In this mood of hesitation and reconsideration – cramped in a ball on a couch before a TV in Putney – Hopkins felt his young marriage come apart. Peta loved him, he was in no doubt, but, a friend says, 'He could take love, provided he could cut it off. Commitment was OK to a point. But he had to have a door to walk out of. He couldn't just stop there. Not then anyway.' With Peta in the next room, Abby at his feet and a mortgage to wrestle with, there was no door. No room. No haven. No silence. No isolation. 'Also,' says the friend, 'there was not enough pain. He was on his way to insulating himself, and that was no choice for an artist. Sooner or later he had a critical decision to make.' Peta kept trying. The house was big, but filled with activity. Mrs Channing, the sitting tenant, was good-humoured and properly unimpressed by the peaks and troughs of the actor's life. Peta initially hoped to maintain her acting and engaged a German au pair, who lived in and brought a sweet, smiling efficiency to the business of tending to Abby and navigating the rocky spaces between the couple. However, later Peta decided she did not want someone else to bring up her baby, and six months after Abby was born, following work on a TV play, she gave up her acting career for good.

Hopkins 'critical decision' was delayed first by director Tony Richardson's call requesting him to join the cast of *Hamlet*, to be performed for a few weeks at the Roundhouse, Camden Town, before being filmed 'live' for cinema circulation, funded by Columbia Pictures. Hopkins would have cast himself as Hamlet – it was a role he was already telling Page and others that he wanted to play now, before age defeated him – but Richardson had another vision, casting Nicol Williamson, who was more broadly experienced and well-versed, in the lead and Hopkins as Hamlet's uncle and stepfather, Claudius, the eye of villainy in the play. Hopkins was uneasy with this casting and quickly fell foul of Richardson's inventive reanalysis of the play. They started coolly, ultimately argued about approach, and Hopkins described the two-month commitment as a 'terrible experience'.

In casting Hopkins, Richardson perhaps saw more than Hopkins saw. Richardson's reputation was that of iconoclast – he was director of the film versions of *Look Back in Anger* (1959), *The Entertainer* (1960), and *The Loneliness of the Long Distance Runner* (1962) – and his re-evaluation of *Hamlet* began with young, untypical casting. But Hopkins, youth apart, was brilliantly 'on the nose'. Was there ever a young actor so firmly on the cusp of vital success, so emotionally primed for the moderation-remorse-bravado-guilt of Claudius, Shakespeare's subtlest villain?

Pray can I not,
Though inclination be as sharp as will:
My stronger guilt defeats my strong intent,
And, like a man to double business bound,
I stand in pause to where I shall first begin,
And both neglect.

Marianne Faithfull, hitherto British rock's sole sex totem, was a siren Ophelia, Judy Parfitt a muddled, deeply 'sick souled' Gertrude, Gordon Jackson the paragon Horatio. Still, the play nudged the outer limits of the broadest *Hamlet* interpretations, reducing his moral plight crucially – and fascinatingly – by shadowing it under the conceits of court conspiracies and political expediency.

Hopkins hated all this, though the evidence of the time suggests he hated more Richardson's refusal to allow directorial interference. Unlike his other recent directors, Harvey and Pierson in particular, Richardson was a veteran of difficult temperaments and the jigsaw discipline of film construction. He was also not fond of 'collaborative' production. 'Richardson and I didn't see eye to eye,' Hopkins told the *Guardian*. 'I nearly lost my mind when he said, "And what piece of genius is Mr Hopkins going to bring to rehearsal today? . . ." I hate all the "Did Hamlet sleep with Ophelia?" type of theatre. All the theorising by over-intellectual directors is dehydrating for actors. All that playing cricket before rehearsal to get the correct reflexes – it stinks.'

It had been twenty years since Olivier's screen *Hamlet* had illuminated the newest medium for Shakespeare, and in that time nothing had come close to his accomplishment. Tony Richardson, in cashing in his commercial chips for a Columbia-financed Shakespeare movie, addressed himself to the previous adaptation failures and opted for a new approach – miles from the lavish Olivier – shooting the entirety in close-up on the Roundhouse stage.

Hopkins stayed for this – barely – and proved himself second, if not best, of a highly emotive cast. Shooting took less than seven days, with all scenery blanked out, suggesting, ironically, a vastness and moving timelessness to setting and plot. Williamson and Hopkins hogged Gerry Fisher's flat-focus camera, staring balefully, wryly, jadedly into infinity, filling the void. It was electric stuff, vindicating Richardson's daring (though ultimately crawling through a box office sated with James Bond and the limitless *Carry Ons*), and most critics took it to their hearts. In the *Monthly Film Bulletin*, Noel Andrews relished its quiet, subversive cynicism and judged it a 'tour de force'. Williamson won top honours: '[his] intense absorption and driving intelligence make [the soliloquies] seem more than usually like spoken thoughts', but Hopkins was in the final frame too: 'Anthony Hopkins' Claudius speaks throughout with a regal confidence and swagger, betraying only in his eyes . . . a recurring and haunted anxiety.'

In due course, when *Hamlet* was released within months of *The Lion in Winter* in 1969 and both films fused in a broad-ranged showcase of his classical talent, Hopkins revised his attitude to the months with Richardson. Calmed down, he thought the movie 'inventive' and worthwhile, though he still had no regrets about refusing the chance to join the play's transfer to Broadway. While all the cast had met the transfer with enthusiasm, Hopkins had told Richardson he was tired, and that he had done all he could with the role of Claudius. He was also personally troubled that tensions at home – as Peta increasingly objected to his drinking in Abby's company – had interfered with his recent stage playing. He was, he said, 'irregular' in the last Roundhouse shows – sometimes vigorous and intact, more often 'going through the motions': he was doing neither Richardson nor himself any favours by chancing a New York transfer. Richardson was livid and allegedly joined the expanding club of 'Hopkins knockers' that Ronald Pickup and the friends from the National were aware of. 'You cannot stretch your capabilities and break new ground without earning enemies,' says Pickup. 'By then Tony was beginning the great stretch that took him into his extraordinary growth.'

Back home it was atrophy, not growth. Nineteen sixty-nine was a mixed-up year: the year of Abby (which thrilled him literally to tears), but the year of very little forward momentum. All he was doing, he felt, was impersonating a star and a father.

As Peta drew her line in the dust – no more drunkenness in front of Abby – the marriage tipped over the precipice. Not two years old, it was as good as over. Hopkins drew tightly into himself, talking to Page more than anyone, nibbling the amorphous future for sustenance, blanking past and present. He ceased all efforts to communicate and repair. Mrs Channing, the sitting tenant, expressed no surprise. 'He always blew hot and cold,' she said to Peta, repeating herself like a metronome, counting them out.

Chapter 7

WAYNE 201 – HOPKINS 4

The dilemma was that while Anthony Hopkins was learning his trade and vacillating throughout the sixties, the sun had risen and set on the British film industry. The decade that had slipped through his fingers had seen the British cultural revolution and ancillary international bushfire. Transatlantic film deals ensued – inspired by the successes of the New Wave and the originality of directors like Lindsay Anderson, Karel Reisz, Joseph Losey and Tony Richardson – and spawned glitzy, internationally marketable epics, the first of their kind from Britain. The huge success of *Tom Jones* in 1963 – funded by United Artists when Tony Richardson's company Woodfall failed to raise the cash in Britain – marked the start of a floodtide of American-funded British exports. By 1966, 75 per cent of British first features were American-financed, and this had risen to 90 per cent by 1969. American money meant American distribution and accordingly British actors and directors were delivered nourished and packaged not just to the Gaumont or Odeon chains, but to the world. In this way, the sixties granted instant international status to Albert Finney, Michael Caine, Sean Connery, Julie Christie and Richard Harris. Feeding on the novelty, genius and the abhorrence of censorship in British films, Universal, for one, poured £30 million into them between 1967 and 1969. But the well was bound to run dry and the sudden string of failures gives witness to unforgivable over-indulgence. *A Countess from Hong Kong, Work is a Four Letter Word, Three Into Two Won't Go* and *Can Hieronymous Merkin Ever Forget Mercy Humpe and Find True Happiness?* all proved expensive failures and foreshadowed the withdrawal of American film investment in Britain.

By 1969, all the Hollywood companies were in debt, many as a direct result of over-investment in the emaciated British product. By then, the re-emergence of native Americana had begun. The glamour of the Beatles and Bond had abated, Britishness no longer spelt bankability, and films like *The Graduate* (1967), *Bullitt* (1968) and *Butch Cassidy and the Sundance Kid* (1969) reasserted American instincts and Hollywood's pre-eminence in the lingua franca of international entertainment. By 1970, only Columbia Pictures had any semblance of a production slate in Britain. All the others had fled. The British film industry was ailing, destined shortly to die in the coming recession and the reversion to traditionalism that accompanied the re-election of Conservatives in government. What chance for Hopkins, then, the Hollywood stardom he dreamed about?

For a moment he contemplated abandoning his mortgage and, in the words of Adrian Reynolds, winging it: 'There was no question but that he would develop internationally. The issue was *when*?' But he froze to the notion. Reflecting on the American rejection troubled him. One close observer believed that 'it really flattened him, it drove his confidence problem sky-high'. He was, he knew, completely unsuited to LA networking: he had neither the social grace nor the patience for it. Worse, the observer believes, 'He knew he wasn't the stuff of the young male lead – he would never fit into the shoes of James Coburn or Steve McQueen or Robert Redford. He was more a Charles Laughton, or Edward G. Robinson . . . and they don't make star movies for Eddie Robinson any more.'

During the long period of unemployment following *Hamlet* – relieved only by the curiously ineffectual reprisal of *The Three Sisters* for BBC television and an unseen role in an independent short film called *The Peasant's Revolt* – Hopkins disentangled himself from his marriage in a subtle adagio. There were no intimate friends with whom to share the anguish – indeed, beyond the usual daily rows there was no final showdown with Barker, just the distinct sense of finality. Neither had wanted the marriage to fail, asserts Barker, but she was determined to raise Abby in a normal home with a conventional, sensible lifestyle. Her husband, however, was pursuing other things.

Domesticity clung. As Hopkins hit the casting trail with a vengeance he was still, to outsiders' eyes, playing husband. He relaid the parquet hall floor himself, affronted by the huge estimate from the local flooring company; he tended the garden, invested in furnishings . . . but it was all a cover-up. He knew, as she knew, that what he yearned for was an invitation to move on.

Against the odds at this parlous time in British films, the opportunity came from close quarters – from a quasi-British film set up by a maverick American agent-turned-producer, Elliott Kastner. Kastner's film was Alistair Maclean's *When Eight Bells Toll*, shrewdly primed – though Kastner is slow to admit it – to inherit the international market spot recently vacated by Sean Connery's British-based Bond movies. The Connery Bonds, financed from the US by United Artists, had defied all previous British thriller records and become the biggest grossing film series in history. In 1967 Connery had stepped down in a blaze of arguments with producer Harry Saltzman. In the hiatus after Connery, Kastner saw a hot market opportunity and launched his sub-Bond thriller, featuring dour agent Philip Calvert, with the quiet hope of a potential hit series. Kastner had already scored a major box-office success in 1968 with Maclean's *Where Eagles Dare*, starring Richard Burton, so was superstitiously attracted to the idea of another Celtic lead in the mould of Burton or Connery. He looked at a number of British actors – notably Michael Jayston – before deciding, after a screening of *The Lion in Winter,* to offer the role to Hopkins. Kastner says,

I came to England in the middle sixties to make *Kaleidoscope* with Warren Beatty, and stayed. The reason for my staying, primarily, was Alistair Maclean. I'd read Maclean's first novel *HMS Ulysses*, and I loved it. He had written four by that time, all sold to the movies. I rang him and said, 'I want you to write a movie,' and he said, 'Big deal, why?' He was very intimidating, called himself a businessman not a writer. But I'd made another movie with a novelist doing the screenwriting – a guy called William Goldman, no less [the film was *Moving Target*] – so I gave Alistair that script and *Kaleidoscope* and I said, 'Look at the economy in a script and do it. You can do it easy. And you can keep the book rights or whatever you do' . . . which was about the dumbest thing I ever said, because he wrote a great screen story – *Where Eagles Dare* – and we had a colossal hit movie two years later.

On the back of that success, Kastner immediately commissioned from Maclean two more original stories for the screen, a western and a swashbuckler; then Maclean offered him the just published novel *When Eight Bells Toll*.

I looked at it and liked it immediately. There was a strong character and a great adventure in there. The movie I envisioned was a kind of *Guns of Navarone*. A combination of *Navarone* and *Gunga Din* and *The Treasure of the Sierra Madre*. I saw the agent-hero Calvert as a potentially very exciting characterisation. A lot could be done with him. But I didn't want a Tony Curtis. I didn't want a star. I wanted a classical actor. A real actor. Once I saw Tony, there was never anyone else for me. I had seen him on stage. I thought he had marvellous rhythms. I said, I want him and I went with my first gut feeling.

'It was bizarre, bad casting,' says Ferdy Mayne, cast as Lavorski, the secret villain of the piece. 'Hopkins was a tubby little fellow then, and all of us so-called veterans who had been around Kastner for a while thought he looked like a puppy. He was carrying this excess weight, and while he was very very pleasant, he hadn't, I felt, the cultured way you might expect from a suave lead.' Mayne was one of Kastner's 'rep boys', spotted by the producer in Peter Sellers' *The Bobo* (directed by Robert Parrish, in 1967) and booked for a series of films. 'Elliott tended to operate on a family basis. If he liked you he was faithful and supportive. In that sense Anthony knew he had a real chance here. Elliott was making big box-office movies. *Where Eagles Dare* made a fortune, so the possibilities of another Alistair Maclean blockbuster were terrific and it was, on the face of it, an invitation to stardom.'

Kastner gathered around him the strongest production team, many of them from the Bond units. He chose 37-year-old Etienne Périer, whose family ran Sabena Airlines, to be director. Kastner recalls,

> He was a lovely chap, but he was probably the one mistake I made on the movie. He was very educated, very charming, very engaging. I met him in New York and he talked me into giving him a chance. He wanted to do big things and I thought, OK, let him have a go. But he was a European intellectual and, I ask you, what European understands the rhythms of American product? Polanski maybe. But that's the one exception. Etienne wasn't right for our movie – but he gave it his best shot and he didn't throw us in the toilet.

When Hopkins first met Kastner in Tilney Street the producer didn't mince words. According to producer Marion Rosenberg, 'He told him straight that what we had in mind was action-man stuff and Tony was too fat for it. If he wanted the part, he had to slim down.' Kastner laughs at the memory: 'Yeah, I might have said that. But I had Bob Simmons [stunt director from the Bond films] there to put him on a regime and knock him back into shape. He was the actor I wanted. I was ready to do whatever had to be done to fix him.'

Simmons advised a plan of diet and an intensive workout at Forest Mere Health Farm, combined with training in sub-aqua swimming, as required by the script. Hopkins was, he himself judged, a lousy swimmer. He had learnt as a young boy with his father on the beach near Margam, but had had little opportunity since to keep in practice. Now, faced with the competition of James Bond, he had every intention of catching up. More: he had been waiting for nine months for the chance to reverse and rearrange his life. He had grown fat waiting. This was the signal to build a new Tony Hopkins, a Tony Hopkins for the Coast. He told Tony Crawley during the production: 'Bob Simmons brought me out of it [his inertia]. He happens to be a very good friend of mine now, the best friend I've ever had. Because he drives me into the ground. He told me, 'You're soft. You're not a man. You're a girl.' And it was bloody true. I'm still soft. I'm a big girl. I don't want to be tough, I don't want to be a daredevil . . . but I don't want to die young from thrombosis . . . I want to be in this job a long time.'

After ten days at Forest Mere, Hopkins had lost a stone and the production was ready to commence at Mull in Scotland, co-starring Jack Hawkins, Nathalie Delon and, says Kastner, 'Robert Morley for the light relief'. Hopkins was dutiful and calm, fastening himself like a limpet to Simmons' brotherly care. He still boozed, but Simmons told him, 'That's OK. But if you drink tonight you'll pay tomorrow. More exercises, more jogging. Your choice.' The fee Kastner paid him was a lean £8,000 (Connery's last Bonds had paid him around £150,000), but, Kastner is at pains to point out, this was fair for a newcomer playing his first lead role. 'I took chances,' says Kastner. 'The British film industry was American money. I get so pissed off when Attenborough and Puttnam and all those fuckers talk about British this and British that. I didn't get a penny in Britain for movies like *Eight Bells*. I'll tell you how I got it: I rang up a guy I read about in *Fortune* magazine and I went and saw him and said, 'I need one point eight million dollars to make this second Alistair Maclean project.' And he heard me out and wrote me the goddam cheque. That is how the so-called British movies got made. I paid Alistair Maclean fair and square, and I paid Tony Hopkins fair. And I made a movie that tripled its cost at the box office.'

By the time Périer and cinematographer Arthur Ibbetson ('he was the one responsible for the film's style and look') started shooting in Scotland, Hopkins had hit a survival routine that would last sixteen intensely physical weeks. This involved regular sessions with Simmons, counterbalanced with nightly binges in the company of fellow actors Maurice Roeves and Leon Collins at the Western Isles Hotel and other venues. Kastner visited the location but saw nothing alarming in Hopkins' boozing. 'Look, I made five pictures with Richard Burton,' says Kastner. 'When you do that you learn how to adapt. But Tony wasn't a troublesome boozer. In fact, I have no recollections of any boozing problem.' Others remember more. Robert Morley disdained what he felt was over-indulgence on the part of Hopkins and the younger actors. When he complained, he was admonished by other cast members. Hopkins was, after all, the featured star, 'carrying' the film. It was his first try. The hard drinking was an understandable pressure release. Some still remember Peta and Abby arriving on location. 'He reacted badly to their presence,' says one observer. 'He wasn't comfortable. And when he wasn't comfortable he got someone to get him some beer and he hid himself in a bottle.'

At Pinewood, ten weeks later, Ferdy Mayne observed a docile, very eager-to-learn film actor who reserved his biggest show of emotion for the arrival of his parents on the set. Dick and Muriel had come by invitation and were introduced to Périer and all the stars. 'They were nice middle-class people who seemed to only half grasp that their son was the middle of this grand blockbusting thriller. They were probably as uncomfortable in this fantasy setting as he was.'

Hopkins later said he loved the experience of making the film, but never quite got to grips with the text. 'I didn't take [the learning of] screenplays very seriously. It seemed such a different discipline, a lesser discipline, than the stage . . . so I improvised a lot.' Kastner was aware of this, but saw no reason to object: 'Hopkins was obviously an actor in his blood. Etienne wasn't necessarily a director in his blood. So the actor comes across to bridge the gap. He fits what has to be fitted.' Ferdy Mayne saw great weakness in the director and the execution. 'There was insufficient discipline, too much intellectualising from Périer. He should have been a stronger director and it would have made a better film.' Hopkins himself commented that 'Etienne loves the violence. He says, "Heroes never sweat, never bleed. But Calvert does. He gets frightened, hot, cold, bleeds. Inside he's a dead man. A sadist. A masochist. He could be a homosexual . . ." This, I don't know.' The confusion, it was suggested, arose from the director's dimly focused personal fantasies, loftily discussed among the cast and crew, but never quite grasped.

Calvert of the film is a Naval commander investigating gold piracy in the Irish Sea. He discovers that Dubh Sgeir castle on a starkly beautiful Hebridean island is the base of the villainy and launches a ninja-like attack on Lavorski and his pirate crew, killing them all but generously – and ambiguously – allowing Lavorski's wife Charlotte (Delon) to escape, with one gold ingot for memory's sake. It was pulp fare, albeit sublimely photographed, but Hopkins wasn't about to knock it. He admitted to Tony Crawley that 'all due respect to Alistair Maclean, the characters are cardboard, two-dimensional'. But he followed every step of its course, partook in all the stunts ('I did almost all the underwater stuff – good fun, but you have to be careful about getting punch drunk from the tank') and even watched the daily rushes carefully ('Just to see if I'm losing my extra chin and my extra tummy . . . Which I am . . . I am pleased about that!'). When questioned by journalist Jack Bentley about what his 'Shakespearian colleagues' thought of this venture into mass-market entertainment Hopkins almost exploded: 'To hell with what they think. I'd never be ashamed of breaking away from the Shakespeare set. Nobody makes money playing Shakespeare. Now I can pay off the mortgage on my house, buy my wife some extras, and give my daughter a good education . . . '

It was another cue for change.

'Somewhere in the middle of my movie,' says Kastner, 'Tony Hopkins fell in love with one of my production assistants, Jennifer Lynton. I don't know whether he acknowledges it: I gave him his first lead, and a new wife.'

Lynton was, says Kastner, 'an excellent movie assistant – bright, fit, eager'. She had worked for his associate, Denis Holt, on a few productions and was valued – 'though not at all a likely candidate as a romantic partner for Tony. I was aware of no chemistry, nothing at all. They seemed to me worlds apart.'

Born in Rustington, in Sussex, and educated at boarding school in Kent, Jenni Lynton developed a girlhood crush on Dirk Bogarde and decided conclusively at fifteen to pursue only one career: a life in the film world. By dint of pestering Rank for Bogarde posters, she landed herself a job in publicity, and was regarded as a conscientious but very self-effacing girl, perhaps too inclined to shyness to do much good on the promotion ladder. Subdued as she was outwardly, Jenni Lynton hosted great ambition. Her constant pastime was the cinema and she read film magazines avidly. A publicity woman who knew her comments, 'She was sugar-coating over flint – very mousy and average when you met her, a real goer underneath.'

After four years with Rank, Jenni left, temped for a while, then took a job as a trainee on the *Look at Life* documentary series at Park Royal. Within a short period, through friends, she manoeuvred a secretarial job at Pinewood Studios, forty minutes outside London, where she was then living. Kastner's frequent employee, the production supervisor Denis Holt, grew to like her and took her on as his personal assistant in the pre-production for *Where Eagles Dare*. Here she bloomed, and though she made it clear that her ambition was to work on the movie sets doing continuity, Holt knew he had a perfect PA and he guarded her jealously. A frequenter of Pinewood during the time recalls, 'Jenni was your perfect production assistant in that she wasn't obtrusive, but she had an air of authority about her. Maybe that had to do with her primness. She was terribly conservative – always dressed in very dull brown clothes or grey clothes – always rushing about, carrying some-one's life in her hands.'

While *When Eight Bells Toll* filmed in Scotland, Jenni Lynton remained at Pinewood, assisting Holt in paving the way for the pro-duction transfer to studio shooting in early October. Her responsibilities were many, ranging from the preparation of call sheets to organising transport. Despite her months on the production she had not met the star Hopkins when, on the first Saturday of the month, she received a panicked call from production manager Ted Lloyd requesting that she collect Hopkins and Leon Collins at Heathrow at 5.30 p.m. The entire production unit in Mull was already en route to London but Hopkins and Collins had been drinking and missed their flight. Lloyd warned Jenni that Hopkins was 'a wild one'. He told her straight that there had been drinking problems, that Hopkins' wife and daughter had visited, which only served to make matters worse. 'He's not in a good mood,' Lloyd advised. 'So watch out.'

Forearmed, Jenni drove to Heathrow to be confronted by a drunken, aggressively argumentative Hopkins who looked at her, but didn't appear to see her. Hopkins raged. He had, he said, been deserted in Mull. It was appalling, insulting! He wanted Ted Lloyd or Holt's number to tell them what he thought of them. Jenni, ever the diplomat, hedged. Hopkins later told Michael Parkinson that this romance that was destined to change his life 'started with a row' at Heathrow that dark afternoon in October 1969. 'I was feeling under the weather and gave her a mouthful of abuse. She took an instant dislike to me, but we got together later, at the party to celebrate the end of the movie.'

Jenni's memory differs. According to friend Adrian Reynolds, she recalled that after the red rage at Heathrow, she decided instantaneously that Hopkins was the man she would marry. That same evening she wrote to a friend explaining the 'funny thing' she had just experienced.

On Hopkins' request, Jenni drove him home to Putney where, in Hopkins' published account, he stayed 'two minutes' before walking out finally on Peta and his fourteen-month-old daughter. According to the *Sun* newspaper, Hopkins left in the middle of the night, without speaking to Peta, leaving just a six word note that read: 'Now I feel nothing for you.' Peta scoffs at this, insisting that there was no note, no sudden situation. He'd had a choice to make. He'd made it. It was as simple as that: she really wasn't surprised.

Hopkins initially moved in with Leon Collins in west London, then accepted Bob Simmons' offer to take up residence in his spare room. As Peta expected, there was no looking back, no second thoughts, no calls in the night. When he was gone, he was gone. Now resolute that she wanted a new life as a mother, Peta gave up acting and bore no regrets.

Jenni Lynton received all this second- and third-hand. In the final weeks of *When Eight Bells Toll* Hopkins calmed a little, became sullen, but displayed no more shrill emotion.

In November, the Thursday before the production concluded, Jenni chatted again to Hopkins at the wrap party in Pinewood's bar and then later when the party transferred to her Kew flat. There was no earth-shaking candour or show of emotion, but they got on well and Hopkins, uninvited, called at Kew the next day – sober – and asked her to the cinema. They went to see James O'Connolly's low-key adventure fantasy (with prehistoric monsters by Ray Harryhausen) *Valley of the Gwangi* – for no other reason than that Alistair Maclean's former daughter-in-law was in it. Two weeks later, Hopkins phoned Jenni and asked her to spend Christmas with him in Dublin. He was missing Abby, feeling raw from the failure of his first marriage, unwilling to submit to the inevitable told-you-so of Muriel and Wales.

In Dublin, they stayed anchored to the bar of the Royal Hibernian Hotel in Dawson Street, hardly communicating, wishing away the festive revelry. Jenni described the trip to author Quentin Falk as 'miserable', but passed no judgements on Hopkins. When they returned to London, she said, he barely spoke on the way to her flat. He dropped her off, bid goodbye and disappeared to his own hideout. A couple of weeks went by, then he called her and said sorry. By the spring of 1970, they were sharing her rooms at Kew.

Showbiz collided with Tony Hopkins' world in the winter of 1969–70, as he manfully squared up to promoting his first starring feature. Fleet Street beat a path to his door, intoxicated by the scent of an aspirant James Bond, and eager to beat the drum.

Hopkins seemed ready. In the eyes of some who knew him he had been waiting all his life for this moment. A woman friend says, 'Secretly he loved to be the centre of "starry" attention. He had a subtle way of exaggerating his successes in the early days. He wanted it so badly that he puffed it up . . . so the big mill of publicity when it came can only have satisfied him.' Others remind you of his breathless race to celebrity: Brian Evans' memory of him spoofing about Flora Robson auditioning him in Cardiff, and of him later casually dropping the word in Wales that he was staying in London with Dirk Bogarde; plus his premature claim on the National which ended in embarrass-ment at the Liverpool Playhouse. When the call came, then, it was hardly surprising that he was a willing, effusive and sometimes arrogant interview subject.

The journalists who met him at the time recall a stout, fidgety man who smoked cheroots endlessly, twitched like an eel and limited his conversation to one thing: his *raison d'être*, his career. He rarely smiled (though, Tony Crawley remembers, he was massively good-mannered), savoured the word 'fuck' but seemed strained in projecting the hell-raiser insolence he embraced. Films pleased him, and in the various interviews he was ready to dissect endlessly *When Eight Bells Toll* and all Calvert was and might be. But there seemed a flaw in his appreciation of the cardboard stereotypes and the films they inhabited. Sure, he was keen to do a sequel and make it as kiss-kiss-bang-bang successful as he was certain *Eight Bells* would be. Maybe, Tony Crawley suggested, they could let Calvert die in the second film? 'Or third,' Hopkins rejoined. 'Let's get a little cash out of it first.' Minutes later he was lamenting, through angry clouds of cheroot gas:

> I don't want to be an image . . . People with bloody images are the most boring people in the world. What the hell have they to live up to when you take those images away? Nothing. They're just Cockneys from the East End with a Rolls-Royce and a contract in Hollywood and their own pair of glasses. Do they do their jobs? No. Any fool can stand in front of a camera and steal a billion and so on. Where's the work? Nowhere! Get a couple of suits, a good wardrobe, couple of million dollars and you can do anything and get away with it.

There was a sardonic swipe at Michael Caine in the accent when he added: 'You know what I'm talking about, don't you? Next thing you're reading in the paper what colour their pyjamas are and what aftershave they use.' Talk of Calvert plunged him, addictively, into the deeper quest: '*Eight Bells* is a nice little adventure story. It calls to mind the old Stanislavsky principle for the play – Elia Kazan uses it as well, and Strasberg. When you are on stage – or when you're on film, whatever – what you are doing to the audience is telling them a story. People need to be told stories just as children need to

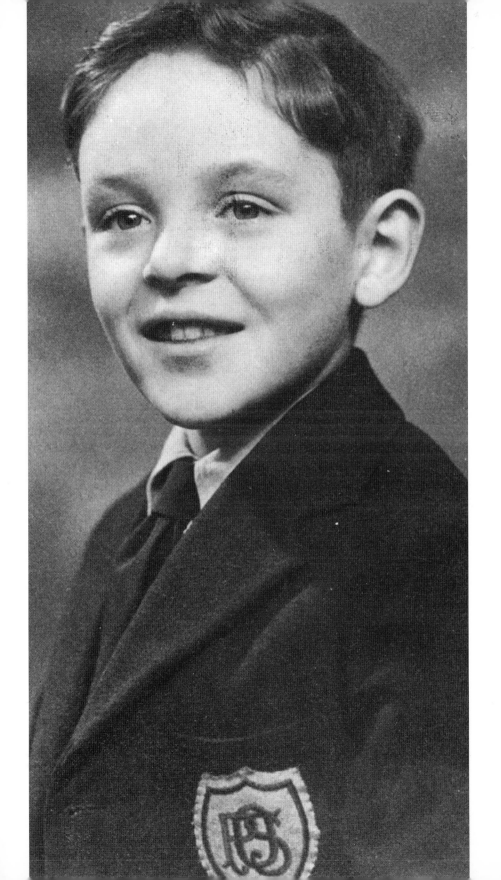

Previous page: Hopkins commences schooling. Two junior schools and two high schools lay ahead, but he would never be comfortable with formal tuition. 'He certainly found no pleasure in his work,' said teacher Peter Cobb.
Author's Collection

Left: Hopkins on the sports pitch at Cowbridge Grammar School, not far from Cardiff. Idwal Rees, a famous Welsh international rugby player, was headmaster during Hopkins' stay, and encouraged students to compete in the scrum. Hopkins preferred to play piano in the assembly room and read Trotsky at night.
Howard John

Left: Hopkins with his mother, the former Muriel Yeats, daughter of a steelworker from Wiltshire. Muriel's influence was lifelong. After the death of Dick, Hopkins' father, the actor spent several years persuading his mother to join him in his Los Angeles life. She finally settled there in the late nineties, and died in 2003.
Author's Collection

Right: Hopkins' first wife Petronella Barker, an actress of distinction whose relationship with Hopkins began in the converted Nissen huts of the emerging new National Theatre, to which both were contracted. She reckoned him a man of passion – though not in the area of personal relationships. They married when he abandoned his National contract for a movie opportunity in 1967 and were divorced in March 1972, not long after the birth of their daughter, Abigail.
Mirrorpix

Right: With second wife Jenni Lynton, a production assistant encountered on the production of *When Eight Bells Toll*, his first lead-starring international movie chance, in October 1969. Their subsequent marriage lasted 29 years, formally ending in July 2002.
Mirrorpix

Above: The first big break, chosen by Peter O'Toole and director Anthony Harvey to star opposite the Hollywood legend Katherine Hepburn in *The Lion in Winter*, filming in England and France through 1968. Hepburn was the first person to teach him camera technique, said Hopkins.
Avco Embassy/The Kobal Collection

Below: Rehearsing Peter Gill's production of *A Provincial Life* at the Royal Court, 1966. Gill believed he 'challenged' Hopkins, thereby minimizing the actor's tendency to mannerisms.
Author's Collection

Right: In Manfred Wekwerth's and Joachim Tenschert's radical 'Brecht version' of *Coriolanus* at the National during 1971, the film transition year. 'There was confusion right through rehearsals,' said fellow actor John Moffatt, who personally judged it 'a disaster'.
©John Timbers/ Arena PAL

Right: More from the National transition year: Victor Garcia's bizarre experimental production of Spanish iconoclast Fernando Arrabal's *The Architect and the Emperor of Assyria*, a major controversy in 1971. Co-star Jim Dale said, 'We learned so much. We were different actors after it.'
©Donald Cooper

Right: Anthony Hopkins as James Bond? Well, almost. Hopkins played the sub-Bond Philip Calvert, a creation of thriller writer Alistair Maclean, in producer Elliott Kastner's *When Eight Bells Toll*. He tried hard, losing weight and working out daily, but it was on this movie that he first recognised his incipient alcoholism.
Winkfast/The Kobal Collection

Above: Diana Rigg was Lady Macbeth in 1972's disastrous National version, where Hopkins, cast in the lead role, walked out in mid-performance. Whatever tensions resulted between the actors were finally laid to rest in 1982's BBC production of Ibsen's *Little Eyolf*. After a stand-off, said director Michael Darlow, 'something clicked and the tension passed.'
Empics/PA

Left: As Pierre Bezuhov in John Davies' marathon BBC version of *War and Peace*, shot over one year (1972) in the former Yugoslavia. There were many inducements: escape from a lost marriage, the companionship of new friends like Alan Dobie (playing Prince Andrei) and, more than anything, the opportunity to explore a Russian classic he'd long admired.
Everett Collection/ Rex Features

Below: By the end of the 1970s, he had a dozen feature films behind him, but the greatest triumph was his sobriety: he hadn't had a drink since 29 December 1975. 1978's *Magic*, directed by old pal Richard Attenborough, was unquestionably his best celluloid performance to date. Ed Lauter (pictured here) became a close friend: 'We had lots in common,' said Lauter, 'and we were both huge Hollywood fans.'
Author's Collection

Above: Directly after *Magic* came David Lynch's *The Elephant Man*, where Hopkins played Dr Treves, a character he would later refer to in establishing his vision of Hannibal Lecter. Above, Michael Elphick suffers Treves' wrath.
Author's Collection

Below: David Lynch was undoubtedly the most eccentric and adventurous film director Hopkins had yet encountered. The initial unease was quickly dispelled: 'It's one of the best experiences I've ever had,' said Hopkins from the set. 'I've found out how to be as simple as possible ...'
Paramount/ The Kobal Collection

hear about the three bears . . . Calvert isn't new but he's as big a challenge to me as playing Hamlet or King Lear.'

The very neighbourhood of classical theatre inflamed him and now, with a willing media to carry his voice, the manifesto was issued, with a jab at the National regime.

Sir Tyrone Guthrie once said: 'If an actor hasn't played five of the major parts, which essentially means Shakespeare and Molière – Othello, Hamlet, Lear, Macbeth – by the time he's thirty, he's just going to be a working actor.' Which is probably true. In the days of the Old Vic – the old days – people like Olivier and Gielgud and Richardson had marvellous opportunities to get the Romeos and Hamlets off their chest at the age of 25 or 28. But today, now, at the National Theatre, for example, there just aren't those chances. There are so few young actors who are allowed to play those parts – Ian Holm, maybe, but he's over thirty – and the Royal Shakespeare Company is so dehydrated, it's just the Cambridge wits who get in there. I love the film industry, but I want to go back to the stage. I want to have the opportunity to do something really good, because the real acting opportunities are only on the stage.

Taking his cue from the successes of the likes of Richard Harris and Richard Burton, Hopkins divined quickly that the demands of mass market entertainment and classical theatre weren't mutually exclusive. The pop press liked the controversy of contrast and had a soft spot for actors of integrity and substance. From early on, Hopkins staked his claim. When he talked he juxtaposed his name with the greats, with Olivier, Bogart, John Wayne, Burton. This was the year of Wayne's 201st film; it was Hopkins' fourth. He had, he told Jack Bentley, never met Burton (sic); but he admired him a lot. In the midst of promoting *When Eight Bells Toll*, and the hopes of a series starring Calvert, he was hot for his pet project: 'I want to do a sort of thing about Dylan Thomas . . . I have three or four people plugging for it and I hope to get my oar in before Richard Harris does his. If Richard beats me to it, it won't be a loss to anyone, but it will be a loss to me.'

This nod of appreciation to Wales was the closest Hopkins got to backward glances. He was not, journalists learnt quickly, a man for anecdotes or memories. Wales mostly bored him, or appeared to. He never spoke Welsh, knew no Welsh songs, had no interest in Welsh rugby or Welsh nationalism. Very shortly he would return on one of his biannual visits (to acquaint Jenni with the family and face the problem of converting Muriel) and would speak about Welshness openly at a mayoral dinner in Newport.

According to the *Western Mail*, Hopkins met the charges of disloyalty to Welsh theatre head on in his speech at the King's Head Hotel. With Dick, Muriel and Jenni in attendance, and his confidence unusually high, he pulled no punches. The *Mail* reported that 'the subtle call for such an accusation was [he felt] that he was not prepared to pay lip service to anything he could not be sure of absolutely. There were one or two very notable members of his profession who paid enough lip service already and he was not prepared to join the ranks'. If he did pledge to Wales, he declared, he was bound to break the promise, because 'I have never laid claim to being the sole discoverer of Wales, as if I owned the place.' There was muted, equivocal applause in the banquet room as Hopkins defiantly prodded at insular smugness. Raymond Edwards was in the crowd and smiled agreement when Hopkins said, 'The principal of Cardiff College of Drama, Raymond Edwards, and I have discussed this many times. It is no good crying over the spilt milk of our Welsh culture, declaring Wales a cultural disaster area. It is in the schools, colleges and universities and needs only practical thinking, application, will, determination, common sense and a great deal of honest commitment and cash [to express it].' He concluded by emphasising that he saw himself primarily as an internationalist.

In the aftermath of *When Eight Bells Toll* and for the duration of 1970, Hopkins was more sanguine and relaxed, fulfilled to some extent by the hairpin turn in his personal life and by the freedom of expression attendant on film lead casting. The future, though, was nebulous as ever and while he pressed Richard Page for opportunities of any kind, offers were thin on the ground. Throughout 1970 the best they could net was a succession of roles for TV – Ferdy Mayne recalls that *When Eight Bells Toll* did not give Hopkins the bonus he expected: 'I know that there were high hopes all round for a Philip Calvert thriller series and that Tony was optioned for it. But it became a talking point round town that Kastner decided not to go ahead with it. The word was that Hopkins had fared just OK, that the high hopes were really unfounded and there was nothing too special about him, or about the movie.'

Hopkins cannot have missed the signal reviews. 'Disappointing,' said the *Sun*, while the respected *Monthly Film Bulletin* admired Hopkins' 'tough unconventional agent'. 'You never know with films,' Hopkins said, cautioning himself. 'You do your thing and then it's up to the director's touch, the music, the editing room. You hope for quality, but you have more control in theatre.'

Before the jury came in on *When Eight Bells Toll*, to Hopkins' considerable surprise, he received a call from Anthony Quayle, who was preparing Simon Gray's adaptation of *The Idiot* at the National. Quayle was aware that Hopkins had left under a cloud and that the peace hadn't quite been made with Olivier. But he – and Olivier – were well aware of Hopkins' progress: indeed, could hardly avoid it. There seemed a positive burying of the hatchet in the offer of significant casting in *The Idiot*, opposite Derek Jacobi as Prince Myshkin. An actor believes, 'Derek was a very measured, no-nonsense actor who was considered by many the heartbeat of the National, the old reliable workhorse who could always go in at a moment's notice. The thing was, he wasn't madly fond of Hopkins, who had given off this grand impatience from the start. Derek saw the newcomers come and go, and it maddened him when he saw rudeness of the kind Hopkins showed on his first contract.' Peter Gill counters: 'I don't think Derek had anything against Tony, but I don't think their relationship can have been enhanced by the experience of *The Idiot*.'

Hopkins was elated at the offer to return and took his script to rehearsals full of optimism. Then he noticed that his script was markedly different from that of the other cast members. His role of Rogozhin was far more slender than he had been led to believe. Abruptly, with no apologies, he walked out, enraging Jacobi and Quayle who thought him 'inordinately insolent'. In turn, Hopkins objected to Page, claiming 'misrepresentation' and, says an actor, declaring emphatically that he 'wouldn't work at the National again unless Larry came and personally begged him'.

Hopkins did what he always did in turmoil: he boozed. Sharing the fireworks of his neurosis this time was Jenni Lynton. The Kew Gardens flat had grown too small for them and they were now living in better-appointed rooms in Epsom, sharing their social hours with David Swift, or Bob Simmons and his sister, and behaving at least some of the time like average young marrieds. But when Hopkins erupted, there was still the loathsome fall-out of ranting speeches and door-thumping and aimless brimstone threats. Jenni differed from Peta, however, in that she didn't fight back. Barker had grown up in a household where shouting matches were not unusual, where, as an only child, she sometimes found herself acting as referee. She had learnt to shout and saw it as a healthy way to dispel grievances. Jenni rarely raised her voice, was used to the sideline seat, the expectation of tolerance and patience. But there were limits of acceptability to 'artistic temperament'. One friend believed that Jenni stood no chance: 'I felt that no woman would stick it out. He really made life hell for his women. Given the choice, it was always the pub – as if all the answers lived there. He turned his back on his daughter, whom he really adored . . . so what chance had any woman? I thought Jenni would last a few months and see the error of her ways, or rather, his ways, and just move out and leave him to it. He was an alcoholic, but he just wouldn't admit to it.'

According to Hopkins, the first inkling of dyed-in-the-wool alcoholism came during *When Eight Bells Toll*. It arose from a passing comment by a veteran actor at the Western Isles Hotel during the Scottish shoot. Hopkins was drinking with his usual vigour alongside Robert Morley. Morley, as usual, criticised but was admonished by the veteran actor who remarked philosophically that 'Maybe Tony needs to have a drink now and again.' Morley asked did the veteran drink, to be told, 'I can't. I'm an alcoholic.' The shock of confession – coming from so gentle and conservative a personality – rattled Hopkins for days. Could it be possible? Alcoholism, the latent, potentially fatal disease? Alcoholism as the root – or if not the root, the main branch – of his tangled neuroses? Alcoholism as the rot? He filed the incident, never forgot it and would recall it when, years later, he met the veteran at the BBC and shook his hand in thanks for that first untargeted warning shot.

In 1970, as he railed against the manipulative, hypocritical, unfeeling, unjust, impolite, unimaginative, irresponsible National – the Olympus that neglected and misunderstood him – His Majesty the Monstrous Baby stalled for one fraction of recognition: an alcoholic he probably was.

Chapter 8

WAR AND WAR

'Of course they are monstrous children, physically and morally, prisoners of an abnormality that seems to relate to the author himself. Sadists and masochists, torturers and tortured, they come and go in search of themselves, in these privileged places to which adults have no access, foreign and distant lands. Such is the island, the imaginary meeting place, far from God and men, where the Architect and the Emperor conduct their eternal dialogue . . .'

Pierre Marcabru, in the programme of *The Architect and the Emperor of Assyria*

Theatrical agent Janet Glass cannot resist laughing: '*The Architect and the Emperor of Assyria* was one of ours, an exercise in the most outrageous theatrical anarchy by an author who couldn't speak English and a quite wild director, and a wilder designer. Ken Tynan wanted to do it passionately at the National, but Edward Woodward turned it down. That's when Tony came into the picture.'

The play, a first at the National for Spanish playwright Fernando Arrabal, was the choicest cut for His Majesty the Monstrous Baby at this

stalled and rutted time. Arrabal, together with his dewy-eyed matador of
a director, the Spanish-speaking Argentinian-born Victor Garcia,
planned an all-out onslaught on theatre convention in the guise of avant-
garde – and Ken Tynan bought it. Just before Christmas 1970, Tynan
rang Hopkins and begged him to come back. The tone seemed to have
changed. Apart from the Arrabal experiment, the National's most
consistently successful director, John Dexter, wished to cast him in the
spring as the second lead in Thomas Heywood's *A Woman Killed with
Kindness*, which was, said Tynan, Joan Plowright's baby. There seemed a
new respect – or at least curiosity – for Tony Hopkins. Cautiously
Hopkins agreed to meet with Tynan, who wasted no time by having
Garcia present in his office for the meeting. Tynan said it straight: Garcia
(though he couldn't speak English) was a genius. Arrabal was the toast of
Paris. The play was a must-see, the ideal casting was Anthony Hopkins
and Jim Dale. Hopkins was in thrall of Tynan's excitement and intrigued
by the notion of playing what was described as 'a very intimate, ground-
breaking two-hander' with an actor he'd long admired for his comedic
skills in the *Carry On* movies. Hopkins knew that Dale had had an
illustrious run at the National, that he was liked by Olivier and Tynan and
Jacobi and many of the leading players, and had appeared in such hits as
Peter Nichols' *The National Health*, *Love's Labour Lost* and *A Good
Natured Man*. His sense of competition was immediately teased.

Jim Dale thrills to the memory of the partnership:

> Tynan called me in and said he wanted to do this amazing play that would
> shock the National. It was an outstanding, arcane, mysterious text – like
> unearthing something alien and exotic from a half-remembered culture.
> And it was outrageous, with scenes literally requiring the actor to defecate
> on stage. Tynan wanted the play done like that, naturalistically. But he
> didn't reckon on Victor Garcia who sidled on to the scene and claimed he
> couldn't understand English – and started this extraordinary game with
> us, really forging an entirely separate work, a very strange something that
> wasn't what Tynan wanted but was nonetheless the most devastatingly
> original thing that the National Old Vic ever witnessed.

Hopkins and Dale met for a viewing of Garcia's cinematic short based on Genet's *The Balcony* and both, as Tynan predicted, were utterly entranced. Dale remembered:

> It was very whimsical and strange, but powerful. But Garcia left something to be desired. He encountered us from the beginning through a haze of dope and booze. He was about four feet high – and Arrabal, when he eventually showed up, was about three feet tall. So you looked at them and thought: Tweedledee and Tweedledum. But it was illusory. They were both dynamic people with very different artistic visions. For which we, the actors, paid the price.

Dale describes the process of conversion to Garcia's vision as an exercise in psychological thuggery the likes of which he had never previously experienced, and never would again. The fact that the actors survived the 'profoundly disturbing' punishment, marked for both a personal triumph but has a further resonance: Hopkins had turned his back on what he perceived as abuse or neglect at the National before; now he held fast. The response spoke volumes for his integrity of purpose in all the carping about withheld opportunities. It signalled conclusively that here was an actor pure, a committed craftsman bound for the edge, who would risk – literally in the days to come – his life for the creation of a worthy role. Dale admits,

> It was hell because Garcia kept us in the dark about the meaning of what we were doing all along. He would request us to do the most bizarre things – deeply disorienting and sometimes humiliating things – and then say to us, through his translator, I will tell you the meaning tomorrow. Customarily, actors don't accept direction like that. They need to know why. And this maddened Tony and me, maddened us so much that I broke down in tears at times and Tony was equally lost. Some days, we performed the entire play from the tops of step-ladders on stage, while wrapped in flowing parachute silk. Some days, we did it from under several layers of animal skins, lying there, rattling into each

other's faces as five or six stage-hands dropped heavy beams of wood from a height that came thundering down around us – all this while two LPs were playing from turntables on either side of the stage, one playing jazz and one classical music. It was manic, insane. Tony and I were at it day after day, day and night. We knew that damn text inside out and we did what Garcia demanded of us and then one of his two translators would scream at him, telling him what we were saying, and he would scream back at us – drugged out of his head – in Spanish. Again, we would beg, 'What the hell is this all about?' And Garcia would do his usual, 'Tomorrow I will tell you what it all means.'

After a week or two, Garcia took to delaying his arrival for rehearsals and insisted that the actors study the *I Ching*, the Chinese book of divination which is the source of much of Confucian and Taoist philosophy. In it the reader pursues fundamental truths by consulting at random any one of 64 hexagrams. Hopkins was enraptured and took to the text with more enthusiasm than Dale. 'Finding answers' was a phrase that tripped frequently off his tongue in those days. In the wake of his split with Peta, his loss of Abby, the confusing seduction of showbiz, he needed a new frame of reference, a code of analysis that would help him place himself in what he described to one friend as 'the unreality' of his life. Bob Simmons' physical endurance tests were cherished – he still jogged weekly, if not daily, as he had done since *Eight Bells* – but the intellectual vacuum horrified him. 'The why was always the great issue with Tony,' says Adrian Reynolds. 'Not just the motivations of a given role, but his motivations. Why was he doing it? More. Why did he *want to do it*? This is a universe beyond any Method, and Tony had a need to tap into it.' At this time he had briefly visited a Harley Street psychiatrist, but the slick sophistication of paternal superiority and the falsely congenial setting had irritated him. The very consultation sickened him, drove him across the street to the nearest pub, where, he says, he 'got drunk out of my head and put it all behind me'.

Jim Dale saw no drunkenness. 'Never. Not once during the play . . . and by God we had reason to fry our brains with Garcia's behaviour. Instead, yes, we went to the pub down the street from the Old Vic and lined up some pints and put them down and said, 'Wow, will we get out of this one alive?' But I had the impression that Tony was troubled and I admired him for the great discipline of his handling of Garcia and our play. He took his drinking home. He took those personal troubles elsewhere, because he knew we could not accommodate them there.'

Garcia came up with another idea. This time he took the actors to an abandoned warehouse and instructed them to perform the play in pitch darkness. Dale shudders:

> I was standing in this great barren place, scared out of my mind, to be honest, doing the lines. Then Tony and I hesitated because we heard a noise. A very peculiar and ominous noise approaching, swerving, darting all around us. Like a bomber getting ready to disgorge its lethal load on us. And it wasn't a bomber – it was a bloody forklift truck. And the driver was driving in pitch darkness, round and round this damned warehouse. We could have lost a foot . . . or we could have lost our lives.

The play opened in February 1971 to a perplexed, riveted and often angry audience. Garcia didn't stay for the opening. Instead, says Dale, 'He took his National money – a huge bag of loot – and got the National driver to take him to the airport. And when he was leaving he turned to the driver, grinning from ear to ear, and said, "Tell Tony and Jim that I will tell them what it means tomorrow!" The bastard left like that.'

A freewheeling, by all accounts indescribably visual play, *The Architect and the Emperor of Assyria* depicted two characters (or maybe just one character) confronting each other on a deserted island, or in another reality, or in the mind. They appear to be polar extremes – one perhaps the survivor of an air crash, the other a simple island native – but then weave and interchange personalities. The Emperor (Hopkins) is the survivor, the Architect the primitive one. They chase and debase each other, enacting ethereal relationships – mother and son, tyrant and slave, executioner and victim – performing semi-naked on a stage stripped to its barest, flanked by mirrors and stapled down by searchlights that drill into the audience and blind the viewer, or stun the cornea into producing images of four actors in place of two. Dale says,

> The actual construction of the play, in the way it is dressed and the magic of the technicalities, was all thanks to the National's technicians spending their budgets. That's how Garcia worked the so-called magic effects. He told Tynan to go out and buy the effects. From these he chose his searchlights and his forklift truck that dominated the second act. It all seemed random, and reflected nothing of what was actually in Arrabal's text. This, of course, utterly insulted Tynan, who wanted the urination and the sex-fair and all the rest that Arrabal wrote about.

Olivier and Joan Plowright watched the preview and came backstage with pale expressions. Then they faced Dale.

'Jesus, baby, it's a disaster. How long did it run?' Asked Olivier.

'Four hours.'

'It has to be cut, Jim. What can you take out?'

Dale felt no loyalty to the absent Garcia; nor did Hopkins. Arrabal stayed dumb: he told Dale that the best performance of the work he had ever seen had been in Paris, where the rep company had read the play back to front. Dale told Olivier how he could cut a long monologue or two . . . or three.

'How much will that relieve us?'

'Two hours.'

'Do it. Fuck Ken, just do it.'

Dale looked at Hopkins, who was trying not to laugh. 'I could tell what he was thinking. So we just damn cut it – and fuck Garcia.'

The reviews were, without exception, fever-pitch. The play was loved, or loathed. Felix Barker in the *Evening News* called it 'pompous trivialities from a pretentious fake' and extended his sympathy to Dale and Hopkins, 'victims of the author'. J. C. Trewin was in accord: '[The play] is thrust upon the Old Vic with a kind of blazing defiance . . . the two parts are performed by the brave and tireless Anthony Hopkins and Jim Dale. I feel very sorry for them.' Arthur Thirkell in the *Daily*

Mirror opined that 'The National Theatre should get this load of nonsense out of its system as quickly as possible. Apart from giving employment to two actors and a forklift truck I can't imagine any reason for its production.'

But others thought differently. Philip Hope-Wallace in the *Guardian* surrendered to the essential anarchy of the mind at the centre of the play. He wrote, 'What Lilian Baylis would have said about last night's doings on the stage of the Old Vic hardly bears contemplation but if she had expostulated, and no doubt she would have done with a "Not here, dears", one would have to point out that the cannibalism and mutilation are no worse than those in *Titus Andronicus* and poor Tom in the hovel in *King Lear* . . . The production is irritating, if brilliant. Mr Dale, with his endearing clown's face, is by far the better actor . . . but between them [the actors] achieve a tour de force of memory, of acrobatics and of discipline.'

Dale dodges the *Guardian* compliment.

> I was the one experienced in comedic rhythms. Even Larry called on me to show him a bit of slapstick choreography. Between Tony and me there was no competition. Rather, there was the closeness and inter-support one finds with friends facing adversity. No matter what faced me afterwards, I had lost fear. I think Tony experienced something not dissimilar. We had faced this actor's nightmare: the burden of a deeply complex script, just two of us, no serious direction from a director. We faced it and found it and made the play. It was a turning point and, I believe, we emerged from it stronger actors, or stronger men.

Certainly Hopkins moved forwards with confidence and control. His next assignment, rehearsing while *The Architect and the Emperor of Assyria* ran, was directed by the commonly feared John Dexter. *A Woman Killed with Kindness* was the diametrical opposite of the Beckett-like Arrabal. First staged in 1603, it marked something of a departure for the prodigious Thomas Heywood, whose domestic tragedies relied till then on horrific calamities; this play, considered his best, depicted realistically the loss of domestic serenity caused by a woman's infidelity. Dexter's revival treated it with classical reverence, vigorously accenting the common humanity of the work while leaving room to appreciate its historical dimension. Irving Wardle in *The Times* believed that Dexter had substantially addressed, and to some extent overcome, the problems of staging this semi-rigid Elizabethan play but, 'the production does not leave you with any clear impression of why the play was thought worth reviving'. Hopkins, though, assuming his first lead casting in an Elizabethan play, was 'the most arresting' of the cast: 'This is something much more violently anarchic than the study of a rightfully enraged cuckold . . . it is a thrilling performance.' Felix Barker thought Hopkins' work 'beautifully restrained' and J. C. Trewin enjoyed 'a compelling night with performances by Joan Plowright and Anthony Hopkins that are rich in sympathy and truth'.

Dexter cannot have delighted in Hopkins outshining him. Always outspoken, beloved by some and hated by some, he had come to know Hopkins during his first contract at the National, though they did no substantial work together. Dexter was aware of Hopkins' reputation for temperament and saw this as the key asset in casting him as Frankford, the cuckold of the play. In Hopkins' volatility, Dexter believed, the subtexts of Frankford would emerge. The problem was, though, that Dexter was mercurial and, in some regards, megalomaniacal. Ronald Pickup says, 'When John was bad he could be very bad, very cruel and relentless. But when he was good he had genius – and that was why Olivier and the National loved him.' Jim Dale professes all-forgiving affection but admits, 'Dexter needed a dartboard. He needed a target to humiliate and focus the negativity on, in order to demonstrate and lead. I loved him for his leadership and brilliance. But I thanked God I was on the right side of whatever chemistry we generated. Tony, I think, sometimes, was not.'

After the Heywood play, Dexter said he admired Hopkins but 'He wasn't fully in control of his craft then. He was insecure. He tended to overanalyse and that slowed everything down.' Dexter stayed outwardly indifferent, congratulating Hopkins after the Heywood but, says a company actor, 'inwardly storing a kind of resentment that Tony hogged the stage, much as he did at RADA . . . There was an element of "wait for me till I work this one out". And John hated that. John liked an actor to rely on instinct or experience and do the fucking thing. He wasn't a great one for other people's anguish or other people's demons.'

On the surface, Dexter and Hopkins' relationship was off on a sound footing. Regardless of who won the honours, *A Woman Killed with Kindness* was a notable success (Olivier sincerely admired it) and it was clear that they would work together again.

The last of the trio of Hopkins' plays for the season was to be Buchner's *Danton's Death*, about the French Revolution. But, in the final rehearsal days for the Heywood play, Dexter called Hopkins in and told him there was a change of plan: the Canadian star Christopher Plummer had been voted off the company's new *Coriolanus* and he – and Olivier – wanted Hopkins to substitute.

John Moffatt, in his last months of a three-year run with the National and cast as Menenius, recalls:

> It was chaotic – a spoilt opportunity for a wonderful play. We, the company, believed we would be doing the conventional Shakespeare text. But Tynan had other ideas. The German directors [Manfred Wekwerth and Joachim Tenschert] arrived with their Brecht version, which had been well received when performed by the Berliner Ensemble, and which had previously been seen – in its German version – in London. We then learnt that this, in translation, was what we were about to do. There was great discord immediately, though as conscientious company members we were ready to do what we were asked to do. But Christopher Plummer had rather a different response. He argued like hell with the Germans and eventually they walked out. This greatly distressed Olivier – though I am quite sure this *Coriolanus*, which was so different from the great text he had so memorably played, didn't much appeal to him. He then called the company together between a matinée and an evening performance of *A Woman Killed with Kindness* and asked for a vote: should Plummer go, or should the Germans go? Plummer went.

Plummer's sacking reflected many things, not least the company's favourite crib – that major roles were too often passed to 'starry bright lights' outside the group. 'Tony would not have been alone in feeling that opportunities within the company were too scarce,' says Moffatt.

With 'just a few weeks' for rehearsals, Hopkins became muddled and frantic. 'I am never terrific when pushed into the deep end at short notice,' he later said. 'But I knew this was important for me.' The importance rested in the fact that here, at last, was lead casting in a National Shakespeare, a chance to set down his *Coriolanus* alongside the legendary London performances of Olivier and Burton (the latter, in Gielgud's belief, the best).

'Tony didn't object to what the Germans were doing in this Brechtian thing,' says Moffatt, 'but there was a division in the company – a fifty-fifty division – of for and against. There was confusion right through rehearsals. Tony sweated and did his best. It was all deeply uncomfortable.' The main objection was the political content – unashamedly, says Moffatt, Communistic:

> I don't think people realised what they were getting, I don't think they
> understood it on its first time round. All sympathy with the Patricians
> was excised, so that one completely lost the beautifully argued balance
> of the original. My character, Menemius, is the wise elder statesman
> who redresses the balance all the time. But in this version he was
> reduced to a doddery old fool. Vast sections were cut. Fragments of
> *Antony and Cleopatra* were stuck in. Quotations from Plutarch were
> projected on a screen . . . It was a total upending of the original, slanted
> as a piece of pure political propaganda.

Duty kept Hopkins from leaving, but he was furious that his first big chance had come with so little preparation time, and that Olivier seemed oblivious to his anger.

Olivier lay low for the first night, a performance memorable to Moffatt for its aching discomfort. 'The entire production was painful. The heavy suits of armour. The bareness of the sets. The great white walls. The

glaring lights – so bright that we could see the back row of the stalls.'
Moffatt remembers Hopkins vividly 'standing primed in the wings,
sweating and shaking, very nervous and agitated, which is really no
surprise when one thinks of the shortness of rehearsal time and the
offensiveness of some of that approach'.

Reviews were not as bad as most of the company expected, though
Moffatt adamantly calls it 'a disaster'. Only Philip Hope-Wallace of the
Guardian refused to be moved by Hopkins: 'He is quite without the
sovereignty of nature which is so much insisted upon.' This said more
about Hope-Wallace's blind spot than anything else (he was the one
who had given the laurels to Jim Dale months before) because, even to
those like Moffatt who disliked the play, Hopkins had been masterful
and dignified, despite the cartwheeling efforts of the script to present
him as a thug. In the *Daily Telegraph* John Barber welcomed Hopkins'
'striking, eye-rolling performance' and Felix Barker in the *Evening News*
marked a moment of theatrical history: 'The part of Coriolanus presents
Anthony Hopkins with the greatest challenge of his rapidly soaring
career. He responds with a star performance, clear and infinitely
calculated. It is full of telling pauses – a brooding stillness [that]
contrasts the fierce outbursts.'

Hopkins wasn't happy. After two weeks the play came off and, in the
midst of this bleak triumph, the news was broken that Christopher
Plummer would take over the role planned for Hopkins in *Danton's
Death*, a role for which Hopkins believed he was ideally suited. He
erupted and stormed in to see Olivier. 'I think he overdid it,' says one
actor. 'He was getting lead roles. He was making great headway inside
and outside the National. *Coriolanus* worked for him. But it really wasn't
enough. He had authored for himself a role alongside Gielgud and the
best of them . . . I suppose you have to hand it to him for cheek.'

Hopkins raged in front of Olivier, saying *Coriolanus* was a travesty, and
Danton's Death should be his. Olivier just shrugged. 'Maybe. But that is
the way it is.'

Hopkins pummelled the desk.

'You want to hit me?' Olivier said. 'Go on. Hit me.'

Hopkins reserved a bigger dose for Plummer. On the opening night of *Danton's Death*, while Plummer's dressing room was filled with well-wishers and flowers and party mood, Hopkins burst in – drunk – and launched a storm of abuse. An actor says, 'Chris was mortified. He heard all the pent-up criticisms – the big-headed Hollywood-prat stuff, the "Who-the-fuck-do-you-think-you-are?" stuff . . . in front of all his friends and admirers. I think Larry was privately very pissed off with Tony and I remember one of the stage-hands saying something to the effect of, "He [Hopkins] is a fucking lunatic. He's Dr Jekyll and Mr Hyde and I'll lay down any money that you won't see him darken this door again. Dexter thinks he's a prick, Larry thinks he's a prick. He's a goner."'

The actor Alan Dobie – a 'plain-talking Yorkshireman with not much time for fey art', in his own words – had met Hopkins the previous year when both were cast by BBC director John Davies in his *Danton*, scripted by Arden Winch. The rapport then was instant and deep: 'He was, outwardly anyway, gregarious. I was not. He played Danton, I played Robespierre. It seemed fitting, we agreed, that we were – personally – opposites. And that ultimately helped that little BBC play, which we were proud of.'

A year later, Davies and producer David Conroy (whom Dobie had worked for in the adaptation of Tolstoy's *Resurrection*) summoned Dobie and offered him the role of 'the chilly Prince Andrei' in what would be the television epic to end all epics: eighteen hours of *War and Peace*. Dobie welcomed the invitation, especially since his casting was alongside Hopkins, whose progress he was carefully watching.

'On *Danton* we had not got close. Part of the game plan had been to maintain the separateness of Danton and Robespierre. But on *War and Peace* we became friends and I took great comfort in him as a friend because I was rather frightened of company and he was a wonderful conversationalist.'

The production, which would span a full year's shooting, was neatly divided into three tactical phases. Phase one was the summer shooting at Bela Crkva, one hundred miles from Belgrade, in Yugoslavia. This mostly involved the big battle scenes, in which more than 1,000 Yugoslav soldiers would participate. Phase two covered the (hopefully snow-draped) winter campaigns. Phase three would be the videotaped interiors at BBC studios in London in the spring of 1972. Dobie found himself getting reacquainted with Hopkins at the converted hospital where the huge BBC unit was stationed at Bela Crkva.

> He did not present himself to you as a complete man, he held back. I do not mean to denigrate in any way, because I was not critical of it, I enjoyed it. Yes, of course he was going through a tough time – later he would confide to me a lot of the upset about his failed marriage and his daughter – but he had, I believe, developed a facility for coping. This wasn't something we discussed, and it is just my personal opinion, but I noticed he would immerse himself very fully in the person he was sitting down to lunch with, or dining with, or having a drink with. I enjoyed what I call 'speculative philosophising'. So Tony joined me in endless hours of shared philosophising. I don't think he was hot-footedly looking for answers as such, but he was keen to speculate on the hows and whys. Why are we here? What is the purpose of creation, of the stars? What is our destiny? Astronomy fascinated him, especially in its connection to *why*? He seemed endlessly knowledgeable and thirsty for knowledge. There was no fatalism, no overt unhappiness. He wasn't despairing for the future of man – none of that. He was just keen to speculate, and lose himself perhaps in the speculations of another. Maybe he was burying himself and his own dissatisfaction with his life in the idle musings of someone else. Or maybe it was a little of both: distraction from his inner unrest and the pursuit of some great mystical answer.

The production days were laborious but, says Dobie, 'David Conroy had planned the production so painstakingly that it moved along well enough.' Dobie was already familiar with *War and Peace* in novel form but found Hopkins more than well prepared. 'This was something I never ceased to marvel at, then or later, when I worked with him in the theatre. His preparation was almost frightening. He had read the script and whatever background he could lay his hands on and was always teasing it . . . but privately. He wasn't a nuisance to the director or to his fellow actors. He just meddled till he found the Pierre Bezuhov he wanted to be.'

In Hopkins' own account of the time, he sought relief from the tedium of the battle scenes of Borodino and Austerlitz in cheap Yugoslav brandy. Alan Dobie saw nothing of this:

> Maybe he shared that with his friend David Swift [who was playing Napoleon] or someone. I saw nothing that would be faintly described as alcoholism or incipient alcoholism. We had a drink or two, but that was it. He was never drunk. But perhaps this again was a reflection of his control of his personal relationships. Perhaps he showed me only what he wished me to see. For instance, I had no knowledge of his musical leanings until, about six months into the production, when we were back in England, I invited him and Jenni to my home in Kent for Sunday lunch. They came, and after lunch we strolled across the field outside my house to the little Saxon church there. Tony went in and sat at the little organ and started playing beautifully well. I thought it was odd that he hadn't hinted to me in any way about this very great musical talent.

The Hotel Turist was the mecca of comfort and revelry during the boiling summer months – temperatures averaged 95 degrees Fahrenheit – but no one took much joy in its undependable water system and dubious food. Hopkins had just recently abandoned Bob Simmons' workout advice ('Out of sight, out of mind,' Simmons told a friend) and had returned with a vengeance to his great passion: doses of old-fashioned English-style food.

The colossal logistical jigsaw of *War and Peace* was new to Hopkins and, Dobie saw, he applied himself to learning all he could, pursuing conversation with crafts people, camera crews, costume makers, runners. 'He was,' says Dobie, 'quite insatiable and I never ceased to admire his curiosity. He was like someone who has to learn about things faster, faster. As if time was against him.' The special effects and dressing area especially intrigued him. The production's budget was almost a million pounds, engaging a cast and crew unit of two hundred and stretching BBC wardrobe and personnel resources to the limit. Casting seemed always in flux. Michaeljohn Harris was in charge of special effects and organised the supply of more than a thousand rubber muskets, 'disappearing bayonets' and rubber limbs for the battlefield – 'designed to be lightweight in order to limit transport costs,' he told Hopkins. The battlefields would be littered with dummy heads – 'doubly economical, because if you look closely you will see that we put French characteristics on one side of the face and Russian characteristics on the other'. Hopkins loved all this, playing practical jokes with the dismembered limbs and Rice Krispie 'open wounds'.

In December, the unit returned to mainland Europe to shoot the snowy scenes of the retreat across the Steppes – but the promised snows of Novi Sad didn't come, necessitating several wasteful moves and burdensome overtime. Then, back in London, the complex fibre of the drama began shooting, in two-week rehearsal, two-week taping runs. Morag Hood, playing Natasha, found Hopkins 'embarrassingly well prepared. He'd read it all, knew it inside out.' Director Davies delighted in his choice of casting. For him, Hopkins *was* Pierre Bezuhov.

For Hopkins himself, this moment, this part, was hugely significant and he sank himself into it in a way that was new. Till then, Simon Ward had often observed, there was something of mad abandon in his analysis of a role; now there seemed an intellectual surrender. All his life, Hopkins had romantically courted the Russians, blindly following his grandfather's lead, always idealistic, not always understanding. Now, in Pierre, he saw himself. He told the *Radio Times*:

> Pierre had become like a brother to me in this last year. He's a huge, ungainly, lumbering man. Now look at my bull's head, thick chest and short legs. I feel we share the same lack of physical grace and the same two-sided nature, part gentle, part violent . . . When the story begins Pierre's greatest weakness is the typical one of youth – that lovely, beautiful weakness of sensuality. He drinks and womanises obsessively.

It's not until he meets the peasant Platon Karatayev on the retreat from Moscow that he realises how to lead the sort of life he wants. He reaches the sort of crossroads that Tolstoy reached when he renounced all his worldly goods. Pierre is a waffler. He waffles his way into the Battle of Borodino, getting in everyone's way . . . and later is taken prisoner. At one point he confesses to Princess Maria that he's always loved Natasha, but it takes him seven years to approach her. He's still dreaming at the end of the story, when he's married to Natasha and living a well-ordered family life that he has come to love. He comes home from Petersburg full of ideas for a new liberal Socialist order, but when he tells Natasha about it, she just says, 'Come to bed, I'm tired . . .'

'It all sounds like some mega-milestone,' says Alan Dobie, 'but truthfully, while we were making it, *War and Peace* was just another long, long BBC2 serial commitment – not greatly paid, but not bad. Actors often covet the long run because it means regular employment, but *War and Peace* wasn't that well received critically. I recall a sense of minor disappointment, or indifference – though I was happy with my work in it, as I know Tony was happy with his – and I know that I was unemployed for nine months after it. So it was no milestone.'

For Hopkins, though, the production reaped rewards. None of the contemporary critics adored it – 'Solemn, reverent . . . too slow and too long,' said Leslie Halliwell – but it scored in the ratings and was transferred from BBC2 to BBC1, the channel with a wider audience, after a short time. Subsequently, Hopkins won his first professional award, as Best Actor, from the Society of Film and Television Arts. John Moffatt, like Ward, remembers noting a breakthrough when he saw the first BBC2 transmission: 'I immediately thought that Tony had found his niche. On stage with him, in my view, one could often see the mechanics of what he was doing. But suddenly it struck me that he was the perfect film actor. In Pierre it came through so powerfully. All the things Tony was and Tony did worked. The internalising, the life in those blue eyes, the eloquent mannerisms seen more economically on film. I thought: *this* is his medium.'

War and Peace brought Hopkins a national TV audience in the middle of 1972, hot on the heels of *Young Winston*, his fifth movie, in which Richard Attenborough – whose work he always liked – cast him in the prominent cameo of Lloyd George opposite Simon Ward's young Winston Churchill. It was, once more fortuitously, the perfect fusion of a broad appeal part at the perfect time. 'He was very well placed after that,' says Dobie. 'The heavyweight papers were full of [his] leaps and bounds at the National and now he was in all the magazines and tabloids. But he was very extended. Perhaps too much extended.'

Simon Ward saw first-hand Hopkins' widening power.

> I hadn't really seen him in seven or eight years and you wonder about people, how they have learnt and grown, or otherwise. *Young Winston* was terribly important to me, my first really major movie role. Dickie left no stone unturned making sure he had the right people. For example, I was screen-tested three times, and then endured a running test, and a horse-riding test. Tony came with his own qualifications and had only about three days on the movie at Shepperton. But in those three days he cut his mark. I'll never forget it. He had one simple scene with Anne Bancroft that I watched from the wings. It went well and then suddenly Tony introduced a certain pause, a wave of the hand, some gesture of expression, and I knew, I knew. I said, 'Oh hell, he's stolen the scene, he's stolen the picture.'

But Ward saw that while Hopkins' acting bag of tricks grew fatter, so too did the self-doubt and self-punishment. After the screening of the early episodes of *War and Peace*, Ward and his friend Neil Stacey, who had appeared in a minor role in the BBC epic, joined Hopkins and Jenni for dinner by the river at Kew.

> It was extraordinary for me in a way because he was still plagued by doubts. He was a mess. He drank like a fish – though I probably wasn't far behind him that night – and he had a fondness for putting himself down. I remember that he said he hated *The Architect and the Emperor*

and all that. He said it was a load of hopeless tosh . . . but then he wasn't patting himself on the back about anything. He was what he always was to me: the mad Celt.

The work offers were coming thick and fast but Hopkins was wriggling in his skin and hungry for the National. 'It was as if he couldn't let the National get away with it,' says Adrian Reynolds. 'He wanted to do the classical greats and get Larry's respect.' In the late spring, to his great delight, Jonathan Miller offered him a radical Petruchio in his upcoming Chichester Festival version of *The Taming of the Shrew*. Hopkins judged this as much a gesture of appeasement and respect from Olivier (who blessed the idea) as one of confidence from Miller. He grasped it, joyously, and despite an abiding tiredness drove south and rented a secluded forest cottage where he and Jenni would spend the summer. The mood was not, however, one of retreat. Hopkins liked Chichester and the play but was, says an actor, wary of Miller's cynicism as filtered through Shakespeare, and highly sceptical of yet another 'working over' of the classic text.

At rehearsals, he was rigidly attentive, prying and prodding Miller, more often scowling than smiling. Miller, an actor says, alternately fascinated and bored him but kept the whole business fluid by dint of 'a very hard-working humour'. As the actor tells it, few among the cast were smitten by Miller's deromanticised approach: his vision was to return the play to the wider Tudor mores and ethos normally overlooked in modern stagings. His reference text for the reinterpretation was Michael Waltzer's *The Revolution of the Saints*, in which the rigidity of Puritan marriage was evaluated. While denouncing the American predilection for styling the play as 'a test case for feminism', Miller stressed that his modernisation was 'not in the sense of putting it in the present, but of looking much more carefully, through contemporary eyes, at what it was saying in the past'. In his reflective book *Subsequent Performances* (Faber, 1986), Miller details the prevalently Puritan society that Shakespeare was writing in and opines that though one way of looking at Petruchio was as a bully, 'If you represented Petruchio as a serious man, you can take and develop the implications of lines such as "To me she's married, not unto my clothes" and " 'Tis the mind that makes the body rich" and see how consistent they are with the Puritan view. 'Casting Hopkins, he wrote, was especially appropriate because 'his personality as an actor seemed to conform to that image'.

Among the cast, playing Petruchio's manservant Grumio, was Harold Innocent, a portly, good-humoured actor carried nightly on stage by Hopkins. 'Olivier visited early on,' says Innocent, 'and told Hopkins that no leading actor should be burdened with the penance of hefting Harold Innocent around stage every night. I was no featherweight, but Hopkins never complained.'

Innocent was among many who expected a rather more forthright production.

> It became clear that what Jonathan had in mind was a very dark vision, cynical about marriage, aggressively challenging on every level. In rehearsals, he spoke about the misogyny concept, of the different angles arising from the truer contemporary scene. He was illuminating, but it was a black, black approach. I like Jonathan very much, but one did rather feel like an idiot when he was around. I don't think that really roused Tony. But I think perhaps the darkness of the approach did.

Joan Plowright played Katherina Minola, but Innocent saw no consequent unease in Hopkins, despite the very focused attention of Plowright's husband, Olivier, who visited quite often while he himself was filming Anthony Shaffer's wordgame *Sleuth* nearby. 'It didn't disarm Hopkins in any way, because Joan was one of the boys, really. When Olivier came to watch rehearsals she perked up, because she strove to maintain the dignity that befitted *his* position, and that was what he expected from her. She was in a bit of a bind, really. Joan was and is very down-to-earth. She liked to go out with the gang and have a few drinks at the end of the day – though she didn't do this when Olivier was around. But Tony found her – as did I – very genial and good company. There were no tensions there. She was a very positive presence in the circumstances.'

In Innocent's view, Hopkins and Olivier seemed, relatively, at peace: 'They had a good, though not extraordinary, relationship. There was obvious mutual respect and I suspect Olivier had a special regard for Tony, because it was generally felt that Tony was an inheritor, that he was on his way to dominating the English stage.' John Moffatt says,

> I don't know whether Olivier was pleased with him or not. Tony seemed to represent a new development in theatrical leading men. Till then the leading men had been less, well, pugnaciously male. Olivier. Richardson. Gielgud. Tony wasn't like that. He had a rugby-player element to him, a brazen masculinity that called attention to itself. Olivier was nearing the end of his run as artistic director. Tony was on the rise. It was a time of complete change.

Hopkins, meanwhile, was increasingly exhausted. Sensing the changes, courting Olivier's blessing, straining to excel, he immediately agreed to sign an extended National contract that would cast him in *The Misanthrope*, *The Bacchae*, *The Cherry Orchard* and – the overwhelming benediction – *Macbeth*, to be directed by Michael Blakemore. Jenni had her doubts about over-commitment: to top all this he had signed to play the taxing Torvald in Patrick Garland's film version of *A Doll's House*, attracted mostly because Claire Bloom, the object of a childhood crush, was playing Nora; there was also the TV Lloyd George in John Davies' forthcoming episode of *The Edwardians*. It was, on the surface, a dizzy, flattering time, a time to make hay, to bank cash against the plan to buy a new, large house on a common somewhere, or by the river, and start a family. It was fulfilment time, but Hopkins was far from fulfilled.

Harold Innocent became another of his compartment friends, close enough for general confidences, but not close enough to be shown the inner workings. 'There was no sign of alcoholism – nothing like it.' For him, Hopkins was a 'man with a great sense of humour, a man with a funny, odd mystical aura about him, a complex man'. Nonetheless, the pressure cracks were increasingly visible. In one revealing incident Innocent saw the Mr Hyde flash dangerously: 'We were rehearsing a piece and all of a sudden he said, "See that fellow over there? I hate him. I'm going to kill him."' Innocent was shocked. 'I looked around and saw some young fellow in the company looking at Tony with reverence, in the way young novices look at the leading men. The boy was full of hero-worship or something and Tony wanted to hurt him. I really thought, at that moment, he was near the edge. So I said, "Come on, let's take a walk."'

Chapter 9

THE BEAR IN FLIGHT

'They have tied me to a stake; I cannot fly,
But bear-like I must fight the course—'

Macbeth Act V, Scene VII

In ten years, Hopkins had passed through three stages of acting approach: the initial apprentice mimicry, the bastardised Method of Fettes and Yat Malmgeren, now a sophisticated Romantic acting of instinct. All had won him admirers, none had satisfied him. He felt, he said, as though 'acting is a mystery, a new game every time'. Squaring up to *Macbeth* he seemed unusually doddery. Interviewed by Hugh Herbert of the *Guardian* in the bleak rehearsal rooms of the Old Vic in November, he wriggled. Pale, wrinkled beyond his years, twitchy, chain-smoking and coughing, he extrapolated nothing from the years of quest. No, he had never argued with Stanislavsky or the Method. Only with 'the dehydrated Cambridge intellectual approach'. He was an actor 'from the gut and from the head' but, 'perhaps I don't trust my gut. I have to work it out rationally before I fire off my guns. And usually if you find the right objective within the text and the line of the play, you're in a better position to start acting from the gut.' Gut, however, should be in quotes. 'I don't trust that part of the Celtic nature that says it is all in the heart.' From where, really, did it come? What was it *saying*? Had he corralled it? Did it matter?

The bonds to a normal life, to an English life, were slipping. In March 1972, after months of anguished phone calls and assiduously avoided showdowns, Peta was granted her decree nisi on the grounds of Hopkins' 'adultery' with Jenni Lynton. Neither Hopkins nor Jenni appeared in court before Judge McIntyre, nor was any contest offered. Custody of Abby was given to Peta, with an order for Hopkins to pay costs and provide upkeep.

Peta admits she was shattered by the divorce and frantic to put a distance between him, and it, and the old life. Back home in Wales, those who knew him detected an inner withdrawal and the hardening of some vague, private resolve. Muriel liked Jenni and was coaxing, friends say, for a formal marriage. But Hopkins demurred. Brian Evans remembers visiting the Ship Inn and being told by Dick Hopkins that his son was 'down by the river, doing the usual reading'. Evans saw Jenni interact with Dick and Muriel in the most agreeable, natural way and perceived 'the best woman in the world for Tony – exactly what he needed – an organised and happy woman with a glint of optimism in her'. Usually, Hopkins was at his most extrovert and active on these Welsh trips home. He helped out at the bar and went shooting with local farmers who were customers of Dick's. Now, Brian Evans found him burrowed in his script, studying. 'He hadn't a lot to say, to be honest. I think he was under a lot of pressure. I suppose it was the price of his success . . .'

Apart from the emotional and physical duress of the hastening work offers, Hopkins was at war with himself about deserting Abby. A friend believes that 'he desperately wanted to see the child, but seeing her meant visiting with Petronella and he knew that would mean rows and remonstrations and he didn't want to reopen it all. So he stayed away.' The self-exile burned him badly through 1972 and he only forgot the pain when he buried himself in work. Another says, 'It was an open wound, so you didn't talk at all about kids in his company. We felt that he and Jenni might get hitched, that they were perfect for each other, but he was in no rush. Someone asked him straight: 'Will you two tie the knot?' And he said, "I've fucked up royally once. Do you really think I'll go through that again?"'

Simon Ward saw this as a flash of bravado: 'He really needed to be tethered to the ground. It didn't need a genius to see that. And Jenni tethered him. There never was a woman so well matched for a man.' Jenni resolutely bit the bullet. She saw herself as a mother figure, but those close to Hopkins insist that she had little in common with Muriel other than a sometimes visibly smothering love for him. Jenni told the *Sunday Mirror*: 'I'm sure I am too much the mother in many respects, because he is in a lot of ways like a child. You have to look after him, do for him all sorts of things, take responsibilities that normally a man would take for himself. Like having money when you go out, or having a front-door key, or a cheque book, or a handkerchief . . .'

While Hopkins continued to speak openly of his devotion for her, Jenni longed for some move forward. Hopkins told the *Sun*: 'I know I'm impossible to live with. I can think of a thousand things that would drive a woman away from me. The moment when we loathe each other, I can take. But once we start to irritate each other, I know it would be time to leave. I have no intention of getting married for a long, long time. But I have a lovely girl at the moment, and when I do marry I hope my wife will be like her.'

'Given the choices,' says a friend, 'he stayed more involved with his work than with any relationship. I remember thinking, I hope Jenni doesn't get her heart broken, because Tony is really upside down. He doesn't have a clue about where he's going.' Alan Dobie refutes this: 'He had a score to settle with himself – perhaps it had to do with finding international recognition, a proof beyond doubt of his capabilities. But I spent time with them and I knew that, whatever happened next, Jenni would be in the frame.'

His back firmly against domestic uncertainties, Hopkins flung himself into *Macbeth*, undoubtedly his most challenging Shakespeare to date. Academically, director Michael Blakemore found him more than ready, but he was also, said Blakemore, 'frightened by the role' and intimidated by taking it on in this, Olivier's, theatre. Very shortly, unwittingly, Ralph Richardson would fire a confidence-killing blow by telling Hopkins, during the shooting of *A Doll's House*, that *Macbeth* was 'a nightmare to play'. 'That's the worse part I've ever played,' Richardson said. 'It takes twelve men to play it. I'd willingly have blacked the boots of the entire company rather than go on stage in that.'

Jittery and jaded, Hopkins kicked out in every direction. Gawn Grainger had been cast as Macduff, with Diana Rigg as Lady Macbeth and Ronald Pickup as Malcolm. Grainger became Hopkins' new best friend and, for the duration, they shared confidences and ciders, sometimes in the stage door pub, more often in Grainger's flat in Islington, or in the market pubs of Smithfield, where Hopkins indulged his taste for fry-up breakfasts at dawn. Grainger watched him wrestle with the demons and clearly become his own – and *Macbeth*'s – worst enemy.

'He really wasn't too happy with the play,' says Grainger, 'and there was a personality clash with Michael Blakemore. Blakemore is a very defined director, and his angle on the production was crystal clear. Tony had other ideas, speculative thoughts, notions he wanted to tease out. Sometimes they clicked, sometimes they didn't.' The rows were legendary. Blakemore grew tired of Hopkins' desire to analyse and poach from other texts and evaluations. They clashed, simmered, stood on an unquiet peace. At one point Blakemore told Hopkins that he had an undue respect for others' opinions. Hopkins exploded and walked out – to the pub, said Blakemore.

'Yes, we were drinking for an army,' says Grainger. 'We would rehearse all day at the Vic, go back to Islington, debate and argue all night – then Tony was knocking on my door and asking, "Let's get breakfast." Which was our cue for another stormy day.'

Olivier focused Hopkins as never before, carefully monitoring every phase of production, not commenting when Hopkins' complaints brought about the firing of fight arranger Bill Hobbs, but drinking it all in. As Hopkins wallowed in academe, Olivier despatched his note of clarification vis-à-vis the core of the play, the relationship between

Macbeth and Lady Macbeth: 'The man knows everything. The woman knows nothing.' Hopkins felt the pressing shoulder of Olivier, and went honourably with the flow. 'Ah yes,' he told the *Guardian*, 'Lady Macbeth is like a Kleenex, used and thrown away . . . she's silly. There she is saying, You get the key to the executive lavatory, and we're away, baby. It's a Rolls-Royce for us. And he is saying, No, baby, no. Look what we're doing. And look at this gas bill . . .' Whether Diana Rigg bought this pocket psychology is doubtful and Hopkins later said that she and he 'did not get on'. 'I don't think Diana and he ever fell out,' says Grainger. 'But Tony was picking fights with himself – so these things got said.'

Occasionally Hopkins would visit Ronald Pickup's flat at Shepherd's Hill, Highgate, and while Pickup was aware that Hopkins 'hated' the production-in-preparation, he observed 'not so much a tendency to fight, as to go the other way. When he was deeply unhappy – truly, seriously unhappy as he sometimes was then – he would become non-vocal and withdrawn. Very depressed.' Pickup, whose last National production this was to be, was in no doubt as to the root cause of the dejection.

> Meaning no disrespect to the designer Michael Annals, or the costumer, it struck me that Tony just wasn't happy about the set or the costume. This sounds like a camp, actor's affectation, but the reality I myself experienced when I did *Richard II* with director David Williams and Annals. Shakespeare can be particularly difficult when you have to put energy into negotiating set and clothing. I had that trouble. And so did Tony, on *Macbeth*. Add this to Tony's other basic trouble: his lack of belief in his own ability to play Shakespeare, and you confront a very serious obstacle. I'm not saying there was no way around it. Like Olivier always said, 'If you don't like the costume, baby, change it.' I make a mental note to myself of that these days. But Tony was feeling quite fragile with the role, and the mountain of set problems and tights problems really unhinged him.

It didn't help that Olivier's attention had a finger-wagging intensity about it. Gawn Grainger recollects a moment that heralded what was, ultimately, a breakdown. 'It seemed to be going along all right, slowly but sure enough. Then one morning Olivier arrived to watch rehearsals. Tony had just done it quite well and suddenly, with Olivier watching, it all came apart. He just wasn't relaxed.' Another actor says, 'He didn't have the diplomatic skills, or the patience, to hold it all together. He had a point of view on it, and naturally so too did Olivier and Blakemore. It's just that he wasn't very good at putting over *his* ideas, or convincing anyone else.'

The first night of *Macbeth* in November was muffled somewhat by the din of preparation for two other projects: the TV film of Ibsen's *A Doll's House*, to be shot over three tight weeks in December at MGM-EMI Borehamwood Studios and, immediately after, John Davies' episode of *The Edwardians* about Lloyd George, to be taped at BBC Studios. Imminent, too, were rehearsals with the irascible John Dexter for *The Misanthrope*, and outline discussions on *The Bacchae*. In the run-up to the opening, Hopkins' new flat at Castelnau, Barnes (which he shared with Jenni), was knee-deep in scripts and background study material and, to counter the pressure, he was smoking and drinking more than ever.

The opening night, Ronald Pickup says, 'was OK', but the reviews were a maze of contradictions, as perhaps befitting the tangle of conflicting opinions aired – and never quite resolved – during the rehearsals. John Barber in the *Daily Telegraph* and Harold Hobson in the *Times* approved of Hopkins and the play. Clive Hirschorn in the *Sunday Express* and Felix Barker in the *Evening News* tore it to pieces. For Barker, Hopkins' Macbeth was 'a Rotarian pork butcher about to tell a dirty story' and generally way off the mark.

All the cast witnessed Hopkins' distress at the negative reviews, which he interpreted as evidence of his failure at this, one of the critical Shakespeare parts. 'I didn't see it at all as a failure,' says Pickup.

> Yes, it was scattered, but it was developing. There had been excellence in rehearsals, and maybe on the night it wasn't so good. But that isn't unusual with major actors. Tyrone Guthrie wrote about [Charles] Laughton having the precise same trouble. His *Macbeth* was sublime in

rehearsal and very shaky in performance. For my money, watching Tony even when he is less than wonderful is a joy. I am not promoting anarchy for the actor, but Tony's individualistic way of doing things – sometimes within the text, sometimes not – is hugely entertaining. This isn't true of all actors. Actors need to hold on to the structure of technique. But when they move like Tony – that is something else. With rare actors, like Tony, every performance carries a value . . . But he didn't see this, with *Macbeth*. He just kept on saying, I hate these fucking tights.

As the play ran on Hopkins seemed to slip further into trouble. Pickup's National contract terminated at Christmas so he lost touch with events before the final crisis. Nevertheless, he sensed it was coming. 'The frame of mind he was in,' says Gawn Grainger, 'nothing would have surprised any of us.'

Macbeth was dropped from the National programme while Hopkins laboured at Borehamwood on the American TV-targeted *A Doll's House* with Claire Bloom. This film was essentially a restaging of the Broadway version of a year before, which had starred Bloom and was produced by her husband, the LA-based agent Hilly Elkins. Patrick Garland had directed the Broadway play – his speciality was theatre (he was later artistic director of the Chichester Festival Theatre), though he made some very successful TV films, among them the previous year's *The Snow Goose*, starring Richard Harris – and opted for very few film concessions. This was both lucky and unlucky for Hopkins. Lucky, in that the film was sound-stage bound and less physically taxing for that; unlucky in that the density of text and the rhythm of filming with Garland had all the rigours of discipline of a National play.

Garland found Hopkins imaginative and dependable – 'his phrasing was special' – but clearly stressed. Hopkins himself admitted that he behaved badly during this shoot and later apologised to Garland. Hopkins said he had long harboured a crush on Bloom, whom he first saw at the Plaza in Port Talbot, but a technician says, 'He wasn't fazed by her in any way – he was very much the star on the rise and a kind of equal to her.' Others believe that Hopkins was so worn down – by overwork, by his drinking, by the absence of Abby, by his uncertainty about another marriage – that nothing short of an earthquake would have moved him.

Garland's film was the conventional Ibsen story of the strong woman determining her own destiny, without frills. Unfortunately, a rival, bigger-budgeted version, directed by Joseph Losey and starring Jane Fonda and David Warner as Nora and her husband Torvald Helmer, entered production at the same time in Norway. Ultimately Losey's film would win all the attention and applause – deservedly – while Garland's found its quiet screenings in English-language TV markets over the next year or two.

In January, Hopkins came back to *Macbeth* on a short fuse, agitatedly chewing over Ralph Richardson's comments that the play was 'a nightmare to do'. Immediately, he was at war with Blakemore, who insisted on him wearing a false beard to replace the shorn locks required for the TV Lloyd George. Hopkins tried the beard, hated it as he hated 'the fucking unwearable Jacobean hose' – and flung it in the bin. Blakemore raged. A vital part of Michael Annals' set was the gallery of giant portraits of the leading players: in his, Hopkins wore the agreed (natural) beard. Now, performing clean-shaven, he looked out of place.

Hopkins refused to give in. 'I had been taking Valium to try to slow me down, but it wasn't working. I was racked with doubt about it, not sleeping.' He spelt out the bursting tension for Tony Crawley: 'Weeks of success, of building up, and being dumbfounded. I talked to Olivier a long time afterwards about the inefficiency of the stage management. I will never be intolerant of human error but this was plain stupidity, crassness and stubbornness on the part of a very ornate production that didn't work. But I made the mistake of saying yes, then, instead of standing up and saying it's just not going to work!'

As Blakemore pressed the beard on him, Hopkins walked out. Jenni told the press sometime later, 'He dreaded every performance . . . One evening I had a call from his dresser, saying, "Tony says can you come quickly. He doesn't think he can go on in the second half. He's in a terrible state . . ." I got to his dressing room and found him very nervous, a bit shaky. Things had gone wrong again on stage, nothing to do with him, and he couldn't cope. All I did was listen to him and assure him that it was going to be all right. And he went on.'

But early in January, he made what he called his 'screw 'em' decision. Gawn Grainger remembers that it was in the middle of a matinee, with the house half-full. 'I am Macduff and I come on, declaring, horror, horror, horror, just after the murders. All of a sudden – on my line – an ambulance from the station right beside the Old Vic went screaming past with its siren blaring. I heard it and I know Tony heard it, and the audience laughed. The word was that Tony was outraged and stormed off. But he was certainly gone, because when he walked out that door the National didn't see him again for ten years.'

Ronald Pickup met up with Hopkins to commiserate. 'He wasn't in great shape, to be honest, and, as you do in those moments, he was pointing the blame – mostly at the tights. He felt a terrible failure, and there was not much I, or anyone else except Jenni, could say to help him. He said, "That's it, I've had it with the theatre. Fuck it, I'll do films."'

Michael Blakemore shuffled Denis Quilley in as a replacement Macbeth and lamented his failure with Hopkins. Despite the mud-slinging, Blakemore believed that Hopkins was a good actor, 'a romantic actor, in the style of Kean'. But the dispute had been more than a personality clash: 'He doesn't like directors . . . He rejects the technical requirements you need to tackle the great verse parts, trying instead for intuition and feeling. If you do Shakespeare like that you land in trouble.'

Hopkins reeled. On an impulse, over Christmas, he had decided on marriage and proposed to Jenni much in the same offhand way as his proposal to Peta Barker. A date of 13 January 1973 had been set and this – perhaps not coincidentally – turned out to be the day after the National walk-out. Some friends believed he would postpone, even cancel, the wedding: but Muriel and Dick were on their way from Wales, about 150 guests had been invited and, anyway, he was in liberating flight. Brian Evans says, 'I don't believe for one minute that he would have cancelled. He had botched it in Muriel's eyes the first time round. Nothing could have stopped him making it as right as possible this time.'

Alan Dobie and his wife drove from Kent for the ceremony at Barnes Methodist Church around the corner from the new flat, and were not surprised to see both John Dexter and Michael Blakemore at the reception. Others were. In walking out of the National, Hopkins was ditching Dexter's plays as well as Blakemore. 'Whatever personality crisis he was experiencing,' says Dobie, 'Jenni was the rock, the life raft, the moderating influence. So it was probably she who had a lot to do with [Dexter and Blakemore] being there. Her attitude would have been, Why make unnecessary enemies? She was always the deeply practical one.'

Hopkins himself told friends that he had quit the National 'before they got me first', which, according to Peta's testimony, was exactly in character with his mania for having the last word. But this time there was more to it than scoring points.

As Hopkins guzzled beer and moved skittishly through the crowd, hugging Muriel, toasting Jenni, joking with his Welsh cousins, more than one guest saw the plaintive evasion of recent events, the cracked voice and twitching eyes, and wondered: was he over the edge?

'What does an actor do when he cannot identify with the character he's playing? For openers, he doesn't stop trying . . .'

This glib introduction to the press handouts for *QB VII*, Hopkins' recovery vehicle after *Macbeth*, conceals a blistering truth: he had lost it.

After a Lake District honeymoon and a few days spent at Caerleon, Hopkins faced up to one of his longest periods of inactivity, killing time in Barnes. A friend of the couple observed Jenni's plight: 'He was anti-social but he wanted an audience. He drank at home because he didn't like parties, but when he went to parties, you couldn't get him out. He disliked driving, was a terrible driver, so Jenni took him everywhere and had to wait around till he satisfied himself that he had had enough drink, which was usually when he was well gone and locked in a row with someone.'

Simon Ward, among many friends, refused to acknowledge the grip of alcoholism.

Theatrical life is social and that era, the end of the sixties, the early seventies, seemed particularly a time of indulgent partying. I remember Dexter bringing me to a party in Chelsea and' stepping over Allen Ginsberg lying in the hall, a whole revolution generation was there. People took dope or took booze. I chose booze, which seemed safer, and I think Tony did the same. Sure, it camouflaged his troubles – or he pretended it did – but I never believed he was that deeply in trouble. Then again, maybe that's half the problem. People conspire to think the best, or hope the best, while all the time you're going down.

In March, Hopkins was offered three months on Screen Gems' six-hour Leon Uris mini-series, to be shot at Pinewood Studios by Tom Gries, the fifty-year-old veteran director of American pulp like *Batman*, *Checkmate* and *I Spy*. The prospect immediately put his values, and career vision, under the microscope. Adapted by the ever-active Hollywood hack Edward Anhalt, *QB VII* told the tale of the fictional Kelno, a Polish physician accused by hard-nosed author Abe Cady of voluntarily performing surgical operations in a Jewish concentration camp during the Second World War. The titled referred to the Number Seven Court of the Queen's Bench Division in the Strand and the story was based, very circumspectly, on the actual lawsuit that followed Uris' publication of *Exodus*, when Jewish doctor Wladislaw Dering accused Uris of libelling him in the novel. In *Exodus*, Dering was mentioned directly as being responsible for medical experiments at Auschwitz, which he denied. In the event, after a protracted trial, derisory damages of one halfpenny were awarded to Dering and Uris had his concept for a new novel.

When Anhalt's script was forwarded to him, Hopkins stalled, disturbed by the morality of the project and the lack of definition in the character of Kelno, the part on offer. 'I had doubts about doing the role at first. I couldn't understand any of Kelno's experience in the concentration camps. It was a world completely unlike any I related to.' This was polite jargon that masked a multitude. Adrift from the National, from the purity of the 'great roles' he sought, what was his direction, his philosophy, his artistic intention? Even he wasn't sure. The only clear message relayed to his agent, to the actor friends who asked, was that the 'establishment theatre' was cockeyed, in the hands of idiots, a waste of time. So was it time for the glitzy surrender? *QB VII*, on the face of it, distilled all the problems inherent in an alternative establishment – the Hollywood system. Hollywood's appetite for product was insatiable. News stories were (and are) the easiest fodder, controversial court cases headed the list. Stories could be assembled from anything, and frequently strained the boundaries of taste and decency. Hopkins was often to be heard deriding Hollywood 'tosh': with a few drinks below the belt he would rail against 'pagan bio-pics' and 'bullshit histories, where they don't bother to get the facts, or find out whether the guy died of syphilis or a gunshot.'

QB VII trembled on the brink. Exploitative? Probably. Informative? Partially. Relevant? Marginally. Acceptable . . . ?

Hopkins told producer Douglas Kramer that he needed time to decide. Here was the irony – the Hollywood gilt-edged invitation card turned to dross in the eye of his self-doubt. Jenni coaxed him, but it was something he had to handle alone. Finally, in the pursuit of background research reading, he found the answer. It came in an out-of-print book by a Polish Jew called Dr Nyizhili, who prostrated himself in guilt and admitted that, while acceding to the SS experiment demands, he endured by carrying out the work 'as if he were going about business as usual'. Hopkins swooned to the notion of the 'switch-off' emotional defence and called his agent to accept the role. 'Suddenly I understood how I would play the character,' he told the Screen Gems publicist. 'He then became fascinating to me.'

Committed to three arduous months at Pinewood in what was a courtroom drama that regularly opened up to flashbacks of a two-family, multi-generation story, Hopkins was the most energetic actor on set. Ben Gazzara played the writer and the traditional American prestige cameos came from John Gielgud, Jack Hawkins, and, as Kelno's wife, Leslie Caron. Throughout, Hopkins never lost sight of the sorrow behind the pulp story. He continued to read and discuss, and was humbled by conversations with actual concentration camp survivors like Anna Maria Pravda, who had a small role.

Duly, in its ABC network screening on 29–30 April 1974, *QB VII* achieved high ratings (it was, in fact, the precursor of the mini-series on US TV) and washy reviews. Hopkins was about the best thing in it, but Clive James, among many, doused a 'specious conflict in the mind of a Hollywood mediocrity'.

What *QB VII* had scored for Hopkins, though, was the confidence that came with defining a work ethos for mainstream American film. It was unclear whether he had what he called 'the charisma' to succeed in American films, but now, he felt, he had the knack. The pursuit of a character's truth was all that mattered. Throughout the Pinewood shooting Tom Gries had been a strict, sometimes bullying director. Hopkins admired his clarity and energy. But he was not beyond calling a cut himself, and dictating the pace when he felt he had issued enough lines for the day. Gries trusted him and didn't argue about it. And it worked as well as the groaning superstructure of *QB VII* – no better, no worse than standard $10,000-a-minute TV stuff – allowed. This course he would follow: to satisfy himself first.

The high publicity profile of the Uris mini-series, aided in no small part by the controversy of the National walk-out, landed Hopkins a brace of mostly lightweight film parts through the remainder of 1973 and 1974. The first, Universal's *The Girl from Petrovka* directed by Robert Ellis Miller, took him to Vienna and – at last – a Hollywood sound stage. Cast opposite Goldie Hawn, Hopkins admitted to a fragile on-set relationship in which he suddenly 'found my feet in the scheme of things'. Despite bouts of overtime and delayed schedules, the production unit still found time to grind to a halt for Goldie Hawn's birthday celebrations. 'A huge cake was baked and wheeled on, and there was I standing by, appreciating all this. Then the photographers arrive to snap it all and one of them waves me out of the way, saying, who's that asshole? Which kind of put things in perspective.'

Never distributed in UK cinemas, *The Girl from Petrovka* was, according to Hopkins, 'The worst film ever . . . I didn't even see it. I played the Russian boyfriend, but it was just such an awful, awful, thing.'

Dick Lester's *Juggernaut* followed. Shot partly aboard the liner *Britannic* in Southampton, otherwise at Twickenham Studios, it represented the straightest, least inventive of Lester's films, a hackneyed yarn about a ticking bomb on a transatlantic liner finally defused by a wooden Richard Harris. Critic Jonathan Rosenbaum admired it for Lester's savvy cutting, and little else. Here, as elsewhere, Hopkins' police superintendent hero – a blend of twenty TV cops – earned no notice. Hopkins didn't seem to care, or if he did, the irritation and angst were adequately held at bay by Jenni, and by beer.

Lester, like Tom Gries, Hopkins liked. At Pinewood, Gries had used a set-up of four simultaneous cameras – 'maybe not a lighting cameraman's dream way of working, because you get flat light, but Jesus, we had it down [the trial scene] in two weeks.' Lester favoured the same cut corners. 'He was the fastest director I ever worked with,' Hopkins recalled years later. 'He had three cameras there and you shoot when he says shoot and you really have to be on the ball. It's great, but I suppose it's a bit crazy. I suppose he's in too much of a hurry. I mean, we filmed *Juggernaut* in four weeks under schedule, which gavè us four weeks with nothing much to do . . . But he has great charm, a nice sense of humour.'

The luck of amenable, easy-going directors didn't last. In the spring of 1974, still in the honeymoon mode of escape from the National and of well-paid reinvention in appropriately invisible film roles, Hopkins was offered an amusing script written by Hugh Whitemore based on the hugely successful vet novels of James Herriot. Simon Ward had already been cast in the co-lead, playing the apprentice Herriot, finding his feet in the Yorkshire farmlands of the late 1930s while assisting the gruff Siegfried Farnon. 'You cannot imagine a more pleasant scenario,' says Ward. 'Yorkshire life at a lazy pre-war pace, gentle moors, villages, streams, trees, twittering birds. I went for it like a shot.' Hopkins was delighted that his old flatmate had signed, and the script and the well-experienced director appealed. He accepted the role of Siegfried.

'Claude Whatham was the director,' says Ward, 'and he had a reputation for his flair for working with children and animals. So I was told. Now, when someone tells you somebody has a reputation for children and animals you should bloody well know that when you walk into town with that person, dogs will start barking, babies crying and cats will throw themselves suicidally down chutes. It really is a recommendation for caution.' Whatham's screen credits were sterling: in a short but rapid career he had directed the estimable British successes of *That'll Be the Day* and the family classic *Swallows and Amazons*. He seemed, on the face of it, the peerless choice for a film targeted at British Bank Holiday audiences.

> It started as the best prospect and we were all desperately happy. It was such a joy to be working with Tony, we all liked the script, it was April – the spring, the best time of the year – and it was to be a bland little movie, but a treat none the less. But Whatham couldn't stand that, couldn't stand it that we got on and were all so content. His idea of film-making was that it must be tough. It must be *uuugh!* – and *aaggh!* – *ggrrr!* And it wasn't. Or at least it didn't start out to be. So it turned to mud before our eyes. Awful confrontations – daily in my case – that we bore up as much as we could.

Ward and Hopkins attempted to insulate themselves against Whatham's bullishness by immersion in friendship.

> Tony was so good to work with, so attentive, so inventive, so patient and spontaneous. He drew out the best in one and one learned from him every day. He had a fine comedic skill that took off before your very eyes. My favourite all-time scene is one in which he and I, as the vets, drive up to the wrong farm, ready to perform some gruesome emergency operation on a pig or something. And, as the old sweetie opens the door, Tony says, like a maniac, 'Give me the carving knife! Let's start cutting!' I've seen that four hundred times and I still roar with laughter. I cut it into a documentary I made about changing practices in veterinary science, really because it is a moment of classic comedy, the very greatest you'll see.

After several rocky weeks, though, Ward found himself physically restraining Hopkins from attacking Whatham. 'It was bound to happen. Tony was his usual mercurial self and Whatham was goading him. One day Tony and I were standing behind camera feeding lines to another actor. The actor kept slipping up, forgetting his lines. After a while Whatham turned to the lighting cameraman, Peter Suschitsky, and said, "Looks like I'll win my bet – I knew we wouldn't be out of this location today, not while Johnny here is doing his thing."

'Tony went berserk and made a go for Whatham, roaring. I grabbed him and tried to stop him killing Whatham, which I more or less managed to do.'

Incensed as both actors were, neither opted for mutiny. 'It was an attractive proposition, but Tony was essentially very disciplined, so we just kept our heads down and got on with it. But it ended up a deeply unhappy memory, especially for me, but also, I think, for Tony. And that was a real shame. Tony and I worked well on screen and despite the harrowing style of Whatham – whom I believed was basically a man who liked making problems – we held it together. The picture actually turned out all right and it went on to earn a bag of money.'

Co-financed by EMI and Reader's Digest, *All Creatures Great and Small* was a pre-Christmas success in 1974 but all it really did for Hopkins was to reaffirm the partiality of British audiences – and, worse, of British producers – to his quirky delivery of stock screen characters. On the plus side, the film did stir his first fluent fan mail (he admitted the 'addiction of ego' in various subsequent interviews) and, certainly, no critic overlooked his contribution. *Photoplay* notched him as 'a star to watch' and the *Monthly Film Bulletin*, while ditching the whole, singled out Hopkins, whose 'bluff, irascible veterinarian shines like a beacon amidst the otherwise dull characterisations'.

Hopkins finished *All Creatures Great and Small* in a suppressed panic. Intuitively he recognised another, fiercer watershed, but was profoundly unsure of where it would, or should, take him. In the eighteen months since the National desertion he seemed to have hardly moved forwards at all. Sure, he had distanced himself from the indignity of marital collapse and achieved the maturity of a less raging life with Jenni – but what was that but a diversion, a camouflage to what he really was, and really wanted? The money was improving all the time – but what was money when all that satisfied him was his books, and his breakfast fry-ups and his beer? Jenni told the *Sunday Mirror* in detail about their marriage, about his dependency on her and her passive, supportive response. In an article entitled 'He needs me so much, that's what counts', she spoke of the job mania that denied them any sort of normal social life: 'Unlike many men Tony has nothing in his life but his work. He is obsessive about it.' She wasn't complaining, but, said the *Mirror*, 'being a Superwife isn't all that super'. Jenni said: 'For me it means being alone, reading or watching television . . . but our good times together make up for all that. To me the best times are when he is between jobs. Then we'll catch up on films and plays, visit his parents in Caerleon, go shopping for clothes.' The *Mirror* described Jenni as 'a mature-sounding 29 . . . dressed quietly in camel and beige with a reassuring presence. There's something safe about the girl.' But Jenni was no mouse and her candour revealed the core of rationality and self-honesty that was the secret of her attraction to Hopkins: 'There are times when Tony is working so much that his sexual energy is sublimated into the work. But I don't get paranoiac about it. Sex is part or our marriage, but it's not the thing that keeps us together.'

The TV roles continued to pour in – he made four TV plays between *QB VII* and *All Creatures* – but they mostly irritated him: 'TV is always a hurry, always a shoestring budget, always incomplete.' In response, it seemed, he powered up the boozing. Now, insidiously, it was two bottles of Bordeaux and not one with dinner; it was spirits to perk the beer, or beer to perk the spirits at the boring, mindless BBC parties around Shepherd's Bush, or the actors' land of Barnes and Putney and Hampstead. This, though nobody saw, was the fatal slide. Peta Barker knew his tendency to burrow in a chair and sink, and drink. It was a creeping, invisible cancer, a soft shift from domestic inertia to stupor . . . and a small step then to insane abandon.

Jenni's suspicions and fears grew, but she kept them to herself and hedged when Muriel queried on the phone, or when the best friends called to say, 'Was Tony OK last night?' Hopkins later said, 'I was going down and down, fast.'

Ironically, in these fraught days, when the flight from the National had become a void of purpose that neither knew how to address, a role in a TV play – the discipline he least liked – gave him the first arse-kick of serious warning about the decline of his mental and physical health. The role was that of Theo Gunge, a boozy actor teetering on suicide (who eventually shoots himself) in David Mercer's *The Arcata Promise* for Yorkshire TV. David Cunliffe, the play's director, became close to Hopkins in the two-month preparation of what he calls 'an extraordinary exercise in art copying life'.

Cunliffe was the young buck, prominent and especially successful at Yorkshire TV in his partnership with Mercer, who was himself widely seen as among Britain's top five TV playwrights. He recalls:

> *The Arcata Promise* was a simple television commission in the days of television's childhood. In those days, you called in someone like David [Mercer], told him you wanted an excellent ninety-minute play with so much film and so much studio tape, and he got a one-third commissioning fee and you waited, and got your play and went out and cast it. You had confidence in quality because of the purity of your sources and your intention. Without sounding pompous, commercialism didn't come into it.

Both Mercer and Cunliffe wanted David Warner for the lead role – 'He was then Britain's Golden Promise' – but Warner became ill and was unavailable, so Hopkins took his place. 'I can't say I immediately knew he would be right,' says Cunliffe, 'because, when he read it, he gave a monotone, colourless reading that kind of frightened me. It was only later I realised how he stores it, and how he uses it . . . I have to say his intensity was amazing, and he was the most intensely focused, most well-prepared, well-read-in-context-of-the-play actor I had ever worked with.'

Immediately, Cunliffe saw the boozing, and it worried him. 'The trouble was, both he and David loved the jar and didn't appear to know how to stop. There was a tendency to go on till three in the morning and while that was bearable when we did our six weeks of rehearsal in London, at Harlesden, in an awful decrepit church hall called the Crystal Rehearsal Room, I feared it would bring us down at the actual taping in Leeds, which was more or less live.'

However, Cunliffe did warm to Hopkins – was, he says, 'fascinated' by him. 'Jenni was there all the time, but *all the time*. Like his shadow. A wonderful, giving woman who would say, 'OK, I'll get you another bottle, but do you really want it?' He seemed completely to depend on her, and he also seemed completely afraid of women. Like all men, I suppose, he loved the idea of a pair of big tits crossing the room to him, engrossed in him. But the reality of it made him wilt. This sensitivity was interesting, and it had a dark side.' Cunliffe found himself comforting co-star Kate Nelligan when, after one of many flare-ups, Hopkins made her break down and cry. 'He had a matter-of-fact way, a confidence in what he was doing – though I knew this was on the surface and underneath were crazy doubts – but he attacked Kate with an attitude of, "Oh for Chrissake, what's the problem doing it like this? Just get on with the damned thing!" She couldn't handle him at all, and he was relentless.' Some hated Hopkins for this on-the-sleeve openness; Cunliffe felt it was the 'expression of a private agony'.

Though Cunliffe lacked the boozing stamina of Mercer and Hopkins he enjoyed great shared conversational candour and was one of the few intimate observers of the beginnings of a sea change. 'He was writhing. There was a colossal resentment of British theatre and the opportunities. He felt hard done by. All the striving, the labour, the love, was for nothing. So he wanted an end to it. I remember the phrase he used to me. He said, "I want the limo now." Meaning, he wanted the bonuses of Hollywood and not the £650 we paid him for *The Arcata Promise*.'

Cunliffe wondered would 'the pain' unseat his production. 'We moved to Leeds, where we all checked into the same hotel for the taping. The drinking had me at the proverbial edge of my seat. Finally it came to the night before the shoot – which would be virtually a one-day affair. I was terrified, thinking, the two of them will go crazy at it tonight and tomorrow I'll be scuppered. So I said goodnight to them quite late and went to bed, praying all would be all right on the morrow.' The next morning Cunliffe was awakened at eight by hammering on his hotel door. He opened it to find Hopkins slumped on the jamb, drooling, barely coherent. 'Apparently I fainted. That's what Tony insists, anyway. Myself, I don't have a great recall – other than remembering feeling, *I've had it, it's dead, it's over, sunk*. Then, after a beat, Hopkins springs alive and says, "Ha ha, fooled you! Are you ready? Let's shoot it!" – and he was stone-cold sober.'

The play, by contrast, was a drunken orgy in which Gunge swings from fantasy projections to agonised self-torment. On its American screening in 1977 *Variety* wrote: 'Theo is nothing more than a marginally animated corpse, bitterly contemptuous of his own self-pity. He is a festering hulk with memories running through his head 'like a bleeding film'. He is infuriating and disgusting but, in a dazzling performance by Anthony Hopkins, he is perversely mesmerising.'

It was easy to see why Hopkins had fallen passionately for the play, and for Mercer's vision of the self-annihilatory capacities of actors. Later, in 1981, in his second theatrical directing venture, he would produce the play at the California Center of Performing Arts. 'It was a good script, a good play. In it Theo says, "I am a dipsomaniac." I loved that word. I thought it was a marvellous word. *Dipsomaniac!* But I forgot that that was what I was. I was that dipsomaniac.'

The Fates were dealing irony and decline. Burton, about whom he had already expressed quixotic ambivalence, whose career started earlier and rose higher, who played *Hamlet* and razed Beverly Hills, who met Bogart, whom Olivier was jealous of – Burton, too, was at his alcoholic gallop. In 1976 Burton told the *New York Times*: 'From 1968 to 1972 I was pretty hopeless . . . I was up there with John Barrymore and Robert Newton. The ghosts of them were looking over my shoulder.' In fact 1974 – Hopkins' unhinged year – was Burton's climactic year, the year that saw him rushed to St John's in Santa

Monica for emergency treatment for 'bronchitis' and 'influenza' that was actually chronic alcohol poisoning.

In May of 1974, Elizabeth Taylor filed for divorce from Burton while he was still undergoing hospital treatment, citing irreconcilable differences and signalling the curve. In September of that year Hopkins made a final mad grasp for America, accepting – with the gravest misgivings – John Dexter's invitation to take over the lead from Alec McCowen in Peter Shaffer's *Equus* in its Broadway transfer.

It was the brink of death for both men, and a swapping point. Here was the occasion of accession for Hopkins, muffled and distracted by hysteria, by crises, by the flapping of wings.

Part Two

FLYING

'We walk through ourselves, meeting robbers, ghosts, giants, old men, young men, wives, widows, brothers-in-love. But always meeting ourselves . . .'

Ulysses
James Joyce

Chapter 10

THE WAY TO SEXY DEATH

At 36, Anthony Hopkins bore the appearance of a middle-class business-man. 'He was never strictly a rebel,' says Alan Dobie, who recalls a hunt ball in Yugoslavia during *War and Peace*, when 'I came very informally, with an open shirt and casual trousers and we were turned away at the door. Tony, to my great surprise, was actually embarrassed on my behalf. They wanted to give me a tie and he said, "For God's sake, put it on," and it struck me that he had a need to conform.'

Arriving in New York and checking into the Algonquin with Jenni, Hopkins was still blindly adhering to the vestiges of boarding school propriety and an actor-idol manqué image based loosely on Olivier. Underneath, he hated himself, his face, his fatness, the limitations of mortality and education, and was racing through philosophical literature for answers. 'On the outside,' he later wrote, 'I probably looked all right. But those close to me sensed that all was not well. I was committing suicide on the instalment plan because life was not living up to my expectations and was disappointing me deeply.' In this frame of mind, flagrantly suicidal, undertaking Dexter's *Equus* was a do-or-die bid for the ultimate American acceptance, which he saw as some mystical elevation that would repair him. Wary as he was of his 'bad chemistry' with Dexter he saw no other option but to tackle the dragons and demons head-on.

The fact that Dexter called him 'Miriam' was just another cross to bear; but soon it would be a cross too many.

Equus, in its National run since July 1973, had won Dexter fair reviews, best encompassed by Matt Wolf's conclusion of 'mighty theatricality and swift production'. Dexter himself had no quarrel with this consensus. For him, the play was 'an invitation to theatricality, a command to do something unique in a unique way . . . It wasn't film material and it required the fullest expression of theatre, which is how it was with Alec McCowen and Peter Firth in London.'

Equus was a barbed, emotionally jolting play, yet another variation on Shaffer's constant exploration of conflicts – between logic and passion, mediocrity and genius, man and God. In it Strang, a stable boy, blinds six horses who witness his frustrated sexual adventure, then faces the interrogation of a 'self-laceratingly literate' psychiatrist, Dysart. The play mirrored in a curious way the dialogue between intellect and passion that raged in Hopkins. Dysart was the frustrated, erudite oracle, controlling passion, who is, as one critic observed, 'prick aroused' by the boy's capacities; Strang is the unapologetic reactor – hugely powerful and resonant – apparently untouched by mortality, morality or destiny, who spits in the face of insanity; each infiltrates the other, seemingly detrimentally, bringing about utter emotional collapse.

Rehearsals started well and Dexter was initially pleased with his lead actor, which gave Hopkins great comfort. All along Hopkins had been dreading some acid onslaught in repayment for the abandonment of the National, and of Dexter's plans for him. In Vienna, where they had first met up to discuss the possibilities of Hopkins replacing McCowen, who did not wish to transfer with the play, Hopkins had come clean and spoken of his reservations about the National's 'Machiavellian regime' and the weakness of Blakemore's team on *Macbeth*. The axe had seemingly been buried, but one never really knew with Dexter. Hopkins told a friend, 'John is a bastard. The one thing I've learnt is not to turn my back on him, and not to let my guard down. Just when you think you're pleasing him, he'll make mince paste of you – just in case you stop trying.' Jenni queried his commitment to Dexter, asking why he wanted to put himself through this tension and fear, Hopkins said, 'Because this is my moment, this is where I take on America and make it work. And then everything will be all right. I'll get my health in order, get my life in order, fix everything.'

In no time at all it turned bad. Hopkins told *Time Out*: 'One morning he screamed at me: "Come on, Miriam, these are the only decent fucking lines that Ruby Shaffer has written in many a decade, so let's have the bloody things right! None of this backstreet Richard Burton acting!"' Hopkins cracked, went back to his hotel, threatened to leave. Jenni reassured him, and he went back. In her autobiography, actress Marian Seldes, cast in the play as the magistrate Salomon, recalls, 'The temperature changed. Discontent. Looks. Avoidance of looks. Directions given with a cruel edge in Dexter's voice . . . Selfishly I took pride in the knowledge that although Dexter could go after Hopkins, it would not happen to me . . . I had been warned by Tony that the warmth and brilliance John Dexter was lavishing on the company might change without warning.'

Hopkins locked horns with Dexter and stubbornly refused to retreat. He dug in. His contract was for nine months and now, determinedly, he took an apartment on East 45th Street, between Park and Lexington, and furnished it with his paperback library. He was here to stay, and he drank with fury to keep the pace, cheering himself with a digestible new discovery, spritzers, in Charlie's Bar. Dexter seemed to turn on and turn off the pressure, reeling in the performance he wanted like a big game fisherman. At one point, seeing Hopkins' discomfort in rehearsing with the play, Dexter dismissed Firth and allowed Hopkins to rehearse with the understudy Tom Hulce. Then, in subtle tribute to Hopkins' endurance, on the afternoon of the final run-through, Dexter requested Hopkins play the various scenes as a sequence of famous star impersonations. Hopkins obliged, mimicking Brando, Burton, Olivier and James Cagney. 'It was so funny and brilliant,' said Marian Seldes, 'and it broke the nervousness of opening night.'

The worries and the wars seemed immediately justified when the Broadway *Equus* opened at the Plymouth Theatre on 24 October 1974.

Clive Barnes of the *New York Times*, whose word inspired profit or closed a production overnight, deemed it 'very important' and Martin Gottfried in the *Washington Post* called it 'a devastating experience' in which Hopkins showed 'a staggering inner power'.

Hopkins appeared light-heartedly ecstatic and celebrated with Muriel and Dick, who had flown over as his treat, Peter Firth's parents, Lauren Bacall, David and Paula Swift, Rachel Roberts and Burton's first wife Sybil, whom he had known briefly in Port Talbot. Here was triumph! Not just to draw a theatre to its feet in ovation, but to be fêted in caviar and Bollinger with Bogie's widow, to see one's name in Times Square, to hear the cacophony of leading agents' interest, the rustle of new friends and new scripts overnight. Clive Barnes' blessing seemed to copper-fasten his American future but, as Hopkins was quickly to observe, he was not yet that rarefied commodity, a film star.

As the play lurched on, the rows with Dexter rumbled and roared, then diminished; but Hopkins seemed worn out by them, and stood on the thinnest ice with his self-confidence. He later said:

> *Equus* was a major success all thanks to Dexter and me and the cast. But Elliott Kastner came backstage and said, 'Tony, it's fantastic! Jesus, I loved it. Tony, you were just fantastic! I'm coming back to see it again today!' So there and then I knew that he was going to make a film of it and in the computer of my brain I summed it up and realised, well, I'm not a movie star, so it's unlikely I'll get it. Pete Shaffer asked me, 'Would you like to do it?' 'Yes,' I said. 'But I'm not going to be asked, surely.' He said, 'Oh my dear, of course you are.' And I said, 'Peter, come on, Jack Nicholson is on the list. I hear that Brando is up for it as well.' Peter had the grace to flatter me . . . but I wasn't a movie star.

Gawn Grainger and Simon Ward were among the friends from London who visited *Equus*. Grainger got 'pissed drunk on vodka and Scotch' with Hopkins, and Ward took a serious step backwards: 'That was when I started to get worried about Tony. I was shocked, to be honest. He wasn't taking care of himself at all and he seemed to have no safety control. We went to Sardi's, a big group of us, and there was no stopping him. I remember thinking, what a waste. He's reaching his peak, and if he keeps this up he's dead.'

When Dexter left New York, Hopkins apparently had all the ingredients for contentment – but this didn't materialise. Awarded Best Actor citations by the American Authors' and Celebrities' Forum, the New York Critics' Desk and the Outer Critics' Circle, Hopkins was still hot for the bottle. He later wrote:

In 1974 I travelled to America pursuing the Goddess of Fame and Fortune and arrived in New York to take on the world. I was in a very successful play and I was riding the crest of a wave. The sweet smell of success! All my ambitions and dreams were coming true. And then for some puzzling reason all hell broke loose. I was in the grip of full-blown alcoholism. I had a tiger, not the world, by the tail. I remember sitting at the corner of the bed one night and saying to my wife that I didn't know what was happening to me: I think I'm going insane, I can't stop drinking.

The greatest of all ironies at a time of ironies was that Richard Burton would shortly assume the Broadway role of Dysart, following Anthony Perkins' replacement of Hopkins on completion of the contract run. [Burton would also win the film role.] Hopkins finally, formally, met Burton, in the closing days of his *Equus*, backstage at the Plymouth. But it was a strained and brief meeting that did little to assuage the competitive and inadequate feelings Hopkins harboured. Though Burton's notices would pale beside Hopkins', one friend believes that 'it did him no good to meet Dickie. He was in awe of him in the worst way. He was vulnerable, he was nothing beside Burton'. David Cunliffe knew that 'all that really mattered – the only yardstick he seemed to want to measure himself against – was Burton. He came clean with me on that.'

As Burton's career switched off that winter with the botched drunken slurry of *The Klansman*, Hopkins' apparently began to gather momentum. The William Morris Agency, one of the 'big three', whose representation in LA virtually guarantees employment in films, offered two projects for shooting in the summer of 1975 – a TV film remake of the 1939 weepie *Dark Victory*, about a socialite (a TV producer in the remake) dying of a brain tumour, and an NBC mini-series of *The Lindbergh Kidnapping Case*, to be directed by Buzz Kulik. Neither was *Equus* quality, nor exactly the pedigree he judged himself worthy of, but *Dark Victory* carried a fee of $80,000, which was twice his former rate, and the *Lindbergh* fee was equally good. In truth, the decision to grab LA was no decision. Though Jenni had come to New York with the vague hope that they would return and resite in London, Hopkins had wasted no time in applying for green cards. 'I didn't actually think about moving to LA,' he said. 'I just knew it was the right thing to do.'

While working on Broadway, Hopkins had continued to pay the higher rate British taxes and, with the high overheads of maintaining a high-swilling New York life, had just $1,200 left in the bank when *Equus* finished. This was all the more reason to convince Jenni that only one path lay ahead: the road to Hollywood. Accordingly, in high summer, he and Jenni flew to the Coast and took up residence in a small, noisy Kodachrome-sunny apartment on Wilshire Boulevard at Westwood, near UCLA, arranged for them by their new American friends Shel and Arlen Stuart.

In more than one subsequent interview Hopkins has described his frame of mind at the time as 'hazy'. He told *Time Out* that his departure for the Coast was an exercise in quitting: 'I woke up one morning and I said to myself, I don't want to be an actor any more. So I went away for eleven months which became eleven years.' To Tony Crawley, he described his geographical leap as part gut-drive, part pilgrimage. 'The first few weeks I felt a bit out of things. We didn't know anyone and I didn't drive. Jenni drove. So it was a little depressing . . . but gradually it all began to fit into place.'

With Jenni's tuition he passed a local driving test, but still wasn't 'a sound or safe driver'. (Alan Dobie recalls that Hopkins' driving skills terrified some people. During the tour of the 1985 play *The Lonely Road* Hopkins offered the cast a lift into London from Epsom. Dobie declined, as he was heading home under his own steam to Kent, but the other cast members accepted. Dobie says they later described the trip to him as 'pure horror'. Hopkins drove 'at about ten miles an hour in a low gear, hugging the kerb' – giving the passengers the distinct impression that, in fact, he could not drive at all.) Yet he continued to drive, indeed loved it, looked upon it as mobile therapy – loved the Pacific Coast Highway especially, with its wide, fast, free access to a far rocky coastline peopled by seals and monarchs, and the open deserts.

He also loved to drive to bars, to drink alone. He told Tony Crawley that he befriended Carol Burnett, that he occasionally enjoyed the Polo Lounge of the Beverly Hills Hotel – 'except when I had to sit there with guys who have projects, saying, "Say, Tony, can you act comedy? What we're really looking for is a Richard Burton, a new Richard Burton . . ."' Mostly he was anti-social and chose to avoid at all costs 'the British Colony, the ex-RADA people'.

The best part of Hollywood for him was the ancient lure, to the heartland of dreams: 'I wanted to find out where Humphrey Bogart lived. Holmby Hills. It was a hero thing . . . And to chase up people who knew him, worked with him. Patrick O'More. Dane Clark. Dane is in his sixties, he was a young kid in Bogie's day . . .' Crawley observed iridescence when the talk was of Hollywood gossip, as opposed to Hopkins' own work. When he spoke of *Dark Victory* or *The Lindbergh Kidnapping Case* he was monosyllabic. But when he talked of the epic Hollywood of yore he was thrilling: 'Dane told me about the days of Hollywood contract players. He said that if you were a contract player at Warners it meant that you weren't over five feet three inches tall. Because over at MGM, the joke went they made them by the yard. Warners had all the short-arsed starts.' Mining and storing yarns about Bogart and Cagney was the priority, as if somehow, in his study of them, he would understand better the esperanto of Hollywood playing at which, he modestly contended, he was hardly adept.

Meanwhile he worked on the NBC film and drank and drank and drank. Jenni told Quentin Falk that his drinking wasn't consistent – that it took the pattern of a three-day stint, or a week here and a week there, with never 'a lost weekend'. Still, it was a worsening situation that, for the first time, put a distance between them and, says a friend, 'brought Jenni to the point of saying, "Make your mind up: either stop, or I'm packing and heading home."' The friend says,

> He was beyond the point of being the embarrassing drunk. He was completely unreliable in that he would go off drinking alone, to some downtown bar, and not show up till dawn. He would drink anything – tequila was a favourite, or vodka, anything. Then when he was drunk he would be utterly unreasonable and offensive. Jenni had a lot of covering up to do, a lot of apologising for his crass rudeness, and a lot of worrying. If he insisted on driving after drinking sessions, she would stand up to him. But he did what he wanted to do every time. It got to a point very quickly [in LA] where he was walking the line every second day. I used to think, you'll hear tomorrow that Tony Hopkins has been killed in an auto accident. He'll never survive this, going round with his Ray-Bans, pretending he's James Dean.

Hopkins told *Time Out* that, then, he was frantically looking for 'the Key of Life'. No, he said, during this 'trip through hell' he 'had not the guts' to try LSD – but it did fascinate him: 'I was on my way to Mexico once to find out about those magic mushrooms Carlos Castaneda was going on about. I was going to have the ultimate trip . . . but I must have got side-tracked. I wasn't so much a heavy drinker as a lousy drinker. I'd drink anything that was going, but couldn't take it.' He told Jim Jerome of *People* magazine: 'I used to space out and hallucinate. I was a lunatic, very hyper and manic. I was drinking all the time to kill the discomfort and self-contempt.' At one point, during the autumn of 1975 he was chasing the sunsets on the Californian freeways daily, aimlessly freewheeling, often losing his way. Since his friends were so few, Jenni took the brunt of all this.

It is hard to pinpoint the crisis of unease that was, effectively, a full-blown nervous breakdown during that autumn-winter. Hopkins himself has described it as simply 'ego', or an inability to cope with what he called 'quick, early success'. Others generally concurred. Sir Peter Hall,

Olivier's successor at the National, was appalled by what he saw as the actor's collapse and tried to caution him against destroying his career. 'He had gone crazy,' Hall said. 'I told him, whatever you do don't cut yourself off from the great British tradition.' But Hopkins had passed the point of tactical analysis and, indeed, rationality. Ten years later in the *Sunday Telegraph* he believed that

> Some kind of critical mass was building up in me. The stress was so terrific that I was reading Zen, Yoga, Indian philosophy, everything and anything. I was so desperate and I couldn't find an answer. Success wasn't it. I hardly ate and I couldn't sleep. I drank like crazy and drove my car like a madman. I think I was trying to destroy myself or get off the planet . . . I was so unhappy. I just didn't want to be here. If a person puts himself under pressure like that, I think he'll crack up or take a quantum leap and go through a kind of wall. I can only think that this is what happened to me.

The grip on business affairs seemed tenuous. Though William Morris represented him in finding TV and film work, he disliked the agent personally assigned to him and would shortly fall out with him over an episode of the TV series *Columbo*, which Hopkins liked and which was offered to him, though, he said, the agent did not pass on the offer. Lee Winkler was his business manager, but he was hardly stressed as the work offers after *Dark Victory* and *The Lindbergh Kidnapping Case* were thin on the ground. David Cunliffe spoke to him briefly on the phone and learnt that 'He was desperately unhappy, really seriously, terminally unhappy. He said the work offers were dross. He might have got the limo, in principle – but it was no substitute for work he could feel good about.'

The publicist Jerry Pam who, in an agenting capacity, has guided the American career of Roger Moore among many, offered himself as a guardian angel and took Hopkins to lunch 'because we had to talk about a career that was going down the toilet'. Pam had been 'keeping an eye on Hopkins' and believed that his best hope of saving a decent Hollywood career was to 'go out and be seen. Seen at parties. Go around seeing the people who matter'. But Hopkins was beyond listening to reason. He said, 'I was past all this, fed up, recognising that I had lost myself in this jungle where people wake up each day and say, "Oh, I must get to Ma Maison and make sure I get the right table." Part of me loved America for the way that you are taught to express your anger there. But they forget that, to express your anger, someone suffers. In my case it was someone I loved very much and I was not able to face the contradictions and the price [I was paying]. It was quicksand.'

For a while, in the autumn, Hopkins had returned to Wales to visit Muriel who was ill in Gwent Hospital. Now it was Jenni's turn to leave for home. As Christmas approached, according to a friend, Jenni did as she had long threatened to do and packed a case. Hopkins, the friend says, was too self-absorbed to respond. Jenni went to see her parents, to catch her breath and judge afresh, from a far perspective. As with the crisis with Peta, there was no blistering row, just a resonant and unmistakable adieu. Hopkins initially held his ground and, in her absence, spent the Christmas holiday in a nomadic boozing spree. A couple of days after Christmas, he rang her in a tearful panic. He was in Phoenix, Arizona, and had woken with no idea as to how he'd got there. Jenni was reassuring but firm. The writing was jumping off the wall: he needed to stop, and he needed professional help.

In a fugue, Hopkins drifted through the next few days. Michele Lee, an actress from *Dark Victory*, threw a seasonal party to which all the cast was invited. Hopkins hit the bottle, and blacked out. Lee's agent Ed Bondi drove Hopkins home to Westwood and couldn't resist passing an opinion: in his Hollywood years he had seen talent aplenty wither on the vine; Hopkins was something special, it was shameful to let this talent go under. Bondi gave Hopkins general information about alcoholic self-help groups and the number of one he knew about. 'Call them,' Bondi said. 'You've got nothing to lose.'

Hopkins has variously described his introduction to the Alcoholics Anonymous network as 'a moment of enlightenment' and a 'road to Damascus experience'. In all accounts, the last days of 1975 are etched as a religious turnabout, the hinge of his existence and awareness when all that went before and all that was to come moved from murk into clarity and he found God. The last drink, he recalls, was in Westwood, in a flat, garage-cluttered Hollywood suburb – 'not in some upmarket lounge, but in a rather seedy bar' – on 29 December 1975. After it, at half-ten on a bright azure-skied Hollywood morning, he rang the number of the local AA group and made an immediate appointment. At 11 a.m., he was in the nearby Westwood office chatting with Dorothy, the contact counsellor. She asked him whether he had a problem with drink and received the mandatory admission. 'But I don't know what to do about it,' Hopkins said. Dorothy told him to leave his phone number, and someone would call him shortly to offer advice.

As Hopkins walked back out on to Westwood Boulevard, he says, he heard the voice of God. Dorothy's last words to him were 'Trust in God' and later he admitted, 'I had been waiting for someone to say that to me all along.' As he ambled down the boulevard, half-sober and half-hungover, he says, he heard a voice whisper comfortingly in his ear: 'It's over. You can start living.' A calmness flooded him and, 'I knew that was when my life began.'

The battle was won but the war had yet to be fought. Superficially, Hopkins' 'conversion' seemed spontaneous and miraculous: indeed, almost all the friends who speak of his recovery talk of 'the miracle' of it. The truth was different. What that December day marked was the beginning of a five-year reorienting programme that was never much more than fragile. Though, he said, he found God, he did not cease searching for spiritual answers and in the months to come would sink to a new, unparalleled despair that would prompt him – temporarily – to quit his marriage.

On the night of his first AA contact, Hopkins attended a self-help group meeting at a Catholic church in Pacific Palisades which had the usual cross-section in attendance. What impressed him most about the meeting was the upbeat nature of the exchanges and the 'birthday cake presentation' to one member in his seventies who had quit drinking forty years before. The man stopped at the age of 38 – the same age Hopkins was now. During the meeting Hopkins was approached by a well-dressed, urbane man with laughing eyes called Bob Palmer. Palmer already knew Hopkins, having been introduced to him on the set of *The Girl from Petrovka*. He was a publicist of high repute, and an alcoholic who was four years 'dry'. The men hit it off instantly and, next day, Hopkins visited Palmer's home for lunch, and again for conversation in the evening. In Palmer's account, Hopkins was, like most alcoholics, 'hanging on one day at a time' and in need of companionship. With Jenni still in England he needed comfort and talk, and the Palmers – Bob, wife Nancy and son Chris – gave it to him. As that first evening of what was to be an enduring friendship and business association ended, Hopkins was in tears – of laughter or anguish, Chris Palmer couldn't tell. He had spent the night seeing a curious, distorted-but-true mirror image in Bob's life story. Where Hopkins had hid from himself in the fifties, emulating James Dean and hiding from his heart, Palmer in the sixties had sported tie-dyeds and carried a guitar. Outwardly conservative and looking 'more the Ivy-leaguer than anything', in the words of writer Larry Grobel, the consequence of Palmer's identity crisis seemed eminently understandable. Hopkins saw himself, his conservatism, the rigid mould of only-childhood, or boarding school, or middle-class Welshness – and the suppressed inventive, radical imp within. He had been two people. Now he might be one.

Hollywood is a small town, an incestuous town, where news travels fast. In a very short time Hopkins had rattled Broadway, won over William Morris and created the general illusion that he was Burton's inheritor. Within months, on the Coast, the word was that he was too like Burton, that he carried the same inherent flaw, that he was unsafe. Ergo, the deluge of work offers predicted earlier dried up.

As he knuckled down to twice-a-week AA meetings and spent more time with Bob Palmer, Hopkins re-evaluated the geography of his life and his attitudes. Burton was no longer a thorn because, living out the ritual of 'success', he could see for himself the horror and the sacrifice:

I think that most actors have a self-destructive power in them, a capacity to tear themselves to pieces – even the best ones, Olivier, Brando and Burton – when things go wrong. When a marriage breaks up, or something, this naturally affects their work and then the critics have a go and a terrible thing starts, and it takes over inside. [The actor] then says, 'Right, let's do shit, let's wallow in garbage so they can't get me. You want to see how bad I can get? OK, just watch.'

The autobiographical hint was tempting, but Hopkins had never quite slipped as far as Burton. Though the climax of abandon had stopped him in his tracks and unquestionably induced a kind of paralysis, he had been fortunate in that it came in the hiatus, between film projects. David Cunliffe, John Dexter and a host of directors gave testimony that Hopkins' boozing never thwarted his work. So the breakdown, in its way, was timely and, in Cunliffe's view, spoke volumes for his sense of propriety and purpose, functioning as it did as a failsafe switch that guarded the growing career.

In the spring of 1976, as Hopkins underwent the early AA therapy in Westwood, *Dark Victory* and the *Lindbergh* mini-series were aired on NBC. Both did well in the ratings and *Lindbergh*, in which Hopkins played Bruno Haptmann, the man who kidnapped and killed the aviator's child, surprised everyone by winning Hopkins a special Emmy. It still wasn't enough to erase the stir of rumour, though.

What Hopkins most needed was time, patience, friends – and luck. He got it all. When Jenni arrived back in early January, she applied herself with renewed energy, 'deeply relieved' and revived by his courage and by the alliance with the Palmers. As Tony grew close to Bob, so she grew close to Nancy, and they forged a circle of surrogate family that was the most auspicious development since their arrival in LA. The next step, Jenni judged, was replacing the late-night bar scene of Westwood with a more conventional family situation. Her personal choice would have been London, but Hopkins had made his bed and intended to lie in it. He told Cunliffe, 'LA is my home now.' With Lee Winkler's help a number of realtors came into action and moderately priced properties around the Hollywood Hills, overlooking the smog, were short-listed. Initially, this seemed harebrained. Hopkins' LA overheads had been high and since the previous summer he had lived on the $150,000 earned from the NBC tele-films. Could he possibly afford an LA home of his own?

Before the doubts took hold the whisper of new film offers began. The first, *Victory at Entebbe*, was a hurried ABC actioner, meagre fare with a measly fee; but the second had all the indications of a workable lifeline – this was to be a Cornelius Ryan epic, shot in Holland by Richard Attenborough with headlining stars like Robert Redford and James Caan. Emboldened, Jenni kept up her coaxing and, after touring a few properties, Hopkins suddenly lit on 1672 Clearwater Drive, off Benedict Canyon Road, a quaint, cramped bungalow, by the style of the environs, but prettily perched on a scrubby hillside, with cacti in place of a swimming-pool garden. Hopkins paid his deposit of $50,000 to the owner, a psychiatrist called Gillis, and loaded up his Westwood furniture.

The offers that broke the tense gloom of alcoholic recovery both resulted from an old acquaintanceship. Eight years before, footing the bill of Hopkins' first LA trip and screen-test, David Wolper Productions had promised to 'fit him in somewhere, sometime'. The somewhere now was as a jaded Prime Minister Rabin in the frenzied forest of cameos that was the all-star recreation of the Israeli onslaught on the hijacked Air France jet at Entebbe of earlier that year. Elizabeth Taylor, Burt Lancaster, Richard Dreyfuss, Kirk Douglas and Helmut Berger filled out the erratic plotline and ensured the right ratings but the film was, as Hopkins always knew, scrappy and unworthy. Hopkins – immersed in studying himself and his neuroses, straining to lose weight and reactivate his jogging, consuming endless Coca-Colas from a stack of cans by the TV, in the bedroom, in the garden – shrugged it off. Privately he called it 'crap' and told David Cunliffe, 'Well, you have a number of options, one of which is saying no and staying at home. I might die of many things, but I won't die of boredom.'

The next one in line was the real test – and more. *A Bridge Too Far* was to be the pay cheque that justified Clearwater Drive and, far more importantly, would give a double insight: into his abiding strength without booze, and into the appetites of American film audiences. This was the fulfilment of a promise director Richard Attenborough had made eight years before during the making of *Young Winston*. Then, Attenborough had, he said, been 'wowed' by Hopkins' improvisational genius on film: he had vowed they would work together again, very shortly.

In 1973, true to his promise, Attenborough approached Hopkins with what he then believed was the ideal project for them both: a bio-pic about Mohandas Karamchand Gandhi, the Indian political and religious leader. Hopkins had immediately been doubtful – 'I was too fat, the wrong race, the wrong face' – but Attenborough persisted. When finally the finance fell through, Attenborough swiftly bounced back with the blockbuster film that producer Joe Levine suggested as a substitute, *A Bridge Too Far*. Duly, one of the first actors Attenborough called on was Hopkins.

According to Attenborough, he was very aware of Hopkins' alcoholism and made a studied research of his progress before booking him – which seems fully justified when one considers the scale and risk of the upcoming production. *A Bridge Too Far* was, according to Levine, his post-retirement baby. Knocking on seventy, Levine was suddenly inspired by the challenge of depicting the heroism and self-sacrifice of one of Second World War's greatest tragedies – the daring, flawed attempt by Montgomery to end the war in one coordinated thrust through Holland. Levine engaged William Goldman, who had broken through with *Butch Cassidy and the Sundance Kid*, to script the film and as early (or late, in Goldman's view) as the summer of 1975 was announcing publicly that his film would premiere on 15 June 1977. Goldman described this deadline as misery: the scale of the reconstruction was bigger than Darryl Zanuck's earlier *The Longest Day*, another Cornelius Ryan history class, and this production would necessitate at least six months of very complex location shooting. Given writing and rewriting time, casting searches, military logistics, mounting and post-production, was it really feasible to make this blockbuster inside two years?

Attenborough's flair, they said, was energy. And it came to the test as never before on *A Bridge Too Far*. He went at it, said Goldman, 'with a fury', criss-crossing the globe from his London home base to New York, where writer and producer were based; to LA, to court the big-name, big-ego stars; and throughout Europe for location scouting and military purchases. Hopkins, of course, was detached from all this. What mattered to him, initially, was his fee – the healthy six figures were the salvation he needed to continue his LA life, but they were peanuts compared with Robert Redford's $2 million, and the million-plus fees of as many as six other co-stars. Actors' wages on the film reputedly accounted for more than $15 million of the $35 million budget. The rest was swallowed by a 300-man crew and as many as 1,800 paratrooper extras in every variety of war scenes.

Very early in the production Hopkins and Jenni flew to Holland and camped at Derventer, 40 kilometres north of Arnhem, where the unit was based. Hopkins was calm and challenged, grateful to Attenborough for the trust, and for the importance of the role of Lieutenant-Colonel Johnny Frost, the legendary 'fighting hero of Arnhem', which was virtually the film's lead. Olivier had also been cast in the somewhat less showy role of Spaader, but when the men met again there was nothing but warmth between them. They lunched together, talked of everything and anything but the National, and Olivier told Hopkins, who was sporting Frost's Gable-like moustache, a little sourly perhaps: 'My God, you look like Hitler. You're miscast, lovey. They should have you as the boss.'

Johnny Frost joined the unit on location and Hopkins found this on-the-spot expertise both helpful and vexing. Frost was amused by the set-up, but never short of commentary. At one point, as the production wheels turned and the bullets started flying, Frost collared Hopkins about running from cover to cover while in action. 'He told me he never ran. He said it wasn't a soldierly thing to do. If you run, you get excited, you fall over. Also, if you are leading a platoon – as he was – it panics men. So he said, "Don't run." And I said, "But it makes good movie action." And he said, "Well, it isn't *true*. Johnny Frost doesn't run."'

For William Goldman, *Bridge* was the most physically taxing production he had ever seen:

For over ten months [Attenborough] lived on the second floor of a small twelve room hotel in Derventer. On an average day he would be up by six, be on set well before the morning start time of eight or whatever it was, stay till late afternoon when shooting was done . . . Then he would go back to the factory the company had found empty and turned into a construction area and cutting rooms. There, in a makeshift theatre, he would watch rushes of people – production designers, the special effects staff, the location heads – whoever was vital for the next day's shooting . . . Following this, at nine, ten, whatever, he would return to his hotel for a bite of dinner along with more meetings – production problems, cost problems, staff problems – and after that meeting, eleven, twelve, whatever, he would go to his room, try to study whatever the shooting would cover tomorrow, make notes to himself . . . then to bed.

In his autobiographical *Adventures in the Screen Trade* Goldman concludes that directing was hard but 'I don't mean hard like it was hard for Van Gogh to fill a canvas or for Kant to construct a universe. I mean hard like coal mining.'

Vying only for screen time with fellow exile Sean Connery, whom he quite liked and who was playing Major-General Roy Urquhart, whose tragic task it was to command the Rhine bridgehead, Hopkins proved that the rigid work discipline of his previously alcoholic days was undiminished. Though he had momentary lapses of tension, insecurity, the shakes, Jenni was by his side to shore him up and, without illness or incident, he put in three solid months of eight-to-ten-hour days. Attenborough was delighted:

In another film, at another time, one might have coped with or drawn the best from an inebriated actor. But on *A Bridge Too Far* I had no margin of error, no luxury of time. There were simply too many walking bodies, too many cogs in the machinery. Tony performed with the deadly, precise artistry I expected from him. Perhaps he had, in some oblique way, benefited from whatever release or disinhibition the booze had previously given him. He could tune into a deeper self. But, for me, then, he produced the goods. He was just terrific.

The end result, premiered as Levine ordained on 15 June 1977, proved neat and accurate and thrilling, but its box-office business sent up some curious signals. Critically, especially in America, the film sank. In Goldman's view, it was the sterility of authenticity that killed it: weaned on John Wayne and James Cagney, American audiences apparently wanted heroes who ran . . . and jumped and dove and cartwheeled and still shot straight. 'One finds oneself angered and harrowed by a film that can make something like *A Night of a Thousand Stars at the London Palladium* out of such an unforgettable military tragedy,' wrote Penelope Gilliatt in the *New Yorker*. But this, of course, was the voice of reason. What American audiences wanted was cheap, sexy death.

Chapter 11

CORKY SPEAKS UP

The idealised America that Hopkins dwelt in confounded him as much as his own demons. It was an amalgam, part Norman Rockwell idyll, part tough-guy haven, where the most appalling spillages of crudity and rudeness were taken as 'free expression'. 'I hate the British tendency to always apologise,' he told Tony Crawley. 'In America they don't ask for that.' Which was probably why, only in America could he bring himself to the voluntary admissions of AA: arguably in the British 'system' he would never have surrendered himself, as he never surrendered himself to the demands of Cowbridge, or the Army, or maybe even the National Theatre. But the reality of his newfound America, his freeing force, didn't connect readily with him. He stayed apart from it. All around him in Clearwater Drive were the living icons of his dreams. Jack Palance lived down the road. Orson Welles. Glenn Ford. But he saw none of them, indeed only sporadically saw LA. Where in the beginning he was keen to disinter Bogart, now he was happy to let him lie.

His habit was his garden, claustrophobic, dishelleved, unHolly-woodish – as was the house decorated by Jenni in the cautious, dull colours of an English autumn. He never gardened. Instead he sat and read, or reflected, and when the demons took him, got in his Caddie and roamed the highways. He was, he said, always pinching himself about being settled, and now owning two cats called Clemmie and Winnie, in a little house that winked down on LA. 'Did I belong? I never knew. I avoided the Brits and I found myself avoiding explanation of my Welshness. "Where's Wales?" people would say. I would answer: "You know Ireland, it's just beside Ireland." It was a very disconnected existence in some ways. I used to look down on the city and say to myself, Well, you did it, here you are. But I never quite believed it all.'

It was a tenuous existence, an impasse of isolation that couldn't last and it is a credit to him – and to Jenni's unflagging belief in him – that he maintained sobriety in what he called 'the awful waiting times when the phone didn't ring and you thought, that's it, the work has dried up, it's over.' Peta Barker believes that Hopkins loved his career more than he loved alcohol, more than he loved anything in fact, and that passion alone was what held him together.

The Hopkinses' green cards had come through, but it was evident to them both that, unless a major breakthrough of acceptance in the American market came, they would be hard pressed to stay in LA. These were scary days, amplified by the AA tightrope and always shadowed by the fear and loathing of the tomorrow. Before the release of *A Bridge Too Far*, Hopkins was already impatiently sketching alternatives for drawing attention to himself and his work. Though his agents were reluctant to offer him up to the lesser market of episodic TV, Hopkins had no false pride. If TV was to be his regular income, so be it. Still a TV addict, he watched most of the main network drama series and particularly liked James Garner, whose *Rockford Files* was scoring high. If nothing better came along, he told William Morris, he would be interested in a *Rockford*, or its type. Failing that, he should perhaps look for a theatrical sponsor and stage a Shakespeare to defy the idiots of the National – show them how it's done, in hip, unapologetic LA.

Once again, luck intervened in the shape of a project tailor-made for his mood and the moment. This wasn't just another utility mini-series, but rather a major American feature for United Artists, directed by one of American film's folk heroes, Robert Wise. Wise was 65, had started as a trainee editor on Orson Welles' *Citizen Kane* and *The Magnificent*

Ambersons, and had then graduated to directing at thirty, in the mythical 1940s of Hopkins' fantasies, steering cult classics like *The Curse of the Cat People*, *The Body Snatcher*, and, in 1951, *The Day the Earth Stood Still*. In the sixties, Wise hit his peak, winning Oscars for *West Side Story* and *The Sound of Music*. Now he was back to his directorial roots with a modern-day supernatural story called *Audrey Rose*. Wise recalls:

> I was working at Universal, completing *The Hindenburg*, when Phil Gersh, my agent, sent me a script by Frank De Felitta, whom I didn't know, that was all about the 'other side'. Now, I'm not an overly spiritual person, but I'd made those science-fiction films and the psychic aspect of our existence is something that interests me – as I was to learn, it interested the two people I wanted to lead this film, Tony Hopkins and Marsha Mason.

The studio legend was that De Felitta, who would co-produce the film with Joe Wizan, had one day been shocked to hear his six-year-old son, who couldn't play the piano, suddenly rattle off a very coherent ragtime ditty. De Felitta had read about what he called 'reincarnation leaks' and was prompted to research the subject further, which in turn gave him the bones of what would become a best-selling novel, and now a screenplay. 'There was some stuff that Frank hadn't yet worked out in that script,' says Wise. 'But I was pretty electrified by it and on our first meeting we worked out that it was Marsha and Tony we wanted, so we called them in.'

In the story, Hopkins' character, Elliot Hoover, becomes obsessed with Mason's daughter Ivy, believing her to be the reincarnation of his own child who died in a car crash ten minutes before Ivy was born. Ivy's parents (John Beck played Mason's husband) resist Hoover with scepticism, and are ultimately forced to defend themselves against a dangerous mania. What unfolds is an education for Mason (and the audience) in the theory of cyclical life and a haul through the lexicon of parapsychology. To Wise's great surprise and delight, both Mason and Hopkins were widely read in the background areas and embraced the project with fervent enthusiasm. 'This was an incredible bonus, because neither Joe nor Frank nor I had any idea what their respective areas of interest were. But it turned out that Marsha was just back from India and was deeply involved in exploring the psychic world and Tony was evidently going through his own spiritual quest.'

As Wise booked both actors, he was advised of Hopkins' drink problem but immediately saw this as no problem at all.

> I don't think that Tony was permanently damaged or reduced in any way by his alcoholism and his fight to overcome it. But it perhaps left its mark. I had seen him in *The Lindbergh Kidnapping Case* and thought he was very concentrated and remarkable. When I met him and began to work with him, I experienced an intensity the likes of which I don't believe I have ever, in a long career, experienced with any other star. It was almost disconcerting, but it was to good effect. It was a practical intensity. For example, he was one of the most prepared actors I've known. The back of every page of his script was covered in tiny notes – prompts for himself, and character observations. Jenni was there all the time, looking after him, but there were no special privileges because he didn't need any. He was, to me, a very stable man who talked about his trouble – but talked about it in the past tense.

Before the eleven-week shoot, which would be based on a sound stage at the old MGM studios, Wise persuaded UA to allow a week's intensive rehearsals. 'I felt Frank's script demanded it. It was wordy and informative and needed a cohesion between Marsha and Tony, and to some extent John Beck. So we put them there and did it, in the recreated New York apartment, and Tony was exactly what I wanted from an intelligent actor – ready to pull a line, or suggest dropping a scene if the play needed it, but never awkward, never combative.'

Once the filming started, the difficulties of the unresolved screenplay were revealed, but Wise is a far-sighted, even-tempered director who keeps a tight rein on rewrites. 'It's been said that there were endless rewrites and improvisations, but that is not the case. Sure, there were some. As we shot it, we had no clear ending. But that was good, that gave

Marsha and Tony scope and gave us time to find out what we wanted to say, what the final message was.'

On the surface, Hopkins had no row with this director. As part of his on-the-wagon re-evaluation he seemed to have shifted his attitude from bull-headed cynicism to a learning mode. But this, some judged, was no more than the newly acquired trait of tactical diplomacy and he was still perfectly capable of shrewdly authoring a change that took the character, or the story, down a road of his choosing.

Wise says, 'There was one scene, a bedroom confrontation that hadn't been quite worked out. So I said to Tony and Marsha, "Just go for it." We put a tape recorder in there and let them fly. What they came out with was superb – Tony was very inventive – and Frank took that tape and took it home and rebuilt the scene and some of what followed in the storyline and then we did it again, more formally, and it worked fine.'

Golden opportunity that it was – and hard as Hopkins tried – *Audrey Rose* was resoundingly not the American breakthrough he sought. Wise says, 'Personally I believed Tony was exceptional but the way it all came together just wasn't enough. After *Audrey Rose*, I suspected he would accelerate quite fast in his career but our reviews were only fair to good and it didn't make much money, or impact, at all.'

Back home in Britain there were those who thought *Audrey Rose* the best thing Hopkins had ever done. At the National, John Moffatt believed it 'pretty much defined his direction from then on, and his strengths as an actor'; Simon Ward admired it; Adrian Reynolds did too. And some of the reviews were flattering: Richard Combs commented that, while Wise lacked irony, he had managed to present the tale as 'a perceptual conundrum' in which Hopkins did well enough. Even better, in the *Los Angeles Times*, Charles Champlin backhanded all praise to Hopkins: 'His desperate conviction as he tells the story comes close to overweighing its coincidences and making it credible.'

Not at all mollified, Hopkins spread the blame. In an interview he stated that Wise had been ill during the film and suffering desperate leg pain: 'I think he was very tired. He knew his stuff and he didn't shout or scream but I think the subject matter got him down a bit. I think it also wore him down that the writer, who was also the producer, kept fussing about and taking it too seriously, so it became overblown.'

Other perceptive observers have commented that *Audrey Rose* missed its mark because of its timing. Undoubtedly intriguing, and eloquent in its treatment of what Combs called 'the mystical beatitude of the East', *Audrey Rose* ultimately targeted an audience fed to surfeit on *The Omen*, *The Exorcist* – indeed, on Wise's own template psycho-shocker, *The Haunting*. As a character study of a man amiss it was riveting stuff; but as a parapsychological thriller it was too economical on special effects, too slow and too tame.

The aftermath for emerging Hollywood star Hopkins (as the trade papers were suddenly wont to describe him) was penetrating silence. Attenborough was back on the phone talking quixotically about on-again, off-again *Gandhi* but, apart from that, nothing happened for several months. Hopkins clung to AA and moved to his fallback: theatre. As he had sworn, he had his agents put the word out and almost immediately received a positive response from James Doolittle, director of the small but prestigious Huntingdon Hartford Theatre in Vine Street (now the James A. Doolittle Theatre) and the West Coast's longest-serving theatrical impresario. Doolittle invited Hopkins to lunch and listened patiently while he proposed his theatrical return in a radical *Hamlet*. Doolittle recalls:

> He had this text he had written himself, stripped to the bones, reducing the play to fourteen or fifteen parts. But I said an emphatic no. I had already put on *Hamlet*, in a very dramatic adventure with Nicol Williamson, who, just before the first night, went out and got drunk and got knocked down by an automobile, which led to a well-publicised first night in which the damned understudy played *Hamlet*! We had recovered from that and did OK with Williamson's *Hamlet*, but I didn't want to do Shakespeare again. Shakespeare is OK for the Coast. But it is limited. It doesn't make money.

Shortly after, Doolittle talked to his friend the actress Judith Searle, who, like Doolittle, had seen Hopkins as Dysart in Dexter's *Equus* in New York and 'been numbed by it'. Searle suggested a revival of *Equus* but Doolittle hesitated since he had only recently scored his most successful LA run ever with another *Equus*, starring Brian Bedford as Dysart and Dai Bradley – the Yorkshire kid discovered by Ken Loach in the movie *Kes* – as Alan Strang.

> I was dubious. Brian is a tremendous actor who had had massive success in his particular *Equus*. But then I thought: Tony Hopkins has something very different from Brian. I remembered that his *Equus* was a powerful volcano of a thing – and I told him this. I told him: 'I felt you were brilliant on Broadway, better than Dick Burton. But I felt you were held back in some scenes . . .' And he said, 'Yes, yes, that's right. Dexter held me back. It was awful. There's more I could do with it.' So there and then, I said to him, 'Let's do *Equus* – again – in LA.'

Any momentary stalling was overcome by Doolittle's bold offer to allow Hopkins to direct. 'I said, "Let's mount it together. I'm on my way to New York. The sets will be in storage. They're no use to anyone. So let's take those New York sets and stick 'em up and you just dive in."'

It was the lure Hopkins couldn't resist. Not just the challenge of outdoing Dexter, but of finally expressing himself in the totality of a director-actor voice. It was no decision: he jumped at it. As Doolittle headed for New York a new pressuring factor came into play: Dickie Attenborough's friend Bryan Forbes was on the phone offering a major role in the MGM-financed *International Velvet*, a late sequel to *National Velvet*, made in 1944. The film was due to start shooting in London in mid-September which gave Hopkins and Doolittle just eight weeks to mount, cast, publicise, rehearse and perform *Equus*. Fast decisions were made: to cast the play with actors familiar with the lines from previous *Equus* productions – and to settle for a three-week run from 12 August 1977.

Judith Searle was one of the only cast members new to the play. 'I wanted badly to work with Anthony Hopkins,' she says.

I'd seen him at the National in *The Architect and the Emperor of Assyria*, and in *Equus*, and I thought his power was outstanding. So I begged Jim [Doolittle] to put me up for an audition and that's what happened – an audition for the role of Hester [Salomon] the magistrate, before Tony alone, at the Hartford Theatre. I was so frightened of him, but I learned to love him. We got on right away and he cast me and I experienced the most educative and fulfilling two months of my life.

Hopkins' approach was to 'lift' the Dexter treatment in terms of text and sets, but 'open it up' in terms of character interplay. 'It was quite different from Dexter's *Equus* in which there was a rigidity, a resistance for the actors to connect on stage,' says Searle. 'Tony changed the dynamics in terms of performances, but it was subtle, it was beautiful, it was effective.'

The one failure of the early phase was Doolittle's refusal to continue with the boy Hopkins had chosen for Strang. Tom Hulce was drafted in as replacement and the boy demoted to understudy. 'But there was no friction,' says Searle. 'Yes, Tony could explode. He had a tendency to *exercise*. But it was controlled, and always to productive effect. There was no bullying – nothing of what I'd heard Dexter had imposed.' Doolittle concurs:

I knew Tony was just off the juice and the battle was raging. You could see the spikes of temperament, the nerviness – but it was all subjugated by a very clear direction. Once he got going with me he was utterly passionate. Immediately we started to talk about other things we could and should be doing. He kept telling me he wanted to do that damned *Hamlet* – and I kept saying no. But we planned a way to go forward – a new theatre venture with him as my artistic director. I had worked with Tyrone Guthrie. I'd envisioned something similar with him. But then he wanted to do *Grand Hotel* in New York and I backed away from that one. I felt the audience identification with the movie casting would complicate it, kill it. It did. It bombed. With Tony I said, 'As soon as you get this movie out of the way we'll do something else.' And we were so clear about it – he wanted to do it so much – that we started publicising it, even in our *Equus* programme. But I'm sorry to say it didn't materialise. We were on our way to a smash with Tony's three-week *Equus*, but after it he did the bullheaded thing and put on his damned Shakespeare, doing *The Tempest* for John Hirsch at the Mark Tapor Forum – and it was a disaster, just like I knew.

During the rehearsals for *Equus*, Judith Searle and her boyfriend became close friends of the Hopkinses, sharing lunches, dinners, secrets:

He was totally candid, a lovely friend. We never went to Clearwater, though I knew all about it – as I knew about his big obsession, which was his commitment to the AA group. I never met a man of such compassion when it came to alcoholism. Through the years since I have heard countless stories of his selflessness in supporting alcoholics – not just friends, but people he hardly knew.

As an actor he was the same. Giving, prodding, exploring. Yes, there was temperament and impatience. I recall, for instance, that I had to take him aside once because he had lost his cool with one actress who had honest difficulty with her lines. He became downright abrasive. I took him away and said as sisterly as I could, 'Now, Tony, be reasonable. She's trying as hard as she can. Calm down.' And he did. At the bottom of it was a serene fulfilment in his role as director. He had fought with directors – he told me horror stories about Dexter's pushing him around. But now he had no one to fight with but himself. It seemed cathartic. More than that. It seemed an historic moment, a moment when he was working through various concepts of himself, and of what he could do. He was at full extension and I like to believe that that play was pivotal in his whole life.

While rehearsing *Equus*, I saw that he was an actor who had to intensely work out every nod of the head, twitch of a pen, every gesture and emphasis. We would do a scene again and again, even when it seemed perfect. I couldn't see what he was looking for. It was visible only to him. But now I think he was refining his art as never before. Very shortly afterwards I watched Tony on film and said, my God, it's

different! He had found it! A placidity! A life in his eyes! A control of
mannerisms. A peace. I think it was on our *Equus* that he broke through
a barrier – as a man and as an actor – and leapt forward.

Sure enough, Hopkins bloomed during rehearsals and went on, in the
rushed three-week run, to supersede all previous stage performances and
win virtually unanimous praise from the critics. Sylvie Drake in the *Los
Angeles Times* applauded a director who had 'intensified the drama'. And
the critic Charles Faber wrote: 'While actor Hopkins builds his
performance as the good doctor in demonic intensity, director Hopkins
is shrewd enough not to allow him to dominate the play.'

'It was the hottest ticket in town,' says Doolittle, 'and it set a record by
being the first reprised play of its kind to do full houses. Tony took scale
[basic theatre wages], about $700 a week. But the money didn't interest
him. He had some point to prove – something LA actors don't feel they
have to prove – and he proved it.'

As Judith Searle hugged him goodbye, she was aware of ambivalence
about his future:

> He wanted to do *Hamlet*. He'd say, 'Let's do *Hamlet*. We'd be great doing
> that . . .' But it never materialised. I always thought that the saddest
> thing. Right there was his chance, his point of no return. After that, it
> was too late. But Jim didn't want to do it, said it wouldn't do the business,
> and so Tony's great dream died. At that time he was so ripe, so ready. And
> when I said goodbye to him I thought, I suppose we've lost you to the
> movies now.

Liberated by his personal *Equus* Hopkins crashed into Britain like a
meteorite. Homecoming terrified him and he told David Cunliffe, 'They
hate me here. I have insulted so many people and no one harbours
grudges like the Brits. Let me back to LA.'

Thus conditioned, *International Velvet* shaped up like another
nightmare. Bryan Forbes, former Head of Production for EMI and the

author/director of a colourful array of successful pictures in many genres
– from *King Rat* to *The Stepford Wives* – had scripted the project earlier
that year on the invitation of his successor at MGM's Borehamwood
Studios, Richard Shepherd. Originally, Shepherd had wanted Forbes to
remake the Enid Bagnold classic more or less as filmed by Clarence
Brown in 1944 with Elizabeth Taylor as the twelve-year-old precocious
Velvet, in training for the Grand National. Forbes rejected the concept,
judging it 'pointless – what is the sense of doing what has been superbly
done and has become in its modest way a cinema legend?' Instead,
Shepherd settled for the later-life sequel in which Velvet is a mature
childless woman, pining for the challenges of 34 years earlier. Into her
life comes an orphaned American niece, Sarah, wild and unresponsive
until she finds the common love for horses and embarks, with Velvet, on
a scheme to compete in the British Olympic three-day event.

Though not fond of horses – a phobia he shared with Hopkins – Forbes
engaged John Oram, one-time manager of the British Olympic team, as his
adviser and set about a strictly disciplined twelve-week shoot on location
in Birmingham and at Elstree Studios. Forbes' casting choices reflected
his eclectic film vision: Hopkins would be Johnny Johnson, the Olympic
selector; Tatum O'Neal would be Sarah; Nanette Newman, Forbes' wife,
the grown-up Velvet; and Christopher Plummer Velvet's writer-boyfriend.
Also among the cast was Peter Barkworth, for the first and only time
playing in a film alongside his erstwhile student from RADA.

Hopkins' discomfort seemed many-layered. He hated the horses (a
consequence of the broken arm on *The Lion in Winter*), was less than
fond of certain co-stars – 'I had absolutely nothing in common with
Tatum O'Neal so no, I didn't particularly talk to her' – and prone to open
arguments with the very clear-visioned Bryan Forbes. In one interview,
Hopkins damned what he saw as Forbes' tendency to chastise with the
command: 'OK – now act!' And Hopkins, never submissive with
directors, always hit back. One observer said,

> Tony is a big presence. He also has a big voice. Directors of a certain style
> pissed him off – especially the 'Now, now, boys, let's shape up and do it!'

type of director. He would say, Fuck off. It was as direct as that – women, men, didn't matter. People said Dexter pushed him [over the edge] and after that he drew the line. But he was not the bossy, my-idea-is-better-than-yours kind of man. It was just, Don't patronise me, and don't dare push me around.

Forbes today insists that any exchanges were grist to the mill: that, in fact, he and Hopkins got on and worked 'harmoniously. But to most, the less than stoical attitude was hidden no longer. This time around, Britain was as he always knew it was – only worse: the same boring, backward-looking values, the same anachronistic style of film-making, the same old boys' system. His conditioning, exaggerated by the liberations in LA, was evident when, just two weeks back in Britain, he was pouring his venom on any journalists inclined to listen. The *South Wales Evening Post* bore witness to the most savage public decrial. Under the bluntest headline – 'Anthony Hopkins to Quit Britain' – it reported:

> Port Talbot-born actor Anthony Hopkins is quitting Britain and joining the growing ranks of tax exiles.
>
> He and his wife Jenni are going to make their permanent home in America. Hopkins, who has been living in Los Angeles, says he has no intention of working in Britain again.
>
> Between shooting scenes of the film *International Velvet* at Birmingham University, Hopkins said that the attitude in Britain is one of constant grudge and moaning.
>
> And he said that everyone in Britain seemed so humourless.
>
> Hopkins said that people in the States got on with the job and that was what he wanted to do.

The reviews, when they came, graphically, validated Hopkins' growth in exile, contrasting his vigour with the current staidness of British film product. *Time* magazine made him the clear winner, giving quality credit only to him: 'With the exception of Anthony Hopkins', all the performances are flat.' And the *Monthly Film Bulletin*, never complacent in reporting the canker in the home industry, tellingly berated a 'horse-mad Girl Guide's wish-fulfilment fantasy . . . in which one inconceivably clichéd situation follows another in pursuit of a fatuously predictable climax, and for which Bryan Forbes has produced dialogue of supreme banality ("Go out there and prove how wrong I was"), well matched by his direction.'

In December 1977, as *International Velvet* moved towards completion, Hopkins was at work in preparation for another American film, this one again for Joe Levine, to be directed by Attenborough. *Magic* was Attenborough's first truly American feature, based on a William Goldman novella about a ventriloquist's insanity. Attenborough's first choice for Corky Withers, the insane showman, was Jack Nicholson – but Hopkins was a close second-best. A technician says, 'Joe [Levine] wasn't enamoured of Tony in the early part of *A Bridge Too Far*. In fact, it was rumoured that at one point Joe wanted to fire him. But by the end of that film Tony was the apple of Joe's eye. He turned it around and it wasn't hard for Dickie to swing him into *Magic*.'

In December, Attenborough gave Hopkins the script, and offered to arrange local lessons in magic tricks and ventriloquism. This was to be Hopkins' third outing with Attenborough and, he joked to Tony Crawley, 'three times was enough'. In fact, he loved Attenborough, judged him a visionary beyond the standard British super-conservatism that succeeded the too-briefly adventurous sixties. More: Attenborough, an actor of measure himself, understood the paranoia of the profession. Hopkins recalled:

> What makes a good director? I don't know really. But on *Magic* [Attenborough] worked it all out before we started a shot. He made it very easy for me. Technically this was a very demanding part and when I first saw that dummy I had to work with I thought, oh Christ, I'll never do it. And I came out in a cold sweat every odd half-hour. But he reassured me. He said, 'It's going to be easy . . .' And I believed him. And I'm glad I believed him because it looked hard but it was one of the easiest jobs I've ever done.

What Hopkins rose to was Attenborough's empathy – but, equally, the prospect of the favoured American milieu, American top-notch crewing and American co-stars like Burgess Meredith, Ed Lauter and Ann-Margret. After *International Velvet*, *Magic* represented the healthy oxygen of Hollywood, the true nurturing ground.

Throughout December, Hopkins applied himself in the customary way to dissecting Corky. Magician Michael Bailey was the expert engaged by Attenborough in support of Hopkins' quest for perfection. Hopkins recalled:

> Every Saturday morning I'd go around to Michael's house in Kingston-upon-Thames and we'd sit in this room at a table and he'd show me all the basic moves. How to do a French drop, the Knuckle Roll with coins, how to split a deck one-handed – all of it. And because there was no pressure, except that by a certain date I had to get it down, and because somebody was having trust and confidence in me, it made life much easier. And I think that that is what worked so well.
>
> Coming back to the subject of directors: that's what makes a good director. To be able to give actors confidence. I've had enough of the crap that says, to be a good actor one must suffer, and one must be critical. I think it's destructive. There are critics and directors who can destroy someone permanently. As far as critics are concerned, I won't read them any more. I just keep going straight ahead. If someone doesn't like what I'm doing, so be it. Sometimes my agent bothers to tell me what my notices are. I say, 'Shut up. You do your job, I'll do mine.' I've learnt in the last few years to be very cut and dried about it, because I don't want to waste time making myself sick.

Tunnelled, Hopkins headed back to LA in mid-January and met up with ventriloquist Dennis Alwood who guided him on the use of Fats, the 16-lb dummy that begins the film as Corky's stage prop, quickly assumes an alter ego persona, then insidiously invades the insecure Corky, turning him into a murderous madman. The technicalities of ventriloquist technique apart, the challenge seemed a curiously apt one for Hopkins.

Throughout *Magic*, the gentle Corky and the manic Fats ebb, flow and interchange. There are few static moments and the suspense is built entirely on Corky's struggle to control the sinister force in him that is articulated through the foul-tongued, destructive dummy. In the end Fats wins, Corky is beaten, tragedy follows.

Hopkins boldly saw the central reference point and later told Quentin Falk that Corky was 'a personified version of the alienation and insecurity' that he felt when he was younger. He said, 'Corky is destroyed by his own inadequacies to cope with other people. He's too egotistical to talk to anyone. He's such a perfectionist that he mistakenly believes he is unique, just as I did in my youth until one day I realised I was just emotionally growing up. So I identify with Corky.'

That identification, the admission of it, was more evidence of his healing and his growth. It was also – actors from Judith Searle to Ed Lauter believe – the key to his power in *Magic*, and beyond. It was self-understanding, a recognition of the smouldering destructive Fats inside him – and a step on the road to the clarity and objectivity that would yield his greatest performances: Lambert Le Roux in *Pravda*, René Gallimard in *M. Butterfly*, Bligh in the new film of *The Bounty*, Lecter in *The Silence of The Lambs*: misfits all, but – more – beacons to a vision of the darkness in the human soul.

Ed Lauter, the American character actor favoured by the likes of Hitchcock (he had just finished *Family Plot* and had been ear-marked for Hitchcock's 54th – but never made – film, *The Short Night*), was to be the sacrificial lamb of *Magic*, playing the obnoxious husband of Corky's true lost love, Peggy, portrayed by Ann-Margret. Lauter recalls: 'It was a very ordered experience, and out of it I made a great buddy – Tony. It started as neat as it went on. I was with ICM [the agents] and I was called in for a meeting with Dickie, and Joe Levine was there, and Dickie said, "There's the script and I want you, but you're a brute, so you gotta put on weight." I did. Fast. I wanted to work with these guys and I felt the script was something special.'

As Lauter fattened up on a junk-food diet, Hopkins, whom he had yet to meet, worked on his American accent with voice coach Patrick

Watkins from Brooklyn. Here again was a profound test: to transcend 'Britishness' and become American. Hopkins recognised the significance and worked on it frantically. For Fats' voice, he decided he wanted a role model – he chose Las Vegas comedian Don Rickles – and a higher pitch. 'Ventriloquism is like driving a car,' he said. 'Once you learn it, you have it. I think it makes it easier to do it at the higher pitch because you can project it better in a microphone or to a theatre audience. All those dolls – Charlie McCarthy, Mortimer Snerd – all of them have a high nasal sound. It's that little boy quality that makes them rather bizarre.'

When Ed Lauter finally met Hopkins, he was immediately struck by the ingenuity of the manipulation of the dummy. 'He was one very, very smart actor, a brilliant mimic who could do all these weird voices like it was no trouble. He took on Fats like he took on, say, aping Rod Steiger. And he did that so well: I know he even did Steiger for Steiger and it was hard to tell the difference. But that Fats – wow, man – weird. There was something deep going on there that was beyond genius.'

Simon Ward admired *Magic* and shrugged off the extraordinary dark reach of the Corky/Fats persona.

> It's like that experience of him during RADA. The hypnotism ability. The almost supernatural – and I don't use that word lightly – intuition. I remember once sitting with Tony in Bertorelli's, eating spaghetti, and suddenly he jumped up and said, 'Something terrible has happened back at RADA – someone has broken a leg.' And when we went back, sure enough a student had fallen off stage and broken his legs. It was magical. Dark and magical. I don't know where Tony drew it up from. I don't know what mystical forces are at work there. I'm embarrassed to talk about it. But he had a doorway to something, and it emerged wonderfully in *Magic*.

Magic started shooting on location at Ukiah, a remote area in Oregon, doubling for the Catskills. Lauter says,

Tony was a revelation in my experience. The discipline was awesome. There's a picture I have of us that sums it up. There I am, sitting in a boat on the lake with some crew people around, and Tony at the other end of the boat. I'm chatting to the guys and Tony is huddled up in himself, concentrating, working out what comes next. He taught us all something on that picture.

The unit was small, camped in two rustic hotels, and bound by the intimacy and pressure of time-is-money film-making. Nevertheless, says Lauter, 'vibes' were great. 'There were things said about Tony and Ann-Margret not getting on, but I didn't see it. Ann is a doll, very kind and open and vulnerable – I wouldn't hear a word against her. But Tony is also a very compassionate and giving actor.'

The oft reported row centred on Ann-Margret's reluctance to do the nude bed scene with Corky that brings their long-lapsed relationship to a crisis. In the story, Corky, on the brink of TV success as a ventriloquist but out of control with the demonic Fats, flees to the succour of Peggy, his childhood fantasy who now runs Finast Cabins in the Catskills. Scarred by her boring marriage, Peggy welcomes the comfort of Corky, but the love is too late – Fats is in command and shortly brings about the murders of Corky's caring agent and Peggy's husband.

According to Hopkins, he was relaxed for the bed scene but Ann-Margret was not. Attenborough was pressing him to get on with it and he finally said to Ann-Margret: 'Come on, they're paying us a lot of money to do this, so let's get on with it.' Ann-Margret conceded, they got into bed (with Hopkins keeping his trousers on, and Ann-Margret her knickers), but, claimed Hopkins, the actress 'would not get into the spirit of the scene'. Finally, to Attenborough's alarm, Hopkins announced, 'Fuck this!' and walked off the set. After sideline coaching, Hopkins came back and completed what ended up as his, and Ann-Margret's, most sexually explicit on-screen scene. Ann-Margret's topless cavorting was later the subject of a vain court action when the actress sued *High Society* magazine, the crudest of America's mass-market soft-porn monthlies, for publishing frames from the film in which her naked breasts were on show. New York Judge Gerard Goettel ruled against her as 'a woman who has occupied the fantasies of many film fans over the years, and who chose to perform unclad'.

'I think Ann was in pretty fragile shape when we did *Magic*,' says Ed Lauter. 'She had just recovered from that infamous bad fall where she broke her jaw [some years before at Lake Tahoe, when she fell off a twenty-two-foot stage and sustained many injuries], and I for one was conscious of not wanting to hurt her in any way. In the script, in my big scene with her, I'd to slap her. But Dickie agreed this wasn't wise. So I just flung her onto the bed.' Lauter admits that Hopkins told him, 'I had a tough time with Ann,' but suggests: 'They had the intense scenes, they were stuck together for a big chunk of that movie. It was a lot easier for me.' Adrian Reynolds later discussed the controversy with Attenborough, who told him, 'Yes, I had a really tough time with both of them', but offers in mitigation, 'I met Ann-Margret sometime after and learnt that she was an excessively shy person. And Tony is basically shy. So I've no doubt it was just a case of the worst deep-set embarrassment.'

For Lauter, Hopkins' resistance to booze and his humour were the big qualities.

As we went on we became close. Both of us are big movie fans – as, say, Bob Hoskins is. So all our talk was about the great stars – Lancaster, Cagney, Bogie. We would do these impersonations all the time, and we still do, on the phone to each other, even today. Tony would say to me: 'You know where Bogie lived, his last house?' 'Sure,' I'd say. 'OK – where?' 'Mapleton,' I'd say. 'OK – where on Mapleton, what number?' 'Number 234 Mapleton.' And he would be blown away. Both of us had this in common. Big fans of the big boys. I remember once he told me he just drove up to Mapleton and parked that Caddie he had and sat there, looking at Bogie's house and thinking about all the joy he gave us. But underneath, Tony wasn't a flash star type. He said to me: 'That Caddie – it's not me.' And it wasn't. He was a very humble, ordinary guy who was excellent at what he did, really ace. I played a lot of sports. And it struck me that that's where Tony shines. He's so alive mentally that he's like a ball-player. You create something and you toss it out to him and he always grabs it, he always returns it. And that may or may not be what makes great acting, but it sure makes great movies.

On completion of the film, says Lauter, there were high expectations for the awards circuit. Everyone, not least Twentieth Century-Fox who had chanced the modest $3-million budget, was suddenly prepared to stick their necks out. Attenborough believed Hopkins had 'broken through some barrier and done some remarkable work' on the film. He told an American paper, 'If he isn't nominated for Best Actor this year at the Oscars, I think I'll be even more disappointed than him.' Fox pushed hard. A six-figure budget was extended to cover a worldwide promotional junket, taking in the States, Europe and Japan. At the press bash in the Ritz Casino, in London, Hopkins had the dummy Fats on his lap, looking like a sinister twin (the facial features were copied from Hopkins') and 'speaking' on his behalf. *Films Illustrated* commented, 'He looks as though he devoutly wishes to be somewhere else, but gracefully halts to accept compliments on his astonishing performance. He is calmer and quieter in his self-confidence than in earlier years – a product perhaps of his years in America, and his marriage.' Ann-Margret was conspicuously absent from much of the press tour – 'Nobody can quite agree on the reason why,' said *Films Illustrated*. But the general nod was towards her equal breakthrough performance. 'Isn't she wonderful?' insisted Attenborough, while Joe Levine's son Richard, pushing the box office, reminded the expectant throng: 'She walks like she's got ball-bearings in her arse.'

Magic gave Hopkins, at forty, America. Overlooked for an Oscar nomination (against which it is hard to justify the subsequent win for Jon Voight in the pedestrian *Coming Home*), Hopkins settled instead for a Golden Globe nomination and a deluge of sizable reviews. Though Ann-Margret pipped him in the pop press stakes, the likes of Felix Barker and Alexander Walker unequivocally marked this moment of maturity and waved him on his way. Even the *Daily Mail*'s usually unimpressed Margaret Hinxman swung, deciding that 'he gives a sweaty, anxious performance I'd never have believed he was able to manage'.

The immediate work reward, it seemed, would be the massive epic *Gandhi*. Attenborough was sure that now, on his run of recent successes which included a quasi-British John Wayne picture, *Brannigan*, American money would entrust him with his great enterprise. He hugged Hopkins and, said Hopkins, told him, 'Now is our moment, Tony. Now we do *Gandhi*. It's a piece of cake. The funding is no problem. Just wait and see.' Hopkins demurred:

> I went off to a health resort. I'd done the publicity tour for *Magic*, and I'd never done anything like that before. So I went off to Mexico and sat in the sun for about ten days and got myself fit and then, suddenly, started getting into these terrible depressions. I didn't know what was the matter. Everything was going well, but I was depressed. I'd be running up a mountain and doing all these exercises and I'd think, well, I've got *Gandhi* to look forward to. But then, one day, I looked in the mirror and said, I can't do *Gandhi*. And then I thought, no – positive thinking, please! But every time I'd look in the mirror it didn't work. I looked at the future and I thought, I just can't go through a year on that macrobiotic junk diet. I like my food too much. I like living too much. I enjoy life. I'm happy now.

Pacing the garden in Clearwater Drive, attending AA twice-weekly, Hopkins abruptly rejected the escalating tensions. He called Bob Palmer, his AA anchor man. 'I wanted to talk about it. So we went out and had some coffee and I said, 'Tell me your opinion. This *Gandhi*, I'm going to do it and it will drive me insane? I've given my word: I have to do it.'

Palmer reminded him of the step-by-step calculation of AA code: 'Ask yourself, Tony, is it beginning to make your life miserable?'

'Yes.'

Step two: 'Why?'

'Because I'm scared of it. Terrified. I can lose the weight but that won't be enough. They need an Indian actor. Dickie is making a terrible mistake.'

'Well, you must tell him.'

'But I promised . . . '

'Why be miserable?'

The worst of it was Attenborough's clinging devotion to an image of Hopkins, the star he helped mould, as Gandhi. 'I wish you could see the tests we did with Tony,' he told David Castell. 'He lost a lot of weight, held his cheeks in like this [he demonstrates] and wore a bald cap. He was unbelievable!'

The 'new' Anthony Hopkins, the self-directing, self-honest Anthony Hopkins, the Anthony Hopkins who – too briefly, as it turned out – could separate Corky from Fats and rationalise, spoke up. He took the wisdom of Palmer, called his agent, then called Attenborough.

'Richard,' he said straight, 'I can't do it. You must get somebody else because I will ruin this film for you.'

Attenborough, he later said, was shocked, but practical. He didn't flare. 'Why, Tony?'

'I will die. I will go to India and I'll suffer malnutrition and I'll either die on the film or I'll let you down. I don't want to do either. If I fail you I'll never forgive myself.'

Hopkins told Tony Crawley, 'He was wonderful about it. He said, "I understand – as long as you are comfortable." I realised I'd made the most awful mistake. I let vanity get in the way. After *Magic*, he thought I could do anything. And if I'd done it I think all it would have proved was that I could cosmetically change myself. I would have had to lose three stone at least. I can't. I'm built like a Welsh rugby scrum man and that's all there is to it.'

This was more than career decision, this was soaring spirit: he had found himself. But was Fats dead or sleeping?

Chapter 12

RUNNING ON EMPTY

'It was a mess, a disaster, a bloodbath. He had enemies coming out his ears and, bless him, I ached for him. He was in pain, going down in flames, he was on his own.'

James Cellan Jones, Head of Plays at BBC television, director of *Magic*'s follow-up, the brilliant Sartre play *Kean*, speaks without rancour or apology when he describes his sole experience of Hopkins. They had met before, at Sardi's during the Broadway run of *Equus*, when Jones had spoken of his ambitions for BBC Plays and they had celebrated their mutual Welshness.

> When I met him it was just before his famous dry-out. He wasn't eating, wasn't smoking, wasn't drinking. He wasn't in great shape, then, but he was, I thought, on a high of abstinence. He said, 'Yes, yes, let's do things.' Sartre was my baby. I had wanted for ten years to do this bizarre and tricky play about Kean, the fabled, tragic nineteenth-century actor. So I called Tony's LA agent who said [mimics the drawl]: 'Tony ain't interested in TV no more, he's a movie star.' I thought, sod that and I wrote to him, a long, impassioned and explanatory letter. Tony called me. He said, 'Don't ever listen to agents.' And I said, 'Well, you know what I want. I want you to come

back to Britain and do *Kean* for us.' And he didn't hesitate. He said, 'All right.'

It was an impulse answer that both men would regret. *Kean* was an emotionally charged play about an actor on the brink of breakdown. It was also, though Hopkins hesitated to imagine it, strictly BBC, a production corralled in 'the system' and peopled with actors whose comfortable habitat was the system. Its budget was £200,000, with a rehearsal schedule of five weeks, a shooting schedule of one. 'It couldn't have started better,' says Cellan Jones, whose serials and plays routinely racked up Emmy nominations and high ratings (he directed, among many hits, *The Forsyte Saga*, along with David Giles). 'But it was downhill from there. To begin with, Tony was doing it for very little money – which is always a good sign as it spells commitment. Or so I thought.'

As Head of Plays, Cellan Jones was in the curious position of assigning a producer – David Jones – who would effectively be the production boss. 'David is a very sweet chap and, after him, I put together what I considered to be a terrific cast: Robert Stephens, who had been with Tony at the National, Sara Kestelman, Cherie Lunghi and a young actor who really hadn't done much called Julian Fellowes.' Hopkins rented a flat in Earls Court and, in a move that with hindsight seems significant, attended rehearsals at 'the Acton Hilton' – the BBC's purpose-built rehearsal rooms in North Acton – without Jenni's company. 'Jenni wasn't around,' says Cellan Jones. 'But, in context of that rehearsal room atmosphere, maybe it wasn't so unusual – although I had heard that she was his right-arm person, very carefully guiding him through his alcoholism recovery. Anyway, the Acton Hilton buzzed with good work. It was an awful place, but full of the energy of good people being highly creative.'

The first days lilted along. Hopkins seemed to have buried the hatchet about his English past and appeared to be enjoying the camaraderie. Then, in an instant, the peace was shattered.

We were seated at a table, working through the text, and Diana Rigg was at another table doing the Greek Tragedies. Tony was all right, and then suddenly Di made some loud remarks about him. Tony thought he heard, 'There's that bastard who walked out on the National.' Loudly.

He was crushed. The effect was dramatic. He didn't fight back, didn't lose it. But everything changed. I personally thought the cast rallied around him well, but I'm not sure he did. The dire effect was immediate. From that moment on he went down. Here he was, back from America with his victories, the past buried – but it was coming back to bite him. My relationship with him altered. You always know when the relationship between director and actor is wrong. There is a glazing of the eyes . . . and that signals mayhem.

Hopkins continued to attend rehearsals but the fury was uncontainable. He avoided Cellan Jones' company, contested the smallest things, irritated Cherie Lunghi with endless evocations of how her part must change.

It was hell. I couldn't reach him. He went into a corner and gave this gabbling performance, with his eyes shut, to the floor. He had made himself, or decided that he was, an outsider. I was very alarmed because I saw that he was in danger of losing whatever kinship he had achieved with this fine cast. It was souring. Bob Stephens' patience wore out. They did not get on from that point. Everyone was on rocky ground except for young Julian Fellowes who was, then, very inexperienced and very starstruck and inclined continually to kneel at the feet of the so-called 'stars'. Julian was supportive of Tony and was rewarded by a subsequent friendship.

In Fellowes' and Hopkins' published memories of *Kean*, the system – or what Fellowes called 'the Gang' – was to blame. Hopkins later elaborated: 'Jim didn't do his homework on *Kean*. He didn't prepare properly and that was the problem.'

With a deep forgiving sigh Cellan Jones rejects this: 'That wasn't the problem. I was ten years preparing for *Kean*, which was a little longer than Tony.'

As the shooting week approached, Cellan Jones obsessed about how he might draw a performance from Hopkins.

I didn't want to give him a bollocking, I wanted to be sympathetic and urge him on. So I called in the technicians and lighting people, as one does, and had the cast rehearse it for them. [The performance] was as bad as I expected, so I drew them all together and said, 'Look, these [technicians] are artists like yourselves. Who the fuck do you think you are, giving them anything less than a good performance? We owe them the courtesy of it.' And right there and then, Tony said, 'That's it, I'm leaving.' And he did. He walked out on us.

Cellan Jones, known, like Robert Wise, for his even temper and easy-easy directorial manner, was forced to take a sharp intake and gather all the cast. 'I told them, "All right, we have a problem. We obviously can't do anything without him, so let's just wrap now and I'll go around to his flat later and talk him back."'

Robert Stephens, senior to Hopkins by several years, would have none of it. 'No, you will not! You will not lower yourself to this blackmail.'

'Oh, come on,' Cellan Jones said. 'I'm not proud. The show must go on . . . so . . .'

'Shut up,' shouted Stephens. 'If anyone has to wallow in this, let it be me.'

Overruling Cellan Jones, Stephens went to Earls Court and 'did what had to be done.' The next day Hopkins was back, but grumpy. 'It was the same old thing, the gabbling, the wanting to change every blasted thing. I felt so sorry for him. He was in such pain, such embarrassment, and he was fighting it internally. He shut off friends, just as he tried to shut off foes.'

Another few shaky days passed, then Hopkins walked out again, bridling at Cellan Jones' emphatic demands regarding one small sequence.

It was then that the entire cast, as one, turned against him. It was horrible but unavoidable. Bob Stephens was livid, livid, and it was all a director could do to keep them together on a stage, doing a coherent scene. I know Tony has said he doesn't like directors. But that's bollocks. All actors say that. My great friend Cyril Cusack, whom I'd known for thirty years, and whom I adored, said that all the time. But he still pinched things from me to use in his own productions. Actors need directors like directors need actors. Tony was posturing when he said that. But this was beyond director-actor conflict. This was a humiliating wounding. We had such a splendid cast. Yes, the Acton Hilton was like a little outhouse of the National, with all those ex-National actors around. But *that* was what killed us. Tony couldn't handle those memories, and he certainly couldn't handle Di Rigg. If she hadn't been there, we might have gone on OK. But as it worked out, there was nothing any director could have done to fix it.

The echoes added to the hurt. In the *Daily Express* Rosalie Horner, who had evidently been talking to cast members, reported that the play 'produced more traumas and dramas' than any of Hopkins' productions. 'He has stormed and shrieked, been weak with despair at himself.' Hopkins confessed to her: 'Acting drives me mad. It drives me up the wall. I just feel crazy with this part. It's such bloody hard work. It's the most emotionally demanding thing I've done . . . Kean can't see the difference between reality and what is on stage. I suppose I'm like him in parts. He is one of the greatest actors of his day, but also a chronic drunk who died at 43 a shattered man. I usually get to play this kind of crazy wild character. But it is immensely disturbing.'

There was no concealing the bitterness. The system was to blame, the Gang, the BBC. During an interview with the *Los Angeles Times* before the American screening, he told Cecil Smith, 'On the final night of the recording people kept watching the clock. I was told that if we didn't finish by ten, they'd pull the plug on us. There was one scene we had to do over and over and time was running out. People were in an absolute panic. You could feel it. We did the scene and we finished just two minutes before ten. Then I was told that if we didn't finish by that time, we'd have had to wait three months to get into the studio again to do the scene.'

The cold reality, says James Cellan Jones, was 'a botched, bad performance, a mess that was made even worse by the American TV programmers who cut it to fit scheduling time and lost whatever good was in it.' The good – scant as it was – comprised the momentary pieces of magic (in fact, literally, since Hopkins employed some sleight-of-hand tricks learnt for *Magic*) when 'that booming Welsh voice took *Kean* into opera'. Cellan Jones liked best the sequence taped at the Regency Theatre in Bury St Edmunds, where Kean rants *Othello*.

> That, for my money, was extraordinary genius. There was Tony in black tights, with blacked-up face, working some wizardry that had all of us bowing in admiration. Even Bob Stephens liked it. Sometime later Tony did *Othello* for Jonathan Miller on TV and I thought it was misjudged, wrong. I felt, as most of us felt, that Kean's *Othello* was the way. In the moments Tony really gave into *Kean* he was brilliant. But maybe *Kean* was real madness, and maybe that was all too close to home.

The critic Roger Lewis wrote, 'Kean, in Sartre's play, laments that, as an actor, he's nothing: a clothes-horse and a gramophone; he's baptised by the storm.' The storm, in the play, is Kean's degeneration as a human being, surrendering his personality and his capacity to feel in the pursuit of sensation and celebrity. 'I have nothing,' says the indigent, hunted Kean. 'Nothing keeps me here. Everything is provisional, I live from day to day in a fabulous imposture.' But, Lewis observes, 'Kean's dispossession is self-possession: the actor unencumbered by boring realities. By refusing to settle debts, he's liberated from the responsibilities of ownership; and he wants to make sacramental his obtuse asceticism, his disinclination to belong to his belongings.' 'I am a priest,' Kean says, 'and every night I celebrate Mass.' A theatrical performance, then, is a sacrifice at the altar of his own personality.

Which is how it seemed with Hopkins. He who undoubtedly found the actor in himself indivisible from the rest and whose quest continued to be – obsessively, almost masochistically – the search for the root of his character and motivations; who would, it seemed, pay the price; and who, too, demanded for his particular asceticism and suffering, sacramental respect. For John Moffatt, 'It was probably easy for Tony to play Kean because he is an Edmund Kean-type actor, a grand illusion, an outsize actor.' The inference implies a core of instability: which is how Hopkins surely was, now more so than ever. Returning to Britain so quickly on the heels of eventual Hollywood acclaim – no, the heels of that vital inner conciliatory resolution – had been the worst mistake. He was fragile, still coming to grips with the AA group and its dictates, still high on the tightrope. Amplified as the experience was by the counterfeit of *Kean*, the game Hopkins played as a counterweight to living and by Kean's resounding failure, the three-month venture crushed him and arguably wounded the emerging embryo, the Corky, the rationalist, the Boy before the Fall.

Disoriented, Hopkins headed back to a long, distressed period of near unemployment in LA, fixed only on one real goal: staying sober. One actor who knew him says,

> He was very unhinged and unguided. More than once Tony has lapsed to madness. He admits this. On *Equus* Dexter talked about it. On [an upcoming TV mini-series] *The Bunker* the director George Schaefer admitted it. Later during the play *Pravda* he himself told [director] David Hare that he was mad. Well, he was mad then. And angry. Very angry . . . which came out in this brute behaviour. He was blunt and rude. Leaving a room in mid-conversation. Being utterly insensitive to people around him. Not shaving, not giving a shit. He barely left the house on Clearwater. He played the piano Jenni had got him and fed the cats. He was known as the oddball and outside of Bob Palmer, Nancy, Julian Fellowes and his wife and David and Paula Swift and his family, there were no friends. There was a big gulf between him and the real world.

Listless and vicious, but – miraculously – still fast to the AA group, Hopkins shuffled into an unready and pointless Prospero in John Hirsch's production of *The Tempest* at the LA Mark Taper Forum, an elaborate auditorium of the Music Center that Hopkins mockingly called 'the Edifice Complex'. James Doolittle had attempted to steer him safe: 'I told him it wouldn't work. I didn't believe in it for a second and I thought he should have been working a better strategy, taking it in stages. I was disappointed that a better partnership hadn't developed between us – but he was hellbent on that damned Shakespeare, determined to knock it into shape, to overcome it. I thought he wouldn't let it lie until he did a successful *Hamlet* or *Macbeth* so I got out of his way.'

Judith Searle saw the play with dismay: he was a far better actor than his Prospero showed; he still seemed to be trying to 'push through some wall of self-understanding' – but this time he was acting on the run. In his frequent way Hopkins picked an immediate target: Hirsch.

> I have no patience with directors. I've tried all the ways. I've been polite. I do this, I do that. But I've had some appalling directors and I worked with the worst on *The Tempest*. Just a dreadful man . . . [who] made a terrible production. It was overdressed, overfussy. He imposed such outlandish ideas. He was a very good talker and I was taken in by him in the first week or two. But what he was really doing was impressing us with his tremendous intellect. And it wasn't really an intellect at all. He compared *Dante's Inferno* to *The Tempest*. And *The Iliad*. And they are not similar at all. He was arrogant and pedantic. And [inclined to] interfere with the story-telling, which is the worst sin of all.

He was also the most suitably invigorating challenge Hopkins could now find, the spur against the inertia of serious depression. Hopkins swam to the best of the wreckage of his recent self-analytical breakthrough: his control of acting technique through the medium of director. In the multiplicity of his troubles, this one held fewest fears. Only three weeks of rehearsals had gone into *The Tempest* – 'because they wanted the money returns fast' – and it was clear that the production worked on no level, playing to what James Doolittle called 'pathetically empty houses from the start'. Hopkins belligerently cut off from Hirsch's theorising and urged Stephanie Zimbalist, playing Miranda, to rehearse privately with him in order to find an alternative sense in the text. Hirsch objected but, says an actress, Hopkins 'rather savagely threw the towel in his face and said, "I'm the director. My way or no way."' Hopkins later said, 'I was just going to do it by myself, in my way, without interrupting the flow of anyone else on the stage. I wanted to gather together my own performance and make it grow.'

Zimbalist, said Hopkins, first supported, but soon retreated. 'It ended up with her calling me a bastard. She said, "You are a monster." And I said, "Yes, and it's going to get worse [because] I want to get it right." She said it wasn't that important to her. And I said, "Well, there are lots of girls who want to do this part. So either do it, or let somebody else do it. If you don't want to do it well, get out."' Zimbalist hung in – not that there was much blood shed, as the production lasted only a few weeks – and Hopkins marked what he saw as a personal victory of spirit and technique. 'It succeeded *for me*. And that clinched it in my own mind. That I can direct . . . I have the intelligence to be a director.'

The pugnacity held him together in the face of appalling notices (and – worse – few notices) but it didn't help when he went home to Jenni and a silent telephone. The wounds to his confidence were visible now in a tangle of contradictory decisions and a new spate of home rows. For a period of eight months he was unemployed, with the brief exception of *The Tempest*, and he was almost tempted to pack in the business. One journalist, also a part-time studio publicist, says,

He was behaving in the stupid egotistical manner of a former heavy-weight champion. In fact, he reminded me of a boxer, with his bug eyes and thick neck and that underlying threat when he talked to you. He talked about nothing but movies, really. Everything else was no-go. Did he have a daughter back in England? I never knew it. You didn't get close to him – ever. No one did. But his patience with stardom was wearing out and he wanted to change his agents, which he did, and he wanted all these agents working for him, making him a star. Not tomorrow. *Now. Today!*

During *The Tempest* came the best film offer since *Magic* – the lead in the big-budget *The Island*, an adaptation of the modern-day pirate romp by Peter Benchley (the writer of *Jaws*), which would ultimately star Michael Caine. Hopkins told Tony Crawley: '[Richard] Zanuck called my agent and said, "Where's Hopkins? I want Hopkins." The agent said, "He's in a play." Zanuck said, "Well, get him out of it. What the hell is he doing a play for? Is he crazy or something?" But I wouldn't do it. I didn't deliberately set out to be inaccessible, but [Hollywood] can't understand that.' [*The Island* directed by Michael Ritchie for Universal, was an £8 million flop; but it did earn Caine a £650,000 fee.]

The consequence was more months of sunshine idleness and a thin sham about getting fit again. He jogged a little, walked on the beach – and fought addictively with Jenni.

> Finally, in my impotence, I was sitting in the garden, looking up at the sun, thinking, What the hell is going on? Rather than turn all this anger in on myself, I was taking it out on Jenni and my agent. So I said to him, 'Get my anything. Anything!' There was one particular thing that's on late-night television and it's so awful but I said, I'll do that. I phoned up a friend of mine who worked on the show and said, 'I'll do it, can you get me anything on it?' I had this perverse longing, thinking to myself, *I will grovel*. I will show them how debased I can be. It was really just a long-drawn tantrum, like a child when his toys are taken away. It was me saying: *I'm not going to play now because I'm not being treated right*.

But even in this deepest distress, uninsulated by booze, there was no diminution of ego. As he reviewed this crisis – with journalist Tony Crawley as elsewhere – he reminded himself constantly and subtly of his proximity to Burton, Olivier, Gielgud and Brando. When he spoke of acting, his allusions were always to them and accordingly, convincingly, in dinner conversations as in the influential trade papers, his name still came in close juxtaposition to theirs. Misunderstood and misused, he was still a viable (though, he insisted, inadequately tested) artist, sacramentally committed to Great Acting.

The new revival chance – for that is what his career had turned into: a non-stop series of blow-ups and revivals – came in a pseudo-British production, directed by the iconoclast David Lynch, and cast with a mould-breaking grab-bag of British types. *The Elephant Man*, a true-life social tragedy told as a sympathetic monster picture – even down to the soft-edged, black-and-white photography reminiscent of James Whale's momentous 1931 *Frankenstein* – had started life, absurdly as it seems, in comedian Mel Brooks' hands. Brooks' regular co-producer Jonathan Sanger had bought the film rights as soon as he'd read the 'spec' [uncommissioned] screenplay by Eric Bergen and Chris De Vore. The writers had taken as their source material a medical autobiography, Sir Frederick Treves' *The Elephant Man and Other Reminiscences*, which had been published in 1923. Treves was a society surgeon in London, knighted by Edward VII, whose claim to fame was his fosterage of John Merrick, a bright, impoverished young man deformed by neuro-fibromatosis and otherwise destined for the life of a circus freak.

On Sanger's recommendation Brooks immediately agreed to structure a production, shot faithfully 'in the idiom' in a London milieu, but striving for qualities of uniqueness beyond commercial cinema, which would, one critic wrote, 'have tended to cast it with John Travolta as Merrick and Dustin Hoffman as Treves'. Brooks and Sanger threw out a wide net but landed all their first-choice names: Lynch, who had just directed his oblique and extraordinarily spooky début, the black-and-white *Eraserhead*; John Hurt, nominated for an Oscar the previous year with *Midnight Express*, John Gielgud, Wendy Hiller and Anthony Hopkins. Hopkins says he initially hesitated at the offer, having already committed himself to upcoming TV work – but missing it would have broken his heart. In the producers' vision Hurt was Merrick (although thirteen years older than the actual *Elephant Man*), and Hopkins Treves. The film would probe for truth, for sympathy, for understanding of the horrors and mores of the time. It would be far from the staple schlock of contemporary favour, far from what Hopkins called 'a standard Rank-cast piece of trash'.

From the start *The Elephant Man* was a strange, almost surreal experience for Hopkins but, equally, the most opportune invitation to explore his own film acting techniques. Initially, there was trouble with Lynch. Hopkins described the director in the early days as 'nervous' and admitted to conflicts and confrontation. Lynch's penchant for wearing oddball clothing – a tall brown trilby, Dracula cape and tennis shoes – irritated him, as did his truculent command. Hopkins had taken it on himself to grow a beard, as befitting a Victorian gentleman. On day one, shooting on location in London's dockland with Jenni close by, Lynch ordered the beard off. 'You don't mess with David,' says a technician. 'He isn't aggressive, but he has a long memory. He was young, a new boy, and Hopkins was the old hand. But it cut nothing with David, who also had Gielgud and wasn't impressed by any of that old-school British crap.' Regardless, the beard remained.

Hopkins told Sanger to nudge Lynch: 'Tell him, why doesn't he get that fucking hat off and stop playing at being a director and damn well direct!' Later Hopkins confessed that the anger was misdirected, that Lynch was 'one of the most pleasant directors I've worked with'.

Nevertheless, in his volatile frame of mind, every glitch was a holocaust. Lynch's way was quiet introspection, slow scene-setting, delicate camera moves. Hopkins saw this as a personal affront, 'a rather arrogant lack of communication'. The rows this time were hushed, but he told Tony Crawley that he and the director had 'agreed to differ' on various interpretations of scenes and – vitally, during a long, on-location interview – that the eight-week shoot was turning into 'a private little trip for me'. What this trip entailed, once again, was a focused reconstruction of his film-acting style. In what Crawley calls 'the longest, best – or second best, after Clint Eastwood – interview of my career in film journalism', on the set of the film at Lee International Studios on 27 November 1979, Hopkins painstakingly analysed the bones of his craft. Crawley recalls:

We went on for five or six hours, through lunch – whitebait for him and steak for me, and he paid – and he opened up in a most endearing way. As we spoke he moved in and out of his dressing room as he played scenes with Gielgud, in a frock-coat, beard, very Chekhovian, much grey in his hair. His room was populated with actorish things and the oddments of his health regime – much honey in sight, Veno's honey-and-lemon cough mixture, Gale's honey, Visine eye drops, his gold Gucci watch on the dresser. When he wasn't working he wore sneakers and told me this was all part of his current stay-well routine. That morning he had run three miles, along the Embankment. The previous Monday, he said, he did seven. Ran down Cheyne Row, up the Strand, along the Embankment, past Big Ben, over Westminster Bridge, up to Waterloo, over the bridge, back along the Strand – all this at 5 a.m. His wife said he was mad.

As Hopkins excused himself, moving on and off the set, Crawley perceived the tensions of ongoing disputes with the director but a general air of control. 'A kindly-looking man,' Crawley recorded in his notebook. But, memorably, one 'hypnotised by the business of acting'. Lynch might have other ideas, but Hopkins saw Dr Treves clearly:

It's a fascinating piece, one of the best experiences I've ever had and one in which I have learnt a lot about myself. I've found out how to be as simple as possible. Just actually speak the lines. Play the situation as simply and honestly as one can and get the balance right. It would be so easy to run riot in this role, churning out false emotion. Treves, for example, cares about the Elephant Man and is a victim at times. He takes him home and gives him comforts.

Now, the temptation is to play a caring man all through the film. But it's not like that. I think there are moments when he actually hates the Elephant Man. I had a discussion with the director the other day and almost entered into an argument about taking everything so literally. [He suggested] that because I care about the Elephant Man I must give soft-eyed warm acting all the time. But I remember when we were doing the BBC *War and Peace*, the scene where the old peasant Platon Karatayev is dying on the retreat from Moscow. I went back to Tolstoy and he describes Pierre's reaction as disgust and anger because the old man is dying. Pierre is pushing the cart and hears the dog's howl echoing out – and then Platon is dead. When you read it, you want to cry. He wrote how all that Pierre could think of was how many miles to the next town and how he wished the dog would stop howling. And I think there will be moments like that in *The Elephant Man*. What I'm trying to do is to gradually bring all this into Treves without making him too complex just for the sake of it. One can quickly fall into generalising and all Stanislavsky ever said was: Avoid generalising.

Though he hadn't researched much, he said, he had (unlike John Hurt) read Treves' book. But he was going cold on the idea of too much research: 'Because it can weigh you down.' Instead, the concentration was on putting 'reality' on to celluloid.

Bogart actually said, 'Acting is experience and something sweet behind the eyes.' In *The Elephant Man*, the plot is so simple that you can't do much with it. Treves takes on the Elephant Man, puts him in a hospital, experiences some opposition and that's simply it. So you find the situation and respond with the inner voice, instinct. For example, talking broadly, if there's a situation where a man suddenly comes in here and shoots up the entire bar with a machine-gun and kills the barman, I don't have to act horror. Put that scene on film and I don't have to do anything. I can sit here and do . . . nothing. The audience does the rest. Take a scene we've been doing today, a short scene, but a dramatic turning point. They've found Merrick [who has been missing from the hospital, forced into a freak show], and a problem is resolved. There's a big close-up reaction shot of me sitting at a desk, reading. And somebody comes in and says, 'It's all right, they have found him.' Blank face. If somebody comes through that door and says, 'The Ayatollah has bombed New York,' and the reaction is [raving] *What!!!* – it's bad acting. The computer works faster than any brain. The brain takes time. But, the trouble is, a director always wants you to show more. They always want you to act. But it's wrong. Once you show them more, it's bad acting.

As Hopkins dissected 'the approach', Crawley reminded him of a previous long interview, during *When Eight Bells Toll*, and asked the actor to comment on the distance he had travelled personally and artistically.

> I think what happened was I saw *Eight Bells* and saw it was a good film, but I had contempt for it. Because I wanted to be a – quote – more serious actor. But now ten years have passed and maybe I feel more secure because more work has come along. I think it was John Dexter who said to me: 'Get on with it.' He is a very savage director, but that was one of his things: just get on with it. I don't really take any notice of directors now. Actors are in charge of what they do all along, and I think that is how it should be. I have given up on the 'yes' trap. I don't like being a nice person any more. I used to be so keen on approval that I would do anything to avoid confrontation. But now I don't care so much. I still don't feel that comfortable or secure, but now I say: 'I don't agree.' But a few years ago, after *Eight Bells* and the National experience, I was afraid to say it. What I'd do then was make the mistake of accumulating all my resentment and then I'd explode. And that is very confusing and dishonest. I did it last year in *Kean*. That was a big lesson. Now I don't do it.'

When Crawley asked about booze Hopkins was equally conclusive: it was the past.

> I'm married, happily married, and I think I'm through my particular crisis. I went through a bad time, a bumpy time. I always wanted to be like the bunch at the Royal Court. The Angry Brigade. The Grim Lot. I thought the only way to succeed was to be grim and angry and to punch people in pubs and get drunk. But a lot of those people are dead or unemployable. I say that with humility and gratitude because I found that it is not necessary to be like that. I'm very square and I live a quiet life.

Though Crawley found Hopkins 'putting up a good show of being a very changed, tamed character', the riddles of confusion remained. Though he pledged serenity he was in fact in continuing turmoil and Peta Barker, who by now was back in casual (usually phone) contact with him, attests to his continuing, obsessive desire to win over English theatre. According to Barker, she urged him to return to the National to 'win a knighthood', and shortly afterwards he did come back, to do *The Lonely Road*, *Pravda* and *King Lear*. Disappointingly for Hopkins, however, he was – initially, anyway – awarded only a CBE in the Queen's Birthday Honours List: Barker says they always joked about 'a knighthood, nothing less'.

Despite the brave face extended to Crawley and the media in general, as *The Elephant Man* concluded, Hopkins was already on the slide, heading for what he later called 'another black hour that lasted half a year'. To his delight – by whatever dominance or compromise – Lynch's final assembly of *The Elephant Man*, exquisitely rhythmed, evocatively shot by Freddie Francis, hauntingly scored by John Morris, displayed his greatest movie performance to date. Universally admired – it won eight Oscar nominations (though not one for Hopkins), three British Academy Awards (for Hurt, for Best Film and for Best Design) and numerous minor citations round the world – the film elevated Hopkins' standing in the eyes of the top-notch critics. Pauline Kael had never much liked Hopkins, finding him, as almost all negative reviewers did, mannered and twitchy. In one review she wrote, 'Hopkins never dazzles you, he dazzles himself.' But here was forgiveness: 'John Hurt and Anthony Hopkins – both specialists in masochism – might have leaked so much emotion that the film would slip its sprocket. But Hopkins comes through with an unexpectedly crisp, highly varied performance – the kind you respect an actor for.'

Before this invitation to euphoria, though, Hopkins' impatience to 'get on with it' had him pushing for and accepting pat a series of highly paid but somewhat less than sustaining American TV roles. From John Gielgud he seemed to have poached a survival philosophy:

Gielgud is 75 and I think he's getting younger. I want to be around as long as him. He said to me: 'I'm going to Budapest to do a film. I don't know what the part is but they tell me it's awfully good.' He does it for the money and because it takes him all over the world – and yet he still commands respect as one of the world's great English-speaking actors. I think he decided at a point, ten or twelve years ago, to move with the times. This means he is not always caring about the quality of speech, and I think that's good. It's like somebody asked me, at the University of Oregon when I was doing the publicity tour: why did I do *Magic*? I said: 'To pay the rent.' Now I have such a full year ahead, and I'm so pleased with it. I know that the scripts aren't *King Lear*, but they're all right – and I'll have a lot of fun.

The fire in him, though, wouldn't settle. To friends he spoke of gems in the offing: David Lean had called him and asked him to play Captain Bligh in a double-feature based on the true story of the Bounty mutineers; before that might be a D. H. Lawrence adaptation, *Priest of Love* – 'to be done in the summer with Liv Ullmann'; after that a film with 'my idol' Bette Davis. None of these immediately ensued (though *Priest of Love* was made, starring Ian McKellen) and instead came the dross of *A Change of Seasons*, a rickety Bo Derek vehicle for Columbia, and a bunch of TV mini-series that took him, among other places, to Paris, Maine, Athens and Rhodes.

'The bard is ever present,' was Hopkins' hopeful but somehow hollow parting shot to Tony Crawley on the set of *The Elephant Man*. In reality, the bard was out of view. His dreamt-of *Hamlet* was past the sell-by date; he had failed with *The Tempest*; Doolittle wanted a theatrical partnership – but not with Shakespeare projects; the National, and London, seemed more a coven of enmity than ever before. Hopkins told Minty Clinch of *Photoplay*,

Shortly after I was 42 I became ridiculously self-important, questioning endlessly who and what I was, making myself more miserable and confused by the minute. I became a recluse. I kidded myself that I was a loner and that life was more interesting that way. I said no to every invitation to dinner and when people came to dinner I'd want to go to bed the moment the meal was over. I expected my guests to do the same. If they didn't, I switched off the lights and would go upstairs without a word – leaving them, and my wife, seated in the dark. I don't know how she put up with me.

This well-parcelled remorse – snugly recapped during 1986 in a dawning era of genuine stability – skirts the near-disaster of the early eighties. In truth, Hopkins was more deeply frustrated than ever. The absence of drink left what he described to one friend as 'a gaping hole in my being'. He told her, 'Without it I see things clearer, but what I see leaves me in more doubt than ever about myself. I feel physically fitter – the demands of Hollywood romantic lead-playing make me keep on top of that – but my spirit is weak.' Unfailingly, he attended his AA meetings, but it distressed him that Jenni would not participate in the family-support group meetings. The friend says, 'Jenni believed that it was unnecessary. She herself is quite shy and not a great mixer and, on the other hand, she saw this great progress that Tony was making, alone and with the help of Bob [Palmer] and Julian [Fellowes] . . . but Tony resented her absence and it came between them.'

The legacy of domestic tension came on to the film set. A *Change of Seasons* had started life as *Consenting Adults*, under the direction of Noel Black for Martin Ransohoff Productions. Hopkins had in fact committed to it before *The Elephant Man*, but the project was shaky even then. Based on a screenplay by Ransohoff and *Love Story* author Erich Segal, the film had no distributor in place and spent six months staggering through a variety of rewrites before finally being given the go-ahead with $6 million raised by Ransohoff from the Guinness Film Group, early in 1980.

Slated for shooting at Dartmouth College in New Hampshire and co-starring Shirley MacLaine, the film lurched, and fell. Within weeks of the start of shooting, Black was fired, according to rumour at the behest of Bo Derek and her husband-manager John (who later denied this). Richard Lang took over and quickly found his hands full attempting to keep afloat the egos of MacLaine and Derek. Derek had just made her popular breakthrough with Blake Edwards' *10* and seemed, said crew members, determined to wrestle control of the production for herself. This complemented the problems with MacLaine, who had just wrapped on a very similar 'consenting adults' picture called *Loving Couples* with James Coburn. She perceived the film as 'hers' and was clearly – and vocally – no admirer of Hopkins. Early on MacLaine complained about Hopkins' speech, claiming that he spoke too slowly. Later she was ruder. Hopkins called his friend Renée Valente, who had produced *Loving Couples*, and asked, 'Is it her or is it me?' When Valente told him, 'Shirley needs a lot of love,' Hopkins raged, 'Don't tell me she needs a lot of love! *I* need a lot of love! Don't tell me she's insecure! I'm terrified!'

From there it was downhill. That same morning, in the critical bedroom scene, MacLaine boldly challenged a smarting Hopkins: 'Is this as good as it gets? Don't you know about timing?'

Hopkins shouted back, 'If you think I'm going to be paralysed by my respect for you then you've got another think coming. If you want Dick Van Dyke or Jerry Lewis or Jack Lemmon, then be my guest. Just get off my back. If you don't want me, get me fired. I don't give a shit.'

As Lang played peacemaker the film managed to wrap – overtime, overbudget and, grievously, overbaked. Though Hopkins had, as pledged, started avoiding reviews, he was not surprised to hear the roar of unanimous derision. David Denby, much respected, pressed the nerve, calling Hopkins' work 'the worst performance by a major actor since Richard Burton roared his way through *Bluebeard*. Hopkins' way of playing an adulterous intellectual is to fiddle with his glasses and to hem and haw and clear his throat, thereby stretching every banal line of dialogue out to twice its length.'

After it, without vacation or post-mortem, came *The Bunker*, a mini-series for producer David Susskind and director George Schaefer, who had previously given him a few weeks' work on a very low-key CBS tele-film, *Mayflower*, shot in Maryland in the run up to *The Elephant Man*. *The Bunker* was a three-hour co-production by CBS, Time-Life Films and the Société Française de Production, funded by the French government. Based on the straightahead account of Hitler's last days written by John O'Donnell, an American army officer who had visited the

Führer's bunker in July 1945, the film offered the distraction of ten weeks in Paris and the opportunity to repay Fellowes' personal support by swinging him on to the cast. Though it came with the highest pedigree – Hitler's surviving armaments minister Albert Speer, with twenty years' incarceration in Spandau behind him, contributed to the production design and authenticity by supplying personal photographs of the Chancellery building and his own (unpaid) notes – Hopkins was sceptical of it and 'the Madame Tussaud effect of this kind of historical film'. Added to that was the fact, not escaping his notice, that Alec Guinness had recently portrayed – definitively, some felt – the defeated Hitler in an exact replica version called *Hitler: The Last Ten Days*, endorsed by the acknowledged Hitler expert Professor Hugh Trevor-Roper and directed by Ennio de Concini.

Biting the bullet, Hopkins dutifully worked his stint at the SFP Studios in Joinville, a suburb of Paris, and filled his evenings by getting into character at a German restaurant called Au Vieux Berlin where he consumed endless plates of Wiener schnitzel 'because', says co-star Martin Jarvis, 'he chose to live, eat and drink Hitler's Germany'.

The $4-million production, when finally aired, was creakily impressive and, in its final sequences in which the broken Hitler rants, subsides and concedes defeat, memorable for Hopkins' unrestrained hysteria, a 'madness' that shocked even George Schaefer. In due course, Hopkins was nominated for, and won, an Emmy for this performance – his second Emmy in five years. For another actor these Emmys – the TV equivalent of the Oscars – might have been the salve, the cure-all. But Hopkins didn't see it that way. 'I suspect,' says David Cunliffe, 'that the greatest plaudits from TV would not have been enough for him then. He had stated his case: he wanted to outdo Burton and he wanted the movies. The mania didn't at all surprise me. Until he found that Hollywood niche, he would never be happy.'

The third in line in this exhausting treadmill of TV projects was MCA's *Peter and Paul*, directed by Robert Day and co-starring Robert Foxworth, which chronicled the Apostles' crusade of faith from the Crucifixion to their deaths three decades later. Shot mostly in sunny Athens, and well paid as it was, this mini-series only served to remind Hopkins of his rapid progress to nowhere in particular. During it he befriended the veteran Herbert Lom, an actor whose humour and erudition he much admired, and though he seemed at ease, the underlying boredom did not pass unnoticed.

The success of *The Elephant Man*, premiered worldwide in November 1980 and showered with praise, brought him renewed attention in the UK. The results seemed immediate. Before the print ink of the approving reviews was dry, a new BBC offer was on the table, from Jonathan Miller and producer Cedric Messina, to star in Miller's *Othello*, which would be part of a BBC summer 'Bardathon'. Hopkins accepted with alacrity – with relief, perhaps – for this was surely a chance to reapproach 'the system' and do it right, to once and for all lay the ghosts. 'I think *Othello* probably became a target,' says James Cellan Jones, 'because he had been fooling around with it since his pre-National days and he'd undoubtedly perfected an aspect of it in our *Kean*. It was probably the central challenge of his Shakespeare and he was, age-wise and in every way, perfect for it just then.'

As soon as *Peter and Paul* concluded in the Painted Desert of California, Hopkins headed to Wales, to spend some family days, exhausted. Apart from the quick-change jobbing in TV there was, now, continually on his mind, the state of Dick's health. A year before, during a Christmas break while shooting *The Elephant Man*, he had journeyed to Wales with Jenni in the hope of a week's recapping and indolence. While he was there his father had suffered a mild heart attack. Now, in January 1981, it was clear that Dick's health had drastically declined. Hopkins had been constantly in touch with Muriel throughout the shooting of *The Bunker* and *Peter and Paul*, but her cautious information had not prepared him for this. As he knuckled down to learning *Othello*, Hopkins found it hard to concentrate. Dick was still mobile, still fond of the long walk – but it was now a breathless saunter and not the brisk constitutional of old. Hopkins might have imagined what was to come, but he cannot have imagined it so soon.

In March, while rehearsals for *Othello* commenced in London, Dick was admitted to St Woolos Hospital in Newport. Hopkins kept a brave face but walked out on the preproduction when he heard that Dick had slipped into a coma. He journeyed back to Wales with Jenni, to be told by Dick's consultant, Dr Jones, that the end was near. Hopkins took Muriel home to the new house in Newport to which they had recently moved. In the early hours of that morning, 15 March, the call came that Dick was slipping away. By the time Muriel and her son reached the hospital, Dick Hopkins was dead.

His father's death turned Hopkins in on himself and, though he continued to prepare *Othello*, he admitted later that 'Miller had problems with me. I couldn't concentrate. It's not so unusual. It would be hard for anyone in that situation.' If Miller, or anyone else, wished to offer their condolences or comfort, Hopkins had a stock response: silence. He drew up the drawbridge, refused to talk about it.

Instead he went home with Muriel and pulled the lounge curtains and walked back into the murk of the past.

He did his *Othello*, and then went back to LA to study the sunset and think. His first major decision was to leave Jenni.

Chapter 13

SURRENDER AND WIN

Here was the fusion of truth, triumph and disaster, the two imposters served on the same plate. *The Elephant Man*, at last a film of unqualified international acclaim; *Othello*, at last the retention of balance in Shakespeare; and the death of Dick. Tired as he was from three years of tail-chasing, it flattened him. Pam Miles, who knew better than most the power of Muriel, speaks with surprise about the reflective Hopkins of later years: 'When I see him on TV, when I read the interviews, it is always Dick he relates to, not Muriel. He adores her, but it is always Dick and Dick's life he muses about.' But that wasn't so surprising. It was Dick who offered the telescope to the world, Dick who told him about London, about Russia, who showed him the constellations in the sky and the traces of German bombers. It was Dick whose blind work ethos he followed, whose mystery became his. 'I never really knew him,' he told a woman friend. 'He worked so hard, there never seemed to be enough time.' Dick's passing, too soon, was the passing of a torch, a generational shift of responsibility and expected maturity, a crossing point.

Othello was apt, so mystically apt perhaps that its coincidence unbalanced his tired moment. Approaching Miller cautiously this time, Hopkins found the expected innovation. Miller's first thought, he later wrote, was that this *Othello* could be resited to Cyprus, during the EOKA unrest of 1954. Othello might be a Sandhurst-trained Indian officer, Iago an army sergeant. But the vision shifted. Miller selected instead a figure based on King Hussein of Jordan – 'a Hashemite warrior, drilled in British Army manners, who married a white woman'.

The casting of Hopkins proved controversial on racial grounds. British Actors' Equity had protested the original casting of the black American James Earl Jones then, ironically, complained about Hopkins. Miller pressed on, casting Bob Hoskins as a rabid Cockney Iago and mining an extraordinarily fresh relationship in a curious Elizabethan-dressed Jacobean mould. Tony Crawley summarised:

> A very Welsh Othello [by Hopkins], no accent other than his own, hardly any make-up either, which made various text references odd – not to mention his bright blue eyes. Best, as usual, in the quiet passages, and he made more of them quieter than most Othellos would. When being loud, he sounded much like Olivier, though minus the accent; instead just the inflection, and the height and the breadth. Penelope Wilton, his Desdemona, badly cast, looking at times like Joyce Grenfell. Bob Hoskins superb . . . No reason, of course, for Hopkins to sound African, as the Venetians don't sound particularly Italian. But odd costuming . . .

On its American showing, the *Los Angeles Times* critic Cecil Smith was unequivocal: 'Hopkins, one of the most gifted actors of our age, is a brilliant Othello. It's the performance, not the make-up, that counts. He begins quietly, a precise, aloof, military professional. We watch his jealousy slowly rise like bile within him until it explodes in terrible rage.'

In April, home again in Newport to comfort Muriel and chew on another BBC offer – a tricky, sensitive one to play Alfred Allmers opposite Diana Rigg in Ibsen's *Little Eyolf* – Hopkins outwardly displayed placidity. When the *South Wales Evening Post* called to the 'comfortable, stylishly furnished semi', Hopkins sat in the velvet armchair beside the aspidistra, took tea from the onyx table on which Muriel laid the polite tray and refused to speak about Dick's passing. 'You see, my father was very full of life. It has hit my mother hard. He was a real character, and very restless. He had a huge lust for life . . . and I suppose that is where I get my wanderlust from.' Restless as he was to get back to America, he was proud of *Othello* and uncritical of his recent work. 'I had a tremendous sense of peace playing *Peter and Paul*. I could not have been happier. Actors are very lucky [but] luck is a question of choice in many ways.'

Bearded, thinner than recently, he was willing at last to discuss some intimacies of his domestic life, though it seemed less an opportunity for insight, more an awareness of the media demands of the moment and an urgency to get it over with. 'Although he has a natural relaxed manner,' wrote Alexis Patt, 'the constant pushing back of the hair gives away some nervousness and feelings of self-doubt.' Hopkins fidgeted with his shirt buttons and sketched his private life: Abigail lived in London with her mother and was 'turning out to be a first-rate classical guitarist'. He and Jenni were 'very happily married', but there would be no more children: 'You see, I am very single-minded about acting. I put all my concentration into it, and if we had a child, I wouldn't be able to. You could call us selfish. But we couldn't do our travelling and I couldn't do my acting and give it the commitment if we had a child.'

The Welsh may have wanted to speak of Wales but Hopkins, it seemed, had a truer home. As Muriel drifted through, silent, dutiful and resigned, Hopkins openly hungered for escape to LA. 'I'm looking forward to getting back to America – we've got a beautiful grand piano at home – but I haven't been back for seven months.'

By the accounts of those who saw it unfold, *Little Eyolf* and the dreaded face-to-face with Diana Rigg was an anti-climax unparalleled. 'I gritted my teeth in anticipation,' says Michael Darlow, the assigned BBC director who had come to the project – a play he long dreamt of directing – when a major feature film fell through in the planning stage, leaving a hole, and an opportunity, in his schedule. 'Jim Cellan Jones told me: "What! You're going to do this Ibsen, this most difficult and sensitive Ibsen, and cast Tony Hopkins with Di Rigg? That's insanity! He's a bastard to work with and Di and he just don't get along!"' Darlow held firm. 'Di had had a similar feature let-down and her agent had called to say she wanted a juicy role for the Beeb. But, to be honest, as soon as I selected Tony I didn't tell Jean Diamond [Rigg's agent] that we were *negotiating* Tony. I said, "We have him." Past tense. Deal done. Delivered. So, no room for any backing out.'

Darlow lunched with Hopkins, expecting a live wire, but found instead a subdued, sombre, reflective man, very ready to talk about the loss of his father.

> It obviously hit him hard and the effects were there. In a curious way it helped *Little Eyolf*, which is a play about the loss of a child, an intense and fragile play. Tony and I discussed death in the context of the loss of his parent, the way bereavement wounds. He was wounded, and struggling to get upright. It helped. It helped also that Di had little children whose welfare was her obsession and indeed I had just fostered a very difficult boy. All that came together to create the proper workable background.

At rehearsals in the Acton Hilton, Darlow witnessed first-hand what he called a mighty gulf: 'They didn't talk to each other – ever, at all. It was bizarre. For two weeks they played the most intimate and emotional scenes without ever saying one word beyond that fucking Ibsen text. Not a word. At one stage my script girl came up and said, "Eh, have you noticed that they don't, eh, seem to want to know each other?" Now, of course I knew about *Macbeth* and then Jim's experience on the disastrous *Kean* – but I just kept the peace.'

Only once, says Darlow, did Hopkins blow.

> And that wasn't a direct offshoot of the stand-off with Di. In that case we were tackling that very tough start of the third act. Very delicate. It was the third week and I thought, hell, let's give it a try. I asked Di and Tony and they said OK and they did try but it wasn't right. I said, 'Christ, that was crap!' and Di agreed but Tony stormed off to the loo. I was bursting to go to the toilet myself, so off I went, only to be attacked by Tony the minute I entered. He was in there, pacing like a polecat, insane with

anger at being criticised in front of Di. He said: 'Don't ever fucking insult me like that again! Don't fucking dare!' . . . And I, of course, did my director's thing and said, 'All right, let's just calm down. I'm sorry. It was a tough piece, it couldn't have worked first time.' Which was true. He cooled off, that was it.

In the last week of rehearsals, Hopkins suddenly changed. 'It wasn't only Tony. The air changed. Suddenly, for their own deeply hidden reasons, Di and he were at ease with each other. The wound had healed. To be honest, it had been fraught till then. Di works in a completely different way to Tony. She takes chunks of text and has a mad dash at it. Tony is the opposite. He takes a phrase or two, a small section, and fiddles away till it is exact. So the odds were wildly against. But it worked. The tension passed. They neither of them said one word to me about the previous row. I don't believe they said a word between themselves. Instead, they took the bull by the horns – or destiny did it for them - and ironed it out by dint of sheer acting competence and professionalism. The play was then taped – with a splendid cast including Peggy Ashcroft and Charlie Dance – in four days.'

The resolution of the tension with Rigg contributed to Hopkins' developing peace of mind in Britain. Says Peter Gill: 'Tony blew it (the row) up in his own mind. Di was never so bad to him and, anyway, in my view she was an irregular temperament too. It was, I've no doubt, an accumulation of the paranoia inside Tony – the steam kettle principle – and then, perhaps, the steam went elsewhere, so the heat came out of it with Di. I don't believe it was personal. It was competitive. Because this was Tony's drive: to outdo everyone else at any cost.'

Itching as he was to go back to Clearwater and contemplate the tumultuous events of the last half-year, he took another fast job, highly paid and stimulating enough, playing Quasimodo in CBS's tele-film of *The Hunchback of Notre Dame*, adapted by America's best TV writer, John Gay. The inducement apart from money, was the accessibility (the film was shooting at Pinewood Studios, an hour out of London), plus the chance to reprise Charles Laughton's celebrated classic, which he was prepared to cadge from. 'Laughton's work was magical,' he said. 'I would be a fool, and a bad actor, not to have learnt from it. I took sections of it and adapted it for myself, for my portrayal. The make-up at that time was primitive, but I took the posture, the gestures of hiding the face. But I gave to it, I hope, something new, maybe slightly more pathetic.'

The Hunchback of Notre Dame, not much changed from Victor Hugo's (or Laughton's) blueprint, ultimately paid off. *Variety* called it 'a humdinger', and gave copious credit to designer John Stoll (whose recreation of Paris and the fifteenth-century cathedral on the Pinewood back-lot was genuinely dazzling), and to Lesley-Anne Down as Esmerelda, John Gielgud, Derek Jacobi and Tim Piggott-Smith, who played the archdeacon's assistant. For Hopkins there was a note of special merit: 'What might have been given an operatic treatment has been handled with style and imagination and Anthony Hopkins as the tormented Quasimodo establishes his own characterization. Hopkins . . . delivers the goods.'

Arguments apart, the days in London, on the heels of Newport, left mixed feelings. Among the cast of *Hunchback* were the 'system' players Jacobi and Piggott-Smith – one who carried memories of bleaker, immature days at the National, the other, Piggott-Smith, now married to Pamela Miles, Hopkins' teenage sweetheart. Though the opportunity was there, Pam avoided contact at the studios. 'Not consciously, but there seemed not much point to it. I had long gotten over the relationship and the separation. We were children then! What did we know about love, or about ourselves? I had my son [who was then seven] with Tim, so everything had moved on.'

But Hopkins hadn't. Stuck in the groove of depression – a dejection which some believed stretched back to the humiliation of *Kean* – Hopkins slunk back to LA and, in Judith Searle's words, 'got down to some serious contemplation of his navel'.

This year in Britain had challenged every facet of his being: his mental discipline and resilience, his dignity in triumph, his fortitude in tragedy, his feelings for his family, his continuing monomania. What pleased him was his tenacity; to outpace the gremlin of 'the system', to stand firm by

Muriel when she most needed him, and all in spite of his tiredness and distraction. What rankled – anew – was the meaning of it all. The *why?* When he spoke to reporters, or saw himself in the press, he cringed. What were those craven words that came back to him? Who was the soul who spoke them? And how did he measure up – to courageous, never-give-in Dick, who built his family, and his castle, and worked his fingers to the bone to hold it all together? Whose life had more value? His or Dick's?

On a Sunday afternoon, while visiting actress Lynn Redgrave and her husband John Clark at their house in Topanga Canyon, Hopkins was suddenly struck with the notion of acquiring a hideaway property north of LA, a bolthole safer and more secure than his shuttered bedroom in Clearwater. Jenni tried to dodge the idea, but it took hold. The very next day, Julian Fellowes accompanied Hopkins on a round trip of Topanga estate agents and immediately a property was found – a three-level wooden cabin, crudely appointed but with good views across the Canyon towards the far beaches. Hopkins made the acquisition, then fell silent.

A few weeks later, out of the blue, he announced to Jenni that he wanted to 'take off for a long drive somewhere'. He didn't know how long he would be gone and he didn't know where he might stay. Jenni suggested the obvious, the new 'Easy Rider cabin', and Hopkins packed his Caddie with essentials like food, towels, sheets and toiletries and headed north. 'I went for a drive to think about my life,' he told the *Guardian*, 'and I didn't come back for two months.' After the initial absence of several days Hopkins called Jenni and told her he didn't think he wanted to be married any more. Jenni's reaction was calm: if that was what he wanted, then so be it. Later, she told Quentin Falk, she reasoned out that he 'needed space', that there was nothing to be gained by pushing him. When she questioned him on the phone, he said he was keeping fit, jogging, reading, thinking, walking, listening to country and western music and 'getting myself in order'.

Hopkins later explained this period of 'insanity' to writer Victor Davis: 'I nailed myself into a fortress. I would not answer the phone or talk to people. It was weird and silly and in that isolation I started going off my head. It wasn't self-dramatisation. It was just that, when I was not working I didn't know what else to do.'

It was, of course, more. The great liberation of AA was not as sweet as he often depicted it. The insecurity lingered – subsumed at times, it is true, in the creation of 'pure' characters like Corky Withers – but reverberating nonetheless. The discovery of God in Westwood was vibrant but not constant: to Richard Brooks in the *Observer* he would say, 'I'm not a religious person, nor am I an atheist.' And so, with Dick's demise and the reminder of mortality, the quest became urgent. The reading intensified – not for pleasure, or text, or information, but for answers. F. Scott Fitzgerald's *The Great Gatsby* became a fixation: perhaps he was enamoured of the likeness, however oblique, between himself and Jimmy Gatz, the lowly son who repaints himself as Gatsby, the lonely grandee who pays for parties he never attends and shirts he never wears; but in conversation (with friends, and later journalists like Edward Vulliamy and Roger Lewis) he contained himself to the obvious. 'What do you make of the green light pulsating at the end of Gatsby's pier? asked Lewis. 'Calling us home,' replied Hopkins and then, caressingly, with resignation: 'Gatsby believed in the green light, the . . . future that year by year recedes before us. It eluded us then, but that's no matter – tomorrow we will run faster, stretch out our arms further . . . And one fine morning . . . So we beat on, boats against the current, borne ceaselessly back into the past.'

These offered conclusions were weeks, months, away. Now, solo, he pushed through the refuge of his library, through Freud, Jung and Gurdjieff. The latter, an Armenian mystic who espoused a uniquely brutal Buddhism, proved promising. During the 1920s, while living in Tibet, he had devised his great theory: quite simply, mortal man was asleep and acted mechanically according to patterns. These must be broken by vigorous mental and physical exercises: then Man may awaken.

Before Gurdjieff had taken a grip, the theory of *Gestalt* took over. This was the notion of the 'organised whole', developed as an emotional therapy method by Fritz and Laura Peris and popularised in the hippie culture of the Cailifornian sixties. *Gestalt* advocates 'thinking in opposites', rather than pursuing cause and effect, and resolves on the basic existentialist idea of every individual assuming personal responsibility, and living in the present moment.

Conventional Zen Buddhism appeared to win the day and Hopkins applied himself to Buddhist tracts as he did to play texts – learning, repeating, enacting. His performances were mostly soliloquies but from the analytical isolation came the spin twist that would have him shortly telling Edward Vulliamy: 'I've learnt to accept responsibility for everything I do. If you don't accept responsibility for your actions you might as well be dead. There is no justice. If there was, then I should be dead by now. There is just luck . . . and I was one of the lucky ones. We are all just chicken-shit. That is the basis of *Gestalt*. You have to say to yourself each day: *You are nothing, and you are free*. If I am not around tomorrow, of what consequence would that be? It wouldn't be of any consequence at all. I think Bertrand Russell said something like that. When I read that I thought: *That's the answer*. I'd like to hang around, of course, but basically it is of no consequence.'

The fatalism – a blunt, unspiritual reality compounded from the conclusions of great philosophies – finally opened the door for him. A casual friend called Chuck Chamberlain, one quarter Sioux Indian and a retired businessman, took credit for the twist beyond Zen Buddhism. Hopkins later lovingly described Chamberlain, now dead, as 'an old guru to me in my California days'. Other friends frowned and debated and offered the painstaking care of conversational psychoanalysis. But Chamberlain 'simply told me to give up fighting everything and everybody. It took me a long time to take that step forward – but I did.'

After many weeks of his absence, Jenni began to imagine a life without him. It upset her and forced her to re-evaluate their lopsided relationship. Undeniably, he had ruled the roost, dominated, driven their lives. To the eyes of objective outsiders, Jenni's function in the marriage was an elaborate extension of her very efficient and loyal work as a Pinewood PA. She organised Hopkins' life, tidied his schedules, made travel arrangements, photocopied scripts, waited up all hours to hear the confessions of a day at the studios. Simon Ward says, 'She was massively selfless. The root of it was probably her capability as a film production assistant – all that skill at backup support. But, it must be said, she loved him very, very deeply and had more patience for him than anyone.' Alan Dobie believed that 'her very ordinariness' was the power that held Hopkins. 'That and real, down-to-earth strength of character.'

Trouble arose, though, when that very strength rebelled against Hopkins' insistent irrationality. But now, with the marriage obviously waning, she rushed to do what had to be done in an expression of undiminished love. Committed to a future with him at any cost, Jenni immediately joined the local family help group and, on the phone to Topanga, told Hopkins of her progress and pleasure in the early meetings. This wasn't exaggeration: it was honest effort and honest joy. Hopkins hardly commented, but asked her out to dinner in Beverly Hills. A fortnight later, without recriminations or promises, he asked: 'Would you mind if I moved back to Clearwater Drive?'

Jenni had no hesitation. 'Of course not. It's your home.'

Hopkins would remember Chuck Chamberlain's motto: Surrender and Win.

The Bounty was the reward.

More than five years in the brew, contorted from a $17-million double-film, provisionally entitled *The Lawbreakers* and *The Long Arm*, via a seventeen-hour mini-series for TV to – finally – a simpler, manageable remake of the original *Mutiny on the Bounty* films (1935 and 1962) with the accent on Bligh's persona, this was the clearest evidence of a spurt in growth, a comprehensive understanding of film and, at last, a general personal aura of *bien dans ma peau*.

David Lean was no longer involved, which was disappointing, but it was luck that the film came to be made at all. Lean had started prepping it in French Polynesia early in 1977, where he had gone to research a possible project about Captain Cook. Cook had seemed banal, however, compared with the Captain Bligh in Richard Hough's controversial history rewrite *Captain Bligh and Mr Christian* that Lean read en route. Lean diverted, made a deal with Warner Brothers and commissioned Robert Bolt, his favourite screenwriter, to prepare a massive double-script, following Bligh's background through to the pursuit of the mutineers on Pitcairn Island. Shortly afterwards, Hopkins was approached.

'I was home in Clearwater and I got a call from Katharine Hepburn. She said, "Listen, David Lean wants your phone number" . . . So she told me he was at the Bel Air Hotel and I went down there. He'd seen me in *International Velvet*, which was a real sort of loser . . . but when he saw it he said, "That's the Bligh I want." He said it would all work out, that he was going to Tahiti and would see me soon.'

Hopkins never saw Lean again. At Christmas that year, he received a phone call from his agent saying the double-film was off. The project was so big it was proving unfundable and might never happen. In April 1979, Robert Bolt suffered a major stroke. By now, Lean was in partnership with Paramount – and the budget had risen to $40 million, not for two but *one* compacted film. With Bolt ill and Dino De Laurentiis (the production broker for Paramount) edgy, Lean backed off. Confusion followed, uncomfortably colliding with the crisis in Hopkins' private life. 'It all went wrong, I'm not sure how. I think David wanted more time, but it was costing too much for the studio. So they went for a new script, but the second time around he was less enchanted.' The muddle irritated him, distracted him from his own inner voyage. 'I had dinner with [the new producer] Bernie Williams and the second director, Alan Bridges. From that point I disengaged from it. I didn't even read the second script. I didn't want to waste my time on it until they made up their minds. Bernie Williams then rang me and said, "OK, we're not doing the television thing, we're going to do it as one feature," and I said, "Let me know if it happens. But I've got other things I want to do, so don't mess me about."'

Two years later, his new English agent, Jeremy Conway, phoned and told Hopkins he had the part, the film the green-light. 'I didn't believe it. I was puzzled and flattered. I'm no Robert Redford. But [the agent] said, "You've got it." I said, "I'll believe it when I'm standing on the set in costume."'

Hopkins was still unsure of Paramount's commitment, unsure who his director was, unsure of his co-stars, when he flew to Heathrow, to be collected at the airport by an assistant director. 'I asked this guy, "Are they really going to do this film?" And he said, yes. I did costume fittings and then he drove me out to Lee International Studios and there they were, building *The Bounty* sets. I said it again, "Yes, but we have no Fletcher Christian."' Hopkins was invited to dine with De Laurentiis that evening and found at his table Roger Donaldson, a 37-year-old Australian director whose big hit was the 1977 New Zealand thriller *Sleeping Dogs*, and the teen favourite *Mad Max* actor Mel Gibson, another Australian. De Laurentiis stood up and announced, 'Tony, meet Fletcher Christian.' Hopkins' immediate response, he said, was the abrupt mental note of: 'Well, that's all right, we're ready to go.'

The great stimulus for Hopkins on *The Bounty* was Bolt's reinstated, truncated screenplay with its depth of enquiry into Lieutenant William Bligh. Bolt's portrait, based on Hough's, was of Bligh as a rigid disciplinarian who lacked humour but was more misfit than thug. Previous film interpretations – by Charles Laughton especially, but also Trevor Howard – had Bligh broadly as a bully; this interpretation had compassionate roots. It was, though, not fully formed on paper. This was tantalisingly exciting for Hopkins, the self-director, especially as Donaldson was, relatively, a tyro and newer to the project than he. Hopkins later said, 'I didn't know what David Lean wanted to do [with the character] but he's a very exacting director and he wants it done his way. I don't know how I would have got on with that. I hate being given a performance. But when I got the final script I thought: I'm going to make it *my* part. I'll give birth to it, my way.' Donaldson, at the start, was nothing other than supportive. Hopkins had the hunger and the energy. It was a savvy move to let him get on with it.

For wider research, Hopkins read two popular biographies of Bligh, one depicting a monster, the other a kindly, hard-working sailor. Then he met with Stephen Walters, the naval history expert assigned to the production. Hopkins said:

[He's a] very nice man, but eccentric, like all fanatics. He's a Bligh expert. We met at a restaurant in Soho, just before I started the film –

you know those intimate Italian restaurants where all the tables are hunched together. He was moving the salt cellars and pepper pots, describing the voyage. 'Now, here we are on the *Bounty* . . .' It was like [the astronomer] Patrick Moore! Any time anybody was leaving the restaurant they came over to say, 'Well, good luck with the film!'

Hopkins was stimulated, too, by the need to outdo Laughton, an actor he greatly admired and to whom he had often been likened. Peter Barkworth says, 'There are fascinating similarities between Hopkins and Laughton in the sensuality and the undertone of menace.' Hopkins saw this, and sidled away from it. But – as with the case of Burton – the similarities ran too close and rankled. Like Hopkins, Laughton was the son of reasonably well-to-do parents, hoteliers in Yorkshire. Like Hopkins, too, he was socially insecure and given, in his worst moments, to exaggerations of mannerisms and an unconscious self-parodying. Hopkins detested these off-the-cuff comparisons and the expectations they brought, and the questions they begged. His Bligh would not be close to Laughton's:

> I think you have to look at the overall view. I think what happened was that Bligh, having got his men round the Horn, then under Asia, through the Indian Ocean to Tahiti . . . he found the men were pretty desperate. All of their experience had been risk and now they were in Paradise. But they had a job to do and he made them do it. But his rigidity and his aloofness from the men undermined his authority. He was a great navigator, but I don't think he was a great captain, a good commander of men. He was a loner and an introvert. Had he been a little more accessible, he could probably have staved off the mutiny.

There was also the issue of Bligh's personal demons. 'People have read it that he was a homosexual [and that gave rise] to his problems with Christian. I don't think it was that at all. But he felt deeply betrayed. He gave this responsible position to Christian and Christian didn't take it. There are parallels. I worked at the National Theatre with a director who wanted to mould me in whatever way. He had this quirk in his nature. Well, if anyone is in that position, it's only common sense to rebel against it. Eventually, when I finally refused to work with [the director] again, he felt it was a total betrayal. And I think it was the same with Christian and Bligh.'

The remarkable insight into the ultimate rejection of John Dexter's Machiavellian enforcement and its mark on Hopkins arguably echoes the failed relationship with Peter Gill. By Gill's own admission he was 'manipulative' and 'the hungry one', while Hopkins was 'the kindly one'. Hopkins had resisted and fled, and had been fleeing for more than twenty years. In the case of Dexter, the manipulation had been coarser and partial – more a desire to bend his artistry than anything else, but nonetheless a bullying con. Now, in the serenity of facing up, with alcohol behind him and mortality in perspective and God in his place, Hopkins, perhaps for the first time, connected that bullying phobia that Roy Marsden and so many others spoke of with the rawest nerve of his teenage insecurity. Out of it, out of a full circle of self-investigation and understanding, came a definitive, deeply affecting Captain Bligh. Ronald Pickup admired the end result; Harold Innocent admired it; Raymond Edwards, David Scase, Robert Wise . . . All of them saw it as a milestone. 'Really,' says Judith Searle, 'there came a point when he was a different type of film actor.' That point, that dawning, was *The Bounty*.

As the sixteen-week shoot commenced, Hopkins did not debate Bligh with Donaldson. The principal cast members undertook some basic read-throughs – then it was down to shooting. On Stephen Walters' advice, Hopkins unilaterally opted for a soft, West Country accent and played it as he saw it. 'I think the danger is, for many actors, what I used to do at the National Theatre. You discuss your part with the director and as soon as the curtain goes up . . . you've discussed your part away. I used to do it until I decided that I was never going to discuss my part with a director again. Just do it. The thing is to just do it. It is instinct, and common sense.'

On *The Elephant Man*, Hopkins had said, 'I never want to lose my anger.' *The Bounty* showed that while his thinking was clearer, more mellow, he was still delighted to fight for what he judged right. Roger Donaldson – in the studios at Lee, then on location in Tahiti – obviously had his hands full. Hopkins moaned to journalist Stephen Farber: 'I think Roger Donaldson has a very unsentimental approach to things. He is very direct. He came ill-prepared. He was just thrown into the deep end with very little time to get the film ready.' According to Hopkins, Donaldson had told him: 'I'm not interested in your track record. I don't care if you have been in a play with Laurence Olivier. I am going to come down hard on you.' In response Hopkins offered, 'I want to tell you that I've worked with John Dexter and some right bastards in my life, so if you think you can come down hard on me, you can get another actor.'

At times, the steam looked like stopping the production. In Moorea, Hopkins kept himself to himself, staying reclusively at the Kiora Hotel and avoiding mixing with the other cast members. He got on with Daniel Day-Lewis, Philip Davis and Liam Neeson, but the relationships were confined to the working day. The rest of the time he read in his room. His main complaint about the production was Donaldson's constant reworking of scenes, which seemed to others just a quest for quality. Hopkins declared this 'endless filming' unnecessary and said that it offended his 'Welsh parsimony'. That was a fuse to a bomb. Days later came the big blow-up.

Bernard Williams remembers:

> They [Donaldson and Hopkins] weren't getting along and it seemed a matter of time before something dangerous happened. And it happened. It came to the shooting of the scenes where Bligh gets cast adrift from the *Bounty* and from then on the story is told in voiceover, from a series of log-book entries. It was then decided that this slowed the action down seriously, so a fresh approach was taken. We decided that Roger should write some new scenes and he locked himself away to do this. But Tony would have none of it. When he read the scenes he said, 'No way!' He would do Bolt's script – and nothing else. It became quite silly, really. And I was forced to put my foot down and warn him: 'Listen, you're asking for trouble. If Dino finds out this is going on he will use it as a

lever to cut back the whole damned production, and the budget. So stop
it or I'll close the whole thing down.'

An uneasy truce was reached and the production staggered on with
Hopkins endlessly moaning about the 'interminable schedule', but
generally behaving himself. For once, then, it appeared he had learnt the
knack of letting things lie. Nothing much else on the production
bothered him and while co-stars went down with stomach complaints
and fly-bites, he stayed well and active. 'I had no trouble with sea-
sickness or anything like that,' he said. 'I learnt very quickly, from the
sailor experts we had on *The Bounty*, that the problem arises when you
try to keep upright and straight as the ship moves to an angle. They said:
"Keep your eyes on the horizon." This I did and it worked a treat. For the
big storm sequence, the rounding of the Horn, I took some sea-sickness
tablets and I was fine. People were going down all around me, but I was
just great.'

As the film wrapped, De Laurentiis, Williams and Donaldson could
look back on a chequered chronicle – 'not all a bad experience,' Hopkins
agreed – that cost exactly $20 million. Orion, co-funders with a $10-
million investment, expressed themselves pleased with the footage and,
as the final assembly knitted, it was clear that a major film was in the can.
Donaldson and Williams continued fighting each other – a consequence
of Donaldson's interview in the *Auckland Times* in which he said he'd
made the film 'single-handedly' – but Hopkins was pleased to steer clear.
'I suppose,' he told *Photoplay*, 'I've developed a healthy indifference to it
all.' Elsewhere, he said the experience had been edifying: 'Because it
once and for all decided for me that there is no point fighting with a
director. The hysteria is unnecessary. There were times on *The Bounty*
when I ranted and roared [and then] I understood: no, it's a waste of time.
An actor can achieve as much – more – by just putting his foot down and
quietly saying No.' In *Photoplay*, he was emphatic about his altered
consciousness: 'I meditate and don't kill myself with neuroses any more.'

Frustratingly, on release in September 1984, *The Bounty* met with
lukewarm notices and uneven business worldwide. *Variety* called

Hopkins' performance 'sensational' and 'startlingly human' – as it truly was – but the *Monthly Film Bulletin* presaged the voice of an unadventurous audience when it carped, 'Gone is the strutting monster which, in Laughton's wake, is how Bligh is always seen. Gone too is Fletcher Christian as the romantic, Gauguinesque rebel. [Instead] it posits a Renoiresque world in which everyone has some kind of reason . . . Mel Gibson and Anthony Hopkins give excellent performances (the latter uncharacteristically restrained). But *The Bounty* [becomes] a sort of modest *2001*, without the stargate and the epilogue: a long voyage to nowhere.'

It was ironic that this daring, careful film – in which Hopkins was, for the first time, partnered with a genuinely hot youth-appeal Hollywood star, and in which he trailed new ground – was destined for relative failure. The double-irony was that *The Bounty* would mature into an undisputed classic, often referred to in the graph of Hopkins' growth as the cornerstone and, widely, as the best portrayal of William Bligh.

For now, for Hopkins, it was continued realignment and – breathtakingly – a recommitment to work. In the immediate aftermath of *The Bounty* would come a short return to the New York stage in Pinter's *Old Times* and, over the next sixteen months, no less than six major TV plays or mini-series both in America and London. *Old Times* was Kenneth Frankel's staging of the 1971 triangular drama of sexual jealousy, co-starring his *Audrey Rose* lead Marsha Mason. Hopkins was comfortable with it, and with himself – a comfort reflected in the good reviews and in the absence of argument during the seven-week run. What *Old Times* had working for it, perhaps, was the narrowness of cast (it is a three-hander) and the content – what *Time* magazine called 'gnomic meditation' on truth. In the play Hopkins is Deeley, a boorish anecdotalist married to Kate (Mason) who shuffles the truth – as does Kate and her visiting friend Anna (Jane Alexander) – in an effort to control the others. They all fail, and at the end of the evening are rendered in various stages of exhaustion or despair. Hopkins related to the dissection of deception and its emotional implications and perhaps saw in the play a metaphor for his own recently troubled past. During the run, when Marsha Mason chatted to him in his dressing room and asked his advice on helping an alcoholic friend, Hopkins was brutally honest. There were no soft options, instead: 'Let them go, let them hit rock bottom and pick themselves up. There's nothing else you can do. You cannot force someone to take help or enter the AA programme. They have to want it themselves.'

Old Times played to packed houses and endless praise. Clive Barnes saved the best for Hopkins: 'With his sudden mirthless Cheshire-cat grin, his combative bustling and windy aggressiveness, [he] gives a wonderfully devious impression of a man broken by his life and times.' Richard Schickel in *Time* applauded an 'austere revival' in which 'the three stars play Pinter's witty melodies and ironic rhythms with graceful professionalism. It encourages one to conjure with the work of postmodernism's most hypnotic theatrical voice.'

The dash of TV work was less substantial artistically but of vital importance in paving the imminent U-turn change that would, within eight years, win him an Oscar and a knighthood. Before *The Bounty* had come *A Married Man*, a six-hour adaptation of Piers Paul Read's melodramatic novel of sexual betrayal and murder, originally developed as a vehicle for Hopkins by his friend Julian Fellowes, and finally produced by London Weekend Television for the second independent network in Britain, Channel 4. This was pop fare, slickly scripted by Derek Marlowe and laced with sexual intrigue (Hopkins insisted on the removal of graphic sex scenes in which he, as the errant husband, beds his mistress, played by Lise Hilboldt). John Davies, the *War and Peace* director, served this time as a producer, Charles Jarrott directed, but the mini-series seemed to fall between all stools – not quite sure, not quite thriller, not quite memorable.

Next was Philip Hinchcliffe's production of C. P. Snow's *Strangers and Brothers*, scripted by BBC 'heavy' Julian Bond for the BBC network. Then a trio of very variable American pulp offerings – for CBS, HBO and ABC. *Arch of Triumph* was a wooden remake of a schmaltzy Charles Boyer romance, with Hopkins substituting for Boyer, and co-starring Lesley-Anne Down in place of the original Ingrid Bergman. The HBO-led co-production (with France's Attene 2 and Italy's RAI) of *Mussolini and I* then returned him to Bob Hoskins' side for a limp, long mini-series not much admired by either critics or audiences and justified only by his biggest TV fee to date – reputedly in excess of $400,000. Hot on its heels came the ABC mini-series of Jackie Collins' pneumatic tosh, *Hollywood Wives*, in which he played English director Neil Gray ($300,000 this time) who paddles through a grey miasma of filmland intrigue with aplomb only to yield to a heart attack incurred while screwing Suzanne Somers.

Discussing Hopkins' creative endeavours in these – or in CBS's *Guilty Conscience* to come – is a self-cancelling exercise well recognised by Hopkins himself. On *Arch of Triumph*, he said, he'd 'had a ball' and *Hollywood Wives* proved 'more laughs than I've had in a long time, definitely better than Shakespeare.' Between these projects, Hopkins managed to bank more than $1 million, solidly establishing for himself and Jenni the first true nest egg that opened up their domestic options. Without doubt, he was clear-headed about his strategy. It was a time of energy and balance for him, and an ideal time to make hay. The recent theatrical success and (in trade perception anyway) the *succes d'estime* of *The Bounty* had catapulted him forwards. There was, too, the alchemy of his tranquillity and the magic that brought. So it was easy to work a lot. As it was easy to laugh a lot. And laughter begat work . . .

If money was ever Hopkins' incentive, the attraction of LA was all dominant now. With his mottled, brooding demon-slaying legend, his twin Emmys, his Bafta, the quality cachet that followed *Magic, The Elephant Man* and *The Bounty*, Hollywood – at least Hollywood TV – was his for the taking. And he had another advantage. Cherubic in his twenties, roly-poly in his thirties, in his late forties Hopkins suddenly fitted his skin. As the hairline thinned and the jowls slackened his face assumed a slumped beauty in which the delicate blue eyes shone with a plaintive, tantalising light. John Moffatt would remark, 'I envied him for it. All of us grew old. Tony grew sexy.'

Spoiled for choice, Hopkins shocked everyone – even Jenni – by turning for home. The occasion was the offering of a London play by his old RADA mentor Christopher Fettes – he who attuned him to the energy cube and the motivational force. Fettes had been courting him for years with various projects and now there was one they both wanted: Schnitzler's *The Lonely Road*. Hopkins told Jenni that he needed it, that he still wanted London theatre, that a new turnabout had come. They packed for home – but not for another protracted hotel stay or rented W1 apartment.

Hopkins gave poignant meaning to *Hollywood Wives* by selling Clearwater Drive and moving out.

Chapter 14

HOME . . . AND DRY?

Peter Gill chortles: 'I can see Tony there at the National, stuck between these various raving gays, not knowing how to jump and being so damned suburban about it all . . .' Regardless, says Gill: 'He wanted that kind of acknowledgement so badly – not Royal Court favour, or West End, or anything so questionable. But the top of the tree. Larry, no less.'

Peta Barker describes what she saw as his frame of mind in the mid-eighties: accomplished, relatively at peace – but 'hungering for profound British acceptance' and ready to do whatever it took to get it. By that time they were friends again and Hopkins was reconciled with Abby. In Peta's view, he had paid his dues and deserved what was coming. David Hare, the committed Socialist playwright who would shortly spur the glory of 'what was coming', believes, 'Tony had a furious certainty that the British audiences loathed him. Not just disliked. Hated. It was a fixation. He came back to resolve that once and for all.'

Transitional markers were everywhere. In *The Bounty* for the second time, he appeared on the big screen with Olivier who, as Admiral Hood investigating the mutiny, interrogated Bligh. Shot in a day at Lee Studios, their scenes had the roar of history: two great actors, ascendant and declining, separated by age, joined by genius, locked in a quiet conflict that reached beyond their fictional exchange. 'There was undoubtedly a surrogate father aspect to Larry's love for him,' says Gill. 'It wasn't unconditional affection, though. I am certain that Larry was absolutely outraged by Tony's indulgence of whatever demons he was wont to exorcize at the National's expense. But there was manifest forgiveness, and that implies caring – and then it would be remiss not to say that Tony was a very great actor and Larry a sometimes very great talent-spotter.'

With *The Bounty* came another ritual handover. Olivier, now 77, had just five years to live and few roles to play. Hopkins' gift was blossoming. *The Bounty* was a reversal of those strained, anxious first months at the National when Hopkins coveted the world that Olivier held in the palm of his hand. Now it was Olivier's turn to rage. But this was no more personal than Hopkins' early resentment. Olivier, all who knew him insist, kicked against the lapses of his extremis years, hated them. But Gill says, 'He probably felt satisfied by his investment in Tony; it was a tidy outcome, really.'

When Clearwater was sold – too quickly to achieve anything other than a modest profit – to producer Jon Turtle, the Hopkinses rented a house at Draycott Avenue, in Chelsea. Hopkins could certainly afford to buy a London property and the rental arrangement hinted at a pervasive fear of what he was now embarking upon. But he hid it. From December 1984, a day or two after his arrival, he began preparation for *The Lonely Road* and a second – deeply significant – play he had agreed on before leaving the States, David Hare and Howard Brenton's newspaper satire, *Pravda*, due for staging at the new National venue.

First came *The Lonely Road*, written by Schnitzler, the playwright famous for *La Ronde*, a man who once described himself as 'a virtuoso of solitude'. Here Hopkins would be Julian Fichtner, a worn-out globe-trotter returning to Vienna in an attempt to reconcile himself with Felix, his illegitimate son. The irony would be that Felix (played by Colin Firth) has no idea of his real father's identity and, as a result of his cosseted bourgeois upbringing, has himself determined on the life of wanderlust his father once enjoyed. Samantha Eggar was cast as Fichtner's mistress and old pal Alan Dobie as the narrating solitary observer. What thrilled Hopkins was the psychological maze of the story, the shades of Ibsen and

Chekhov – and Fettes' wild concept of openly tuning to the Freudian references by setting it in a psychiatric hospital, where the characters become case histories observed by a frock-coated Viennese doctor.

Dobie found his old friend much the same but 'placid, relaxed, much much much more relaxed than I remembered him.' Dobie also believed that Hopkins had much to do with his casting. 'He certainly was the reason for it happening, as he had cast approvals. So I know he gave me the nod.' As a four-week rehearsal stint began, Dobie observed evident, if subdued, hero-worship for Fettes and a willingness – initially at any rate – to accede to the director's every whim. 'I wasn't so sure about any of this,' says Dobie. 'The radical approach didn't connect with me. It was all too fey. I recall, for example, the first day of our read-through. We all sat around and Fettes put on some bloody music. We listened obediently and he said, "That's it! That is what the play is about!" Which I thought was so much nonsense.'

Dobie continued to enjoy Hopkins' company and friendship, but grew further apart from Fettes and his concept by the day.

As opening night drew near, Dobie was convinced the play was a disaster. 'Tony lay low but I had started to rant and shout and break the furniture. I couldn't abide what this man was doing and I was really very depressed by it. Then, as soon as we opened – very lukewarm – in Guildford, Fettes vanished from the scene.'

Hopkins had apparently been biting back any unease, inhibited by his long-time affection and trust for Fettes and by his newfound pledge to 'cease fighting'. But with Fettes gone, the actor-director moved insidiously into sight. 'We were still at Guildford and Tony very gently came up to me and with that unique manner of his – as when he acts, the way he breaks up sentences and delivers in a hesitant, disarming manner – he said: "Eh . . . ah . . . eh . . . Alan, would, eh, you mind if I, eh, came . . . if I came down here during that line and did my speech facing . . . eh, did it facing, eh, here?"' Dobie was delighted, saw salvation. 'Tony,' he replied, 'you can do what you like when you like.'

The return to the Old Vic stage was an occasion of strange emotions but by that time, says Dobie, the play was 'quite a lot sweeter' and, though

Fettes continued to drop by and have his say, 'things remained pretty much as Tony and the cast steered them. There was no more friction. Tony spoke to Fettes. I didn't. Which suited me fine.' The Old Vic was now under commercial management, run by Canadian Ed Mirvish, the National Company (now under the artistic directorship of Bill Bryden) having transferred at last to its new three-theatre building on the South Bank. 'I don't know whether nostalgia was in mind,' says Dobie, 'but he was certainly comfortable there. It was positively a homecoming.'

The Lonely Road was, glitteringly, the shape of excellence to come. Though the play's Freudian distortion won some criticism, Hopkins' notices boomed. In the *International Herald Tribune*, Michael Billington got straight at it: 'The greatest pleasure lies in watching Hopkins back on the stage. He plays Fichtner like a man aching for human commitment: in one unforgettable scene he stands downstage, eyes slowly moistening, as his son gazes at a portrait of his mother and begins to understand his origins. Hopkins, playing with mature quietness, has the naked-souled quality of a real actor.'

The naked soul was real enough, but now it was a cautious naked soul. Even – yes – a calculating one.

The mature Tony Hopkins squared up to *Pravda* ('truth' in Russian) with the greatest reservations. Burning as his need for the National was, at the last minute, deeply dug into Schnitzler and having burned his boats in America, he thought of pulling out. *The Lonely Road* was playing a final week at the Theatre Royal, Bath, when rehearsals with director-writer Hare began, and Hopkins told Jenni he thought it was all a mistake. The text baffled him, he couldn't 'see it', he wanted out. Jenni and Julian Fellowes reassured him: they read *Pravda* and said he must persist; this was a special role. Some believed that the main reason for his hesitation was purely tactical. One actor contends it was 'a spasm of insecurity, arising from the National he wanted. He wanted something celebrated, classical, as befitting Olivier. *Pravda* was a dodgy new play by two brick-throwing socialists. It was not proven stuff.'

David Hare and Howard Brenton, sure enough, were controversial figures, untypical in the National story. Distinctly socialist, damning of tradition and of recent British history, they formed the cutting edge of a group of social commentators – among them Trevor Griffiths and Snoo Wilson – who came to prominence in the seventies. Hare was the most articulate and active (he is now also a director of feature films) and a founder of the Portable Theatre with Tony Bicat in 1968 and the Joint Stock Company with Bill Gaskill and Max Stafford-Clark in 1974. Serving as literary manager and writer-in-residence at the Royal Court before tackling the bastions of the new National, Hare had had particular success with *Brassneck* (written with Brenton in 1973) and his own *Plenty* (1978), but craved the popular audience. *Pravda* was his tool for that.

Hare recalls Hopkins' arrival: 'We had approached him quite strategically because for many years he was the legendary missing figure of British theatre. Here we had an opportunity to do a play at the Olivier Theatre [in the National complex] of the type not normally done there. A new play. Today the situation is better but, then, the fact that the Olivier had 1200 seats to fill was the big turn-off. But Tony was a controversial, star presence, so he would help to fill it.' Hare was aware of the immediate uncertainty, but insists that Hopkins overcame it in a flash. Cast alongside him were Kate Buffrey, Tim McInnerney, Ron Pember, Bill Nighy, Peter Blythe and Basil Henson, not all of them widely experienced.

'We got straight into that first-day reading and Tony was very, very, very nervous for a few scenes.' Once the brief doubt was passed, says Hare, once a few actors started to laugh at what he was doing, Hopkins spontaneously found the character of Lambert Le Roux, the unctuous newspaper magnate crossbred from Robert Maxwell and Rupert Murdoch. 'Really nothing changed from that first "discovery" of his – it just grew and grew.' What Hare then found was 'unbelievable, frightening energy. I'll give you an example of how much: every day he was up at 5 a.m. to hit the Steinway. Then he'd do a few voiceovers [for commercials] in the studio between 8 and 9.15. He would be in the rehearsal room a half-hour before I arrived and then he would stay there, even if the scenes I was working didn't include him. Because he had ideas not just for how he wanted Le Roux, but for everyone else's characters too. Then he'd do his stuff and when we left in the evenings, he would still be there in the canteen, studying.' (Hare later learnt that Hopkins would usually be in bed – 'out cold asleep' – within twenty minutes of curtain down at the theatre.)

'I learnt something wonderful with him,' says Hare.

> Tony is completely and unstoppably an actor of instinct. He must 'try on' a character more than any actor I know. He must know his character. But once he has it, as with Le Roux, he is boundlessly free and extendable. This is the genius of him. If he doesn't find the character, then his performance becomes the search. And that is a much more restricting and unattractive thing – which I discovered later when we did *Lear* together. But Le Roux he found instantly, and instantly he was having fun and I thought, Well, this might be something.

Hare and Brenton's Le Roux, like the play itself, was conceived 'for entertainment, no more'. But the satirical content – Fleet Street as a moral wilderness, the truth ravaged by incubi who are lionised by the masses – was a central strength. 'But Tony did not analyse the meaning of scenes, there was none of that. Instead his maniacal energy went into refining a great comic performance. He found the 'lean' after about a week. Then after ten days he found the reptile idea as the key to his man.' The 'lean' – a from-the-waist, rugby-run tilt – was based on the posture of producer David Susskind, an executive on *All Creatures Great and Small* and *The Bunker*. Hopkins used a shrill South African accent, taken from tapes loaned by the actor Athol Fugard. 'The reptile was especially fascinating,' says Hare, 'because he expanded it for Hannibal Lecter in *Silence of the Lambs*. Howard Brenton rang me after he'd seen *Silence* and said, "Did you see what he did? On *Pravda* he was only licking [the actors]. On this one he's biting their lips off!"'

Although Jenni was always close by and the marriage had been repaired to a point of closeness acknowledged even by Peta Barker as extraordinary, she was not the perennial rehearsal-room presence of earlier days. This was further evidence of Hopkins' growing control. 'He came without the accoutrements of a star,' says Hare.

> He usually walked from his house to the theatre and if he drove he drove himself. The only problem I had with him arose from his speed. He would say, 'You know me, David, I'm no good in rehearsals.'

One actor believes that Hare drew the sublime best from Hopkins because he neither submitted to him, nor patronized him. Hare says,

> I recognised the drink problem. Tony likes to rake it over endlessly and it creates an instability which, in turn, he's trying to control. One day he is in great shape, he likes what he is doing and loves a particular actor. The next day he can't stand that actor. It shifts all the time. The thing is that he has committed himself to the Alcoholics Anonymous regime, which is about control. So all the time he is fighting to control emotion and with the mania-energy involved there are often imbalances. I didn't suffer it so much on *Pravda*, but *Lear* was a different story.

As the momentous preview approached Hare was confident but Howard Brenton was still unsure. Brenton later wrote in *Drama* magazine:

> I sat in the middle of the packed Olivier Theatre watching the first preview of *Pravda*. David Hare and I had driven each other on to make the play a comedy, committed to laughter or dreadful failure. We had never before attempted as dramatists, either singly or together, to 'go over the top', in the First World War phrase the theatre uses for outright commitment to one thing in a show. A few seconds before the lights went down on the first preview, I had a nightmarish thought: Oh my God, this lasts three hours. What if only David and I find these scenes, lines and foibles of human behaviour funny? And what if there is not a single laugh between now and curtain call?

As it turned out, the preview reception was rapturous – unlike anything Hare or Brenton had seen before. 'Superlatives fail, really,' says Hare. 'There was an ovation as he came on – which put him mentally in the right place and reassured him in terms of assuaging whatever feelings of inbred audience reception there were. And then, well, all I can say is he played Le Roux with utter command. And it brought the house down.'

In the third scene of act one, Le Roux bullets into his personal philosophy:

> What I do is the natural thing. There is nothing unnatural
> about making money. When you are born where I was born,
> you do have a feeling for nature. What I admire about nature
> is . . . animals, birds and plants; they fucking get on with it
> and don't stand about complaining all the time . . .

Hare believes that the bogeyman that Hopkins imagined – monster, misfit and comic-tragic character that he was – 'undoubtedly grew from the dark adventure of his own self-analysis, it was drawn from within'. Hopkins concurred: in his view, Lambert Le Roux was a part of him, a part of everyone, a predator, a creature without feeling, who came 'out of the darkness of everyone's fears'.

On the first night, Hare says, he was hard pressed to find the right words of compliment and thanks. 'The previews just blew us all away, so I wondered what I might say on that first night. So I went to him in his dressing room and said, half-joking, before the curtain up: "Tony, I just wanted to mention this – is there any chance of doing *Lear* with me? If the first night goes bad I won't renew the offer but . . .?" He didn't really reply and then the curtain call came and off we went.'

The first night, like the previews, was electric. Hare went backstage and Hopkins didn't bat an eye. 'Very casually he said, "David about that *Lear* . . .?" And of course, I knew we were away.'

Seven months of *Pravda* followed, not all swaddled in praise (some critics found the play 'shallow' and 'too obvious', though Emlyn Williams rated Hopkins' performance 'the greatest in postwar theatre'), but they unfolded for Hopkins as the most fruitful, satisfying months of his entire professional life. Hare was witness to this unusual state of perfect equilibrium in which, as a man and an actor, anything was possible.

> It was such a long haul, but so inspired. I recall that, about 120 performances on, after I hadn't seen the play for a while, I came to look and it was still drawing the audiences, still doing great. But I thought Tony had become a little stiff and mannered – which wasn't surprising as the character was a very stylised creation. So I said it to him and he went on that night and I watched and saw what I can only say was the best acting in theatre I have seen in my lifetime. Every single gesture had changed. It had become fluid and fluent, and it was completely fresh and completely, devastatingly brilliant. It was as if the hand of God touched him. And I went backstage and said to him, 'How the fuck did you do that?' And he said, 'I don't know. I just don't know. There are nights when it just goes that way. I don't understand how it happens myself.'

Pravda's unquestionable success – packed houses and round-the-block queues every night, a British Theatre Association Award, a Royal Variety Club Award, a *Drama* magazine award – swayed Hopkins' decision to purchase a home in London. Very shortly he would move to Eaton Square, then acquire a new property at Alexander Place, which remained his home base till the late nineties. '*Pravda* made his mind up,' says Hare. 'He came home to see if he could convert a National audience, and he did. Stunningly. That was the point of new direction. That was the homecoming and a new lap of career.'

High on accomplishment, Hopkins worked effectively and happily on three major film projects through the *Pravda* run. One was for TV, two were largely British features. Each showcased a positively 'new' Hopkins – quieter in his eyes, less fidgety, less mannered, fully immersed in that 'less is more' concept he had sworn since *The Elephant Man*. Mike Newell's *The Good Father* gave cause for pause in its subject matter – indeed, Hopkins admits, it made him break down in tears. Scripted by Christopher Hampton from Peter Prince's maudlin novel, the story was of Bill Hooper, an angry marketing executive separated from his abrasive wife and struggling to maintain closeness with his one-day-a-week son. When he fails to control his own impasse he manipulates his new friend Roger, himself separated with a son, to demand and win custody. Emboldened, he makes friends with his estranged wife, but finds that the improved sharing arrangements are a sham: with sadness he realises that it wasn't his wife he was running away from, rather his son.

During the production – packed into five weeks – Hopkins upset Newell by resisting rehearsals. True to his pre-*Pravda* prejudice he told Newell, 'I'm an instinctive actor. Either it's there or it's not. This time, I have it. I know this character, it's me.' The director held his ground and Hopkins did rehearse – 'very profitably,' Newell later said. But when it came to shooting the film, co-starring Harriet Walter as the wife and Jim Broadbent as Roger, Hopkins' kinship to the lead character unleashed unexpected emotion. During the filming, Hopkins later said, he broke down in a bedroom scene where Hooper and his wife argue culpability while surrounded by kiddies' toys. When he left Peta, he said, Abby had still been in her cot. He had absolved himself from the pain by telling himself that he 'didn't need all this – family responsibility' in his life any more. The honesty of playing Hooper brought the pain flooding back and he wept. Newell ordered a cut, then asked for a reshoot.

Peta Barker cannot speak about *The Good Father*. Though she has followed her ex-husband's film and TV career – she especially loved him in the upcoming TV bio-pics *Blunt* and *Across the Lake* – she could never bring herself to watch *The Good Father*, believing it too full of memories and too hurtful. The film was shot on a tiny budget – less than $2 million – and was, perhaps, too sombre to score at the box office, but its truthful heart, and Hopkins' conviction, made it worthy.

The wondrous screen adaptation of Helene Hanff's *84 Charing Cross Road* (developed from her autobiographical book by Hugh Whitemore who had scripted *All Creatures*) benefited too from Hopkins' maturity. Squeezed into the *Pravda* days, this immaculate dramatisation of the letters of friendship exchanged over twenty years between Frank Doel, chief buyer at the antiquarian booksellers Marks & Company (of the eponymous address in London's West End), and Hanff, a New York-based bibliophile, brilliantly encapsulated the inarticulacy and mystery of human love. Hopkins 'adored' Whitemore's script and asked director David Jones – who had produced the nightmare of *Kean* – to convey gratitude to Whitemore at the start. The film was made by Mel Brooks' company on a structuring arrangement similar to *The Elephant Man*. Interiors were shot at Shepperton, with limited exteriors around London and – for one day – at the seaside town of Eastbourne. Hopkins' co-stars were Brooks' wife Anne Bancroft (with whom he'd briefly appeared in *Young Winston* and *The Elephant Man*) playing Hanff, and Maurice Denham and Judi Dench.

Dench played Doel's wife in a role that was absent from the recent stage adaptation by James Roose-Evans, but which assumed a crucial importance in terms of defining Doel's character in Whitemore's romantic, but never indulgent, adaptation. Interestingly, says Dench, she and her actor husband Michael Williams had turned down the offer to play Hanff and Doel in Roose-Evans' version 'because we thought it smacked of a recital evening – which goes to show what my judgement is!' David Jones had been friends with Dench since the early sixties and had cast her unreservedly as Doel's wife – once more against her instincts.

> David and I had worked happily together on good things like *Langrishe, Go Down*, but he knew I am not a happy screen actress. I hate myself, how I look, and that makes film acting hard for me. Before I can contemplate acting as such, I have to get myself comfortable with how I look. Film is unforgiving. It draws the worst out of you. And people have always told me this part of me is wrong, or that part. So I approached that film, as I do with most films and TV things, with great doubts.

Dench knew Hopkins only by reputation:

> No one had ever said to me that he was volatile or difficult but I knew he was one of the Old Vic boys and I was told he had a great sense of humour. And all of this turned out to be true – but I would also learn,

later when we did *Antony and Cleopatra*, that he was incredibly victimised by his temperament. He was absolutely inspiring to work with – but I would not have been able to live with him 24 hours a day. That level of intensity in a human being is brilliant, but unnatural.

Dench met with Hopkins and Jenni at a dinner party at Jan and Gawn Grainger's, then went to work on location at Richmond. 'I was a little overawed. I had seen his *Pravda* and thought, my God, he's a genius, But filming with him was so pleasurable. Humour was his big thing – a marvellous, witty humour, and it was clear that he was very much at ease with film, as I was not. If he was overextended, I didn't see it. He seemed cool, fit, very much in control of it all.' Dench saw no conflict in her approach alongside Hopkins and Jones.

Perhaps Tony dislikes rehearsals. I don't. But I, too, am an actress of animal instinct, rather like him. I avoid intellectualisation. I can't do it. I just sense the character, smell it, do it. David [Jones] interacted well with this intuition. He is an organised director, well ordered and prepared – which perhaps is unlike the man I know on a personal level – but he allows room to improvise and draw out. This happened when Tony and I rehearsed our bits . . . and it made for very satisfactory chemistry, I think, on screen.

Though Dench insists that she 'never, ever, ever' watches herself on screen – 'it is much too painful' – she did attend the premiere of *84 Charing Cross Road* and relished it. 'It was the most auspicious start to a working relationship with Tony. I thought it all worked very well indeed, for me, it was the happiest ever film experience. I loved the warmth of it, and have the nicest memories of dancing in the open air with Tony, in the sequence shot at the old Festival of Britain site on the South Bank. He was so funny, which, I confess, was a little different from the *Antony and Cleopatra* experience yet to come.'

Made for $4.6 million (the sets at Shepperton absorbed much of the budget), *84 Charing Cross Road* maintained Hopkins' progress, winning him the Best Actor Award at the Moscow Film Festival and, according to David Jones, the admiration of the likes of Robert de Niro who, after watching a print of the film, enthused to all and sundry about Hopkins' 'truthfulness'.

Hopkins' life was now a 24-hour, seven-days-a-week acting commitment. Hare speaks of 'a frantic whirl of work', Dench of 'tired eyes'. But he dashed onwards. *Blunt* was next, for the BBC. Here he played a robust, camp Guy Burgess in Robin Chapman's version of Anthony Blunt's subversive activities. Admired as the play was – Dr Raymond Edwards back in Cardiff found it 'vindicating' and 'highly crafted' – some found signs of weariness evidenced by the intrusion of the familiar old, shelved mannerisms.

By mid-summer in 1986 Hopkins was firmly rooted back in London. He was seeing more of Abby, who had now turned her sights to the theatre and seemed immune to the doubts he expressed, and he made it clear to friends that he would never reside in America again. An actor friend says, 'He had all the equipment for happiness but Tony is too complex, too self-punishing to ever be happy. He builds it up . . . and then he destroys it. We called him 'a crisis maniac'. He had to feed on exhaustion, or disaster. He was never stable and, though he looked it after *Pravda*, he was never reconciled.'

In January 1985, returning for *The Lonely Road*, Hopkins told Michael Owens of the *Evening Standard*: 'I always knew I had to get back. I've spent an awful lot of time running away and now I understand that it's time to come back to the realistic side of life. I'd been living up in the mountains of California where I've been able to come to a few decisions. It's that old thing of either you grow, or you go.'

The aftermath of his British rebirth in *Pravda*, *84 Charing Cross Road* and the rest threw those remarks back in his face. *Pravda* and the victory over the National, over 'the system', could only be a hollow one. Life moves on. His vanity was fed, his doubts silenced – but after that came more doubts and another vacuum to fill. Hopkins told David Lewin,

One night, suddenly, standing on the stage I thought, what on earth is this all about? It was halfway through *Pravda* and [*Lear* and *Antony and Cleopatra*] were still to come and I just felt I was wasting my time. I felt panicky and I said to myself, I can't get involved in this acting life in the theatre. It is the group and the family atmosphere, which really leaves me cold. I never felt a part of it. But I was committed, so I stayed. But I really don't know what I was supposed to be doing.

The yawning pain was the chronic one: the inability to surrender himself to the 'family' unit. 'That became very clear to me,' says Judi Dench. 'He felt uneasy with the intimacy of sharing. Not as an actor, but socially and privately. He was kind, but he was not gregarious. He told me straight: he hated team spirit. His vision of life was a kind of constant solitude.'

Still, Jenni cheered him and steered him when he took on Hare's offer of *King Lear* in what would be the National Company's first ever staging of what Charles Lamb termed 'the unactable' play. Late in the summer of 1986 the couple took the Venice-Simplon Orient Express to Italy for a week's vacation with David and Paula Swift. Then, batteries ostensibly recharged, the real graft began.

This time round Hare gritted his teeth. 'It really didn't click. From day one on *Pravda* he had Le Roux. But with *Lear* he didn't. It was the problem of the search. And his inability to tie it down upset him deeply and, I think, made him temporarily quite insane.'

This was Hare's first Shakespeare, a notoriously difficult play in terms of vocal and physical demands and generally judged as a text that actors and directors build up to, usually working through the comedies, then the tragedies, towards what John Barton, the Royal Shakespeare Company director, viewed as 'possibly the greatest play every written'. Olivier, who played the part on stage in 1946 and for television in 1983, recognised the obstacle course of playing *King Lear*. In a three-and-a-half-hour drama, in which eighty-year-old Lear appears in eleven scenes of varying dramatic requirements, all the time sliding towards (lucid) insanity, the actor needed more than talent. Olivier said, 'When you have the strength for it, you are too young, when you have the age, you have lost the strength.' Gielgud, too, found it difficult and advised future Lears to 'get a small Cordelia', alluding to the play's requirement for Lear to heft his daughter's body across the stage after an intense evening's work.

But Hare wasn't fazed by the complexities. Declaring himself a *Lear*-ist, as opposed to an admirer of *Hamlet*, he was invigorated at the start by the Everest challenge.

> Apart from Peter Brook's 1962 production, I have never seen a *Lear* that worked to the fullest. Sometimes four-tenths of it work, sometimes six-tenths. Even in Brook's production, Scofield did just eight-tenths, I think. But I was ready to go for broke with Tony.

While Hare planned a radical reworking, expectations – inevitably because of the National connection – were of the highest. Recently, there had been several *King Lears* of differing success. Adrian Noble's Royal Shakespeare Company version literally roped Cordelia and the Fool together in symbiotic life and death; Deborah Warner's Kick Theatre Company's version was simpler; Ingmar Bergman's Parisian staging invested the play to high degree with sexual wit and political energy.

> But my version was unsentimental about old age and quite direct. Many Lears have shaken and quavered for their effect. Tony did not. He was belligerent, aggressive, combative and active . . . but it was *still wrong*. He just didn't quite get it. Part of it, though, was my fault. I never properly got to grips with the early part [of the play]. He was fantastic in the second act, in the 'Dover beach' bit with Michael Bryant as Gloucester. I believe that will never be better played. He was great in all the moments of tenderness. But for the rest of the time he was flailing, often very desperately, and I can think of no more tragic sight than watching an actor like Tony wandering about the stage, disconsolate, searching, searching. Because he is an actor who cannot cover his pain. He does not possess the trick that British actors have, where, when this disaster happens, they can be quite covert and can bury it by playing off the irony

or their basic technique. Tony doesn't, cannot. When it isn't there, it isn't there. And it drove him crazy.

Hare tried not to be alarmed when Hopkins' frustrated fury came out on other actors in the play. 'He was pugnacious and it suddenly came to him that one actor, a very nice fellow who was having trouble with his part, had actively set out to fuck up the production. It drove him crazy. It was a very dangerous situation. He was on stage, flailing and hitting people and there was certainly a feeling of "on the edge" about it.'

The previews were fine, as was the first night audience. There were ovations all round and the *Independent* newspaper wrote, shortly after the December opening, 'Despite not being a musical, the National Theatre's *King Lear* is the hottest ticket since *Phantom of the Opera.*' Hare was quoted as saying, 'The sense of event is unnerving. After all, it's only a play.' Mark Lawson in the *Independent* opined:

> In the lead role, Anthony Hopkins, who shares a birthplace, physique and vocal mannerisms with the late Richard Burton, [is] attempting to re-establish himself among the first rank of Shakespearean [sic] actors. The problem is that the production is overhyped. In Hopkins' performance there is the stump of a considerable Lear, but it needs about another month and it would have been fairer for the National if it had been allowed to develop more privately. The National needs a hit . . . but there is something about this production which suggests that it will be a *succes d'estime*, and that the touts will not be needed at the later performances.

Other critics were notably kind to Hopkins. For Frances King in the *Sunday Telegraph* Hopkins was 'often thrilling . . . On the debit side, however, must be set his vocal limitations, and his mysterious inability to move one deeply except at random moments.'

Hopkins became increasingly unhinged, believing some nights that 'you have to punch into the audience, you have to attack them, go for it at any cost'. On these nights Michael Bryant and the fellow actors would cringe and circulate the word: 'It's another one of his fucking sex-and-violence evenings!' Hare says, 'It was very difficult for me and we had rows. He hated it and he is a reformed alcoholic and he has investigated the AA regime dictum which says that alcoholism is about anger and the worst thing you can do is turn that anger inwards and let it corrupt your feelings. I told him, "Look, it is not my fault that you are an alcoholic. You are killing yourself and making waves" . . . and then he would calm down and say, "All right, all right, I'm sorry."'

The great friendship forged on *Pravda* waned, and though *King Lear* ran for one hundred performances – a record for a single actor in London – 'and always to packed houses', Hopkins could not wait to be rid of it. Hare says,

> After the joy of *Pravda* it was very sad. But then I got annoyed with Tony. He went off and let his frustration stew and, months later, every time I lifted up a newspaper I would read where he said that *Lear* was a disaster and he was awful in it. After a while I thought, well, enough is enough. So I wrote to him and said – literally, 'Tony, I am sick of reading that Lear was a disaster. I am sick of you taking your anger out on other people. I would rather you go back to being an alcoholic than continue to take this anger out on other people. You may not accept this, Tony, but for one hundred performances we filled every seat in a 1,200-seat theatre. So, although you do not wish to admit it to yourself for your personal reasons, something was happening there and I for one am not ashamed of it.'

Hopkins phoned from Australia, three days later, in the middle of the night. 'He was upset. He had my letter and he said, "David, you're right. I'm so sorry. I don't know why I do these things. I'm sorry."'

All of Hopkins' directors and many of his fellow actors tell similar stories of explosion and contrition. The written or telephoned apology figures large in many recollections. 'I think what that says,' says David Cunliffe, 'is that the turmoil is part of the package. Like molten rock in a volcano, it is the essence – and its effect is the price you pay for the glory of it. Tony knows that in his rational moments. And so, obsessively, he says sorry . . . because, once you know him, you know there is a fundamentally gentle soul in here. Malice doesn't exist in him. He is an artist. That is all.'

Out of *King Lear* Hopkins stumbled, punch-drunk, into a promise to Sir Peter Hall, the current director of the National, to do *Antony and Cleopatra*. Later he said, 'I have no idea why I put myself into that mangle again. I promised, so I did it. But that's it. It's the last. I don't want this agony, this humiliation, again. I proved I could take the National, it's done.'

The humiliation of *Antony* was, says Judi Dench who played Cleopatra, nothing of the sort. 'But I had no inkling of how tired he was, though, looking back it's easy to see why. *Pravda, Lear* – two huge runs – and then those films. But when we started rehearsals with Peter in January 1987, he seemed ready and quite intrigued by the prospect.'

Dench had come to the part 'in the most embarrassing way', having committed to the invitations to play it from *both* Hall and the Royal Shakespeare Company. 'In fact, it ended in a kind of written duel with Peter [Hall] declaring to the RSC, "Well, we made our offer in an office, you made yours at a party." But I wanted to do it, though I know I am not perhaps physically what Cleopatra should be, and I suppose I was instrumental in prodding Tony because I wrote to him and said, "I'm going to take a chance, please do it too."'

In Conference Room 3, at the top of the National, twelve weeks of rehearsals started well enough. 'There was the initial tension and embarrassment of us not really knowing each other well. But Tony was excellent at deflating that. His wit did it. Jokes. Smiles. Very great charm. And then, on the second day, we could throw ourselves at each other as these people did and be passionate.' Hopkins had spent himself on *Lear*. After three weeks, during a lunchtime break, Dench suddenly found the actor at the stage door, sweating, pale, clenching his teeth.

'It's all a mistake,' he told her. 'I can't go through with it.'

Dench was shocked but saw he was in no shape to go on. 'I tried to console him. I said, "You have nothing to be ashamed of. You have done this monstrous load of work. People half your age would drop dead on it.

Please, just go find Peter – get him before we go back into session – and just come clean."'

Hopkins did and was comforted by Hall who told him to 'take a week or two and then see how you feel'.

Hall then faced the cast. Dench says, 'He was very cool and collected and said, "We have plenty of work to be going on with, so let us not panic. He needs a rest. We have nine more weeks, ample time. Let's forget Tony and get on with our work."'

Three days later, after an extended weekend with Jenni, Hopkins was back. 'Nothing was said,' says Dench. 'No analysis, or discussion. We just got on with it and, I felt, developed something quite good, something unique, for this *Antony and Cleopatra*. We didn't want the play "set" – nothing rigid in stage movements – and I think this gave a great fluency in what followed.'

Hopkins was working on reserves. One actor friendly with him adamantly insists that 'he came within a hair's breadth of pulling out. It was a miracle that he didn't do another *Macbeth* disappearing act . . . and the cause was *Lear*. *Lear* proved to him, in his view, that costume stuff like Shakespeare wasn't him. It made him physically awkward and that inhibited his discovery of the character. He told me himself, "I've had it to here with the classics. Fuck 'em."'

Antony and Cleopatra opened to the kind of grudging reviews that had scoured *Lear* irretrievably. Charles Osborne in the *Daily Telegraph* wrote: 'About Anthony Hopkins' Antony I have reservations . . . He tends to adopt a somewhat somnambulistic manner all too reminiscent of those performances Richard Burton used to give in the fifties at the Old Vic.'

Dench says,

I was aware of the anger building. On the first night, before curtain up, I said to him, by way of quietening him, reassuring him: 'All over the world people are dying and being born.' Just those words. And then we went out and did it and, for me, he was extraordinary. More than anything there was this *danger*. I think it was exaggerated by his own inner conflict, his unhappiness with whatever theatre was or was not

doing for him. But it did frighten me. I remember holding the girls and
. . . shaking. I would look at him across the stage some nights and be
genuinely distressed and afraid.

Though Dench clings to her fond memories of Hopkins' kindness – as
when, during a rehearsal, she opened her mail to discover a particularly
nasty 'anti-fan' letter and he ritually burned it before her, thereby setting
off the National's fire alarm – she admits that, as the play progressed, it
became more violent. 'I think it was better for that,' she says, 'and
certainly there was no difficulty with audiences. Because we easily
knocked off a hundred performances, giving Tony yet another
Shakespeare record.'

In the spring Hopkins managed a fortnight off to holiday with Jenni in
Lucerne and in the autumn he ferried to Dublin to shoot the small-
budget feature, *The Dawning*, based on a Jennifer Johnson novel about
the Troubles. But contentment had begun to move hopelessly out of
sight. Even the CBE awarded in the Queen's Birthday Honours List in
June didn't appease him; if anything it upset him.

As Christmas approached so, too, did his fiftieth birthday and the
bitter background reality was that he had burned out on theatre and felt
dispirited, with nowhere left to go. *His* classics were, in his judgement,
second-rate affairs, and though the likes of Michael Billington believed
his and Dench's *Antony and Cleopatra* was an easy match for Ashford and
Redgrave at Stratford, he didn't feel it, and that was what counted. The
CBE augured badly for the quiet hopes of a knighthood, and the
Hollywood offers, he was distressed to realise, had faded to few.

Dench was entranced by his insecurity and his inability to comprehend that 'he was a towering figure, and a master actor, a master of many
media'. As they played on New Year's Eve, says Dench, a blow fell.

I didn't realise it at the time. But the word had come through that I had
been made a Dame, and of course, on the same day it was his birthday.
So when the play was finished, backstage there was great commotion and
excitement. Everyone started singing 'Happy Birthday To You' to Tony

and 'There is nothing like a Dame' to me. It was all wonderfully high-spirited, but Tony somehow didn't rise to it, and he left the theatre very abruptly, which he often did as he disliked the clubby thing among actors. It was only later that I discovered, from an American writer, that he had been very angry about the honours and felt quite neglected at that time. I myself thought my award was absurd. Wonderful, but absurd. I thought: This is for all the work I did in Africa long ago. It was a delight, though I'm not sure how serious I took it. But apparently Tony took it seriously.

As with Hare and so many others, Dench was later to receive a heartfelt letter of apology from Hopkins for his anger and behaviour during *Antony and Cleopatra*. 'But I never took it personally,' says Dench. 'He didn't intimidate me on that level. Sure, the other guy did. The man from a foreign land who loved Cleopatra. That volatile devil. But after the actor, there's the man. And Tony was, and is, a wonderful man who lives every day with the burden of genius.'

Chapter 15

CHRYSALIS

Burton was dead – from a brain haemorrhage in August 1984 (the time of *The Bounty*) at his home in Celigny, in Switzerland – and Olivier was in his last bedridden days. Their passing pushed at the edges of Hopkins' despair, reminding him of his failure in assuming their legacy, in achieving the totality of acceptance that began with Guthrie's five major parts philosophy and rose to the door of the Oscars. Burton and Olivier had been *Hamlet*, had romped through the classics, had won their celebrity, their fortunes and their Oscar nominations. Compared with them what, at fifty, had he truly got? A record of half-successes, a hugely variable film output and a CBE?

David Hare contends that Hopkins didn't fully grasp his celebrity and the currents of emotions it discharged:

I recall that the stage door, during *Pravda* and *Lear*, was always choked with fans. Almost all of them women. One particular woman had this extraordinary devotion. But there were so many. Their presence seemed to surprise him – all the time. And I remember I said to him, 'Jesus, Tony, all these gorgeous women! Why don't you cash in on this celebrity thing as everyone else appears to do?' And he was very chaste about it. 'Oh no, no,' he said. 'Get into that and you get into emotion. I don't want any of that. I want to control the emotional side of things.'

Nevertheless, try as he might to keep his distance, the impact of his stardom – inadequate as he found it – threw him into cauldrons of unwanted emotion. Towards the latter days on *Antony and Cleopatra*, early in 1988, an act of violence against him made newspaper headlines and, says Dench, 'deeply frightened him and made him rage'. Under a headline of FIRE THREAT TO HOPKINS the *Evening Standard* reported:

> Actor Anthony Hopkins has received a series of threatening letters.
>
> Mr Hopkins received the letters during the final run of *Antony and Cleopatra* last week. One of them said his car would be set alight. It is understood the letters came from a jealous rival of Hopkins' continuing success on stage and screen. Welsh-born Hopkins dropped his usual routine of walking to the theatre on the South Bank because of the threats.

Absurd and melodramatic as the report sounded, it was true. Hopkins might have been tempted to dismiss the letters as crank threats, but then security men at the theatre alerted him that a fire had been lit under his car, which they had managed to extinguish. Hopkins called the police and CID officers from Kensington started an investigation. Judi Dench and the cast of the play saw a complete change in Hopkins' persona. One says, 'This was food for major paranoia. This wasn't self-flagellation. This was the real thing. Someone out there, out to get him. You think of John Lennon and Jodie Foster – all those maniac-stalker stories – and you realise he wasn't overreacting.'

Judi Dench says, 'It was horrible. The atmosphere became nightmarish and Tony didn't see or talk to anyone for the last few nights of the play. There was a security police cordon round him and we seriously worried about his well-being. I brought him a gift to mark the end of the show, a Roman coin. But I couldn't even give it to him. I had to hand it to the police to pass into his dressing room.'

By strange coincidence, similar threatening letters had been sent to Peter Gill, who then ran workshops in the studio wing at the National. Gill says, 'I think Tony overdid it. When I heard this was happening I contacted the police and gave them my letters. The handwriting was similar and I think a connection was made. Basically I put it down to rampant loonies. Jealousy. All the usual vile baggage that attends stardom and celebrity.'

According to the *Standard* reports, 'an actor' was arrested but released without charge. Gill counters this: 'It boiled down to a security man at the theatre who was well known as someone given to ideas outside his station. Tony had offended him in some personal way and the man was terrorising him in response. It was a childish personal vendetta that I thought was just a load of old nanny fuss.'

Judi Dench thought otherwise and confesses that the final night's performance was one of the most unsettling of her life. Hopkins told the press: 'It was bloody frightening. There was a coward out there, but I was not going to back off. I thought I might as well go out and give it all I had.'

Dench says his performance was flinty but 'you couldn't help wondering, was some loony about to do something crazy? It coloured everything we did, really.'

When the final curtain call was over, Hopkins made a run for it. 'There was no final goodbyes – nothing. The police guards were flanking him, ready to escort him off. The next day he was on his way to the Lake District, to shoot the Donald Campbell story for the BBC. It was a kind of sad farewell to the play and maybe soul-destroying for Tony after all he had accomplished.'

By the time he joined the BBC crew under producer Innes Lloyd at Coniston, Hopkins had clearly decided that the theatre was his past. He told David Lewin:

There is an ethic in the English theatre that we all have to stand like gentlemen and take our punishment. But I don't believe in all that stuff. Some people have the temperament for it. Wonderful people like Ian McKellen and Judi Dench, who played Cleopatra with me. But to me it is elusive. It has got me into trouble over the years because I would fight with directors and I felt I just didn't belong to that family. I always associated rehearsals with a bunch of badly behaved children presided over by some disapproving director who sneers . . . they take themselves too seriously in theatre. You go into a rehearsal room with all the pictures of the productions on the wall and the director says, 'This is going to be a voyage of discovery for us all.' And I think, *I wish I had never come.*

To Lewin, Hopkins confided that film-making, and regaining momentum in films, was all that interested him now. 'I am very grateful to the National Theatre because it burnt something out of me. Something in me died, in the best sense. What I find I enjoy now is just doing my daily routine: making the film, doing the work.'

The corollary was a hope for film invitations, but that was no reflex certainty. *Across the Lake*, the BBC film depicting Donald Campbell's final, fatal attempt to break the water-speed record – his Bluebird crashed and broke up at 320 mp.h. – was honest fare, well written (by Roger Milner), superbly directed by Tony Maylam, but its international appeal was slight and its fee unspectacular, in the BBC way. Slumping now into what he called 'an alienation relapse', Hopkins staggered and flailed like his blind, questing Lear. A measure of Hollywood's propensity to forget was the lack of weighty offers. Nothing came. Instead, doggedly pressing new agent Jeremy Conway for 'work, any work – or I'll go mad', a variety of limited-budget parts was found in a host of middle-market, mostly TV, films. After *Across the Lake* came Kevin Billington's *Heartland* for the BBC – his first opportunity to portray a Welshman in a play filmed on a Welsh location. Then Graham Greene's posthumous *The Tenth Man*, for CBS and producer Norman Rosemont. Then yet another remake of Dickens' *Great Expectations*, playing Magwitch (who else?) in a bland rendering by director Kevin Connor for Disney/HTV.

The only theatrical film that reared its head was Michael Winner's starchy adaptation of the Alan Ayckbourn comedy, *A Chorus of Disapproval*, a play that had been a National Theatre hit four years before. In this instance, the casting invitation came not from Winner but from Elliott Kastner, the producer of *When Eight Bells Toll*, who had been looking for another project to share with Hopkins for years. Kastner reveals:

> I had no idea of his frame of mind, because we hadn't been in close contact. But I still held him in the highest regard. It was too bad we didn't do anything after *Eight Bells* but maybe it was no bad thing for Tony and his subsequent career that he didn't get bogged down in action thrillers in the seventies. Anyway, for my money he was still one of the best instruments around for creative artistry on screen. Use him right and you get sparks up there on screen. But he's an actor. He's an instrument. And he was in Winner's hands, and Winner didn't play him right.

To be fair to Michael Winner, the play has a confined, delicate rhythm that centres on language and offers limited visual opportunities. It is not a play to 'open out', and though Winner mostly enacted it faithfully, the vagaries of editing seem to stunt it. In the film, Hopkins plays Dafydd, a buttoned-down solicitor (based, he said, on his father) whose current mission is to direct the local drama society's *Beggar's Opera*, which features an attractive newcomer, Guy (Jeremy Irons), who is a widower and much fancied by Dafydd's wife Hannah (Prunella Scales). Dafydd's secret assignment is to find out on behalf of an unidentified client whether Guy's electronics firm plans a local expansion; Guy's intention is to dally with seduction. The consequence is farcical mayhem, not unlike the best West End of Brian Rix.

With a budget of $2.6 million – 'which I paid for, every damn cent,' says Kastner – *A Chorus of Disapproval* was scheduled for eight weeks' shooting at Scarborough, entirely on location for cost reasons. 'The choice of movie was Winner's,' says Kastner. 'But I wanted Tony and Jeremy Irons. I felt they would ensure its success, because firstly they are tremendous actors and secondly there is a box-office advantage with these people.'

When Kastner visited the location at the Opera House in Scarborough, it quickly became apparent to him that Winner's film was not the one he envisaged. 'Everyone seemed happy enough. A great cast. But I looked at what Tony was doing – this marvellous, skilled actor who should have been making the biggest pictures in the world – and [in my view it] was hammy.'

The image of Hopkins that was emerging now in newspaper features and radio and TV interviews was one of immense contradiction. John Dexter once said Hopkins had a tendency 'to invent stories', that he wasn't 'a strict observer of life's truths'. Peta Barker agrees. The journalist Lynda Lee-Potter, researching him for a newspaper profile, confessed: 'Certainly after reading all the interviews he has ever given, the facts do seem to vary, even on issues like how many "O" levels he's got.' But now the wriggling and self-definition seemed wildly askew. In a BBC interview during *Heartland*, he seemed keen to bury his mystical inspiration and his skill as an actor. Byron Rogers asked him was it true that he'd had a vision in which he'd seen the Archangel Gabriel – presumably a reference to his 'road to Damascus' experience in Westwood, much publicised at this time. Hopkins replied, 'No, I didn't see Gabriel. I thought I'd had a kind of religious vision, but I made a mistake. All right?' Questioned about his actor training he was equally contemptuous of the past: 'I just bang away. Fast or slow? Remember Victor Mature? He was playing a gladiator in some film and it was that moment when he becomes a Christian. The director said: "Right, we need a close-up. More of that moment of miraculous conversion." And Mature said, "Look, Mac. I got three expressions. I look left. I look right. I look straight ahead. Which one do you want?"'

An actor who worked with him at this time believes that Hopkins' insecurities were a manifestation of

> what was probably a treatable neurosis. I never knew an actor so intent on self-analysis, so urgent about interpreting a script, and so maniacally private. He seemed to be unsure of the rightness of anything he did. I don't mean everyday doubt. I mean raving psychosis. There is a category of unipolar depression called Endrogenous Depression, a kind of permanent 'blue' state that is chemical and biological in nature. It struck

me that he might well fit that characterisation. I know Burton, towards the end, had a difficulty 'seeing' himself and finding a context for his life's work. Tony had that too. He was unsure even of his voice tone.

In his notebooks published in Melvyn Bragg's *Rich*, Burton wrote:

> Rex's [Harrison] brand of acting and his offstage personality are inextricably bound together. Most obviously, for instance, Rex's normal private-life voice is the same as the voice on stage – only projected a little more. I think mine is. So is George C. Scott's and Gielgud's, so was Coward's, so is Jason Robards', so is Fonda's, so is Richardson's, but Olivier's is totally different, and Scofield's, and Guinness'. Alec and Paul tend to 'boom' onstage though cathedrically quiet off, and Larry Olivier's develops a machine-gun rattle with an occasional shout thrown in 'to keep', as he said to me once, 'the bastards awake . . .' Does it mean that Olivier, Guinness and Scofield are basically and essentially character actors, while the rest of us mentioned above are simply extensions of ourselves? Why one believes in one actor and knows he's blazingly honest and not in another equally dazzling player is beyond my competence to explain. I can only accept it and hope for the best.

With similar fervour Hopkins tried to pin himself down. On *King Lear*, before opening, he contemplated 'postcards and death' in order to induce the necessary insanity. On *Antony and Cleopatra*, he later said, the play was 'hopeless' until, on the 78th performance, shortly before Christmas 1987, he suddenly 'saw it' by virtue of a raw sore throat. He found the rasping voice – a voice that wasn't his – and then he had the play. So was he, as an actor, basically and essentially a character actor, or just continually an extension of himself? Was he an actor of spirit, or technique? Was he *true*? And, after that, was it relevant?

David Scase, his first earnest professional employer, once gave him advice which, Scase today believes, kept him centrally anchored while the madness raged. 'My father was a bricklayer who rebuilt two-thirds of those magnificent chimneys at Hampton Court. When we were children he used to take us down there, to show us his work and I recall saying, "Good Lord, Dad, you're an artist!" But he said, no. All he did was master the craft. So I used to say to Tony: "Forget about art. Concentrate on the craft, the basic technique. Keep it simple. And before you know it you will slip into art."'

Though Hopkins momentarily switched off and surrendered to the likes of Winner at times of spiritual exhaustion, the ongoing quest for resolution – of his acting persona and the discomfort at the core of him – was never passed up. The problem now was an apparent career dead-end of his own making, exacerbated by the inertia of confusion. With no more theatre and an absence of significant film offers, what edifying challenges lay ahead? What chance resolution and fulfilment?

Intuitively, Hopkins saw the need to U-turn, to race back and untangle the past. Fortuitously, at that very moment, John Dexter – the tyrant of his nightmare years, the visible face of his demons – came back into his life.

There are those who believe, like Muriel Hopkins, that the first 'tempestuous marriage' (Lynda Lee-Potter's phrase) was the cause of the crisis of Hopkins' alcoholism. Peta Barker always rejects this; she believes that on the contrary, she was the only one of that time who tried to make him face reality. There are others who argue that John Dexter drove him over the edge, sparked by an indefinable personality clash, driven by a megalomaniacal theatrical vision. 'I don't know what the problem was with Tony's antipathy for John and vice versa,' says RADA friend Adrian Reynolds. 'But I often felt if one could get to the bottom of it, it would explain a lot about Tony's insecurity and self-criticism.' What Hopkins mostly bridled at was Dexter's remorseless public criticism, and his tendency to call Hopkins girlish names, such as his favourite 'Miriam'. Hopkins found this 'deeply offensive'. In Equus, Hopkins claimed he had been 'brutalised' by Dexter, and had been lucky to come out alive. But now – bewilderingly to some – he seemed eager to go back to Dexter's side and work with him on another play, the extraordinary, resonant M. Butterfly, a study, tellingly, of sexual identity.

Previous page: The run of good luck didn't last. Hopkins might have been pleased to be cast alongside the beautiful Bo Derek in Columbia's *A Change of Seasons* in 1980, but the poor on-set chemistry with co-star Shirley MacLaine almost stopped the production. When MacLaine complained about his timing, Hopkins railed, 'If you want Jerry Lewis, be my guest. Just get off my back.'
Author's Collection

Left: For many, the years of emotional suffering and career experiment paid off in 1984's *The Bounty*, regarded in the industry as a landmark. Hopkins' version of Captain Bligh was far subtler that his predecessors, Charles Laughton and Trevor Howard.
Everett Collection/ Rex Features

Left: Jenni and Muriel accompany Hopkins to the palace to receive the CBE, granted in the Queen's Birthday Honours List in 1987, during the exhausting stage run of Peter Hall's *Antony and Cleopatra*, his Shakespeare swansong. Six years later would come the knighthood.
Author's Collection

Left: With Patsy Kensit in Michael Winner's *A Chorus of Disapproval* (1989). The film was a failure, but remains interesting for Hopkins' close-quarters portrayal of a character based on his father.
Hobo/Curzon/Palisades/
The Kobal Collection

Above: After a return to the English stage in the eighties, Hopkin's capacities as an actor seemed grander than ever – though Hollywood work offers were still thin on the ground. The nineties saw in the sea change, starting with Michael Cimino's invitation to play the victim to Mickey Rourke's thug in a remake of the Frederick March-Humphrey Bogart thriller, *Desperate Hours* (1991).
SNAP/ Rex Features

Below: Before reading for producer Mike Medavoy and director Jonathan Demme for the role of Hannibal Lecter, Hopkins spoke on the phone with old buddy, Ed Lauter. Lauter asked him how he would approach the audition, and Hopkins introduced the trademark hiss of '*Hello, Clareeeece*'. 'He was ahead of the game. He had the reptile down to an art,' said Lauter.
Orion/ The Kobal Collection/ Ken Regan

Above: As Van Helsing, the vampire slayer created by writer Bram Stoker and sweetly updated in Francis Ford Copolla's 1992 expressionist movie. *Dracula* was one of six movies starring Hopkins released in the golden 1991–1992 period, a spurt of unparalleled productivity that rubber-stamped his international stardom.
Moviestore Collection Ltd.

Above: Attenborough's *Shadowlands*, based on a BBC play by William Nicholson, and released late in 1993, was an eloquent expression of Hopkins' skill in portraying troubled characters. Based on the late life love and fated marriage of C.S. Lewis, and set amid Oxford's dreaming spires, the film jousted with the Merchant-Ivory production of *Remains of the Day*, in simultaneous release, for honours.
Author's Collection

Below: By the mid-nineties, return trips to the Wales of his childood were no longer anguished affairs. With Muriel close by, he visited the Port Talbot civic centre but hid the Oscar in the rear of his car. 'I don't like to flash it around too much,' he told the throngs of kids jostling for autographs.
Author's Collection

Left: As the erratic Dr Kellogg – he of pink corsets and curative enemas – in Alan Parker's fabulously ridiculous *The Road to Wellville*, in 1995. The corsets, and the self-administered enemas, were bluntly resisted, said Parker. 'He left you in no doubts that he knew what he wanted …'
Beacon/ Dirty Hands/ The Kobal Collection

Left: Oliver Stone flew to London to persuade Hopkins to play Richard Nixon. Hopkins demurred, then conceded – but aspects of the movie's revisionist reality were illuminated, and discredited, by the later publication of presidential papers.
Illusion/ Cinergi/ The Kobal Collection

Left: A curio – perhaps even an ignoble curio – that deserves debate: Hopkins portrays a heartless Pablo Picasso in Merchant-Ivory's unfriendly assessment of the artist, based largely on the work of Arianna Stassinopoulos Huffington (1996).
©Corbis/Sygma

Right: Embracing the young lions. In yet another remake (this time of a thirties fable), *Meet Joe Black* provided its most interesting moments in the nimble exchanges between Brad Pitt and Hopkins. Pitt was one of Hopkins' favourite new actors, but director Martin Brest's intricate attention to detail, and the expansive sets, depressed the actor.
©Schwartzwald Lawrence/ Corbis Sygma

Right: Julianne Moore replaced Jodie Foster in *Hannibal*, the long anticipated sequel to *The Silence of the Lambs* (released in 2001). Ridley Scott's movie was stylish, but savage – and stirred questions about the morality of Hollywood villainy and the boundaries of an actor's responsibility.
MGM/ Universal/ De Laurentiis/ The Kobal Collection

Right: Hopkins' most meaningful work stretches his emotional expression in simple human relationships. Here, finding late life love with Nicole Kidman in Robert Benton's sublime adaptation of a Philip Roth novel, *The Human Stain* (2003), the actor presents a vulnerability hitherto unseen.
Miramax/ The Kobal Collection

Left: Hopkins' relationship with Abigail, his daughter with Peta Barker, has endured roller-coaster years of separations and collaborations. She has inherited his musical flair (she is an accomplished guitarist), and, under the name of Abigail Harrison, continues to pursue the acting career given wing alongside him in small roles in *Shadowlands* and *Remains of the Day*.
©*Randy Bauer/ Rex Features*

Left: Hopkins today with third wife, Stella Arroyave. At last, he says, he has found a companion who loves to share his wilderness drives. They met in Om Asian Antiques furniture store in LA, where Hopkins was shopping for his new Malibu home, and were married a year later, on St David's Day, March 1 2003.
©*Rufus F. Folkks/ CORBIS*

The first tentative suggestion for Dexter and Hopkins to reopen their dialogue came from the agent Jeremy Conway who, of his own choice, rang Dexter in New York and asked him about the possibilities of bringing *M. Butterfly*, the current toast of Broadway, to the West End. Dexter responded that that was the plan, and he was considering Michael Gambon for the male lead of René Gallimard, the French diplomat who conducts a twenty-year affair with a male Peking opera singer whom he wilfully mistakes for a woman. Conway opined that Hopkins, especially after the long-run discipline of *Pravda*, *King Lear* and *Antony and Cleopatra*, was perfect for the role; and, more, needed the challenge. Dexter agreed to lunch with him in London.

Heartland was filming in Wales when Conway rang with the lunch arrangement. With little persuasion, it seems, Hopkins was drawn to the meeting. With hindsight it is tempting to say that momentous destiny was at work: Dexter had less than two years to live and the London *M. Butterfly* would be his last theatrical triumph. Hopkins might have said no and forever missed his moment. But instead, by his own admission, he had decided to confront the past: to face Dexter and beat the devil.

At the lunch in London Dexter came straight to it, asking, 'Why the hell did you walk out on *The Misanthrope* and what was all that hysteria and drunkenness in New York?'

Hopkins came clean. 'I can't work when I'm being hassled. When it happens, I take a walk.'

Dexter asked, 'Do you find me tough to work with?'

'Yes, you behaved abominably. But, I have to hand it to you, you were the best director I ever worked with.'

When the men parted there was little altered in their relationship but both, curiously, had decided to bridge the divide and do it one more time. Hopkins later said that, for his part, the decision was one of 'balancing the books'. 'When John and I worked together before I wasn't fully *compos mentis*,' he told author Quentin Falk. 'This would be the perfect way of getting the old mess out of my system, a chance as it were, to tackle some unfinished business.'

M. Butterfly was entirely about delusion and its consequences in human sexuality. This was the thorn Hopkins now grasped, unashamedly. Those who didn't comprehend the reversal of his decision, so soon, to return to theatre failed to recognise the impact of turning fifty, the stretch of his maturity and the distance he had travelled. Intellectually, he could no longer justify turning away from 'the devils'. If he continued to do so, he would be sentencing himself to a life of intermittent madness and rage and – he seriously suspected – inhibited growth. Facing up to Dexter and the dark aspects of his sexuality was really no choice at all. He had to do it, in order to grow. The real wonder of it was the magical confluence of Dexter and *M. Butterfly*, the devils, merging into one moment – now.

Before starting his text study for the play, Hopkins flew to New York to watch David Dukes as Gallimard. In this way, he absorbed the architecture of the play before returning to London to work on the text. As he read, the energy of his best days came back to him and he consumed research books voraciously. Glen Goei, a 26-year-old Chinese-born, Cambridge graduate was cast as Song Liling, the object of Gallimard's fantasy love, and, in rehearsals, Hopkins' admiration for him bordered on reverence. 'I'm in awe of him,' Hopkins told Janet Watts for the *Observer*. When Watts asked him for a play analysis, he was ready to present conclusions that read like good press but were in fact a crucial illumination of his own mystery. He told Watts that for years he had found it hard to reconcile his work with his background and temperament. Then:

> The Welsh are a very emotional people, but I hate expressing emotion, I can't bear tears or grief. For me, being an actor has been quite a difficult thing, because to strut on to stage is a feminine activity, art itself is a very female, creative thing: and then I go back to Wales and stand in a pub and they say to me, 'Still acting, are you?'
>
> I think that's why a lot of actors are so screwed up. There's a lot of conflict in the awareness that what we are doing is not a very masculine activity.

Hopkins told Watts frankly of the catharsis of the play, without, of course, opening the long barricaded doorways to the past. 'When we started [rehearsals], I have to admit, I thought: How are we going to get around this? And I'd do the defensive thing of making jokes like, "If the boys could see me now!" Yet the play has been a tremendous release for me. It's an area that doesn't scare me any more.'

In their rambling chat, Hopkins touched more of his primal nerves with Janet Watts than he had ever done in a major interview. He had, he told her, considered Jung's theories of the *animus* and *anima*, the maleness within the woman and the femaleness within the man, and in consequence saw the character of Gallimard as 'a man who denied and repressed the creative female aspect of himself' to the point that he falls in love with it in his fantasy figure, Song, the sexy 'woman' who appears in glamorous costumes throughout the play, only to strip naked, to reality, at the end. 'What [Gallimard] is in love with,' said Hopkins, 'is the pure beauty in himself. And what is sad is that he doesn't recognise what it is he loves. He falls into the trap of believing that the answers are outside himself: whereas the answers are always inside.'

No matter that the story was based on a true-life espionage incident (when in 1986 diplomat Bernard Boursicot was found to have conducted an affair with a Chinese actress, Shi Peipu, who turned out to be a male spy), nor that neither writer David Henry Hwang, nor Glen Goei, nor Dexter saw it strictly as a play about sexual identity. All that mattered was Gallimard's connection with him, the adventure of finding him and the huge, far-reaching release of the discovery.

Another concurrent change was inevitable: with his new vision of himself and the unresolved past, he suddenly stepped out from the cowering shell. Suddenly, confidently, not belligerently for once, he was man enough for Dexter. The hiding was over. His meaning was clear. No one could threaten him or bully him.

Everything changed. When Dexter ranted and shouted and told a young actress that she didn't know what the fuck she was doing, Hopkins told him politely to pipe down. When Dexter attempted criticism in those withering, sexually demeaning onslaughts, he could tell him –

calmly – 'Fuck off.' Released, he told the journos who came to rake the embers of the infamous relationship: '*Stand there! Move up there! Get off that door and come back again! Sit on that chair . . . don't talk about it! Show me!* That's the very formal, tough, muscular way Dexter works. I like that. You cannot wander round a stage looking for a moment of inspiration, because it never comes.' Elsewhere, he said, 'John is a bully-boy. But that's all right when you can bully him back. The thing is, he knows what he's doing. And so do I.'

What emerged on the stage – in a trial run at Leicester before a heroic London opening (Hopkins' first in the West End) – was a tough, uncompromising expression of masculinity wryly duped. Milton Shulman in the *Evening Standard* unknowingly cheered the phenomenon of emotional rebirth: 'Hopkins as René charges at his role with all the rampant aggression of the proverbial bull in a real china shop. It is a compelling performance but totally at odds with the concept of a civilised French homosexual mistaking his transvestite fantasy as reality.'

Many of Hopkins' old friends trekked to *M. Butterfly* with expectations reasonably aroused by *Pravda* and the not inglorious Shakespeares of the previous year. Roy Marsden saw the play both with Hopkins and also without him, when he had moved on and been replaced in the continuing run. 'Some American friends were in town and they wanted to see it, so I bit the bullet and went along to see it without Tony. His performance had struck me as being unusually dynamic. Something very electric and eccentric about it. Without him, good as the replacement actor was, the play was nothing. Tony breathed utter conviction and truth into Gallimard and the text.'

Peter Barkworth hadn't seen Hopkins for years but had kept abreast of his career. He attended *M. Butterfly* and was inspired to write that night in his diary:

> The play is wonderfully done, with splendid evocations of China and its captivating culture, with mind fights and authentic music. John Dexter directed. Anthony Hopkins is <u>perfect</u>. He is a perfect actor. Perfect

voice. Perfect gesture. Perfect stance. Perfect ease. Perfect rapport with audience . . .

Barkworth was moved to acknowledge a leap of genius. 'It is about authority. Much of what Tony was doing round that time spoke of extraordinary authority. I recall that in the Campbell film [*Across the Lake*] his power hit me like never before. *M. Butterfly* brought it to another dimension. It radiated into everything then. The TV voice-overs, for example. Insignificant as they seem, they reveal an actor. Ian Holm has a brilliant, evocative strength in voiceovers. But when Tony does them, *now* you believe. When Tony tells you such-and-such a car is this or that, you believe. He is unself-conscious. He has moved beyond himself.'

But old habits die hard and Hopkins was still the perfectionist, still the purist. Such business as voiceovers (his was the TV voice of Ford cars) and the recent low-budget TV was useful because it vented his massive, unquenchable energies, but also mildly irritated him. Under the surface, he knew his capacity; but the Fates had seemingly led him back to the hole of Britain. Revived as he was by *M. Butterfly*, the frustration of career opportunity didn't leave him and, after several weeks as Gallimard on the Shaftesbury stage, he was expressing boredom and uninterest in the play. To one journalist he carped: 'The critics tore it apart' – which seemed a preposterous exaggeration, and – 'I've had enough of it. I went out each evening on stage and found myself thinking, how many more nights of this? Am I really a theatre actor at all?'

The agitation at the end of *M. Butterfly* signalled the wheel had turned full circle. He had started in theatre, humbly at the YMCA in Port Talbot, more than thirty years before, in the hopes of answering some emptiness inside himself. With the storms of adolescence came seeds of neuroses that grew in theatre and – now – seemed resolved in theatre. His Shakespeare had not reached the peaks hoped for, but that was a minor crib against towering achievements – the unsurpassable *Equus*, the glittering *Pravda*, the curative *M. Butterfly*. The complaints were heartfelt, but hollow.

With the liberation of his theatrical conquest and the energy of his ambition it seemed just a matter of time before a major film break-through. Almost everyone who knew him predicted it. John Moffatt says, 'I knew his biggest achievement would happen on film, most of us did.' And Gawn Grainger, his close friend, says, 'There is a breed of actor who has the skill, the drive and the ease of sitting on airplanes and hopping round the world to the casting call. That in itself is a talent. Tony had it all.'

As Hopkins tells it, he was stuck in boredom, mired in the endless run of *M. Butterfly*, when, one non-matinee afternoon, he went to see Alan Parker's *Mississippi Burning*, starring an actor he much admired, Gene Hackman. He enjoyed the film, and coming out of it, thought how nice it would be to land another American film. Briefly, earlier in the year, he had flown to LA and joined a round of Polo Lounge meetings. 'It was the usual rubbish. How excited they were by something that would never happen. I just wanted to get away from it and back to the real world of London.'

At the Shaftesbury, he took a nap, only to be awakened by a call from Conway. Here was luck! Not one but two American films on offer. One was a major feature with director Michael Cimino, the other a thriller to be directed by Jonathan Demme. Hopkins says he was so excited by the chance of Hollywood as an antidote to his lethargy that he begged Conway not to build him up. He didn't want to read any scripts unless the offers were 'for real'.

Initially, says Adrian Reynolds, the excitement was mostly for Cimino. Hopkins said, 'I knew his work, I admired him. He was the class of Hollywood talent I wanted to be working with.'

Demme, on the other hand, was a relative unknown whose greatest success was the previous year's moderate comic hit, *Married to the Mob*, for Orion. The new thriller, called *The Silence of the Lambs*, was again to be for Orion. It was a project that had had a chequered history, beginning life as a novel, the follow-up to Thomas Harris' earlier bestseller *Red Dragon*. *The Silence of the Lambs* was published in 1988, the year of the film of *Red Dragon* (released as *Manhunter*), which starred Scottish actor Brian Cox as the monstrous, cannibalistic killer Dr Hannibal Lecter, a mad psychiatrist. *Manhunter*, directed by *Miami Vice* creator Michael Mann, had been a box-office failure, but was widely admired as an offbeat, if somewhat disoriented, thriller (it later scored on video release) and on its heels Gene Hackman acquired the film rights to Harris' follow-up. Hackman, however, changed his mind about *The Silence of the Lambs* after his Academy Award nomination for *Mississippi Burning*, feeling that he had had enough of the sinister villainy depicted in Parker's Ku Klux Klan film. Accordingly, the rights shifted to the doddering Orion Pictures (they would go bankrupt within two years), who assigned favoured son Demme. Mike Medavoy, head of Orion production, believed passionately in the project and was intent on a particular casting: the female FBI agent who befriends the incarcerated Lecter in this story would be played by Michelle Pfeiffer; Lecter would be Robert Duvall.

Jonathan Demme says he had other ideas from the outset: Tony Hopkins should be Lecter. Medavoy resisted, saying, 'But, Jon, you can't have an Englishman [sic] as Lecter. It's written for an American. And we need someone who can be instantly sinister and terrifying.' Demme argued. He felt that Hopkins' portrayal of Frederick Treves in *The Elephant Man* proved his potential as Lecter. The monstrous element must be subdued, but 'what really counts is the ability to convey humanity and intelligence. Lecter is insidious, and that's where the terror arises – from the distortion of humanity and intelligence.'

In the last weeks of *M Butterfly*, Demme flew to London to dine with Hopkins. Hopkins read the script by Ted Tally, but 'fleetingly, because I didn't want to be disappointed if it fell through for me'. Jenni attempted to read it too, but was repelled by the horror of it. Hopkins says that even as he dined with Demme he was doubtful of the likelihood of his casting. But, a few weeks later, with *M. Butterfly* imminently finishing, the call came from Orion to read the part in New York with the prospective new female casting, Jodie Foster. Pfeiffer, says Demme, had lost interest – allegedly because of the horror content; Foster was Medavoy's replacement choice.

The day after the completion of his Shaftesbury contract, Hopkins flew to New York, checked into the Plaza on the Park and geared up for the Orion audition with a jog in Central Park. In the recent months he was fitter than he had been in a while and had recommenced his jogging 'to clear my head and keep the waistline in order'. Ed Lauter, from *Magic*, had never lost touch and, just two weeks before, had told him on the phone to London, 'You must get this Lecter role, Tony. You gotta do it.' And, prophetically, 'This will be your Oscar.' Now, from the Plaza, Hopkins called Lauter and told him he was on his way to see Demme.

'D'you know how you're gonna play Lecter?' Lauter asked.

'You betcha, Ed. Listen to this . . .' and, says Lauter, the voice drilled up chillingly: '*Hello, Clareeece.*'

Lauter chuckles at the memory. 'He had that reptile thing down to an art. He had every nuance. He knew what he wanted to do with Lecter and I knew, don't ask me how, that his time had come.'

Without question Lecter was Hopkins' clearest spontaneous focus since the creation of Lambert Le Roux. In fact, his Lecter *was* Le Roux, a leech on humanity in human clothing, perverse and unstoppably smart. And the voice? That was easy: 'It had to be detached and disembodied. So I took the computer voice of HAL from Stanley Kubrick's *2001* – cold, mechanical, exact. Terrifying.'

At Orion's office on Fifth Avenue, several scenes were read with Foster and, says Demme, he knew instantly that his casting instinct had been right. 'My God, that's it! Yes, yes!' Demme enthused, and he hugged Hopkins. Medavoy and the Orion executives present stood up, shook Hopkins' and Foster's hands, and agreed.

There was still no conception of the phenomenon that *The Silence of the Lambs* would become when Hopkins flew on to LA to meet with Cimino and commence the Salt Lake City-based shoot of *Desperate Hours*, a remake of William Wyler's 1955 high-strung siege thriller, based on the famous play by Joseph Hayes. Here was spectacular satisfaction: not just to be back in the well-paid comfort of a high-class LA film, produced by De Laurentiis and Fox on a $10 million budget, but to be recreating a role in a Bogart classic, no less.

In the original, Bogart played a jail-breaking hoodlum whose violent gang take Fredric March's suburban family hostage. In Cimino's update, Hollywood's reincarnated James Dean, Mickey Rourke, played the villain and Hopkins the March role.

Cimino had not seen the original *Desperate Hours* in its entirety, though he had tried to: 'I couldn't sit through it. I wanted to, but it was so tragic. Bogart was dying when he made it – it was his final movie bar one – and the pain is in every scene. You see him there, this great legend, dying before your eyes. I couldn't bear it.'

From Cimino's point of view, though, the omission was no handicap. He was regarded within Hollywood's system – a system that has, despite continual claims to the contrary, changed little since the death of the contract era in the early fifties – as a high-risk roller, and nothing less than innovation (or novelty, at any rate) can have been expected from him when Dino De Laurentiis gave him the job.

Cimino's track record was, by any standards, remarkable. New York born, in 1943, he attended Yale, studied ballet and acting, then joined a TV commercials company that brought him to LA in 1971. Cimino's achievement in *The Deer Hunter* ranked him immediately among the fêted *nouveau* film 'brats': Scorsese, Spielberg, Lucas, and Coppola. The hugh box-office returns on this relatively modest $13-million film (it recovered its budget in just four weeks in the domestic market) ensured that the Hollywood powerbrokers, who still defined bankability as retreading last week's hit, offered him a virtual *carte blanche*.

The Deer Hunter won Oscars for Best Film and Best Director, but no such luck was in store for *Heaven's Gate* (1980), Cimino's personal-vision follow-up slice of American Wild West history. *Heaven's Gate* cost United Artists more than $55 million, then a record for a single film. The film's failure, critically and at the box office, shocked the industry. It bombed worldwide, taking just $10,100 in three days at the New York Astor Plaza – which was less than half the cinema's operating costs. Nevertheless, *Heaven's Gate* was important work. Stoutly non-commercial, it angled for naturalism and, resolutely without stars, scored some majestic performance moments.

As a direct consequence of *Heaven's Gate's* failure, Cimino ran into trouble with many of his subsequent projects. Successive ambitious deals fell through, until he made *Year of the Dragon* in 1984, starring Mickey Rourke. This mildly successful thriller resurrected his career, but his 'bankability' was the kind of restrained trust that his ally Francis Coppola would shortly endure in the wake of high-profile flops. Still after the bumpy years, Cimino was 'back on the dog track' with *Desperate Hours*, a film he ostensibly fully controlled (as co-producer and director), but one that would, he insists, be ultimately stolen away from him.

Hopkins was not first-choice casting, which was no surprise, considering the Welshman's absence from the Hollywood scene. Still, Cimino had huge regard for his body of work.

> And that's what's usually the attraction with actors like Tony. The English [sic] actors have this immense advantage over American classics, if only as rep players. With marvellous people like the late Ray McAnally, whom I adored in *The Mission* [McAnally was BAFTA-nominated for it], or Daniel Day-Lewis, one's admiration or recall is not for a specific role, but for the breadth of work. With Tony, I knew the variety of what he had done. And that, I knew, was a great advantage for a director facing a project that would be shot on a very restricted time schedule – a time schedule like they had in the thirties and forties, where a broad ensemble of players of very varying styles were pushed together in an intimate, intense storyline.

The film was to have a six-week schedule, mostly 'housebound' and mostly revolving around Hopkins' finger-wringing, taut Tim Cornell, the Vietnam vet-turned-lawyer whose family is terrorised. Hopkins enjoyed the prospect of the work, despite apparent loggerheads from the start with Mickey Rourke and, says Cimino, a constant mood of unease – even hysteria – on the set. For Hopkins' part, Cimino was 'Napoleonic', presumably on account of the director's diminutive size; but he admired the efficiency. Ultimately, in the actor's judgement, Cimino was 'a very good director, very fast'. Rourke, on the other hand, was a pain in the neck.

Cimino says,

> Tony arrived concentrated. On his very first day, in the very first set-up, he had a very wound-up scene to play, outside the house where he explodes under the pressure of the siege. Well, Tony did it first time and was so wound up that he punched the side of an automobile and dented it. Now this was a BMW, which you don't dent. But he meant business. He just drove himself into a frenzy and did it. He was that disciplined, that prepared. We were all impressed. I had actresses stop in a scene and walk up to him and say,'Jesus, Tony, I just have to say that that was *something else.*' There was a colossal admiration among the American actors for him: young Elias Koteas, Lindsay Crouse, all of them.

Rourke, however, came under different steam.

> Mickey is a completely different type of actor, from another school, another mind set, different motivational wells. He takes time. Tony has such reserves to draw on – and, yes, experience. Mickey works into it very deliberately and slowly. So there was disparity and there was tension. I had to spend time with Mickey. I had to fire him up. He is a tough man, a truly dangerous man. I always joke with him. I say: 'Mickey, why do you need those bodyguards? I've never seen one that you couldn't knock out.' And it's true. He's a boxer. He's hard, and I knew that once I got to that part of him, I would have the danger I wanted from the character Michael Bosworth.

Quite a lot of Hopkins' work was in the can by the time Rourke arrived, calling the set to his own rhythm. 'Rourke is a behaviouristic actor,' Hopkins later told writer Andrew Urban. 'And he's moody. We occasionally exchanged a few words, but he really doesn't say much on the set. He's very violent and uses physical violence to get going. I'd respond and fight back, hoping I wouldn't get any bones broken, or get my face readjusted . . . but I did get a few bruises.'

Cimino remembers one point at which the 'natural antipathy' between the actors almost derailed the production.

> I cannot over-emphasise the polar approaches of these men, and I can-
> not over-emphasise the tightness of that schedule. From the start, Tony
> and I got on. Even in the very early days, when all our contact was by
> phone – he in London, I in LA. The movie had even been costumed over
> the phone. I had sent Tony to Dougie Hayward, my tailor in London,
> and, for speed's sake, had Dougie dress Tony in my fabrics, my style of
> suit. So, Tony is slick and laid back, but Mickey is rough'n'ready, the
> polar extreme in every way.
>
> We had all the scenes blocked out, everything discussed and
> rehearsed precisely before we went on the floor. So each time Tony, in
> his way, was ready to deliver. And being the skilled actor he is, he would
> give it pretty much first each time. Mickey didn't. Mickey, for starters,
> took a long, long time to come out on the set. So there was a lot of waiting
> for him. And then, when he came out, he didn't always deliver. In fact,
> he rarely did first time round. Like Brando, or many of the greats who
> chose to work in that way, you got the take out of him at number fifteen,
> or number 26, or whatever. So Tony, and the others, adjusted to this and
> kept it rolling. Tony was very polite. I have to say that he had tremendous
> emotional and physical stamina to endure long takes of high-pitched
> intensity – and the long delays. But then he blew . . .

The scene was, appropriately, the climax of the film, when Bosworth's siege, and his nerve, are wearing out. Almost all the cast are gathered in the hallway of the house as he explodes at breaking point. Cornell – the Hopkins character – takes the brunt of it. Cimino remembers:

> We were close to the end, and at last Mickey had himself worked into the
> part, so he was pretty angry. Being strong, he was certainly able to deliver
> ferocity. But he doesn't know his own strength. Another actor who shares

this with him is Kris Kristofferson. I recall on one movie he decked a stunt-man – really decked him – because he, too, is a boxer and he knows how to throw a real punch too well. Well, in our case, Mickey had to draw a gun on Tony and go berserk. And he did. He prodded the damn gun so hard into Tony's neck that Tony flipped. I mean, totally lost it.

Hopkins later remembered the 'loss of patience'. He said, 'I just cracked. I said, "That's enough of this shit! I'm out of here!"' He told Andrew Urban: 'I can't work with tension. If an actor rants and raves, they have to get another actor.'

Cimino held firm:

I had experienced a similar moment on *The Deer Hunter* between de Niro and Christopher Walken. Then, as now, I let it ride. As Tony stormed out, I shouted to everyone to keep their marks. There were three cameras running on that scene and I shouted to *Keep rolling!* Everyone stood or sat there, frozen. Mickey was absolutely shocked, didn't know what the hell was going on. And all the time we were rolling, and I was hoping the damn [film] magazines wouldn't run out. It was an interminable wait. And then, as I expected, Tony just walked back on to the set and resumed the scene. Mickey was shaking – off his head completely – but it worked terrifically. Afterwards, they made up.

In fact, afterwards Rourke would write to Hopkins expressing the unheard of compliment that he would like to work with Hopkins again. The antipathy and tension undoubtedly helped the film in some regards, but Rourke's combustibility and tardiness hindered it in others. Cimino admitted:

My regret was that I didn't get the movie I set out for. One of the main reasons I wanted to do this film was to see if I could master the fluidity of long takes on that small set. We built that house especially for the film and I planned every move within it, and rehearsed it, to establish a long, freewheeling fluidity. [The original writer] Joe Hayes was there and helped a lot. And if I had achieved what I set out to do you would have had a movie with six- and seven-minute scenes, very very few cuts, very seamless. But with Mickey that wasn't possible. I had to keep bumping in the close-ups for his reactions, because he missed them in the main take. So it wasn't the movie it started out to be.

On completion of the shoot, though, Hopkins was on a high. He took Cimino aside and shook his hand, telling him: 'Thank you, Michael. In my entire career, this is the first time I have ever been directed on film.' Says Cimino, 'I was touched. Coming from a talent like Tony, it was the highest praise. I knew he was going on to do Demme's film and I felt that his time in Salt Lake City was well spent. And, for me it was good. You never forget or forgive the abuses of power in Hollywood, but you don't keep picking the wounds. You go on.'

The violence of *Desperate Hours*, and the six-weeks of suppressed tensions, doubtless helped Hopkins establish the mood for *The Silence of the Lambs*. As he left Salt Lake City early in December, he had before him the commitment to be in Pittsburgh before Christmas for make-up tests, then a date in New York to join Muriel, Jenni and Paula and David Swift at the Broadway opening of the National Theatre's *The Merchant of Venice*, in which the Swifts' daughter Julie was starring alongside Dustin Hoffman. Hopkins was looking forward to the Christmas break, but more to the opportunity of *The Silence of the Lambs*, a film he intuited as being – finally – perfectly *right* for him. During *Desperate Hours*, for relaxation, he regularly rode his Pontiac through Wyoming and Montana, out into the autumnal deserts, stopping at motels, visiting faraway AA groups, chewing the discoveries of the last six months. Now he got back in the Pontiac and motored slowly through the States he hadn't yet visited – going via Durango to Oklahoma City, to Dallas, New Orleans and Charleston – listening to endless Handel, Mozart and Philip Glass. It was a slow, meandering two-thousand-mile trawl through the senses – a cork in the ocean – moving lazily through the past and inexorably towards the biggest, best film chance of his life.

In January, at the Westinghouse factory complex in Turtle Creek, outside Pittsburgh, Hopkins metamorphosed into Lecter, stunning Jonathan Demme, who had, he told friends, expected 'great invention', but not *this*. From day one, scene one, Hopkins' grasp of the ultimate monster was unprompted and total. Demme told Robert Kiener of *Reader's Digest*: 'Tony was uncanny. He just *turned up as Lecter*.' Across Hopkins' 120-page script were cobwebs of drawings and notes to himself: on how Lecter looked. Dressed. Walked. Smiled. Talked. Laughed. One scribbled drawing had the slicked-hair image now famous from the film. Another, a reptile's eyes. Another sketch had Lecter in a prison boiler suit with the note to himself: 'As fit and fierce as a caged panther'.

Hopkins told *Reader's Digest* that, in order to be comfortable with the script and a character, he read the lines aloud 250 times. 'Only then [could I] start to improvise.' But it was obvious that another dimension of awareness was at work in his creation of Lecter. Jodie Foster openly admitted his presence was 'scary' and set workers studiously avoided him when he was in costume. Hopkins found this vastly amusing, admitting that at the start of each day, he would repair to his cell, grease up his hair and offer the camera crew and props men a lecherous '*Hello, boooys*' to chaotic effect. One unit technician said, 'The best part of it was locking him into that cell. You didn't feel too comfortable till he was safely under lock and key.'

The actual filming was, says Demme, 'one of the neatest, nicest experiences a director could hope for. No arguments, no script crises, good chemistry all round.' Hopkins particularly liked Jodie Foster, playing Clarice Starling of the FBI, the investigator he helps and finally hunts. 'Jodie works like me. She learns her lines, does her job and goes home.'

The professionalism defined the film: but there was something beyond which helps define the coming colossal success. Beyond the dynamics of a *Psycho*-like suspense film and superior ensemble acting was, undoubtedly, some *truth*. And a little black magic.

Simon Ward had read the novel well before the filming 'and before any of my friends'. Its effects made him wish to avoid the film – though he eventually saw it 'more or less piece by piece on various aeroplanes' in various Atlantic crossings. 'It [the novel] damaged me, to be honest. It is a story of such penetrating horror that I read it in one night and wished I hadn't. Don't get me wrong. It is utterly brilliant, as is Tony playing Lecter. But it works too well, and the fusion with Tony is too effective. I recall thinking, well, I know where he draws from, I know he has this insight into monsters and misfits, but I really hope this is not the label he gets known by. It is simply too dark and too lingeringly dreadful.'

Peta Barker concurred. She detected something beyond what she had ever seen in the creation of Hannibal Lecter.

Even before the full impact of Lecter's worldwide success, Hopkins divined it. But wherein, in his judgement, lay the magic? 'I don't know. If you are going to play a vicious, evil character, you have to play him as attractively as possible. I think I am attracted to monsters. I don't like cruelty, but maybe it is better to accept the darker side of your nature than to suppress it.'

Out of the shackles of his long neurosis, Lecter – an act of acceptance *non pareil* – was his first true moment of flight.

Chapter 16

BUTTERFLY

There are only partial answers. There may be fulfilment, but there is no utopia. There is no state of perfection. These things he would learn unreservedly in the glare of the unmitigated success of *The Silence of the Lambs*, a picture of grotesque humanity, whose very fibre called into question the character of heroism and which became, along with Capra's *It Happened One Night* and Forman's *One Flew Over the Cuckoo's Nest*, one of only three films in history to sweep the boards in all the major categories of the Oscars.

In the afterglow of its completion, knowing as everyone knew that it was something spectacular, watching with barely hidden delight as the citations flooded in – the Paul Muni Award for Best Villain, the Critics' Awards in New York, Chicago and Boston, the Best Supporting Actor Award from the National Board of Review, Golden Globe nominations, Bafta nominations, Oscar nominations – Hopkins reached for the benediction of his accomplishment.

Terry Rowley, the chirpy Cockney driver he frequently used in London, took him for a drive into the cinema-studded West End in June 1991 just as the British hysteria for the film broke. The film was playing at the Odeon Leicester Square and breaking all box-office records. His name was in lights – literally – above the title and his face was everywhere, in the tabloids, the broadsheets, on bus shelters, in satirical comics. He was an icon of the times, a joke and a signpost. 'All I ever wanted,' he told Rowley, 'was to achieve this. To get my name up there for the world to see. To be at the top.' He told *Reader's Digest*: 'For years I dreamed of being in a hit film. I'd drive drown Sunset Boulevard, look up at the other actors' faces on those giant billboards and secretly envy them. I thought that that kind of success would make all the difference . . .' But now, driving in circles round the block, viewing the queuing kids that recalled the Plaza, Port Talbot, or the wet days at the *cach* with Brian and Bobby, or the drifting days with Peter and Pam when he hoped to be Jimmy Dean – all of it seemed . . . empty. Terry Rowley asked: 'Well, how does it feel?' and he replied, 'Well, nothing much, to be honest with you.' He told *Reader's Digest*: 'I was surprised and a bit disappointed that I didn't feel changed. Then I thought, I've done it. I haven't got to prove myself anymore.'

Alternatively, in the days to come – in the triumphs yet to come – he would shift from euphoria to his customary quiet depression. The momentum of media exhilaration would carry him forwards but the niggling intrusions of reality tugged the other way, made him stall when he could – when he *rarely* could, because now the promotional demands on his time were unlike they had ever been – and worry at the value of his work, of his very existence.

When he wasn't flitting across the world, riding his adrenalin, he saw the circle of family unity as a fragile, embattled thing. Recently, it had not all been plain-sailing. He was closer than ever to Muriel, who was robust and greatly recovered from her loss of Dick. But Abby upset him, moving close and then drifting, seeming some days like his mirror image and others like a stranger. In the middle eighties, to his horror, she'd told him she had a drug problem. The admission pulverised him until he could balance himself and recognise a certain inevitability and his place in that problem. Abby told Jim Jerome of *People* magazine that her problem, and the subsequent temporary move to live with Jenni and Hopkins, was 'a cry for help and attention'. Hopkins came to his toes. Said Abby: 'He showed enormous compassion and empathised with that kind of Celtic thing, this yearning to be alone. He once said to me, "Both of us will always be on a lonely road."' In the years to come he would labour in many areas on her behalf, ensuring, even, her casting alongside him in a small role in *The Remains of the Day*, one of the key films of the consolidating nineties. But the repair work of full reconciliation would always stay just outside his reach. In 1996, he would hint to the error of the *Remains* – 'I can't do anything right as far as Abigail is concerned' – and wince at the unending complexity of a relationship that was beyond him.

But if Abby's anguish couldn't be repaired there were others he could help. Any number of old associates were touched by Hopkins' sincere efforts to redress the damage of his alcoholism by helping others. David Scase says,

> He became a guardian angel to a lot of people. I know this to be true from one very good friend, and from my personal experience. I myself developed a drink problem some years ago and got myself into a very bad state. Tony heard about this and chased me up, spoke to my friend and said, 'I must come up and help him. Where shall I go?' As it happens, I resolved my alcoholism another way. But I was aware of Tony's attempt to help and I adored him for it.

Judith Searle speaks of the many incidents of Hopkins' subtle assistance to fellow thespians who suffered substance abuse and says, 'It became a crusade, almost of equal importance as his acting. He had caused suffering and he now wanted to pay his dues.' In the coming years, Hopkins' support of alcoholics and the emotionally disturbed would become even more active.

As the Abby crisis calmed and her own acting career stabilised, his attentions turned to institutions in need of support and he became a valued contributor to a multitude of alcohol and drug rehabilitation programmes in London and LA and with Rhoserchan, an addictive-illness treatment centre near Aberystwyth. Here Hopkins visited often, mingling with the patients, hugging them, offering comfort and advice. Joe South, Rhoserchan's founder, says that Hopkins has been 'a real inspiration for people here'. Writer Robert Kiener reported him visiting, giving every resident a bear hug and telling each, 'Hello, I'm Tony and I'm an alcoholic,' then sitting patiently for hours listening to troubled life stories. When one resident, overpowered by his celebrity, gasped, 'I can't believe I'm sitting next to Hannibal the Cannibal!' Hopkins corrected her. 'It doesn't matter who I am. I am an alcoholic just like you.' He embraced her, wrote Kiener, as tears streamed down her face, whispering, 'There's nothing to be afraid of any more . . .'

An actor friend insists:

> *Silence of the Lambs* called him to a halt. It had been his lifelong ambition to have an American hit, and then it happened. He had never been one for romanticising Wales but, after *Silence*, there was a real rethink. A reflection time that brought out a gentleness and – yes – a compassion no one had seen before. The Welsh have a word: *hiraeth*. He had never been one for any of it. He used to say, I hate rugby, I hate men's choirs, I hate Welsh. But now he didn't. Now he became involved. It was an extraordinary *volte face*, like a man putting his affairs in order before he dies. But of course it wasn't that. It was just that he had been on the run from himself for so long, chasing his fortunes. And now it was all settled and he looked outward. Yes, that's it. After *Silence of the Lambs* and all the ballyhoo, he was at last outward-looking.

If he had sometimes lapsed with Wales, Wales had never given up on him. Before him the great West Wales actors were Ray Milland (born in Neath) and Burton. The Welsh identified Hopkins as their legitimate successor early on and never quit on him. In 1988, before *Silence*, came the honorary degree of Doctor of Letters from the University of Wales. Afterwards came the local tributes, the mayoral invitations, even the opening of an extension, the Anthony Hopkins House, at the YMCA building where he'd started. All of this gave him a genuine pleasure, more satisfying in its way than any acting plaudits because, says Les Evans, 'he probably saw the glory of it in his mother's eyes. There is no triumph quite like a triumphal homecoming.'

After *The Silence of the Lambs*, with a fluid confidence, Hopkins cashed in on a movie career. Without a vacation he flew to Mexico to make the TVS/Home Box Office tele-film *One Man's War*, about repression in Paraguay in 1976. This film was a brittle affair, a little too wordy and didactic in the HBO politico-drama way, and considerably overshadowed by the recent, similar, *Missing* and *Salvador*, but Hopkins' performance saved it. The *Hollywood Reporter* acknowledged 'fine' work and was again admiring of the follow-up, a small-budget Australian *Spotswood*, a gentle comedy by director Mark Joffe that was particularly amusing for Hopkins as it was the first time any director ever asked him to 'play yourself'.

Spotswood contrasted *The Silence of the Lambs* in every regard. Budgeted at just $3.5 million, shot in a warehouse in Richmond, Victoria, it told the story of Wallace, a time-and-motion expert who arrives at an archaic moccasin factory and decides its day is done: the staff must be fired and the shoes imported. Entangled as he then becomes in relationships within the quaint, happy workshop, Wallace finds his judgement clouded and events overtake him. This was subtle, though mannered, Ealing-like humour – 'a tragedy of comic proportions,' in Russian-born Joffe's assessment. What made it important in the log of Hopkins' career was both the speed and sensitivity of his adjustment to Wallace so soon after Lecter and the radical adjustment of his technical approach. Hopkins accepted the film – for a very modest six-figure fee – because, he said, he loved the 'wacky, ambivalent, ambiguous script' and wanted to support Joffe's endeavour.

Joffe was pleased. His career till then had been in Australian TV, directing some eighty hours of diverse mini-series from 1978 until 1987, when he made his theatrical debut with *Grievous Bodily Harm*. 'I was sick of being offered projects that weren't ready to be filmed,' Joffe says. 'There are too many being made at second or third-draft stage. The script, to me, is everything.' After eighteen months shuffling the script with Max Dann and Andrew Knight, Joffe had the structure he wanted – and then went for the prime casting. The dust hadn't settled on *The Silence of the Lambs* when he opted for Hopkins, 'because he is the best'. Within three weeks of approaching Hopkins' agent the deal was done by fax and

Hopkins was aboard. Twelve weeks later the actor was in Australia confronting his first comedy since the failed Michael Winner film.

Producer Tim White explained: 'Wallace, the character, is an introverted, uptight sort and called for an excellent actor. He was underwritten in the script, so we wanted someone who was able to say a lot without words.' Hopkins was 'bemused' by the suggestion that he play himself. 'The only way I can do that,' he told White and Joffe, 'is to be very straight and deadpan.' In the magazine *Cinema Papers*, Hopkins reflected that 'playing myself was difficult at rehearsals. But then, on the first day of the shoot, I said to myself, All right, I'll just be me . . . It was the first time I'd dared'.

Responding to the open invitation, Hopkins threw away the rule book. 'Years ago,' wrote journalist Andrew Urban, 'Hopkins would have analysed everything, writing lists of objectives in a very earnest way – 'like a caterpillar learning to walk, putting one foot in front of the other . . .' But John Dexter's dictum had 'set him straight'. Hopkins told Urban: '[Dexter said] just learn your lines. Stop complicating it. You *are* the part. Don't add anything. Don't take away either. But don't add anything.' Once absorbed, the effect was outstanding on *Spotswood*. It was a signal moment: there would be no more tricks.

As Hopkins awaited the release of *The Silence of the Lambs*, he took another part, of what was essentially a long, windy cameo, on the Morgan Creek/Warner Brothers' *Freejack*, an insipid, time-travel film, top-heavy with disco-lights special effects and starring Mick Jagger and Emilio Estevez. This was a stop-gap project, more assembled than directed, which Hopkins took only because, he said wryly, he wanted to meet the illustrious Mick Jagger. Dross that it was, the film still commanded a second look – for Hopkins. Playing McCandless, the sinister boss figure of Immortality Inc, who hungers for a fresh young torso to occupy, Hopkins rendered a sub-*Pravda* characterisation that was manic and comical and eminently watchable.

By now, with the trade bush telegraph prophesying fat fortunes for Lecter, Hopkins' name and image were highly valued promotional commodities. As the *Freejack* publicity machine cranked up, Hopkins' face flanking Jagger's and Estevez's became the logo of a picture which would be pushed hard in all markets throughout 1992. Hopkins would now have no less than four major international features running from mid-1991 into 1992. One at least seemed a guaranteed mega-hit: the die was cast. He was a star.

At this felicitous moment, parrying offers for TV, stage (one was an offer to play Bomber Harris) and any number of thriller features, Hopkins chose the Merchant-Ivory production of the last-but-one E. M. Forster novel to be filmed, *Howards End*. The actor Martin Jarvis, who had known him since RADA, lived round the corner from him in his recent home at Eaton Square and had appeared with him in the CBS mini-series *The Bunker*, believes that this film, and this choice, comprehensively demonstrated 'the genius that ranks him up there with Olivier and Alec Guinness'. Jarvis says,

> You have to get it in perspective. In a very short period of time Tony was compacting American and British films – films inherently different in style, in character, in accent. The mimicry helped. He and I had had great fun together always with our impersonations. I would do Ian McKellen, he would do *everybody*. With Lecter he chose an amorphous American accent and it was, apart from anything else, a tremendous vocal *tour de force*. But then, within a short period of months, he opted to play Henry Wilcox [in *Howards End*] – completely British, vocally mellow and eternally English. Every single aspect of his characterisations within these two movies – made within such a short spell – was different. Every whisper, every flush. Very few actors can deliver that versatility. So few that you couldn't count ten.

James Ivory, the veteran Forster director, whose partnership with producer Ismail Merchant was thirty years old, had some gentle goading to do to keep Hopkins in his film. Though the actor admired the Merchant-Ivory style of film-making and the proffered script, he later confessed to serious second thoughts about undertaking the project. He admitted that he had 'just skimmed though the script' on its submission, then became alarmed by Ivory's surprisingly cool, hands-off style to preparation.

According to Hopkins, he considered pulling out at the last minute, but was told by his agent that the contract was watertight. Hopkins panicked and, when asked by make-up artist Chrissie Beveridge to grow a moustache, refused. 'I don't want one,' he told her, bluntly, Captain Bligh-style. But Ivory wanted the moustache, so a false one was forced on him. Hopkins says he finally felt uncomfortable squaring up to Wilcox, a rigid Edwardian whose strait-laced attitudes clash with the bohemian Schlegels' and who was 'not very warm at all'. The resistance lasted only as long as it took to get the false moustache in place. Till then, he reported, he hadn't been able to 'see' Wilcox: thereafter the character came alive in him. 'It was one of those moments when the great burden is lifted and *you know*. After that it was all easier. I find the process of acting easier now. Maybe it was to do with the accumulation of experience, one's own life's experience. And maybe it has something to do with just accepting things as they are. In my earlier days I fought. Now I just let it pass.'

During location work on *Howards End*, *The Silence of the Lambs* opened with a bang. Heartily consumed by the tabloids who routinely tagged it as 'terrifyingly brilliant', 'shocking' and 'a creepy flesheater classic', the film was initially ignored by much of the serious press. The scales were tilted, though, by rapid and astonishing box-office success that placed it quickly among the top three earners in America and Britain for 1991. In the States alone, in its first half-year, the film took a colossal $130,726,716; in Britain the takings amounted to £17 million, ranking it only marginally behind the *uber*hits, Kevin Costner's *Robin Hood: Prince of Thieves* and Schwarzenegger's *Terminator 2: Judgement Day*. Throughout 1992, *The Silence of the Lambs* continued to maintain its top box-office status throughout the world. Only Japan, Greece and the CIS rejected the film, generating only small box-office numbers.

But there were strong murmurs of significant critical dissent. No one chastised Hopkins who, far and away, won the performance honours. But the nature of the film, and its bizarre social signals, gave rise for concern.

Among the first to wag a cautioning finger was the *Monthly Film Bulletin*, where Lizzie Francke announced the film, ominously, as 'Demme's omen for the millennium', where Hopkins offered 'renaissance man turned mediaeval gargoyle'. Franke dissected the plotline – where Jodie Foster's FBI agent Clarice persuades Lecter to help her locate another serial killer who has kidnapped a young woman – and found it 'most disturbing' on account of Demme's invitation for the audience to 'crawl under the killer's skin'. Hopkins had few scenes in the film, Franke observed, yet won it comprehensively from its true star, Foster. Franke wrote, 'The shift of identification away from the feisty heroine to the obsessive killer pushes the spectator to the very edge of his/her own abyss.' The *Motion Picture Guide* was even more wary. Acknowledging 'one of the most talked about movies of 1991', the *Guide* warned 'the film's accomplishments cannot be endorsed without reservation. While the degree of violence in this thriller is not unusual, the disturbingly bizarre nature of Lecter's face-eating cannibalism and the misogyny may be sufficient reason for many would-be viewers to forego the film's gripping drama.'

In hindsight, the level of success of *Silence* – an unprecedented success for a psycho-thriller – presaged a dark downturn in Hollywood mores. The box-office and Oscars victor of 1991 was Kevin Costner's directorial debut, *Dances with Wolves*, which ably essayed a moral fable about the trials of the Native American Indian. Exciting and moving as it was, there was also a core equilibrium in the film, part history lesson and part revisionist corrective, that lent an edifying wholesomeness. But equilibrium was hardly the order of the day. Beyond the culture and arts scene, the world itself was in turmoil with the international political landscape changing faster than at any time since World War II.

The western consumerist ideology of the 'Me' Eighties was superseded by the revolutionary, global New Man ethos of the nineties and an impatience with big bureaucracies and old regimes saw changes in leadership not just in Rome and Washington, but in Moscow and Tokyo too. The first stirrings of a dangerous new schism in the Arab world rose with the Gulf War, socio-political upheaval overtook the former Soviet bloc, Western Europe kowtowed to the far right – and Americans voted the Democrats back into the White House as a seemingly nervous, yearning knee-jerk.

Indecision distinguished film-making principles at this fluxing time. The 'rom-coms' and 'shoot-'em-ups' beloved of Hollywood continued to thrive (*Ghost, Lethal Weapon*) but other angry elements – the Black Pack of Spike Lee, Matty Rich and John Singleton and the haemorrhage of foreign and 'ethnic' films – indicated an urge for radical change.

The Silence of the Lambs was one of many films that dived unabashedly into the anger of the moment. Martin Scorsese's reputation as a character essayist had been built in the eighties; he soared in the nineties with *Goodfellas* and *Casino*, uncompromisingly savage films whose influence on Quentin Tarantino, the standard-bearer of the millennium cinema, was writ large throughout the rest of the decade. Shortly after taking office, in December 1993, President Clinton abandoned a prepared speech at a Democratic fund-raiser in LA to appeal to 500 entertainment industry guests to think twice about the moral signals of the work they were undertaking. It wasn't hard to see the direction of concern: Tarantino's bloodbath *Reservoir Dogs*, released in October 1992, had been adopted as a teen template; Michael Douglas' *Falling Down*, about the murderous breakdown of an overstressed white-collar worker, was still being debated in the popular press for the numerous copycat shootings of Asian store-owners that it allegedly inspired.

In the months to come, the significance of *The Silence of the Lambs* would be widely discussed. For now, the Hollywood mill and the media that fed it ignored the moral rumblings. Though the film fared indifferently at the Golden Globe Awards (Best Actor went to Nick Nolte, unquestionably impressive, if somewhat shallowly Redfordesque in *The Prince of Tides*), by the late spring *Howards End* had opened and the Academy voters were being deluged with comprehensively positive Hopkins write-ups and the far-flung tales of box-office records. When, in late in March, Hopkins and Jenni flew to LA and joined Bob and Nancy Palmer for the Academy Award ceremony at the Dorothy Chandler Pavilion, they were among the few still sceptical of a major industry gesture. Hopkins says he didn't rate his chances, nominated as he was alongside Nolte, Robert de Niro (for the remake of *Cape Fear*), Robin Williams (*The Fisher King*) and Warren Beatty (*Bugsy*). Apart from the high calibre of the competition (many said, the best in ten years) was the well-publicised factor of too many recent British wins: the previous two years' Best Actor awards had gone to the Brits – Daniel Day-Lewis in 1990 for *My Left Foot* and Jeremy Irons the following year for *Reversal of Fortune*. Weighed against this, however, was the multitude of *Silence* nominations and the not inconsiderable influence of several heavyweight critics, almost all of whom had pulled more for Hopkins than for the film itself.

As Hopkins sat and watched the ceremony unfold he was, he says, detached. Then, as soon as Kathy Bates went on stage to read the Best Actor nominations, he suddenly 'just knew' he had it. Till that moment Nolte was the shoo-in – then, this turnaround. 'I don't know what forces were at work,' Hopkins said. 'But it was like *déjà vu.*'

His name was read aloud, cheered, shouted out. He stumbled for the stage, abandoned his scrap of half-prepared safety script, focused himself in his old-fashioned way by watching 'the dot of toothpaste I had planted on the tips of my old shoes – the same shoes I wore last year [for the ceremony], the same ones I wore for *Pravda.*' His eyes were moistly electric when he waved the statuette towards the phalanx of TV cameras. 'First of all I want to say hello to my mother. She's in Wales watching this on television. My father died eleven years ago tonight, so maybe he had something to do with all this . . .'

The Silence of the Lambs won Oscars in all the major nominated categories, including Best Actress, Best Screenplay, Best Director and Best Film. In the final scene of *The Silence of the Lambs*, Lecter, having guided Clarice in capturing the serial killer Buffalo Bill, escapes to South America, calls Clarice to bid adieu, and walks off hungrily into the sunset. The scene was resonant, citing a new era for Hollywood films where darkness wins – and a new challenge for Hopkins.

He was now a butterfly, flitting on gilded wings from project to project, fat with offers. In the months following his Oscar he winged back to Wales to bask in the accomplishment and in Muriel's adulation. Visiting the Port Talbot civic centre he was crushed by well-wishers, the sons and daughters of miners from the Side, from the Sker bar, from the pained past. He was, gloriously, the baker's son made good, a role model for children with dreams, a symbol – ironically in his heart – of hope. As Muriel and Jenni hugged him, the kids jostled, begging him to open the trunk of what the local press wistfully labelled 'his shiny new car', in which was ensconced the 'glittering prize'. Hopkins thought not: 'Because I don't like to flash it around too much . . . My family keeps my feet on the ground.' There was work aplenty to be done: for his AA friends, and in any number of films. A Robert Maxwell biography might be one film, a version of *Les Miserables* another: 'But my agent has heard no confirmation yet.'

Directly after the Oscar came a cameo for BBC Films' Harold Pinter adaptation of Kafka's *The Trial*, for old friends. Shot in Prague, the producer was Louis Marks, who had enjoyed his experience of Hopkins on Ibsen's *Little Eyolf*, and the director was David Jones from *84 Charing Cross Road*. Overshadowing *The Trial* – which was admired but hardly seen outside Britain – was Francis Ford Coppola's sprawling *Dracula*, at $40 million plus, the biggest budget film Hopkins had ever been graced with and for which he earned his biggest ever pay cheque – in excess of $2 million. For *Dracula*, Hopkins said, the attraction was 'the fascination of working with a genius like Coppola. I would have killed for the chance'.

Coppola's casting net had been wide, the project more painstakingly mounted than anything he had done since *Apocalypse Now*. Cast as Van Helsing, Dracula's nemesis, the selection of Hopkins was, said Coppola, an easy choice: 'He is an actor who can command respect from the other cast members.' The lead role casting, however, proved difficult. Coppola's quirky *Dracula* would be the hybrid of a real-life historical figure, the Romanian tyrant Prince Vlad the Impaler, and the devil himself. 'It's a huge, myth-laden role,' said Coppola, 'and it was never going to be easy work.' Gabriel Byrne, Armand Assante and Viggo Mortensen were all tested before the role of Dracula went to British theatrical bad boy Gary Oldman.

Unlike *The Silence of the Lambs*, *Dracula* meted a fair morality, historically face-lifting the old immortal of Bram Stoker's 1897 novel, but otherwise leaving the plot alone. Hopkins avoided discussions about relative morality in Hollywood's new choices and concentrated instead on observing the inner workings of the Hollywood élite. Coppola was the greatest stylist he'd ever encountered and his working methods were more painstaking than anyone he'd experienced. Based at a state-of-the-art, eight-floors office complex atop San Franciso's Sentinel Building, Coppola was a modern-day Thalberg, a mini-studio unto himself, intent on controlling every aspect of production. Like Thalberg, Coppola's career was one of precocious energies and great lapses. His track record veered from the milestone successes of *The Godfather* series (the first two of which won him Academy Awards) to major misjudgements like *One From the Heart* and, ironically, *The Godfather Part III*.

Dracula had come to him in a roundabout way, from the twenty-year-old actress Winona Ryder, who was touting a script given to her by writer James V. Hart. Coppola liked its quirkiness and brought it to Columbia, who promptly agreed a conditional deal.

All the major studios were wary of Coppola's reputation for running over budget. They also believed, Coppola himself said, that he was crazy. Consequently the only deal he could muster was based on studio dictates in crewing and budget. Coppola fumed, but gave way, determined to prove the studios wrong. He quietly followed his personal vision, determined to present not just a compelling pop classic, but something 'unique'. To that end, the director immersed himself in creative planning with cinematographer Michael Balhaus and an experimentally willing cast.

Hopkins perfectly understood the mania before him when Coppola described his modus, saying, 'I can count to ten, but not in that order.' Another actor may have been put off: for Hopkins it was the territory of his own madness. As it progressed, nothing of the production of *Dracula* was conventional. The story itself was tested out by campus readings around San Francisco where a variety of actors read the roles to invited audiences. Then the actual cast was booked for three weeks of the most detailed rehearsals, the last week of which was taped by Balhaus in order, said Coppola, 'to estimate the value of individual movements.'

Stimulating, too, was the motley approach: all schools of acting were represented under one roof. Some of the cast were theatre trained, some, like Oldman, *nouveau* Method. Oldman stood out and, as Coppola hoped, set the pace, 'living' his *Dracula*, drawing what the director called 'the pain' of his character from primal responses recalled from the death of his own father. Most of the time, according to reports from the set, Oldman was drunk. Winona Ryder, despite her several successes in films as variously demanding as *Edward Scissorhands* and *Mermaids*, deemed herself 'too unready' to plumb the agonies of guilt and obsession required for her character of Mina – in this version, Dracula's mistress reborn – and requested an acting coach. Method teacher Greta Seacat accompanied her on set from then on, priming her for every scene. 'She opened a lot of doors inside me,' said Ryder of Seacat. 'I had always gone on my instinct, but for this you couldn't "phone in" anything.' Coppola, said Ryder, 'badgered, threatened, humiliated, teased and courted' her.

Hopkins came in for his share too. Working the trick from *Howards End*, he decided to base Van Helsing on the Walter Huston character in the film of *The Treasure of the Sierra Madre* and grow a similar wispy beard. Coppola looked and said, 'Get it off.' Hopkins shaved it, only to be told, 'Grow it.' Later Coppola pressed all his cast to reach for Oldman's intense character identification. As Hopkins was playing an incidental scene in which he speculates about the nature of evil, Coppola called a cut and demanded that Van Helsing lecture to the crew and cast. Hopkins went with the flow: 'It was good, really. It made me define Van Helsing more and more. He was not just a shadowy do-gooder who slays monsters. He was a troubled man himself, an absinthe drinker, a drug-taker maybe, who had gone through his personal hell and come through like a rod of steel.'

As the production struggled against the clock – and Coppola's penchant for as many as thirty takes on one reaction shot – Hopkins calmed to the tensions. 'I've been down these roads so many times,' he told a friend. 'And really, it's only a movie.' Gary Oldman took the bad-boy slack. During pre-production he was Ryder's best friend – indeed, she had been instrumental in pushing his casting. But some schism happened – some personal, off-the-set incident – and suddenly, said Coppola, 'she recoiled from even touching him'. Coppola liked Oldman and only rose against him when Oldman 'took over' the set in his moments of ebullience. In one incident, in mid-production, Oldman was reportedly booked and sentenced for drunken driving after a night on the town with Kiefer Sutherland. Hopkins later said, 'I could see what he was going through, all the same kind of energy and intensity. I used to get very angry and upset about things . . . but it just gets dull.'

When *Dracula* wrapped in mid-summer Hopkins moved on tirelessly to a few days' cameo on Attenborough's laboured bio-pic of *Chaplin*, then John Schlesinger's *The Innocent*, a muddled, obviously under-funded film based on Ian McEwan's surreal novel. But late in August, after Coppola's reappraisal of no less than 37 different rough cuts of the film, he was called back to do a voiceover for a new narration for *Dracula*. When it was completed Coppola could hold up his head and announce that his film was 'only a couple of dollars over budget', and the point had been proven: anyone who saw the early cuts marked this new *Dracula* as an important work of art.

Opening in America at Christmas 1992, Coppola's *Dracula* sealed Hopkins' Hollywood A-list rating. Though some criticised its melodrama (RADA friend Adrian Reynolds found his performance 'overblown, unsubtle, I didn't like it at all'), the general consensus was that Hopkins' unashamed grandiose size ideally fitted the gargantuan, expressionist splash that was Coppola's vision. Oscar-nominated director John Boorman selected *Dracula* as his film of the year, if not the decade. For him it was the shape of things to come in cinema – 'a brave, artful, experimental, thought-proking *tour de force*'. As with *The Silence of the Lambs*, the film became a box-office 'event', beating standing records in LA, New York and London, where it took more than £350,000 in its first weekend of business.

In the winter of 1992–93, Hopkins was enjoying an unprecedented popularity, famous beyond Burton across the world, with five films playing to all kinds of audiences. His home base was his magnificent, nineteenth-century, six-storey house at Alexander Place, but he was rarely there, preferring, as he told one journalist, 'to make the best of the moment and travel as much as I can. I love hotels. I love the anonymity. The suitcases. The opportunity to try new Indian and Chinese restaurants in new cities. Jenni prefers to stay at home – but it works out well. I like my space now when I'm working.'

In terms of marital comforts, the arrangement was clearly less than perfect, but what it boiled down to was a case of different priorities. Nancy Palmer remained Jenni's closest friend and the bonds of unity were still tight, but Jenni's work with the local Anglican Church was of more interest to her than the intrigues of Hollywood. 'They put themselves at great risk as a couple,' said one mutual London friend who had doubts about Hopkins' declared contentment. 'Had he been failing in his career it would have been easier, but the *speed* of life that accompanies his type of success is very disorientating. Personally, I had my doubts about that marriage. Precedent was, to say the least, is against them.'

In November, while Hopkins was working the American intrigues, Jenni called breathlessly from London. Hopkins said, 'She sounded worried as she said, "I have some news for you." There was a pause. And then she just said straight, "There's a letter offering you a knighthood!" What for? I wondered. I only thought they gave knighthoods to theatrical actors – the luvvies. I'm not one of them, and anyway, I've been away from Britain for so long.' This offhand, modest summary was misleading. In fact, he loved the honour, relished the fulfilment of what he long craved: acceptance from the establishment.

Almost everyone who knew him, who worked with him, whose voices are expressed in this book, offered unbridled delight at the 'overdue' (Ronald Pickup's word) acknowledgement of his work, which was made public on his 55th birthday, 31 December 1992. Among the actors, Alan Dobie voiced the common subtext: 'There is vanity and competition at the heart of all actors, so I cannot say there wasn't a twinge of envy. But, if anyone deserved it in our generation of stage and film actors, it was him. It was also good to see the reintroduction of theatrical knighthoods.

They appear to have skipped a generation, overlooking Finney, Burton, Bates, O'Toole. McKellen was the first of the "new" lads. Tony was an inevitable follow-on.'

Martin Jarvis recognised a further value in the knighthood: 'At a time when the British film industry is so undernourished, and yet churns out so many wonderful directors, actors and small-budget pictures, it is essential. It calls worldwide attention to our people, our quality – and that can only help the industry as a whole.' David Hare, committed social reformer that he is, chided the honours system. 'But, mark you, if you want to give that kind of decoration to anyone, who better than Tony, for all his work on stage and film? Name me a better actor in Britain? I say, bully for him.'

Interviewed shortly after, Peta Barker saw the knighthood's truest value as something that would galvanise her former husband. As a man of energy and ambition, she believed, he would not sit on the honour, but would focus his attention on more actively 'saving the British film industry'. Another close friend doubted any such commitment, imagining 'the contrary, in fact, because there was still this paranoia or schizophrenia about Britishness and British regard. My feeling was that [the knighthood] will close the book on Britain for him. He has reached the top of the ladder and accomplished it all. Now he will strike out for brand new things. Frankly, I thought he would open a production company of his own in Hollywood, or strike out for directing as a second career.'

But the momentum of the jobbing actor went on: back to Ireland for James Ivory's *The Remains of the Day*, based on Kazuo Ishiguro's 1989 Booker prize-winner about the tragic unravelling of an elderly butler's life; thence Wales for a short environmental film; then back to London and Cambridge to portray author C. S. Lewis in *Shadowlands*. In many circles, there was talk of a new headline return to theatre, but Hopkins demurred. 'I just get bored with the long runs,' he concluded to his friend, the journalist Patrick Hannan, during an HTV tribute, one of many that winter. To writer Robert Kiener he elaborated: 'I'm not interested in climbing the Everest of Shakespeare anymore. He's so difficult and I don't like falling, especially in public places.'

The energies of preeminent success were instead funnelled into *Remains* and *Shadowlands*, two films strongly linked by austerity and by the sublime restraint embodied in the lead characters. In retrospect, this double-header, which would hit cinemas worldwide a year after the Oscar win, represented the true, focused rebirth for Hopkins. In the previous three years he'd run the primary gauntlet, from Mick Jagger to monsters, from Kafka to the grandstanding Hollywoodese of Van Helsing. Now he was intent on the detail of the small canvas, embracing character roles that demanded the finest intensity art film demands.

Comforted by his familiarity with Ivory, *Remains* drew out the masterly best in him, allowing a performance of reticent power that swung the most polarised reviews and, very appropriately, inspired extremes of emotion in its audience. Superficially, the story's appeal for the American market was the tried-and-tested allure of its setting. *Upstairs Downstairs*, the marathon London Weekend series of life in an early twentieth-century London household, was one of the most successful imports on PBS throughout the eighties. Its star was Hudson, played by Gordon Jackson, who dominated the arcane parallel worlds of the privileged and the 'downstairs' staff. Now, in Ivory's most restrained film, Hopkins was Stevens, another Hudson, suspended between alternative universes and adrift in unspoken love for Miss Kenton, the former housekeeper at Darlington Hall.

Despite the success of their previous work together, there was no special chemistry between Hopkins and Ivory, according to crew members: Ivory was loath to give interviews about his methods or his personal feelings about individual actors but, says one technician, 'It was probably the best relationship because it recognised the temporary nature of film relationships, and it was honest.' Another assistant commented, 'They regarded each other like prizefighters, with that sort of sharply defined professionalism.' By all accounts, Hopkins was 'calm and non-argumentative', sanguine from the fragrance of the awards trail. Emma Thompson, who had also starred in *Howards End* and now played Miss Kenton, was also no hardship. She liked Hopkins' company and viewed the film as 'a continuation'. This time round, the route of entry into character was multifold: Ivory had employed a former Buckingham Palace butler as an on-set adviser, which Hopkins found more entertaining than useful; the greater inspiration came from a personal source, from the Welsh recollections of 'Yeats the Traveller', not his grandfather, but a bakery rep who personified restraint and good manners and who looked, said Hopkins, like Sir Malcolm Sargent. Thompson drew from different sources, playing from a deep instinctive eroticism and closely adhering to Ivory's meticulous direction. The combined effect – Ivory's elegiac directing, Thompson's edgy passion, Hopkins' romantic transcendence – produced an authenticity and accessibility beyond the best of Ivory's work. Some reviewers, like the historian David Thompson, experienced the dichotomies as 'torture'; but it was enough to sway the Academy voters to bestow it with no less than eight Oscar nominations, including Best Actor (again), Best Actress and Best Film. Hopkins admirers saw it as full vindication, if any more were needed.

For Peter Barkworth it was 'proof positive' of the leap forward:

> What he did with Stevens, that kind of internalising, is a matter of micro-millimetres [in film]. The crescendo scene [of Stevens and Miss Kenton's relationship] is played in a huge intimate close-up. *Everything* is expressed when Tony closes his eyes – and that cannot be lifted from a script or instructed by a director, no matter how gifted. That scene ennobles the film, and it is the work of a great actor. Maybe *The Silence of the Lambs* released a new wave of confidence. The reward is certainly here: [That scene] is beyond stardom: it's the highest art.

It was clear that the actor had entered a new phase of comfort within himself that put an even higher premium on his instincts. During *Remains*, he told friends, he'd 'cracked the movie' on the very first day with Emma Thompson on the sea front on the north Somerset coast, in the chill of autumn, under lowering skies. The first scenes shot were of the later, fifties-set reunion between Stevens and Miss Kenton. Hopkins told Quentin Falk that the setting reminded him of Chekhov – the ambient light, the quaint ballroom in the background, the poignant strains of a nostalgic *Blue Moon* in the air – and out of this abstraction he and he alone extrapolated the components of romance. 'You know,' he'd told Thompson, 'this [setting] really is heartbreaking.'

That Chekhovian mood was bottled and reopened for the follow-up *Shadowlands*, a Richard Attenborough film version of Nicholson's dour television play, about the sad love life of the author C. S. Lewis, whose fame, derived from children's works like the *Narnia Chronicles*, lent him little joy. Nicholson's play, first filmed by the BBC in the seventies with Joss Ackland as Lewis, was considered an unlikely film subject, not because of its central tragedy – about the terminal illness at the heart of Lewis's late-life marriage – but for its overweening wordiness. 'Movie adaptations [from literary or play sources] require a mad courage,' said Lindsay Anderson, who admired Attenborough and kept an eye on Hopkins' growth. 'I learnt with [novelist David Storey's] *This Sporting Life* that you had to have respect for the source, but no film succeeds by words. In *Sporting Life* we threw away the book and started from scratch. *Shadowlands* needed that sort of irreverence to get it going. Lewis' life was fascinating, but the original play was too much moaning and whinnying.'

Still, Hollywood always had an appetite for moaning and whinnying and *Shadowlands'* essence, as Attenborough perfectly understood, was not a million miles from the beloved tradition of romantic mortality tales, from *Love Story* to *Beaches*, nor indeed from the cookie-cutter Douglas Sirk tearjerkers. What made it special, however, was the authentic eccentricity of Lewis – a genuinely quirky spirit immersed in the formality of Oxford academe in the morally repressive 1950s – and the unlikely attraction to a ballsy American divorcee.

Researching Lewis and revisiting his stories of the kingdom of Narnia, Hopkins found him 'strange', and took that hook on which to hang his characterisation. In the script, Lewis is a neurotic introvert liberated, then crippled, by romantic love. There are strong undertones that amount to an indictment of romantic love, but Attenborough, renowned for his sentimentality, headlined behaviour instead, relishing this chance to focus less on the broad sweep of biopic *à la* Chaplin and concentrate on the vagaries of the heart. Attenborough saw and exploited a happy confluence between Lewis and Hopkins. The reality of Lewis' nature – a Christian essayist whose obsession with the allegorical aspects of religion stunted his emotional development and left him incapable of dealing with the vicissitudes of human relationships – echoed something of Hopkins' neuroses. Beset with self-doubt arising from a chronically unbalanced personal life, Hopkins had been unable to orientate himself to sober living. Acting became the allegorical obsession – until he turned round and faced down the manipulative bullies like Dexter who thwarted his instincts, his sexuality, his sense of self. Prior to the great showdown with Dexter in the late eighties, *Shadowlands* would not have been achievable. The courage to confront his demons was the great shift into art. Lindsay Anderson among several contemporaries specifies the telling scene in *The Bounty* that identified a demarcation point: 'Hopkins is Bligh on the Tahitian beach during the ritual feast to stimulate the gods. The tribal youngsters play out a fornication to excite the gods and Fletcher Christian, of course, is loving it. But Bligh is repulsed by the naked women and lusting men. It is one of the great moments of self-revelation where you sense the actor subsuming and *being*. It is Hopkins who is being repulsed, because that confessional openness of uninhibited sexuality is beyond him.'

After *M. Butterfly*, repression and repulsion were redundant and the liberation of confronting himself unleashed the magnificent control of *The Silence of the Lambs* and beyond. Despite the fact that *Shadowlands* was manifestly a triumph – honoured with a Golden Globe at the same time that *Remains of the Day* was sweeping the boards with Oscar, BAFTA and National Board of Review accolades – Hopkins regarded it with some disdain. He had liked Debra Winger, playing his lover and wife, the New York poet Joy Davidman, but had laboured to pull against her tendency to over-rehearse and Attenborough's legendary, sometimes tedious sentimentality.

Five years later, he would dismiss both films in an interview with the *Houston Chronicle*, condemning the very restraint for which they were applauded: 'All these characters who are dead from the kneecaps up' irritated him, he claimed, but the comment came from the new perspective of yet another self-challenging growth spurt. 'I got the impression,' said Anderson, 'that he peaked intellectually with *Silence of the Lambs*, *Remains* and *Shadowlands*. The industry recognised [this moment] in the multitude of awards thrown at him. But his nature was convulsive, and even though the great personal emotional resolutions had occurred, it was plain to see that he wouldn't just stop and park. It was never that way for Olivier either. You reach the peak, but then you have to look for other places to go.'

The other peaks, for those who knew him, were obvious. Within a week of wrapping *Shadowlands* he was cashing in his Hollywood chips and flying to Canada for *Legends of the Fall* – finally 'the John Wayne deal' that he'd fantasised about since his late teens. His timing couldn't have been better. In the nineties, the cult of the Western, dormant through the previous decade, was reemerging in a series of interesting originals that followed *Dances with Wolves*: *Last of the Mohicans*, *Tombstone*, and *The Unforgiven*. *Legends of the Fall*, based on Jim Harrison's epic of a father's struggle to raise his sons in turn-of-the-century Montana, was hardly original, but it had the staple elements of the Hollywood grand-slammer.

Chicagoan director Ed Zwick, whose Harvard and American Film Institute education, plus ten years' experience in hit television-making, lent him a comprehensive understanding of the Hollywood model, had first spotted the viability of the story when he read it in *Esquire* almost twenty years before. Zwick was, he insists, determined to make *Legends*, seeing a parallel in the 'odyssey' of the fictional Ludlow family with the trials of his own life. Living through the unexpected death of his brother, television success, marriage and children, Zwick related, he says, more and more with the struggles of the Ludlows. Finally, the golden key to pursue the project came through his casual association with a young actor who worked two days on *thirtysomething*. William Brad Pitt was on the brink of the big time when Zwick sat and talked about their respective futures during *thirtysomething*.

The Harrison story involved a father and three sons, the middle one of whom was passionate and dangerous. Before *Interview with the Vampire*, before *Thelma and Louise*, Zwick saw Pitt as Tristan, the great catalyst of the Ludlow story. For two years Zwick sat on the script of *Legends*, but when Pitt read it during *Interview with the Vampire*, he immediately pledged himself. When *Vampire* soared into mega-profits, passing the $150 million bonanza line, Pitt's support sealed Zwick's film deal.

Zwick's 1989 success with the Civil War yarn, *Glory* (which won Denzel Washington a Best Supporting Actor Oscar), reinforced Columbia's belief, but *Legends* was a vast project – spanning decades of storyline and reaching from Montana to the Ypres trenches of World War I – and it was only by the most stringent budgetary 'housekeeping' that the production was green-lighted late in 1992. At Harvard, says Zwick, he learned 'how to work within large, complex institutions and how to manipulate them for your own ends.' In the case of the Columbia deal, the manipulation was worked by persuading Pitt to defer his fees (as Zwick deferred his), and resiting the film to Calgary, in Canada, where at least $2 million could be shaved off the projected $32-million budget.

Hopkins came aboard as part of a mosaic of contrasting talents strategically assembled. His role was Col William Ludlow, the patriarch who would fight to build a life for his family. The very experienced Aidan Quinn was cast as the elder brother, and Henry Thomas, in limbo since his childhood stardom in *E.T.*, became the youngster. Julia Ormond, a virtual newcomer, was imported from Britain and read satisfactorily with Zwick and Pitt in New York. Thus assembled, the ensemble took off in August for fourteen weeks in Calgary, allegedly the driest province of Canada. In fact, for at least half the time, wet weather conditions kept the production reshuffling scenes.

Reports from the front line quickly suggested stress fractures. Pitt and Zwick were, allegedly, arguing round the clock. And even Hopkins was rattled by Zwick's bombast. Rarely sedentary, Zwick's screaming responses to the minor dilemmas of the day's shoot immediately offended Hopkins, who called an assistant aside and urged him to warn the director of his own short fuse. Thereafter, says Hopkins, Zwick was an angel. For Pitt, the arguments were both inevitable and worthwhile. Zwick was nothing if not a perfectionist. His view of film was as a perennial challenge to truth. 'Every moment in a movie is a concession to something *you know* is true,' he once told a Harvard audience. The American West of lore, he stated, never existed. But 'the myths of a culture are sometimes as important as the history. As dramatists, we are as interested in the iconography as we are in the individual truths.'

Pitt was ready for argument because he had his own views and his own truths. 'People want to hear that we were not getting along,' Pitt told a visiting journalist during a food break in Calgary. 'But [the actor] reads things in scripts and envisions them. Remember in *Spinal Tap*, when they wanted the big Stonehenge and it came out tiny? I [don't want] my character to show his cards so blatantly and Ed [does]. So you've got two people who care about the film . . . Fortunately, something good is going to be squeezed out of that.'

For the visiting journalists, Hopkins seemed not just happy to be aboard, but manic. Clad in stetson, boots and a long bright red scarf, with Jenni by his side again, he jauntily boasted that these were the best days of his life. 'I turned up on set the other day and said to the director, I've done Shakespeare, Ibsen and Chekhov, but I've been rehearsing to be a cowboy all my life. The 'jolly 59-year-old' defied the 'generally subdued' hangover of weeks of intense night-shooting that recreated Ypres at the nearby Indian reservation: 'Look at me. I'm not discovering the cure for cancer. I'm just getting paid to play out all my childhood fantasies.' He liked Pitt and Zwick and all the others, but the best part was the unselfconsciousness that came with relived childhood. He had, he said, been smiling all over LA to see himself, at last, for what he truly was – a modern-day cowboy: 'This role gets me out of those stiff English parts and helps me stay on the move, which is what I love best.'

And stay on the move he did, though not very far physically, in accepting Alan Parker's offer to join *The Road to Welville*, an absurd comedic version of the story of the elder brother of the famous Kellogg family, John Harvey, health-guru-inventor of, among other things, the 'orgasm machine' (younger sibling Will founded the Kellogg cornflakes empire, though, Parker insists, John Harvey invented the food). Parker had chosen the project as a counterweight to some of his recent heavy-duty dramas, like *Mississippi Burning*. 'I'd done three serious films, and then I'd done *The Commitments*, which was funny, and I enjoyed doing that, so was looking for something [else] funny.' T. Coraghessan Boyle's novel, based on well-documented reality, was handed to him, and a number of other potential directors, in manuscript form in 1992. 'It was a weird world I didn't know about. I just thought it was very cinematic. Everybody in it was crazy and it was outrageous and I thought it would make good film material.' Having met Boyle and decided to commit to the film 'about this lunatic Kellogg' Parker immediately phoned Hopkins to offer the role. Parker's enthusiasm to book Hopkins – 'I got down on my knees and wept, begging him' – is a measure of the ennobled heights to which he had risen. At first, says Parker, the actor stalled. He had yet to make *Shadowlands*, so didn't want to commit. Parker insisted on delaying the film – whose $22-million budget demanded the endorse-ment of a blue chip star – and was rewarded by Hopkins' usual gung ho. As Hopkins worked on Zwick's film, Parker finished his final draft of Boyle's story and set about recreating a Hollywood studio backlot version of Kellogg's outrageously innovative sanatorium at Battle Creek, New York State, the original building of which, as with the town itself, was now derelict.

On the phone to Hopkins in Canada, Parker was pleased to hear Hopkins' warm reception for the script, but less keen on Hopkins' take on John Harvey Kellogg. There were photographs of Kellogg at the turn of the century aplenty, but, watching Bugs Bunny on television in his Calgary hotel, Hopkins abruptly decided to play the old guru with excessively protruding buck teeth – 'because, after all, he was a vegetarian like Bugs Bunny'. When, weeks later, Hopkins showed up on location in upstate New York, Parker was depressed to see the crew laugh at the set of teeth Hopkins had taken it on himself to get made. 'The crew laughing is never a good sign,' said Parker; but he was compliant because, in his observation of Hopkins, he detected a discomfort, despite the thespian skills, at portraying a dyed-in-the-wool American. 'He needed something physical to get a hold of,' Parker said. In fact, Hopkins was in outright experimental mode, interpreting the 'outrageous screenplay' as bald comedy and applying the kind of age-tested actorly devices so beloved of Peter Sellers, who built Inspector Clouseau – a bumble-brain not unlike Kellogg – from the furnishings of Burberry rain coats, a moustache spotted on an Italian poster ad and a clichéd accent.

Welville functioned as a release of steam, for both Parker, hot from the worldwide success of *The Commitments*, and Hopkins, hot from the best of good runs. The calculation was indicative of a new philosophy that answered the queries posed by many watching his progress, like Lindsay Anderson and Peter Barkworth. Barkworth had been asked to star in *Shadowlands* alongside Hopkins, but was committed to touring Simon Gray's *Quartermain's Terms* and, consequently, turned Attenborough down. 'I really wished I could've work with Tony then, because there was much to learn from him. His career had become transcendent: there is no other word for it. Myself, it took me a long time to master the 'instant' acting of film; not so [with] Tony. He obviously grasped it early on. Then there was the massive spurt. There's no doubt his alcoholism and recovery opened wider doors to him. [By the time of *Shadowlands* and *Welville*] there was an obvious finessing in progress. He knew the ropes, he was the master, and with that wealth in his hands he was not wanting. He pressed every frontier within himself. I began to think: he has given us all these variations of character and ethnicity – where can he possibly go now?'

The Road to Welville and *Legends of the Fall*, opening in cinemas worldwide inside a span of eight weeks around Christmas of 1994, offered Hopkins a conclusive case study of relative film principles. *Welville*, the arty and Englishy picture, cost $22 million and earned a disappointing $6.5 million in its first two weeks; *Legends*, an unquestionably Hollywood-slick work that cost not much more, took $14 million in its first weekend alone, and went on to gross more than $160 million, achieving solid 'hit' status. The lesson learnt was the obvious one: that Hollywoodese was the paying route, the power route. 'I make no apologies for my Hollywood leanings,' he'd said the year before. 'There is no shame in entertainment.'

The full force of recognition of the rewards of Hollywood put an end to the game of boundary-leaping from American mainstream to art house and, yet again, recast Hopkins' direction. But in truth he needed no object lessons: his self-steering new course was already set. During *Welville*, said Alan Parker, Hopkins was emphatically clear about demarcation points. Parker's script required his character, Kellogg, to give himself an enema. 'But he refused to do it. He said, There are two things I will not do. I won't give myself an enema, and I won't wear the pink corset [required in the script].' Parker was in no doubt as to the determination of his self-image. The days of manipulation by his peers were over. It was he, and he alone, who called the shots.

Chapter 17

ISHMAEL AT THE EDGE

The payoff for the consolidation of the American career was a return trip to Wales, by way of personal reward and a farewell. For the last eighteen months the ties that bound him seemed closer than ever, and he had been happy to participate in fund-raisers for the Snowdonia National Trust appeal, and to continue his private counselling support. He had even managed to reacquaint himself with Abigail who, under the name Abigail Harrison, continued to pursue an acting career – though the relationship waned almost as quickly as it warmed. But friendships within the Welsh acting community were warmer than they'd ever been and it was out of such affection the offer came from the prestigious Theatr Clwyd's director Helena Kaut-Howson to work with her group. In February, before *Welville*, Hopkins chaired a Masterclass and encountered the evening's compere, writer Julian Mitchell, who had drafted a new adaptation of Chekhov's *Uncle Vanya,* planned for the theatre's intimate Emlyn Williams auditorium. Hopkins knew the play inside-out, having acted in the BBC's 1970 version directed by Christopher Morahan. During supper backstage, he suddenly told Kaut-Howson, without preamble, that he would like to act in and direct Mitchell's version – and also film it. The film connection came by way of Granada television whose key producer, June Wyndham Davies, another affectionate Welsh supporter, had recently suggested that Hopkins might direct a Charles Wood-scripted version of Rattigan's *The Winslow Boy*, for Granada's film arm. After the supper with Kaut-Howson and Mitchell, Hopkins phoned Granada who immediately confirmed a commitment for *Uncle Vanya*. But there were problems: Michael Blakemore, the director whom Hopkins had abandoned during *Macbeth* at the National had just completed his own film version of *Uncle Vanya*, retitled *Scenes from a Country Life*, starring Sam Neill and Greta Scacchi, which was bound for international release. Hopkins was unfazed: Blakemore had resited his romanticised *Uncle Vanya* to Australia in the 1920s; his would be set in a South Wales village at the turn of the century. It is a measure of Hopkins' gilded status that Granada, the funders, didn't hesitate to support the actor's headlong dash into production, agreeing to shoot the film before the production of the stage play in order to take advantage of the warmth of summer.

Hopkins yet again demonstrated what Simon Ward called his 'innate appetite for hairpin change' in the speed with which his *Uncle Vanya* was cast and mounted. The spurt of energy – astonishing even to those who knew his methods – also produced a self-penned piano soundtrack to accompany the work. 'How does one do that?' Ward mused. 'How does one take off the cowboy hat and become *Chekhov* in a shrug? Name two actors anywhere who can pull that off on that scale.' But there was a strategy afoot. The 'British way', always the irritant, was now a challenge to usurp. He had briefly considered directing the Rattigan, but the overdose of stiff upper lips in *Shadowlands* and *Remains* demanded counterbalance: his Chekhov instead would be bloody and earthy and a universe away from the BBC edition. The title he chose was *August*, the perfect encapsulation of the Chekhovian idyll. The lead actress he chose was equally symbolic: Kate Burton, his idol's daughter, whom he'd met twenty years before, and with whom he renewed acquaintance at a post-Oscars party in Hollywood where, on the spot, he offered her the major co-starring role.

Thirty-six-year-old Burton had studied at Yale Drama School, specialising in Ibsen and Strindberg but, given the opportunity, she told an American interviewer, 'I *always* chose Chekhov'. Here she would play Helen Blathwaite, the enigmatic wife of the professor who, returning from the big city to the Welsh farm whose legacy he shares with his daughter, finds himself the target of the hatred of his former brother-in-law, Ieuan Davies, who manages the farm and has fallen in love with Helen. Ieuan was, of course, Mitchell's version of Vanya, and the delight for all involved was the leap of humour that the writer had invested in this new version, and which Hopkins would milk, emphasising from day one the kind of stellar close-ups beloved of Hollywood but that here would amplify Chekhov's study of the anguish of hopeless love.

Only fully contracted in April, *August* was shooting under Anthony Hopkins' direction on the Lleyn Peninsula, not many miles from his birthplace, in July, with crew well familiar with the actor's work – including Robin Vidgeon, who had been camera assistant on *The Lion in Winter*, as cinematographer – and actors who ranked among his personal favourites. Old boozing buddy Gawn Grainger was cast as Dr Lloyd (Chekhov's Astrov) and Leslie Phillips as the professor; the rest of the cast was a hand-picked ensemble of the best of Welsh theatre. In the judgement of most, Hopkins was nothing if not adept. In his words, he found the discipline of organising a film shoot 'surprisingly easy', so easy, in fact, that he was happy to undertake more than a score of set-ups for the first day alone and, by the end, was several days ahead of schedule and under budget. But the good news stopped there.

During production, Hopkins told several visiting journalists that he believed he'd found a second career. In the autumn, rehearsing the theatre play while cutting the film with editor Edward Mansell, everything changed. One observer believed 'there was an abrupt *volte face* when the realities of editing and dubbing emerged. Film-making is three phases: preparation, which is casting and locations and tweaking the script, and is sociable and fun; then shooting, which is very creative and communal; and then the post-production, which is two or three bodies in a darkened room, with coffee and beer and notes and the ticking clock. Tony had never really endured that full-on. But this is the part where all focus is on the director – this is the moment the dark-room film develops – and executives demand their results. This, on *August*, is where he came unstuck, because he'd been spoilt, and now he was in the deep end.' Sure enough, Hopkins baled out on the edit, asking Mansell to locate discarded footage and drastically recut the first assembly. 'It was just so damned boring,' Hopkins later admitted, while emphasising his gratitude for Mansell's genius. In the end, Mansell handed in a decent, well-paced, 90-minute cut, and Hopkins admitted the clear realisation that 'I don't want to direct films. I'm an actor, that's where my bread is buttered.'

Commercially, *August* was destined to fail miserably, barely seen in Britain and opening at just five theatres in the US eighteen months after completion and, according to the published grosses, totalling receipts of less than $70,000 against its $4-million budget. But there was a residue of glory. The *San Francisco Chronicle*'s reviewer observed the short distance between Ieuan Davies and Vanya – where 'nothing substantial was changed beyond the character's poison of choice shifting from vodka to whiskey' – but failed to notice the shorter distance between Vanya's inebriated imperative and the actor's, each the product of frustrated need. Some, like Lindsay Anderson, saw this as a critical expression of maturity and power. The legend of Hopkins' drinking problem being so well circulated, said Anderson, the study of Vanya/Ieuan 'showed immense intelligence. Whether it succeeded or not is almost by the way. Art is about courage, and playing that close to the edge takes real courage.' In the end the film was not the bold show of control that might shame 'the Brit way', but rather a daring fusion film – the Welsh equivalent of the culture-straddling Bergmanesque work of Woody Allen, like *Interiors* or *September* – and no less significant for that.

The true value of Hopkins' *August* was as a declaration of intent. Though *Silence* had established a massive screen persona, its inevitable limitation – 'the Boris Karloff connection' – would not sustain him. By the end of 1994, with a flood of offers unlike he'd ever seen, the battle lines were redrawn. Fending off the non-stop press queries about a *Silence* follow-up, he allowed the work to speak for itself: character studies of substance stimulated him; Hollywood would have to meet him halfway to keep him in court. 'The attraction of being in Hollywood,' he told Martin Jarvis, 'is the volume of work done there. The rest, in terms of choice, is up to me.' Jarvis recalled: 'Most actors are looking for the Hollywood endorsement, and when they get it, they sell out in some way. Look at the mess Burton got himself into with those pointless action films. Tony took the kind of disciplined character essaying he'd done in *The Bunker* as his template. If Hollywood wanted him as a permanent resident, they were going to get some *big* character showcases.'

Over the next two years, Hopkins parlayed Lecteresque evil into the subtlest projections of darkness in a trio of large-scale, character-study films, each controversial, each flawed, but all memorable. The first, Oliver Stone's *Nixon*, gave him serious cause for pause. Stone's reputation for historical revisionism, a source of outright agitation well beyond the film industry, intrigued Hopkins, but the suggestion, via ICM, of the lead role in a film about the 37th President of the United States floored him. His initial reaction, well reported, was to tell the agent that the proposition was absurd. But Nixon, who had died in April during the run-up to *August*, and was again the subject of enormous academic and street debate, was too juicy a subject to reject out of hand. Stone's choice of Hopkins was unequivocal. 'He *feels* like Nixon,' he told reporters hot on the trail of yet another inevitably controversial docu-drama. 'In *Remains of the Day* I felt his sense of isolation, his sense of sadness. In *Shadowlands* there was an emotional fullness to his character. Hopkins is a *complete* actor. He's not like some of these by-the-numbers TV actors who have their bag of tricks. Tony is sincerely exploring the universe. He's bold, that's what does it for me.'

Stone flew to London, breakfasted with the actor and told him his grand vision: like his *JFK*, the project was less psycho-biography than a contextual study of what he called 'the illusion of power'; there was no 'black and white' in the Nixon story – rather, the fascination was in the grey areas, the hesitations and self-doubts and human flaws that com-pounded to bring about a national crisis. Suddenly the 'absurdity of a British actor portraying the essence of Americanism' no longer offended

Hopkins. Instead, he heard echoes of his own experience and, particularly, of his father's perception of his own failures. The breakfast meeting, though, was not all intellectual engagement, as Hopkins recalled: '[Stone said,] "So you don't want to do it, eh? Chickening out, eh? Well, you can go off and do those boring Hungarian films you usually do that nobody goes to see" – the-son-of-a-bitch! – "or you can take the chance and be bold."'

'I was so sure he was the one for Nixon,' said Stone. 'Others disagreed, but, for me, he had the physical look – the large face, the bulbous nose, the forehead – and the rest you couldn't define. I bullied him. And, it took a little persuasion, but he phoned the next day and said, "OK, all right, I'll do it."'

That Hopkins was assuming the highest-exposure risk – with the corollary accusations of actorly arrogance and the absolute inevitability of Stone-credo controversy – says much for his emotional relaxation. But it was a delicate balancing act that made the first weeks of production shaky. Day by day, as he absorbed the 170-page script written by Steve Rivele, Christopher Wilkinson and Stone, there were frantic adjustments and long, long discussions with Stone.

According to Julian Fellowes, Hopkins was still entertaining doubts till the last minute. Only by Fellowes telling him to imagine a Sunset Boulevard hoarding announcing 'Nick Nolte as Nixon' was the deal swung. The prospect of such a casting outrage, not untypical of Hollywood whim, calmed Hopkins – at least temporarily. Weeks later, during make-up tests, the abomination of a doughy false nose further unbalanced him. Later, with production up and running, a gushing indiscretion from the actor Paul Sorvino, playing Henry Kissinger, brought the shoot to a standstill. Sorvino, an Italian-American best versed in Mafia films, told Hopkins his accent as Nixon – the product of well-tested mimickry, after studying fifty hours of Nixon video tapes – was all wrong. 'That was a nightmare,' said Hopkins. 'That was not a very pleasant day . . . [and it] wasn't a very smart thing [for Sorvino] to do.' For half an hour the possibility of the actor walking off the film became a reality but, said Stone, his 'discipline and humanity' kept him aboard. So too did the friendly voices in the wings. The actor David Hyde Pierce intervened, reassuring Hopkins of his accuracy. And James Woods, whom Hopkins had long admired, playing Nixon's aide H. R. Haldeman, helped. Woods' clear admiration for Hopkins kept spirits high, as did the outright compliments from another key player in the Nixon story, John Dean, who was working throughout as Stone's Oval Office consultant. 'Oh my God, it's weird,' Dean told Hopkins. 'You don't have the nose. You don't have the voice. But you are just like him. You've got the guy. You're there!'

The next twelve weeks – from commencement of shooting in May at Sony's Culver City studios, where all interiors were built, till location shooting around the Washington landmarks in July – were among the most mentally taxing of Hopkins' career. Stone's reputation is as an exhaustively prepared and single-minded filmmaker, and it was just as well because the huge span of the plotline, from Nixon's Quaker childhood on an impoverished California lemon farm through the Ike years to the epoch-defining scandal of Watergate which occupies the last half of the film, necessitated huge modulations in performance. Later, Hopkins widely announced that the production 'finished him' – but it didn't, beyond the mental exhaustion for which he was already, by dint of frequent blow-outs, well equipped to handle. In truth, *Nixon* tested his tenacity to the limit, and the fact that he did recover, and was in the south of France shooting another bio-epic, James Ivory's *Surviving Picasso*, within a fortnight of wrapping up Washington, proved the greatest superstar commendation: not only did he survive a Stone multi-disciplined epic, but he headlined it, 'carrying' a Hollywood blockbuster as the lead name for the first time.

Nevertheless, *Nixon* was a close call in terms of survival. From the start, it was evident that Stone intended a curve ball: a sympathetic rendering of Nixon's personality, as opposed to the conventional catch-all tarring familiar since Redford's *All the President's Men*. Questioned at the time of filming, the director was vague about the belief in Nixon's fundamental decency implied in the script. He was not personally sympathetic: 'Empathetic is the word. He was a man. He lived life in the arena, sometimes right, sometimes wrong. You have to put flesh on the man. Liberals from the sixties still hate him; it's a badge of honour [to hate him]. They won't lose their anger. Maybe they feel their suit of armour will fall off, or they'll lose their identity. It's time to move beyond the ideology and look at *what he did* . . .'

In Stone's view, what he did was potentially substantial: the 'triangular diplomacy' of stroking China and Russia while maintaining a military presence in Asia, for example, was pure genius. But Nixon was compromised by 'the most complex human weaknesses' manifesting as chronic low self-esteem and a deep self-loathing and, more than anything, by his paralysing guilt obsession over recruiting the assassination team that, having failed to kill Cuba's Fidel Castro, later killed JFK for his failure to back the anti-Castro efforts with sufficient zeal. From Hopkins' point of view, perhaps actorly duty was enough; but Stone's persuasion had left its mark. 'I know this is a fiction based on *some* fact,' Hopkins told interviewers shortly after the film wrapped. 'It is only Oliver's and my view of the guy . . .'

The *Washington Post*, always suspicious of historical inaccuracy at the heart of Stone's unending anti-institution/anti-press polemic, could not, at first, see much reason to complain. Stone was, said the *Post*, 'the most Nixonian' of all film directors, a shadow of the President in so many ways – from the 'high octane blend of ambition and idealism' to 'the good soldierly tendency to lead with the chin'. The only insult, sugar-coated with irony, was in the conclusion that, unlike Nixon who could not express his anger, Stone relished in giving vent to his, '[wearing] his wildness like a diamond-studed stetson'. But within two years of the film's razzmatazz opening – and superb box-office, force-fed by exhaustive personal promotions by actor and director – came the crash. Stone's purpose in making so evidently redemptive a film, he'd said, was to promote 'emotional catharsis' within its audience. Suddenly, in January 1998, the core focus theorised to illuminate Nixon's inadequacy was seen to be spurious. Two hundred hours of newly released audio tapes from the National Archive, transcribed by author-historian Stanley Cutler and published in his book, *Abuse of Power*, showed that, rather than suffering survivor's guilt over Kennedy's demise, Nixon had repeatedly tried to publicly disgrace him. Stone showed Hopkins' Nixon trying to conceal tapes relating to the disastrous Bay of Pigs operation sanctioned by Kennedy. The new research proved the opposite: Nixon had obsessively pushed to declassify the Bay of Pigs tapes and leak them to the press. Far from the compassionate dignity Stone 'absurdly argued' for Nixon, suggested the *Post*, 'the man was actually trying to assassinate his rival a second time round'.

Stone, who by then had moved on to *Natural Born Killers*, avoided debate, the better to keep his powder dry. His tacit response was in his long-stated principle: that his work, like others', was the product of the kind of personal Pavlovian response that made all art essentially political. And anyway, as he'd told Charlie Rose, political commentaries apart, one must not forget the first position of film, as a *dramatic* medium; drama dated back to Sophocles, and film dramas like *Nixon* merely trod the same territory, telling tales of metaphor and symbolism that might provoke, but shouldn't be taken literally.

Hopkins too dodged controversy and the speed of his career was such now that, by the time the *Post* was parading the invalidity of *Nixon*, he was fighting new wars.

If, as Frank Rich of the *New York Times* had it, Stone's *Nixon* had sentimentalised a scoundrel, then the next project, stumbled into in true weariness, was a direct inversion. Ivory's *Surviving Picasso* took another legendary figure, the greatest artist of the twentieth century, and spun him into a thug. The emotional and intellectual challenge for Hopkins was obviously daunting but, despite his protestations of exhaustion, strength was drawn from the re-prioritising of his personal life. A new home had been acquired – a two-bedroom bungalow, clinging to a steep slope in Pacific Palisades, surrounded by wooden decking from which, with a telescope, he could study Catalina Island. Along with the house, came a new fitness regime that saw him lose almost 30 lb in weight during *Nixon*.

And along with the weight loss came the rumours. Stoically married in the eyes of the press, there were suddenly whispers of dalliances with a woman encountered in AA. *Vanity Fair* had him as the macho gypsying 'Knight Rider', photographed broodingly by Annie Leibovitz behind the wheel of a steel-blue, two-seater Riviera on a desert road at Amboy, California, announcing, 'I may have screwed up a lot of my life. I'm not a very good husband. I'm not a good father. I'm a roamer.'

'He was more than a roamer,' claims one actor colleague unseduced by this emerging James Dean-like figure.

> He was like [President Bill] Clinton who, at that time, was quietly known to be a rake, but was so swathed in the presidency that you took him at face value. Tony hadn't been a star. He was a relatively anonymous character actor, the kind the tabloids tend to ignore. He took advantage of that anonymity. He was coming out of himself and looking around and saying, let's slow down here, let's smell the roses. He wasn't boozing, but he was into a new social scene with the new level of success and meeting some nice women, and he was open to new relationships.

Another colleague dismisses suggestions of deception and double standards: 'We knew about the "new" Tony because he admitted it. Yes, he'd met someone at AA. But, the story goes, he stood up at a New Year's party [New Year's Eve 1995] and told the partygoers that he was quitting his marriage and starting afresh with this woman. We all knew about the changes coming.'

But first there was Merchant and Ivory's *Surviving Picasso*, a project on its knees before it began. For decades filmmakers had attempted to mount films about the great modernist. Since the early fifties, Anthony Quinn (who would portray Gauguin famously alongside Kirk Douglas' Van Gogh) had been trying. But only one film, Henri-Georges Clouzot's remarkable 1955 experiment, *Le Mystère Picasso*, made it to the screen. The problem, always, was the Picasso family endorsement. Picasso himself loved cinema but had little time for its technicalities.

Warners was in the picture for *Surviving Picasso*, which had started as a pet project of producer David Wolper's. Wolper commissioned

Picasso's forties' mistress, Francoise Gilot, to work with the American-Greek author and socialite Arianna Stassinopoulos Huffington, on a script. Gilot's role in Picasso's life was substantial: she had lived with him from 1943 until 1953 and had two children, Paloma and Claude. But in the middle sixties, she co-authored (with art critic Carlton Lake) a harsh, revelatory book which was the subject of a failed major legal action by Picasso himself in the French courts. The central accusations of the book which Picasso tried to stop seem, in retrospect, banal. The artist was, claimed Gilot, a controlling individual, given to working all hours and, consequently, bizarre mood changes. When they'd first met in February 1944, wrote Gilot, Picasso had told her 'that he felt our relationship would bring light into both our lives. My coming to him, he said, seemed like a window that was opening up and he wanted it to remain open. I did, too, as long as it let in the light. When it no longer did, I closed it, much against my own desire.' Gilot, who later married the polio inoculation pioneer Jonah Salk and settled in America, held this uncontested distinction: she was the *only* woman who ever walked out on Picasso.

Though, from the start, Wolper's development was based on Gilot's work, it was Huffington who drove the project and it was her own book, the controversially racy 1988 biography, *Picasso: Creator and Destroyer*, that informed the final screenplay and started the rot. Gilot's book was partisan, but emotional: even the cloth-eared reader could imagine the mental toll on a 21-year-old *ingenue*, setting up home with an insatiable, chronically-risk-taking 61-year-old. But Huffington's book was remorselessly cynical: for her, Picasso was, simply, a moral bankrupt who abused women. This core notion, embraced by Wolper, was carried into the final script that Ismail Merchant and James Ivory, Wolper's assigned co-producers, commissioned from their long-standing screenwriter partner, Ruth Prawer Jhabvala. Hopkins, for his part, remained, as he always did now, diplomatically neutral, asserting that this Picasso – like Stone's Nixon – was merely 'one interpretation' of the man. His function as an actor was just to enact the screenplay.

By the summer of 1995, both Gilot and her son Claude, who controlled the Picasso Administration which handles exploitation of the artist's work and image, objected to the film and refused the use of the artist's paintings and sculptures. Merchant attempted to intervene, meeting with Olivier Widmaier Picasso, the artist's grandson by Marie-Thérèse Walter, and a consultant to the Picasso Administration, at the Hotel Raphael in Paris, and entreating him to bring Claude aboard. But the approach was in vain. Olivier did try to persuade Claude, but the latter remained adamant – and, wrote Olivier later, with good cause. The resulting film, in Olivier's view, projected 'a vile and sadistic man' who bore no relation at all to the family man Olivier knew.

Nevertheless, there was honest passion for all concerned in the making of *Surviving Picasso* and that was enough to fuel Hopkins. It was Wolper who had first brought him to America twenty years before and who'd promised him some decent roles after *The Bridge at Remagen* fell through. An avid collector of Picasso sculptures, Wolper was unquestionably an enthusiast – as were, Merchant, Ivory and Jhabvala, all of whom had long held their own plans to forge a Picasso film. According to Wolper, he had 'waited a long time [to find] Jim, Ismail and Ruth, who were the perfect team to do this justice'. For Ivory, the wellspring bubbled during his student days at the University of Oregon: 'All the students wanted to be like Picasso, to live like Picasso. I was the same. I came to France at 22 and lived among the American painters in Paris. Picasso had by then moved to the south of France, but his name and his influence were everywhere. Really, for young artists, he was a god.'

Hounded by the Picasso Administration's lawyers, who threatened every device in French law to stop the film, Ivory began filming his code-named *Number Nineteen* (the nineteenth Mechant-Ivory film) surreptitiously in August on the Place de la Concorde. Throughout the press, Gilot was railing, 'Merchant Ivory have turned my life into a soap opera. The script is so below grade, it is ridiculous . . .' But the producers forged on, grabbing Paris Occupation scenes on the back of the film Ivory was just wrapping, *The Proprietor*, and making extensive contingency plans to shoot along the Italian Riviera, if the authorities of the Côte d'Azur, Picasso's real-life stomping ground, facilitated the process servers. To offset legal threats, private beaches and villas at Hyères and Giens were favoured over public places and the first love scenes, shot with fair historical accuracy at Le Lavandou, were shadowed, inevitably, by a fortress mentality.

Emboldened by surviving *Nixon*, Hopkins, however, had little trouble accessing the ebullience required of Jhabvala's Picasso. Later, willingly on the promotional junkets circuit, he would offer an equivocal thumbnail evaluation of Picasso – 'He was obviously complex, a selfish man and probably a generous one, too' – but it was clear that both he and Ivory saw the key as being *energy*. To Quentin Falk, Hopkins would confess to examining Clouzot's film, borrowing mannerisms, then working as 'a minimalist' to create the character. The evidence upholds this: side by side, Clouzot's filmed Picasso *moves* like Hopkins' version; but that is just the starting point. Thereafter comes the human dynamo, manifest from the start, where, in company of the dour male secretary Sabartes he flirts with Françoise at a Parisian café, till the last, when he explodes in rage at her sullen departure. Where, under Stone's direction, Nixon was about internalising while offering a window to depression, this Picasso was all external gestures, lavish even in reflective moments. And this, in career development terms, was significant because, formerly, as Peter Barkworth opined, Hopkins' delivery had been 'concerned in the main part with what goes on *under the surface*. What you now saw was the great expansiveness that comes with the confidence, I don't doubt, of worldwide acceptance. Still, it takes immense strength to play so frenziedly.'

Notable, too, in *Surviving Picasso* was the actor's comfort portraying a sexual icon. Picasso's life was studded with profound sexual relationships and the film gave glimpses into several. While newcomer Natascha McElhone played Gilot, Julianne Moore played the tormented Dora Maar, the woman Picasso left for Gilot, Susannah Harker played the ever-loyal Marie-Thérèse, Jane Lapotaire was the mad first wife Olga and Diane Venora the redoubtable Jacqueline Roque, whom Picasso married after Gilot left.

Weaving among these strong female presences, Hopkins' Picasso was tender, abrasive, childlike – and masterful. The best of these scenes, the one that perhaps most illustrates Picasso's way with women and might equally suggest something of the domestic Anthony Hopkins to come, is the confrontation in the studio between Gilot and Dora. Picasso is on a ladder, tending a mural, when the women argue about their dominion, then physically slug it out. Picasso's/Hopkins' response is to giggle, shrug, and get on with his work. Hopkins later said he 'identified' with the artist's toughness: 'As an actor one has to be pretty ruthless – very tough, very strong. And perhaps I've gotten tougher and stronger over the years. I probably don't waste much time nowadays.'

To many who knew him there seemed a clear personal redefinition – beyond serendipitous muscle-flexing – in this portrayal of sexual confidence. 'Picasso's ferocious energy and relentless sexuality offered a welcome relief [to Hopkins],' reported *Vanity Fair*, quoting the nascent Knight Rider himself protesting, 'America sees me as playing all those restrained parts. I'm not like that at all in real life.'

Neither *Nixon* nor *Picasso* made money at the box office, a likelihood intuited by Hopkins when he signed, not long after the completion of *Picasso*, for a mainstream thriller from Fox, *The Edge*, to be made in Canada with Alec Baldwin and model-actress Elle Macpherson. A project originally intended for Robert de Niro, producer Art Linson and director Lee Tamahori 'jumped at' the chance of Hopkins, once his agent mooted the idea.

After readings with the cast in New York, Hopkins drove to Calgary to commence production in the second week of August of 1996 – and immediately started to come unstuck. The last twelve months, to be sure, had shaped up as another signal year. Not only had he finally taken legitimate starring status in Hollywood blockbusters, but, bit by bit, it emerged that he had effectively quit his marriage to Jenni Lynton. Through much of the French location work on *Picasso*, his companion was 45-year-old Joyce Ingalls, a former Californian model, once Miss General Tire, who had appeared in the Sears Catalogue and in an episode of *Starsky and Hutch*.

In the mid-seventies, Ingalls began an on-off film career, the highlight of which was a small role in *Paradise Alley* alongside Sylvester Stallone, with whom she'd had an affair. For several months, she and Hopkins were, to all intents, 'a couple' but, according to Jenni, who'd been kept in the dark, the affair was over by the time the Oscar nominations were announced in February. On the gossip gravevine, it was known that Ingalls was sharing the family home at Pacific Palisades. Only weeks before, the tabloids were quoting Hopkins on his devotion to his new partner: 'I think now is the time to really start living. I want to do that with Joyce. She has given me back a passion and vigour that has been missing for years.' But Jenni reported Hopkins calling her with the suggestion that she accompany him to the Oscars, where he was again nominated as Best Actor for *Nixon*. There was no apology, nor explanation. The suggestion was that they bury the past and 'return to normal', an olive branch the long-patient Jenni was ready as ever to accept.

Nixon won nothing at the Oscars (Hopkins lost out to Nicholas Cage, for *Leaving Las Vegas*) but by the summer Hopkins' concerns were for his health. The yo-yo dieting, the constant stooped posture applied for *Nixon* and the emotional strain of the Ingalls affair, reported in the media as nothing less than a tawdry fling (Ingalls, it was reported, had a yen for Welshmen and had also had an affair with Tom Jones), all took their toll. By the time he joined the Rocky Mountains location for *The Edge*, said Hopkins, he was a wreck, all but hooked on painkillers for constant debilitating back pain. The prospect of the eight-week shoot that lay ahead filled him with dread. Unlike any of his films, the physicality demanded by *The Edge* was extreme, requiring him to immerse himself in a crashed sunken aircraft, fight a live Kodiak bear (the selfsame bear that had 'guested' briefly in *Legends of the Fall*) and trek the slopes of the Calgary Rockies, doubling for the wastes of Alaska. The plot, by the respected playwright David Mamet, concerned an intellectual, billionaire businessman, Charles Morse, who suspects his wife Mickey (Elle Macpherson) is having an affair with a fashion photographer, played by Alec Baldwin. The men are thrown together unexpectedly when their light aircraft crashes in the wilderness, forcing them to bury mutual antagonism and collaborate in order to survive. Mamet or not, the storyline – originally sold by the writer to Linson as *The Bookworm* – tilted towards pulp, though Hopkins was making no apologies about it.

From day one, everyone knew Hopkins was in serious trouble. Among the first scenes filmed, on 20 August, was the aftermath of the plane crash that necessitated both Hopkins and Baldwin to be underwater in a lake, in borderline-zero temperatures, for hours on end. Both wore wet suits, but Hopkins was clearly in discomfort. Baldwin, a good swimmer, weathered the scenes well, Hopkins less so. 'I did say that it wouldn't be a picnic,' New Zealander Tamahori recalled. 'We weren't going to be shooting on the back of Big Bear. The truth is, the only way for this to have credibility was to take it to a place that was really incredible and make it look like Anthony and Alec were at the end of the earth.'

At the end of the day, Hopkins was driven to a Canmore medical clinic for tests, then given the next day off. Unit publicist Lee Anne Muldoon reassured the media that the doctor's visit was cautionary, and that Jenni's imminent arrival from London was nothing other than routine. Hopkins needed 'his vitals checked', said Muldoon, and the medical prognosis was fine. 'Mr Hopkins is in every scene in this movie, so we can't work "around" him. It was the production company's suggestion that he see a doctor. He's British, which means he's much too much a trooper to expect to be pampered or to raise an alarm.' After 48 hours, Hopkins was back shooting a campfire scene in the Canmore woods, apparently recovered.

But Hopkins knew he wouldn't last the course. He told a local guide, Brew Miller, that he'd injured himself weight-training: 'The clinic first said he was suffering from exhaustion. But he was lame, simple as that. He couldn't hold his neck up. He said he'd been frantically exercising to cut down his weight and he didn't warm up properly and something went "click" in his spine. They did everything – massages, the works – but he was white-faced and slow as an old-timer. Tamahori kept shouting at him to keep his head up. "You look like an old man!" he'd holler. But Hopkins just couldn't keep up.'

Hopkins hung in for four weeks, enduring the 'tingling, nagging kinda pain'. Then, in the middle of September, the real dog work started. The scene where Morse attempts to escape the stalking bear by hopping onto a log suspended over a river always looked risky. No stunt double was possible, since close-ups were required. In the scene, the bear grabs the end of the log and twists it, shaking Morse off his feet and forcing him to hang on for his life. 'The weight of my body was pulling on the damaged disc,' said Hopkins, 'and there were times I thought I was going to pass out because of the pain.' The next day, Hopkins stunned Tamahori by not showing up at all.

Unknown to anyone, he had checked himself into Calgary's Foothills Hospital, consulted neurosurgeon Jack Kreck and elected for micro-surgery to remove three pieces of crushed bone from his neck. Tamahori closed down production for three days, both shocked and, he later said, 'deeply respectful' of Hopkins' single-minded sense of self-preservation. Brew Miller recalled: 'For a couple of days it looked like the movie was a goner. No one knew what happened [to Hopkins] and eveyone assumed the worst. "He's off his head," someone said. "He had a booze problem, and now he's vamoosed." The director was struck dumb.' But Tamahori's relief at the immediate recovery from surgery and consequent return to form quickly reanimated things. His biggest concern, Tamahori later said, was the colossal personal risk Hopkins had taken with elective surgery, since the film's insurance didn't cover him and the potential liabilities, health apart, could have been calamitous.

The importance of momentum was clear from Hopkins' focus through the crisis. As quick as he was back in the spotlight acting – literally within a week of his surgery – he was back on the phone to ICM's Ed Limato debating script offers. *Nixon* was still controversially doing the circuits and *Surviving Picasso*, every bit as notorious, was about to be premiered; their combined high-profile effect, along with the newly applied strategy of hugging the mainstream, excited the interest, he hoped, from the biggest studio players. Dented by the Ingalls debacle in the British press (where the *Sunday Telegraph* billed him a 'bargain-basement Burton' who 'never really seems to have anything at stake in his films'), there was sheer joy now in defying the nay sayers by pegging offers from Steven Spielberg, and from the legendary MGM Bond film camp. The Bond offer – to play the villain Elliott Carver in Roger Spottiswoode's *Tomorrow Never Dies* – was attractive; *Goldeneye*, the previous Bond, was the first in the series to star Pierce Brosnan and the most financially successful so far, with earnings of more than $330 million. But, with no script yet available, Hopkins demurred in favour of another major offer, this one from the TriStar/Amblin partnership headed by producer David Foster, to play the Saturday matinée favourite, Zorro.

This new incarnation of *Zorro* had begun more than five years before when Spielberg, a celebrated fan of all variety of silver screen swash-bucklers, acquired the rights of the *Zorro* series, popular since Douglas Fairbanks' trend-setting 1920 hit, directed by Fred Niblo for United Artists. The story of the effete nobleman, Don Diego Vega, in nineteenth-century California, originally written as a newspaper serial by Johnston McCulley, had been reworked regularly, most famously by Disney in a television series in the late fifties. But Spielberg planned the all-stops-out *Indiana Jones* treatment, and engaged a number of partners to develop it with him, among them the daring Robert Rodriguez, whose reworking of his budgetless bandit romp *El Mariachi* into the major hit *Desperado* was regarded as industry alchemy. Rodriguez failed, however, to find a productive course with Spielberg, who cast his net out again, approaching David Foster, currently partnering the *Goldeneye* director, Martin Campbell. Since Spielberg intended only to produce *Zorro*, the Campbell connection was the big attraction. Campbell had a flair for directing flamboyant action, having mastered the form in cult television series like *The Professionals*, and he was keen, like Hopkins, to broaden his audience. Foster and Campbell were working on a western when Spielberg called, but happily rejigged their schedules.

Initially, said Hopkins, he told Foster that the proposed casting was preposterous. 'I was nearly sixty, looking forward to my old age pension. What were they thinking?' But the role on the table in the script Spielberg liked was a shadow Zorro – not the virile youth, but the old swordsman and justice defender, whose late life's mission is to hand over the mantle to a newcomer. Traditionally played by Europeanised Americans like Fairbanks and Tyrone Power, this new Zorro would, at last, be appropriately Latino: 36-year-old Spanish-born Antonio Banderas would take equal billing as Zorro.

Hopkins went on record saying that he saw the film as 'two hours of popcorn' but he had not given up on the literary merit or quality control in the subjects he took on. *The Edge*, for example, ably answered the critics. Released in September 1997, just months after the completion of *The Mask of Zorro*, it surprised many, not just for its very able box-office (a $34-million return against a modest $7.7-million investment) but also for the impressive dramatic nuances. When it started out, said Art Linson, David Mamet had a simple notion: 'It was just two guys who wanted to kill each other.' But, pulp withstanding, Mamet, Tamahori, Hopkins and Baldwin all invested heavily in the subtext, draining every ounce of potential from a wilderness two-hander that Baldwin predicted might easily be overpowered by its scenery. In Hopkins' and Baldwin's hands, *The Edge* had become a serious existential study, where human values – the philosophy and calculation of Hopkins' character versus the impulse and brute-force of Baldwin's – are measured against the impassivity of nature.

On *The Mask of Zorro*, once again, no stone was unturned. Three writers worked on the screenplay, with input from Spielberg, and, to Hopkins' great delight, Martin Campbell proved the kind of director who labours on the details in pre-production. Much discussion was forth-coming about Zorro's antecedents, about Johnston McCulley's borrowing from *The Scarlet Pimpernel*, and about the plotting variations that might take it away from the sort of one-dimensional Errol Flynnery that had gone before. 'Finally it was decided to break the mould of the traditional Zorro,' said Martin Campbell. 'That story had been played too many times. Instead we took the model of the relationship between King Arthur as a young king, and Merlin, who shows him the ropes. We were striving for a kind of depth, I suppose.'

Hopkins felt himself destined to play the gallant role, even if it was to be the vintage version. Encouraging presentiments showed up during

The Edge. In Campbell's script, the older Zorro would be an expert whip-and swordsman, as per the legend, though only one small prelude scene with the whip was written. On *The Edge*, before *Zorro* loomed, Hopkins' stunt double, Alex Green whiled away his free time practising tricks with a whip, and even presented a gift of a whip to the actor at the end of the shoot. On Hopkins' say-so, Green was engaged on *Zorro* as whip coach, backing up the renowned Bob Anderson, the former Olympic fencer, assigned to teach the critical swordplay.

The one area of concern was Hopkins' health. Facing three months of fencing practice with Anderson, the parameters for a happy shoot were emphatically laid out. 'I don't do stunts anymore because I hurt my back too many times,' said Hopkins. 'And I don't much like horses. Look what happened to my friend, poor Chris Reeve, falling off a horse. So no stunts, no horses. I knew, of course, that those two "no-no's" effectively covered the plotline of *Zorro* from A to Z. But it pays to be sensible. [Alex Green] does the dirty work, and someone else does the dangerous duelling. I stay upright, learn the lines and hit the mark. That's what the studios pay me to do: to stay alive.'

Zorro filmed from January to May in ferocious heat at Churubusco Studios in Mexico City, and then in desert locations around Tlaxcala. On *The Edge*, Hopkins had particularly enjoyed the company of Alec Baldwin, an actor he described as 'a lovely man, beautiful man, with some marvellous ideas in his head'. *Zorro* promised the absolute opposite in terms of cast relationships. Where *The Edge* was intimate, *Zorro* was overflowing with characters, a multitude of whom had scenes alongside the two Zorros. But the kinship was easy: cast alongside the affable Banderas, and playing Hopkins' daughter, was another Welsh thespian, Catherine Zeta-Jones, whom Hopkins already knew, and approved of.

But the best social yield from *Zorro* was the Spielberg connection. On the very first day of rehearsals, Walter Parkes, the executive in charge of Amblin (Spielberg's production company), called Hopkins aside to suggest his suitability for a major role in Spielberg's current directorial venture, the essay on nineteenth-century slavery, *Amistad*. Parkes organised a quick meeting with Spielberg before *Zorro* started shooting, and Hopkins was elated to find himself offered the part of President John Quincy Adams.

'The immediate problem was how to shuffle the deck,' said Hopkins. 'What a thrill to be invited by Steven Spielberg, because he's truly one of the greatest living storytellers on film. But I had my work cut out in Mexico, so it was tough.' With Martin Campbell's compliance, Spielberg arranged for Hopkins and his regular make-up lady, Chrissie Beveridge, to be transported to Universal Studios, where *Amistad* was filming, for three days; then later to Waterford, Connecticut, where an exact replica reconstruction of the US Supreme Court had been recreated on a makeshift sound stage for the film's finale.

The Mask of Zorro was, undeniably, designed to enamour Hopkins (as it did) to the mass, ticket-buying youth market, but *Amistad*, a brilliantly conceived but ultimately unwieldy historical square dance, provided one of the best big screen showcases for his theatre-trained power of command. Originally devised by the black actress-choreographer Debbie Allen in the middle eighties, and based on contemporary essays and journalism about the hijacking by slaves of the transportation ship *La Amistad* en route to the Americas in 1839, the project had foundered with a number of producers until, in the wake of *Schindler's List*, Spielberg sought out a meaningful follow-up.

Allen professed herself gratified and moved: 'The political climate was right. Steven had the courage with *Schindler's List* to say, yes, we pay attention to these injustices in our history, but we do not pay enough attention. *Amistad* was the same lapse, the same need.' David Franzoni's screenplay, coached by Allen and Spielberg, was nothing short of massive – more than 200 dialogue-laden pages covering the mutiny led by Cinque, then the treachery of the crew who claimed they were navigating *La Amistad* to Africa, when in fact they were headed for an East Coast port, where the ship and its hijackers were arrested. The action winds its way to a two-man, political-legal showdown, where incumbent President Martin Van Buren, rabidly pro-slavery and keen to appease the South, determines to see Cinque and his supporters hanged, prompting Adams, retired from his legal practice but committed to human rights, to fight the Africans' case in the Supreme Court.

The extreme contrast in character, acting style and intellect had by now become second nature for Hopkins. In Mexico, he was an old Errol Flynn, candy-coloured and exotic, easing in and out of near farcical comedy moments; in Connecticut, preaching the moral and legal rights of the Africans, he was white-faced, bewhiskered and magisterial. For the oratorical climax, which would take up eleven uninterrupted minutes of screen time, Hopkins claimed he went into a hotel room and read the text 'just hundreds of times, and absorbed all the little bits – and then just did it.' To the Benin-born actor Djimon Hounsou playing Cinque, Hopkins related his theory for effective acting: 'He just told me to forget everything I'd been taught and free up my head and just walk onto the set and "be" Cinque. He was very persuasive.'

John Quincy Adams' speech about freedom and rights held Spielberg himself in thrall ('I just melted. I went back in time. He can do that, great actors do that') and became the potent redeeming part of the overlong and over-earnest *Amistad*, winning Hopkins yet another Academy Award nomination. But if its sublimity spoke of the actor's thirst for intellectual stretch, the decisions he was making, along with his agent and Jenni for consultation, indicated continuing, money-chasing ambitions. There were those, like Simon Ward, who believed an actor cannot be over-employed: 'The skill is versatility. The tradition goes back to the Greeks. You have a story to tell. If you have the time – the *physical* space – there's no reason not to do it. Tony was lucky.' As indeed, Hopkins knew – though his tendency, borne of so many years jousting with the press and learning the risks of its in-built cynicism, was to overstate modesty. '*Zorro* is probably my last chance for a big, virile international hit,' became an interview staple; though the signs told the opposite story. In fact, during *The Edge*, on the strength of the controversies of *Nixon* and *Picasso* as much as the standing body of work, offers at last flooded in, among them two pop heavyweights, one from the respected Martin Brest (of *Scent of a Woman*) and Universal, one from Touchstone, to be directed by John Turteltaub. Hopkins first told his agent that he could only accept one, that his health was down, and he was exhausted after the back-to-back run of *Nixon* and *Picasso*, and then the stressful *Edge*. The better of the two, on first reading, was Brest's *Meet Joe Black*, a reworking of a 1920s Alberto Casella play and a thirties' film starring Frederic March about a businessman's encounter with Death personified. A positive plus was also the involvement of Brad Pitt, whom Hopkins had come to like and trust on *Legends*. He instructed the agent to accept Brest's offer, and then got another phone call: 'He said, you can do both of them. The Turteltaub film, *Instinct*, is going to take a little more prepping. The schedules don't conflict, and it will work out. So, I accepted.'

It must be remembered that when Hopkins accepted these films, the jury was not yet in on *Nixon* or *Picasso*, and his biggest recent money-earner, *Legends of the Fall*, was two years past. In that context, *Meet Joe Black* and *Instinct* were suspiciously like safety ballast to ensure continued visibility. The problem inherent in this buckshot work method, however, was counter-productivity. Never saying no to the big boys not only implied an untypical lack of dramatic discernment but invited the potential for fast-sequenced high profile misfires. And such was almost the case.

Different directors focus on different film principles. Oliver Stone, like Scorcese, is known for his obsession with the acting performance; Spielberg with the 'beats' of the story; but Brest was, allegedly, the sort of director Hopkins had most come to fear: the meticulous all-rounder who can grind to a snail's pace adjusting the furniture of a scene or hairline cracks in a performance. Hopkins started well, joining the production at the end June in New York, having taken a short driving holiday alone to loosen up after *Amistad* and *Zorro*. Once again, the intellectual gear change was colossal. After the lusty grime of Mexico, the world of Bill Parrish, the media millionaire at the heart of *Meet Joe Black*, was elegance itself; beyond that, the intention of the film was the same, subtly philosophical territory as Brest's recent multi-award winning *Scent of a Woman*. Hopkins should have been alerted. Mitchell Leisen's 1934 version of the story, *Death Takes a Holiday*, was all of

78 minutes long. Brest's script – the product of several years' work by no less than four writers – was as fat as *Amistad*: the eventual film would span almost three hours, more than twice the length of Leisen's.

Hopkins loved being back in New York, loved working with Pitt again ('He has a great sense of humour, he's lighthearted. I'm sure he takes it all seriously . . . but he's very friendly, generous, he hasn't changed a bit'). He was also impressed by the thoroughness with which his character was prepared by director and writers.

In the story, Parrish is a widower with two daughters, one of whom, Susan, is on the lookout for love. Parrish is wrestling with his own loneliness, and with the imminent corporate merger that may dilute his proud, self-made empire. But it his time to die and the Grim Reaper, hearing his concern for his daughter's happiness, enters the body of 'Joe Black', and makes a deal: Death will allow Parrish more time, in exchange for the temporal experience of 'living' inside Black for a period. The twist, of course, is that Black, played by Pitt, falls for Susan.

One of the writers, Kevin Wade, summed up the ambition for Hopkins' Parrish: 'We wanted to create another layer to the conflicts Parrish faces. We identified him as a man who has built his business as a dearly held reflection of his own convictions and tastes, and when that legacy is threatened, he finds himself in the toughest negotiation of his life. His struggle to preserve his legacy, and the effect that his determination has on Joe Black, became an integral theme for further exploring and defining their relationship.'

Hopkins hung fast with this and, like Pitt, who praised the 'literate dialogue and smart drawing-room exchanges', milked the subtext. There was, he said, a personal attraction to the material which fired him up: 'My father was a confirmed atheist. In the last days of his life he talked about having seen his own father and friends of his who'd been dead for years. The clincher that something had happened to alter his beliefs came when he remarked that he didn't know what he had done wrong in his life for the good Lord to give him so much pain. That's all the proof I've ever needed to know there's something beyond this life.'

But it was hard, according to just about everyone who visited the astonishing sets built at massive expense in the converted National Guard Armory in Brooklyn, not to be diverted by the dressing of the film. Ever a stickler for detail, Brest had employed the Fellini collaborator-designer, Dante Ferretti, to build Parrish's homes. Ferretti proudly announced:

> Marty and I talked very carefully over every aspect of the set. Before we started working we went to see every penthouse apartment we could in New York, visiting the Cartier Mansion and the home of Lady Fairfax at the Pierre Hotel. We even went to see Donald Trump's apartment in the Trump Tower. The pleasure of working with Marty was that he gave me the freedom to do what I felt was necessary. He trusted me, so that when I began building the sets and I told him that we needed to use real materials or else the sets might look fake, he agreed and gave me carte blanche.

The result was monumental: the construction of the first and second floors of Parrish's Fifth Avenue apartment, filled the 150 ft by 270 ft by 80 ft armory drill hall (larger than a football field) to the brim; later a fully functional, full-sized, heated swimming-pool basement was built; then the production annexed a 'French pavilion-style' seminary at Narragansett Bay near Providence, Rhode Island, once the estate of Senator Nelson Aldrich, where, despite the existing lavish 'Versailles' layout, gardens were resculptured and a huge carved staircase built from a mezzanine to the sea. 'Marty and Emmanuel Lubezki, the cinematographer, wanted a warm, romantic, emotional atmosphere,' said Ferretti – which was just as well since both Pitt and Hopkins declared their belief in the film based on what Hopkins called 'its nice romance'. Finally, though, neither romance, nor deep intellectuality, seemed possible, given the burdens of furniture, and the shooting style of the director. No one grumbled at first as the schedule, almost instantly, lagged. Only later did Hopkins complain to director Julie Taymor, with whom he would shortly work, about Brest's impossible perfectionism.

Unlike Dexter, or the villains of his former experience, Brest, by all accounts, erred not by boisterous bullying, but by chronic distraction. Hopkins said he enjoyed the ensemble work – 'There were just six of us [leading actors], which is small for so big a commercial film, but it was great' – but one visitor to the set saw 'people in a snit, aggravations, silences . . . and Mr Hopkins very red-faced. He has a way with his anger. He takes up a lot of physical space, like many big actors. And he can tell you to fuck off with a twitch of his shoulders. He was so pissed off half the time that those shoulders were working overtime.'

According to Hopkins, he was 'bewildered' by Brest's need to keep reshooting, a burden most evidenced by the Rhode Island party sequence that took six weeks, one *week* of which was dedicated solely to a fireworks display enjoyed by 600 extras, the 100 most prominent of whom had specially designed gowns made by Aude Bronson-Howard and David Robinson. 'Marty really takes his time with wardrobe,' said Bronson-Howard. 'I think he took his time to look at each and every extra at least once . . .'

Hopkins' time on the film amounted to an outlandish four months and when the film wrapped on 12 November, he was furious at the overruns and, undoubtedly, at the lost opportunity. Part of his rage, some believed, was directed at himself, because it wasn't just the over-working of the plotline that finally offended, but its essence. From his earliest view of the rough-cut film he must have seen what discerning critics like *Time*'s Richard Schickel saw – that *Meet Joe Black* was an illogical story. Death, in the form of Joe Black, trades with Parrish ostensibly to learn more about living. But, wrote Schickel, who could know more about life than the figure who confronts us all in our final moments?

> They've sent him knocking on the wrong door anyway. What do people as privileged as Parrish and his family, at least as they are presented in *Meet Joe Black*, know about life? Mostly they are observed dressed to the nines, eating delicately prepared viands and enjoying life in either a Manhattan penthouse, where one prays the swimming pool does not spring a leak and ruin the library's first editions, or a riverside mansion,

where the helicopter pad blends nicely into the landscape. There is no rage, pain or panic in any of these venues, and no wild laughter either. There are only the muttered discontents of the well favoured . . .

A kind of respite came at Christmas, with *Amistad* and *Zorro* in the cinemas and his energies consumed by the major birthday bash – his sixtieth – organised by Jenni at his favourite London restaurant for New Year's Eve. The homecoming was cheered in person by Mick Jagger, Lord Snowdon and a host of London luvvies, though Jodie Foster, who'd also been invited, failed to show. A fellow actor of the National era – who was uninvited – believed the respite, *all respites*, was and would always be temporary. 'I met him. He was grand, very *burnished*, the way you get with the LA sunshine. But he was talking *at my shoes*. I don't think it was "all Hollywood". I think he was very ambivalent about *Zorro* and all that, because they were mainstream movies, and he knew it. I wished him well, but he was really champing to get out of my face, because – and this was like the old times – he really wanted to get out of his own skin.'

By January, Hopkins was in Florida, so far silently venting but eager to push his steam into Turteltaub's bizarrely fused drama, *Instinct*, a noble film of strange origins described by one reviewer as *Gorillas in the Mist* meets *One Flew Over the Cuckoo's Nest*. This time, Sean Connery had been the studio's first choice, but Hopkins wasn't complaining. There was salve, again, in the ambition of the work – unquestionably psychologically and sociologically probing – and, this time, in the plain-talking clarity of a director. On the surface the plot looked as implausible as Brest's film. Hopkins played Ethan Powell, a primatologist who has abandoned his family and retreated to the mountains of Rwanda to study gorillas. Offended by intruders, he kills two game wardens and is imprisoned for seven years, during which he refuses to speak. Facing repatriation, Powell sits down with a keen young psychiatrist, Dr Caulder, played by Cuba Gooding Jr, who takes him through the long flashbacks of his experience and, along the way, enters an intense teacher-pupil relationship that centres round a meditation on human decency.

The real twist was less in the plotline than in how the film story came to be. According to the credits, *Instinct* was 'inspired by' the novel by Daniel Quinn called *Ishmael*. Quinn deserved more. *Ishmael*'s core plot, a feisty philosophical debate, was told in the form of a telepathic conversation between a teacher, Ishmael, who happens to be a gorilla, and a student, and was based on the model of Plato's *Republic*. With it, in 1992, Quinn had won the largest literary prize in history – half a million dollars – granted by Ted Turner, who then acquired the film rights. In succeeding years, Quinn attempted to persuade Turner to make the film, but constantly failed. Quinn himself decided the story was unfilmable, and all but abandoned it, though he continued the teacher-pupil dialogues in further books and on the lecture circuit around the world. Then, to his chagrin, the Touchstone transformation began.

Quinn recalled: 'There were two producers especially who wanted to make a film out of *Ishmael*. These were Barbara Boyle and Michael Taylor, best known for their recent success, *Phenomenon* [which was directed by Turtelatub and also starred the emerging Cuba Gooding Jr]. They took the problem to *Phenomenon*'s screenwriter, Gerald DiPego. DiPego read the book, loved it, and told them that no one will ever make a film based on *Ishmael*. He said, 'Since we can't come up with a movie that *is* based on *Ishmael*, why don't we come up with a movie that *isn't* based on *Ishmael*?' And this is exactly what they did. Here's the story they pitched to Touchstone: An anthropologist kills a poacher and ends up in a prison for the criminally insane. There he engages in a prolonged dialogue with the prison psychiatrist and eventually wins him over to his strange Ishmael-like point of view. To tell the truth, this doesn't sound like much of a movie to me, but it evidently did to Touchstone, which proceeded to buy the *Ishmael* rights from Turner, so they could go ahead and make a movie of a different title, with a completely different story and nobody in it called Ishmael.'

Hopkins avoided the Quinn issue and concentrated on the film, which took the form of a two-hander like *The Edge*, in which virtually all his screen time was shared with Gooding (who, having just won a Best Supporting Actor Academy Award for *Jerry Maguire*, was also sharing top

361

billing). Gooding he liked, as he had come to contentment with the whole new generation of actors. 'Cuba is all energy. These young guys are terrific. They break away from the conventions, which is great. I've had enough of earnest acting.'

Katherine Spafford, introducing him on a university circuit interview shortly after filming, summed up the shifted perspective that made these new films, regardless of artistic value, tolerable: 'Like Yoda to a Jedi knight or Buddha to a monk, Anthony Hopkins is now the wise ruler of the acting world.' Gooding endorsed the view: Hopkins was, he said, an educator, from whom he could glean so much. Turteltaub, whose most publicised hit was the witty Jamaica Olympic bob-sleigh romp, *Cool Runnings*, concurred: what he wanted for the Ethan Powell role was authority, and no one could match Hopkins for that.

There were other in-built advantages for both Turteltaub and Hopkins. Doubtless, Turteltaub welcomed the steely-eyed containment of Lecter; for Hopkins the intrinsic drama of the obsessive neurotic, a persona he was well familiar with, had a special resonance. 'Tony is permanently in the grip of feelings he cannot control,' says David Hare, who still watched his every move. And nothing could have been better fuel for Powell, a character written as an elevated intelligence, a man whose relationship with nature takes him beyond the conventions of contemporary values to a paradoxically savage moral high ground.

Little or nothing of this, though, made it onto the screen. As with the Brest project, which theoretically shone, the film that coalesced from its brilliant primal elements, as Daniel Quinn prophesied, somehow stumbled and fell. Ideally, if the *Ishmael-Republic* ethos had been maintained, *Instinct* would be powerful ecological polemic. Instead, as the *LA Weekly* concluded, it substituted shocks for character development and became a graceless functional thriller: '[Powell] can give me a look at man in his primitive state,' says Caulder excitedly, eyes glittering at the thought of a best-selling case study and seemingly unaware of the weird racial politics underlying this whole setup . . .'

In Quinn's view, the unshakable corruptions of 'La La Land' killed *Ishmael*, and the promotional tour which heralded its opening in June

1999 drove home the point. Turteltaub and Gooding, best buddies now, travelled together on the Disney freebie junket – unassisted by Hopkins, who cried off entirely – and visited cities as far apart as Michigan, Seattle and San Francisco to meet the press. In Michigan, the *Daily News*' Ed Sholinsky noted Turteltaub's observation of the film as a humanitarian tract, 'all about letting things happen, about letting go'. This was something, Sholinsky spied, that Gooding evidently could not himself do, since he chose to recount an incident in which his *A Few Good Men* director, Rob Reiner, rejected him for an audition, assuming some betrayal in Gooding's earlier film, *Boyz 'N the Hood*, which Reiner felt stole a scene from his *Stand By Me*. 'A prick, Gooding called him,' reported Sholinsky. At the glamorous Ritz-Carlton, the *San Francisco Chronicle*'s Mick LaSalle met the promoting duo. 'Of *Instinct*, two things need to be said immediately,' wrote LaSalle. 'It marks a big moment in Gooding's career – his first full-fledged, name-above-the-title starring role. And it's a movie about how career doesn't matter, awards don't matter, success doesn't matter. It's a movie that says we put too much emphasis on those things when we ought to be getting in touch with nature and our inner selves . . .' LaSalle went on to report a rambling, circular argument between actor and director about the 'sentimentality' of the film:

'It's funny,' Gooding says. 'It's always rich people that are the first to say, we've got to save this, we have to save that. Average Joe Schmoe on the construction site, he might say, hey, I shouldn't litter, but fuck it . . .'

'The problem is not the having of money,' Turteltaub says. 'It's the desire for it, the need for it . . . As the Anthony Hopkins character says, "All people have to give up dominion."' Elsewhere, in the confetti of features covering the two-man tour, Gooding was reported bullishly refusing a waitress' delivery of Coca-Cola with his meal, insisting on Pepsi – with whom he had a promotional contract. 'For to do it the other way would be a violation, like Michael Jordan appearing wearing Reeboks.' And Turteltaub leaned over to scoop a spoonful of caviar from Gooding's plate . . .

Hopkins' only insightful words at the time appeared in the *Toronto Sun*. His personal philosophy was intact: 'My hair and teeth are still falling out and the body hurts more with each passing year. And, of course, the older I get the more I realise how inevitable death is. Life is tough, and then it's *adios amigo* . . .'

The silences and omissions spoke more eloquently of *Ishmael* the educator than any junket. But they were also electric with anger. 'I always believed,' says David Hare, 'that every authentic artist has a point of view, some message, some conclusive reality. Beneath his anger, Tony has something important to say.' At the end of the nineties, Hopkins had something to say, and the modus of expression he chose was another swing back to Shakespeare. He chose *Titus Andronicus*, Shakespeare's first hit, the play of rape and murder and revenge that made the Bard the Quentin Tarantino of his day.

Chapter **18**

BAD COMPANY

'. . . *dost thou not perceive*
that Rome is but a wilderness of tigers?'

Titus Andronicus, Act 111 Scene 1

Titus Andronicus has been controversial for almost 450 years. As recently
as the 1980s, the esteemed Shakespearean scholar D. C. Browning was
disowning it, calling it 'a farrago of horror [that] has been reckoned
unworthy of Shakespeare'. Peter Quennell wrote, 'Critics have sought to
relieve Shakespeare of responsibility for it.' But the facts are indisputable:
Francis Meres catalogued it as the Bard's in 1598 and it appeared in the
First Folio in 1623. The cause of the furore was never in doubt: the play
strips human behaviour to its basest, and the actions are rewarded by a
sweeping annihilative violence in which almost no one survives.

Its central protagonist is the Roman general Titus, who begins the play
seemingly exhausted, having beaten the Goths and taken their queen,
but lost twenty of his sons in the process. Exhausted he may be, but he
is ready to face the inevitable when an act of tradition – the execution of
the queen's son – provokes a savage revenge that causes his only daughter

to be raped and disfigured. Titus plays an eye for an eye and entraps and kills the queen's sons who are the rapists, the emperor and his own daughter. He is killed by the queen (who in turn is slaughtered by his last remaining son) but the moral burns bright: evil begets evil, the cycle of grief in violence is endless. In the Elizabethan way, there is no distinct redemptive coda at the end of the play; Shakespeare's assumption is that his audience absorbs the moral from the plot.

But in the early 1990s, a distinguished designer-director, Julie Taymor, accepted an offer to revive the play with a new elliptical structure. Titus' grandson – a child – was taken from the centre of the action and placed in neo-modern scenes at the start, then the end, of the play, personifying the literal damage caused by traditions of violence. In the quixotically remedial culture of the millennium, Taymor was holding up the starkest mirror to contemporary audiences. After the success of the play off Broadway, she took it to the films. Anthony Hopkins was her first and only choice to play Titus, the character who embodies the risk of human ennui.

Hopkins was muddling through on *Instinct*, recovering from emergency surgery on a snapped achilles tendon acquired in a scripted brawl with Gooding at Orlando airport, when Taymor's letter of invitation to *Titus* arrived. Its timing could not have been better. Though he had promised himself he'd never return to the Shakespeare that connoted British tedium, the *Titus* dynamics roused him.

Whatever the personal unease (manifest to all who knew him) in the unrewarding home life that drove him chronically out to the desert, the landscape of his business world had changed disagreeably. During the eighties, as he strove to establish himself, the political universe was as clearly defined as it was in the immediate post-war years. The polarities that Old Dick recognised still stood, the Cold War reigned and western culture ebbed and flowed and ebbed with the self-limiting utopian promises of the hippies, the Space Age and eco-awareness. But after Reagan and the collapse of the Soviet Empire, globalisation brought not homogeneity but vacuity. The nineties seemed a voyage on uncharted seas, with no clear enemies and no clear destination. In the void created by these fusions of multiculturalism, diversion therapies like the movies became globally powerful beyond precedent. Throughout, the movie nineties were financially profligate. The 1990s' *Bonfire of the Vanities*, $40 million of plotless waffle, signalled the era of extreme excess. By the decade's end, *Titanic*, albeit suitably plotful, could burn up $200 million of production costs without batting an eye. Even *The Mask of Zorro*, blithely joyful as it was, cost $68 million – more than twice as much as, say, another template action film like *Goldfinger* (inflation adjusted, with the Bond film's $3-million budget assessed at $30 million). At the heart of many of these big-dollars movies ·was anthropological and historical emptiness; fantasy and comedy seemed sounder diversions for the nineties. But one stream of cinema moved against the trends and kept the discerning on their toes and hopeful for film art.

The independent cinema movement arguably began with the counter-culture of the late 1960s. In the eighties, it became a notable force, corralled and labelled by Robert Redford's Sundance, and offering an alternative to profits-driven entertainments. The success of Steven Soderbergh's *sex, lies and videotape* – winner of the Jury prize at 1989's Sundance Festival – accelerated a trend. Soderbergh's film, made for less than $1 million, well out-sold *Bonfire of the Vanities*. By the end of the decade, *The Blair Witch Project*, made for $35,000 and a handful of goodwill favours, grossed far more, proportionately, than *Titanic*, the film that still holds the record for the highest grosses. [*Blair Witch* grossed $240 million; *Titanic*, which cost $200 million, grossed $1.8 billion.]

Like everyone else, Hopkins was alert to the signs. Independent cinema begat Quentin Tarantino, the successor to Spielberg in terms of populist impact. The fact that Tarantino's 'trick' was stylised violence said less about him than about humanity itself. The eternal verities were alive and kicking in a strand of modern cinema, if not in Hollywood. Hopkins loved Hollywood, had followed the Hollywood dream with a passion. But when he looked over the ramparts at sixty he knew, too, that his power as an actor derived from truth, and his passion for honesty was undiminished. 'I always felt,' said the *Kean* director James Cellan Jones, 'that Tony had the profoundest curiosity about human behaviour . . . no, about human destiny. It made him restless, it made him great, and it made him mean.'

The decision to do *Titus* was dismissed as depressed fatalism ('So they want me to do the Shakespeare tights again?') but was the smartest calculation. Devoted to measuring himself in staking his Hollywood territory, Hopkins had largely avoided the independents through the nineties. Now, typically, he opted for the wide outsider, choosing a project that set itself the task of redefining the ethos of the independents.

Julie Taymor, at the start anyway, was a big inducement for *Titus*. Taymor's gift was always kinetic eclecticism. Originality for her was a wasted concept, 'a late twentieth-century idea that has no real foundation. Nothing is original. You can read in Plutarch the same words Shakespeare wrote. It's just his way of assembling them that becomes poetic and deep.' Since her student days Taymor had been experimenting with animation and film, though she viewed herself as 'a caricaturist', more interested in writing and design. Her 1992 operatic production of Stravinsky's *Oedipus Rex* in Japan initiated a rapid run of major theatrical works that climaxed with the two-Tonys win (for direction and design) in 1996 for *The Lion King* on Broadway. But interest in the electronic drama of television and film paralleled all her theatre work.

Her film of *Oedipus* showed at Sundance and won the Jury Prize at the Montreal Television and Film Festival and another work, a one-hour adaptation of Edgar Allan Poe's *Hopfrog*, called *Fool's Fire*, for PBS's *American Playhouse*, also screened at Sundance. Merging passions launched *Titus* as her major film debut. Having already directed stage versions of *The Tempest* and *The Taming of the Shrew*, she 'devoured' the invitation to radically adapt *Titus* for the Theater for a New Audience group, then became so enamoured of it that she wrote the screenplay in which producers Robbie and Ellen Little persuaded Paul Allen of Microsoft to invest. For Taymor, the excitement was simply in the prospect of the biggest possible canvas for the telling of her tale. Shakespeare, she observed, had taken the idea for *Titus* from the centuries-old legend of *Philomel*. Her version would be 'a compendium of 2,000 years of warfare and violence'.

Hopkins agreed to make Taymor's film within an hour of meeting her. He had seen the dazzling inventions of her *Lion King* (though not the stage *Titus*) and was fired up by the modern imagery in her new *Titus*. Taymor insisted he take time to consider his commitment (though in her letter she had stated, 'This is *your* part'), but Hopkins was already in harness. The shooting schedule was delayed to accommodate *Instinct*, and began with the kind of detailed theatrical rehearsals Taymor favoured at Cinecittà in Rome in October.

There were immediate problems. Firstly, Hopkins didn't want to rehearse. Long experience had taught him the mastery of script and he still adhered to the wise way: 'I like to study the text. I read it 250 times. I don't know why, but that's the magic number. I cannot over-prepare. It just kills the performance because you create the moment . . . it is there, and then it's gone. I save the acting for when the director says, *Action!*' Taymor objected. Though they were in full agreement about the iconoclasm and attention-calling social commentary, the obstacles both faced were, in fact, miles apart. Taymor's challenge was the complexity of her visually enriched neo-tragedy, and also with the diversity of casting, placed relative newcomers and all types of American accents alongside British theatre-trained adepts like Alan Cumming, playing the Emperor Saturninus. Hopkins' problem was himself. He later told friends that he was more than exhausted, that he was despairing of continued energies and ready to quit. He told one: 'It's a hard enough life without this shithole business hanging round your neck like the hangman's noose. I don't want to die in make-up.'

Taymor had brought in one of the stalwarts of Shakespearean theatre, the voice coach Cecily Berry, who had the actors – Jessica Lange as Tamora, queen of the Goths, Laura Fraser as Lavinia, Titus' daughter, Harry Lennix, Matthew Rhys and Jonathan Rhys Meyers – spinning in circles on the parquet rehearsal room floor, puffing out diaphragm exercises. Hopkins stormed out. Later, attending one of the readings, he accused Taymor of over-directing. 'When it gets to the point where you are being directed about body movements, I can't be bothered. I am not that kind of actor, and a director who wants to work like that should look elsewhere.'

When filming finally started in Rome – at Cinecittà and Hadrian's villa – there was appeasement in the hard labour and also a serendipitous magic: Titus, even in the original, is spiritually jaded to the point that it is difficult to interpret the extent of his insanity when he murders Tamora's sons; Hopkins, in the bathroom scene prefacing the showdown and staged at Cinecittà, is anguished beyond acting. The sense of suffering *in extremis* worked wonderfully for Taymor – who professed herself thrilled with the performance despite the confrontations – but finally toppled at the edge.

Suddenly, early in December, with at least two months of filming still ahead, Hopkins was all over the tabloids with the news from Rome that he'd announced his retirement from acting. *Variety* pushed for a confirmation, and was referred to Jenni, and his new agent, CAA's Rick Nicita. Jenni could only confirm her husband's statement. Nicita put it all down to 'exhaustion after years of non-stop work . . . he just wants to get off the treadmill for a while.' Hopkins himself admitted the statement, but later backtracked. He had, he said, been struggling with 'madness, utter insanity' and had been overheard by a journalist on set telling a fellow actor that he needed a year off. The journalist asked did this mean the actor was retiring, to which, said Hopkins, he angrily responded, 'Well, you people are the arbiter of truth. You decide.'

The real problem was explosive anger at the release worldwide of *Meet Joe Black* in mid-November, for which, per his contract, he was allowed promotional days off. Nothing experienced on the *Titus* shoot – not Taymor's doggedly painstaking direction nor the delays incurred by jigging schedules to facilitate Alan Cumming's commuting to New York, where he was also appearing in *Cabaret* – matched the horrors of watching Brest's final three-hour cut. Critically, the film was universally mauled and, despite the fair box-office ($142 million gross against a $90-million budget), the humiliation, after the disappointment of *Instinct*, brought about a mini-breakdown.

Taymor described Hopkins arriving for the second phase of the *Titus* shoot after Christmas as a walking nightmare. She loved and respected him, deeply admired his contribution to her film, but felt him 'different'. From henceforth, the confrontations were worse. Taymor, like Jessica Lange, preferred multi-takes, and conversational reflection after a complex set-up. Hopkins liked to do one, maybe two, takes – and expected, said Taymor, immediate decisions after a 'cut'. 'Sometimes,' said Taymor, 'things can't be like that, and you have to take a moment to consider.'

Hopkins' response, in hindsight, was the same impatience with the machinery of film-making that made the post-production of *August* so distressing. He and Taymor shared an authorly vision in this techno *Titus*. His personal creativity depended on instantaneity; hers was belaboured with the devices employed to showcase the message, from the technically messy blue screens to the crowd-heavy visual in-jokes that parodied Fellini or Leni Riefenstahl.

Still, none of it mattered in the grand scheme because Taymor was a straight communicator, a true 'people's person', according to those who worked with her, and an adherent, first and last, to story values. Though the ever impressive Dante Ferretti – he who had designed *Meet Joe Black* – also designed *Titus*, the sets, magnificent as they were, never overwhelmed the point. '*Pulp Fiction*,' Taymor told the *New York Times* by way of illustrating the difference of her own work, 'is all surface.' *The Times*' Jonathan Bate, approved of the inference: 'In *Titus*, both the characters and the audience go on an inward journey in which the human reaction to violence is of more consequence than the violence itself.'

If Hopkins felt relieved to have vented his late nineties rage in so resonant a social essay, he never let on in any public forum. There were many among his jam-packed industry admirers, like the veteran actor Hume Cronyn (Polonius alongside Richard Burton's 1964 Hamlet) who saw *Titus* as a vital apologia and war cry.

That's *exactly* the role I would have played, with those Shakespearean connections and the fame he'd had from Hannibal Lecter. It's a way of saying, 'Hang on, we are collaborators here. *I* didn't invent violence. I am the product and victim of it, as much as you.' Titus is the victim of the Roman traditions. He kills Tamora's son, and invites these miseries on himself. We are the people who buy the tickets to see Hannibal Lecter. We invite this monster into our dreamlife. The actor is just the myth-image, not the myth-creator.

Whether or not the venting provided some exorcism, it surely restored an equilibrium that put an end to talk of retirement. Instead, abruptly, he withdrew from work 'to allow myself a year to repair and get it all into perspective again'. And this retreat seemed full of direction. From the middle of 1999, the millennium demarcation point, the landscape of his emotional world looked suddenly different. He described himself again and again in interviews as anti-social and relatively friendless. Alec Baldwin he reckoned a close friend, and yet he admitted that they rarely met, unless it was a casual collision at the pool of the Fairmont Miramar, still the favoured LA hangout. But there were new lines being drawn. Forty-four-year-old interior designer Francine Kay became his new 'squeeze' and a staffer at the Miramar saw 'a very busy guy who always likes the company of a good-looking woman, he's never alone for long'. Jenni began to fade from the picture: from the summer of 1999 the regular trans-Atlantic trips ceased completely. And, to everyone's surprise, he suddenly bought a ten-acre Mission-styled estate at Ojai, seventy miles up the Malibu coast from LA, in what used to be 'hippie country'.

Hopkins told acquaintances that the break at the millennium saved his sanity. It also appeared to alter his attitude to his work. In the future, there would be no indulging even the vaguest artistic analysis. His work, he said, was idiot-proof. They gave him a script, trusted his intelligence and mimicry, then let him at it. It was that simple. Morality, art, hard labour didn't come into it. In 2001 he told an interviewer, 'It takes no effort. I should feel guilty. In fact, I'm very, very lucky.'

The new cavalier stance apparently found its feet with *Mission Impossible 2*, a John Woo–Tom Cruise formula bandwagon that steam-rolled out of a Paramount committee room and into fifty locations from Broken Hill, Australia to the desert at Moab, Utah. Rick Nicita's wife,

Paula Wagner, an agent with CAA for twelve years who had cut out into independent production and forged a partnership with former client Tom Cruise, was the driving producer of the *Mission Impossible* series.

The major success of the first film, which grossed $450 million, ensured the follow-up; the assignment of Woo to direct (Brian De Palma had directed the first) ensured the abandonment of all subtleties in the cause of slap-bang-wallop. Hopkins was with Nicita when the agent, cautious of his client's equivocal ambition, coolly suggested Wagner's interest. Hopkins later recalled: 'He said, "My wife would like to know if you'd like to do a small part?" I said, "With Tom Cruise?" And he said, "Yeh, a guest part. Australia for a few days. Would you like to do that?" I said, "Yeh." He said, "Do you want a script?" I said, "No, just tell me, what do I do?" He said, "You're the boss . . ."' Thus 'contracted', Nicita called Wagner excitedly.

'They sent me the pages,' said Hopkins. 'I didn't even know what the story was about. I went down to Sydney, saw Tom, and just spoke all these lines about *chemical formulas*. I didn't even know what the hell I was talking about, and I had no idea what the story was about because the script was so unfinished. But I had a good time.'

But the 'good time guy' persona hardly stood up to scrutiny. More buoyant with the media he might be, more tolerant of the studios' baloney, but his discernment faculties were still, obviously, in good working order. The next job undertaken in self-declared snooze mode was the voiceover role of the narrator in Ron Howard's *How the Grinch Stole Christmas*, a state-of-the-art computer graphics imagery (CGI) reconstruction of the Dr Seuss classic first made for television in 1966 by the Disney-rival animator Chuck Jones.

As with *Mission Impossible* 2, work on the *Grinch* only occupied a few days. But the resonance was unmissable. Howard traded the usual mediaspeak to celebrate the preeminence of Sir Anthony, 'one of our truly great treasures'; but a fascinating confluence was taking place. The creations of Theodor Geisel (a.k.a. Dr. Seuss) always had the morality of great fabulist writing: his Grinch was a representation of darkness, a mean man who hates Christmas ('with termites in his smile and garlic in his soul'), tries to steal it away from the people of Whoville, but sees the light and mends his ways.

In the sixties, Jones employed Boris Karloff, the contemporary King of Horror, as narrator – an obvious admission/enhancement of the fable's darkness. Reworking the classic, Howard opted for the horror*meister*'s successor, not by way of homage, but as a boost to screenwriters Jeffrey Price and Peter Seaman's fresh – and questionable – take on the story.

A comparable work, such as Dickens' *A Christmas Carol*, would surely not stand the moral meddling applied to the millennial Grinch. This version, featuring Jim Carrey in the title role, offered the benefits of our remedial society to the Grinch's history. No longer merely 'bad' converted by love to 'good', Howard's Grinch, is an outsider, the child of an alternative-lifestyle family alienated by a bad press and determined to wreak revenge on the folks who spurned him. Along the way, Whoville is depicted as venal and shallow, a place which exploits the material aspects of all festivities and has as much to learn about the spirit of Christmas as the Grinch himself.

Savvy reviewers cited Columbia professor Andrew Delbanco's controversial book, *The Death of Satan*, which argued that the 'PC' appetite for revisionism had blocked Americans' ability to perceive real evil. The intense opposition to moral and religious metaphors had induced a 'tragedy of the imagination' that absolved everyone of everything and produced the prevailing condition of 'Hollywood grey'. 'Actors and directors, like psychologists and social workers, search for the "motivation" of characters,' wrote the critic Jonah Goldberg. 'This search for understanding can segue quickly into explanation, and from there to excuse-making.' The revisionism had even reached the Devil himself. In the seventies, the *Exorcist* suggested a cogent dark force. By 1997's *The Devil's Advocate*, he was a fallible character not too hard to outmanoeuvre. In a dozen further films in which he featured, from *Bedazzled* to *End of Days*, he was, metaphorically and sometimes literally, killable with a handgun. The passing of the torch from Karloff to Hopkins might have been a nice touch, wrote Goldberg, 'but Hannibal Lecter is no old-fashioned bad guy: The serial-killing cannibal is nasty, but also something of an antihero. In *Hannibal*, the sequel novel to *Silence of the Lambs*, we learn that Lecter is the product of a terrible childhood, just like the Grinch, and it's really not his fault that he eats people . . .'

Hopkins' take on New Age evil in its millennial, burnished, Hollywood version is unavailable. Like Howard, whose promotional interviews centred on the genius of his collaborators – 'You just had to call, *Action!* for Jim [Carrey] to *become* the Grinch' – the sidestepping sound bite sufficed. Howard was 'great fun', the film was 'a hoot'. But there was, many friends felt, something akin to an intellectual realignment under way. The actor Martin Jarvis declared:

> I do not believe that actors like Tony 'drift' with the trends. He is an autodidact and a reader, and the possessor of a very inquiring mind. If Hannibal Lecter came to represent a change in our culture's view of evil, then he'll have wanted to intellectualise that for himself. He will have applied himself to understanding the change, because he is an actor who works from the root. No matter what he says in dismissing the work, it is *work*, and he undertakes it with the deepest seriousness.

The cultural adjustment of *Grinch* foreshadowing a frenzy of media speculation about the imminence of writer Tom Harris' *Silence* follow-up, *Hannibal*, might have been no more than serendipity, but that was enough. Recently Hopkins had begun to see a therapist again, and to read more Jungian philosophy. Synchronicity, he'd decided, answered many woes. 'Things happen because they are meant to happen, and I learned not to query it all so much.' He was also battening down for the inevitable: for almost ten years the same questions had haunted him. Hundreds of times he had fended them off with the same response. Would he reprise Hannibal? He didn't know. Maybe Tom Harris would never finish his long-promised sequel. 'I keep hearing about this Harris, and the fact that he's writing this book, but I've never actually met him . . .'

Emerging from his hippie sabbatical, Hopkins readied himself for a bumpy ride. However he played the return of the cannibal, he would be criticised. Still, the public demand was unremitting and, perhaps, the reflections of his autumn years legitimised a maturer reassessment of the character. Maybe Howard's instincts with the Grinch were right; and if they were, perhaps Harris' rehabilitating storyline would, at least, offer something thought-provoking . . .

As Hopkins bided his time, *Hannibal* rose like a swamp creature from the mire of contractual squabbles. Commissioned by Dell publishers from Harris even before *Silence of the Lambs* went into production, the sequel was finally delivered on 23 March 1999 and published – in an edition of 1.3 million – in late summer.

The slick gloss of the marketing belied the truth: this was a story that had been dragged kicking and screaming into life. The Mississipian Harris had had many second thoughts, but too many interested parties stood to gain too much to let this project slip. Orion, now defunct, had hit paydirt with *Silence*. But it was Dino De Laurentiis who owned the film rights to Lecter, having secured the first deal on the 'prequel novel' *Red Dragon*, filmed as *Manhunter* by Michael Mann in 1986. He was not prepared to pass on this golden opportunity. Neither was Universal Studios, who had leveraged an exclusive option on the Harris film rights. Nor was Jonathan Demme, the director of the 1991 Oscar-winner. The other interested parties – screenwriter Ted Tally, Jodie Foster and Hopkins – stayed silent while the early wars were fought. De Laurentiis and his new wife, Martha, were at the forefront on harnessing Harris, the uncertainty of whose plans drove everyone to the edge. At various times throughout the years De Laurentiis canoodled imaginatively, organising his own pasta chef to fly to Miami Beach to cook for the writer, and carefully tracking his apparent researches which indicated that at least a part of the sequel storyline would take place in Italy. Finally, De Laurentiis received the precious text, but it was only after an intense legal argument between the various parties – Harris's literary and film rights agent, De Laurentiis' lawyers, Universal and MGM and a $10-million advance payment from De Laurentiis – that the viable film was green-lighted. So complicated was the negotiation that a legal summary compiled by the Century City law firm of Greenberg, Glusker,

Fields, Claman & Machtinger, running to ten pages, was all but incomprehensible even to industry insiders.

During the spring of 1999, the debate about the *Silence* sequel became a game of smokescreens in which the conventional foil – displeasure with the script – dominated. But the realities were otherwise. It was true De Laurentiis wanted to maintain as many elements from *Silence* as possible, and Jodie Foster, like Hopkins, was critical. But Foster, as reported, didn't like the implausibly cosy ending of Harris' new book which, while delivering the expected gore quota, joined Clarice Starling, Foster's character, in a bizarre love match with the serial killer. Harris' ending, though, didn't stand. Ted Tally had turned down the chance to draft the screenplay, so David Mamet had a go, followed by the *Schindler's List* Oscar-winner Steve Zaillian. What survived was the body of Harris' book – basically a double-story of the revenge-minded Mason Verger's determination to destroy Hannibal Lecter, and a parallel psychodrama about Clarice's obsession with the killer – and an enormous dose of excessive savagery that peaked with a dinner party during which Ray Liotta's (playing a Justice Department creep) brains are on the menu.

It was now, with a script that might actually appease Foster, that De Laurentiis saw the insurmountable problem. Hopkins' fees, since *Silence*, had been steadily rising, allegedly peaking with the $10 million paid for *Meet Joe Black*. *Silence* had cost $19 million. But the first budgeting of *Hannibal*, as befitted the grander scale demanded by an ever more technically sophisticated audience, suggested a budget of around $80 million. Given the fact that a considerable portion of the story was set in Florence, Italy, necessitating extensive location shooting, and given his already considerable expenditure, De Laurentiis immediately understood the impossibility of retaining *two* lead actors whose fee profiles suggested $10-million pay cheques – each. And then there was the trouble with Jonathan Demme, the stylist who had created the big screen success in the first place. Demme, it emerged, had negotiated himself out of the frame by failing to secure a creative-control clause in his option deal brokered by CAA. Before the script was finished, with the world media focus on the Lecter Show, Demme was withdrawing, further emphasising the chaos. De Laurentiis, meanwhile, already had an alternative plan.

While supervising the completion of a low-budget film, *U-571*, at the studio tanks in Malta, his nextdoor neighbour was Ridley Scott, the definitive stylist. As Scott wrapped up *Gladiator*, De Laurentiis presented him with Harris' original 600-page text and the offer to take the helm. 'I didn't think I'd get the time to read it,' Scott said. 'But I read it in three sittings. I liked everything about it. I liked the fact that it had Hopkins, and that it was original. The action takes place ten years after *Silence*. But it was also written ten years later. So all the sensibilities are different, and so it feels fresh.'

The crunch with actors' fees boiled down to a decision to abandon Foster. According to the best evidence (neither Hopkins nor CAA discusses it), Hopkins was paid $5 million up front and – crucially, for such is where the big bucks dwell – a generous 10 per cent of the gross. In place of Foster, Julianne Moore was approved by Universal and paid, according to a CNN report, a more workable $3 million. To win the race, Moore had nudged out Cate Blanchett, Calista Flockhart, Helen Hunt and Gillian Anderson, among several short-listed alternatives. De Laurentiis welcomed her, describing her as 'sexier' than Foster, to which, one studio publicist countered, 'It's not about sexiness, it's about economics.' Once these contracts were settled, the film finally rushed into high gear and the other lead casting was confirmed: Gary Oldman as Verger, Liotta, and the Italian actor Giancarlo Giannini as the corrupt Inspector Pazzi.

Shooting on *Hannibal* began in May 2000, between the American and UK release dates for *Titus*, a film of substance that found itself in a vivid limelight in the wake of the tragedy at Columbine high school in Denver's Littleton suburbs. At Columbine on 20 April 1999, two gun-obsessed students, Eric Harris and Dylan Klebold, ran rampage in a self-declared mission planned over one year to kill as many students and members of faculty as possible. Thirteen were shot dead and 21 seriously wounded before the students who, allegedly, were marking the anniversaries of other acts of anarchy – the Oklahoma bombing of 1995 and the Waco, Texas Branch Davidion standoff in 1993 – killed themselves. Commonalities were drawn. According to the *New York Times*, Taymor's film 'portrays violence as an escalating fever, an addictive mass hysteria that consumes the characters and turns them into bloodthirsty fiends'; elsewhere it was observed that Harris and Klebold were reflections of Demetrius and Chiron – maniacs corrupted by twisted traditions that drove them to delay the killings by 24 hours in order to mark an even more important anniversary, the 110th birthday of Adolf Hitler. Though, as ever, personal taste divided the critics (Wesley Morris of the *San Francisco Examiner* typified the dissenters, citing Ian McKellen's *Richard III* and Baz Luhrmann's *Romeo and Juliet* as better pairings of Shakespeare with film postmodernism), the general consensus was that Taymor provoked serious reflection – 'a profound exploration,' *The Times* called it – at a parlous time in human society, as barriers in the global village dispersed.

Hannibal, meanwhile, was emerging as a calculated romp, as precision-plotted as a Punch and Judy show and, ultimately, as dramatically inevitable. 'I can't see what all the fuss is for,' Hopkins complained as shooting commenced amid protests alleging vulgarity from the Popular Political Party in Florence. 'What's everyone afraid of?'

Certainly, compared with Harris' book, the Zaillian *Hannibal* was less *surprising*. Ridley Scott, like Foster and Ted Tally, had totally rejected Harris' outlandishly daring finale seduction of Clarice. 'I told Tom [Harris] I just don't buy these two guys going off together, even with Clarice under the influence [of drugs]. He said, fine, see what you can come up with.'

What Zaillian and Scott had come up with was a total inversion of the book, placing Clarice in the story from the start (where Harris downplayed her till past the halfway mark) and emphasising Lecter's madness in place of the pursuit that echoed metaphorical aspects of Shelley's *Frankenstein*. The bad news for concerned sociologists swayed to Andrew Delbanco's argument was that the sophistication of the formula (far slicker than *Grinch*) offered complete absolution to Lecter: this horror film excused itself from the cautionary warning inherent in

Titus, and exulted in the celebration of cinema as the most popular contemporary forum for vicarious violence.

If Hopkins was troubled by this apparent complete accession to self-absolving Hollywood psychology, he gave few signs. But an edge of defensiveness suggested rumbling uncertainties. Of Lecter he said, 'We admire him in a secret way. He represents the unspeakable part of ourselves, the fantasy, desires and dark areas of our lives that are slightly unacceptable to us, but actually healthy, if only we acknowledge them. Perhaps, we'd like to be as daredevil as him. But admiring him doesn't mean we're deeply disturbed, sick people. It means that we're human.' Elsewhere he added, 'We're all flawed, deeply damaged, imperfect beings. We're corruptible, shabby, grubby, great, magnificent and all the rest. That's why we like watching Hitchcock's *Psycho* and *Jaws* and going on rollercoasters. We like to be thrilled, entertained, frightened. We like to see Dirty Harry say, "Make my day" and see the bad guy get his just desserts.'

But wasn't Hannibal Lecter the bad guy? De Laurentiis didn't seem to think so: at one point, dining with Hopkins and trying to persuade him to commit to yet another Lecter film – 'and so develop the franchise' – he likened Lecter to James Bond.

Professionalism slaked his intellectual thirst. Scott was nothing if not a stickler for detail, and the authority of co-stars like Liotta and Julianne Moore impressed him. While Moore, keen to match the legend of Foster, immersed herself in formal training at the FBI's Quantico base camp, Hopkins wandered the streets of Florence in Armani duds and Truman Capote panama, soaking up the atmosphere of the fugitive life and slumming with the locals at bars like La Borsa, round the corner from the Palazzo Vecchio. Here, he spied the bartender as a potential screen 'face', and persuaded him into the film. 'He's really into it,' said Mette Wemmelund, a regular at La Borsa, which was also on the shooting itinerary. 'One thing's for certain: you can't escape Hannibal in this city at the moment.'

Nowhere was impervious. In June, the production moved to Washington, where a sequence was shot at Union Station. *Variety* later reported Hopkins taking time off to dine with an illustrious Washington resident, who had 'rushed from a golf game' to join him. The resident was President Bill Clinton – facing his last months in office – and the meeting had a strange poetry to it. In April, just a month before production, Anthony Hopkins, the film world's bogeyman, had formally taken up US citizenship. In private, Clinton welcomed Hopkins to American citizenship. In public, en masse, American filmgoers opened welcoming arms for the return of the cannibal.

Wales, of course, would have none of it. Or so said the BBC. Widely reported in Britain in the days after the 12 April citizenship ceremony (attended by 'close friends John Travolta and Steven Spielberg'), Hopkins was quoted refusing to parry: 'I don't want to discuss it. Thank you for your interest, but I really have nothing to say.' Port Talbot's postmaster – one Asghar Ali – felt the need to debunk such a gesture of inter-nationalism: 'Sir Anthony is always harping about his Welshness, but when the chips are down he decides to go away. To be honest, I think he is a hypocrite.' Two years later, in a sanguine moment, Hopkins relented, implying his clear understanding of British jaundice, an example of the partisan bigotry he'd come to detest in the System: 'I came here in 1974 to do a play, and then I went to LA. I really *like* living in America. I had been living on a green card, and it was fine. But I really wanted to change my identity. I know you never really change identity . . . My friends are fine with it, but it's the stupid press who called me a traitor. I didn't realise [Britain] was at war with America.'

But the millennial indicators of change had become the rigid new outlook that washed through all his life. In 1999, he had finally persuaded his mother to join him in California. One friend immediately saw the importance of the decision: 'Muriel had been close to Jenni, but that relationship had cooled entirely. Tony didn't want to be in England, and he didn't want English ties. He said, "Life is too short for all that stiff-upper-lip Brit crap. I want rebirth."'

The momentous nature of the changes at hand was evident in the anxieties. First, the house and lands at Ojai were sold – back to the original owner. Then, during *Hannibal*, the relationship with Francine Kay, described in the American media, as 'an engagement', ended abruptly. Reuters reported Hopkins' explanation: 'When I get too close to someone I want to move on. I don't feel ready for any commitment. I've hurt enough people.' Early in 2000, just before *Hannibal*, a serious house fire wiped out one floor of the house in Kensington. Jenni had been out to dinner, but the London Fire Brigade recovered, among other possessions, Hopkins' *Silence* Oscar from the ruins. The event seemed ominous. Hearing of the US citizenship in April, Jenni declared herself bemused: 'He was given every honour going and very rarely had anything critical or derogatory written about him as either a person, or an actor. The only reason I can come up with is that he wanted some excuse to validate his desire to live as a US citizen. But, who knows, maybe that will change some day?'

But any reversal seemed less and less likely. During the promotion for *Hannibal*, released with the greatest tub-thumping fanfare in February 2001, Hopkins admitted his relationship with Kay and, while insisting he wouldn't divorce Jenni, rejected guilt: 'I can't be driven by guilt. Guilt is the great thief of my life.' The following summer, he effected the most dramatic spring cleaning, purchasing a large hilltop home in Malibu and, after months of private discussion, initiating a divorce from Jenni. The extent of the hurt was indicated by Jenni's complete withdrawal, but one actor who knew both commented: 'She got it wrong, plain and simple. She said Britain never criticised him, but it did. There was always that begrudging thing among the theatre luvvies – it works against anyone who makes it as big as Tony did in Hollywood. Jenni chose to stay in Britain, but the writing was on the wall in 2000 when he opted for dual citizenship. That was her moment: she could either go to him, or dig her heels in in London. She stayed put.'

It was a new, harder-mould Anthony Hopkins who rolled out the carpet for *Hannibal* and announced that he was ready for another Lecter film with De Laurentiis. Already Ted Tally was at work on a new screenplay, this one a broad reworking of *Red Dragon*, the Lecter 'prequel', filmed as *Manhunter* in the eighties. According to Tally, his *Red*

Dragon would be a major departure, focusing on Lecter's first escape from prison and his consequent killings, but the gore would be toned down: he would 'never show Lecter eating people. It's just too gross. I just imply it.' His reason for doing the film was simple: Hopkins had agreed to be in it.

Empowered as never before by the surefire returns of committing to the Lecter franchise, Hopkins' film choices continued to surprise. On one hand, there was an all-out engagement with Hollywood pap; on the other, dogged whimsicality. Directly after *Hannibal*, beloved synchronicity directed him towards *Hearts in Atlantis*, a typically machine-tooled Hollywood 'package', scripted by William Goldman from a story collection by the redoubtable Stephen King. Hopkins' reason for choosing the film, he said, was coincidence. In Florence, he had been reading a William Goldman memoir in which Goldman singled him out as one of his favourite actors, and immediately afterwards was offered the King adaptation via his CAA agent, who visited him on the set of *Hannibal*. 'It was one of those moments when destiny speaks.'

Hearts in Atlantis became a showcase of all that was wrong with Hollywood and all that was right with Hopkins. Goldman's facility was always reduction. His work since *Butch Cassidy and the Sundance Kid* was an exercise in refinement, where each succeeding script, from *Marathon Man* to King's *Dreamcatcher*, was increasingly stripped of character and bullet-pointed with action scenes. *Atlantis*, then, unsurprisingly, was more of the same – a leanly written compression of two of the five stories in King's bizarre and spooky collection, linked by the simple overview of a 'rites of passage' education of an unhappy young boy, Bobby Garfield, played by twelve-year-old Anton Yelchin, by a mysterious lodger in his home, Ted Brautigan, played by Hopkins.

Though Hopkins was hugely admiring of both Goldman (who had also written *Magic*) and director Scott Hicks (who had recently scored impressively with *Shine*), he cannot have helped but see the gap between King's poignant source material and the thin quasi-thriller woven from it. In King's stories, the Brautigan character is tormented by the mysterious 'low men', nefarious agents who are chasing him down for critical reasons unspecified. Careful readers of King would find an explanation of the low men in the sixth instalment of the *Dark Tower* series. In Hicks' film, the 'low men' become 'law men', not by scripted intent, but because the loose ends are left hanging meaninglessly. Through benign neglect more than anything, *Hearts in Atlantis* becomes a model New Age Hollywood mystery – at once familiar and thrilling, finally shrouded in vacuous 'meaning'. Its redemption, in its entirety, is Hopkins' performance. Peta Barker admitted that she always looked with interest at her former husband's portrayal of father figures: in *Atlantis*, perhaps tellingly in context of the new maturity of pragmatic acceptance, he transcended all previous performances, turning in a truly touching character that many judged more fitting of Academy Awards nominations than the Presidential cartoons of the nineties.

There were offers of thrillers galore, but the choice after *Atlantis* was spurred more by friendship than money – although the money on offer, given the nudge of *Hannibal*, was considerable. Alec Baldwin, like most actors, had long wanted to direct. In 2000, with the backing of Warners and production partners Cutting Edge, he finally got his wish with a remake of William Dieterle's 1941 minor classic, *The Devil and Daniel Webster*, which he had been developing for seven years. What unfolded – with Hopkins at the centre – was an altogether different kind of classic, a template Hollywood business story of alleged budgetary abuse, mismanagement, egocentricity . . . and lawsuits.

At first, though, Hopkins had been delighted to come aboard. The plot was largely unchanged from the original: Baldwin played a writer who sells his soul to the devil for ten years, in order to secure a *New York Times* bestseller. When the devil comes to claim his dues, the writer disputes his liability, and engages a lawyer, Daniel Webster, to defend him. Production on the film, which was scripted by the novelist Pete Dexter, began after Christmas and ended in March 2001, during which Hopkins worked, according to Baldwin, 'just a couple of weeks'. For his labours, Hopkins received $6 million, an upfront improvement even on *Hannibal* and, it would emerge, a serious bone of contention.

Production itself glided along smoothly. Jennifer Love Hewitt played the devil, and Dan Ackroyd and Kim Cattrall provided sound support. But, according to legal papers later filed, difficulties began when the budget shifted from the initially declared $13.5 million to $28 million. Within two months of the completion of principal photography, with the editing yet to be done, Baldwin was formally announcing his withdrawal from the project and launching a lawsuit against Cutting Edge producer David Glasser for $850,000 of unpaid fees. At the same time, Corinne Mann, Baldwin's producing partner at El Dorado, his development company, initiated her own lawsuit – against Baldwin – citing breach of contract, and owed fees 'in excess of $100,000'. For the next eighteen months *The Devil and Daniel Webster*, which was eventually cut and dubbed, languished on a filing shelf while Warners withdrew and accusations and threats flew. At one stage *Variety* announced that Glasser and Baldwin had reached an agreement 'for the sake of the movie'; within weeks they were back at legal loggerheads and the news service WENN reported that 'federal agents have seized' the reels of film, with the assertion that one of the film's investors had allegedly 'bounced checks' during production and was under federal investigation.

For Glasser, the case boiled down to Baldwin's greed. He said,

> We gave Alec exactly what his lawyers asked for, and he went and filed a lawsuit, which basically comes down to an $850,000 *bonus* he was due only if he delivered the picture on time and on budget. Why, if he was so concerned about vendors getting paid, did he make sure he was paid in full, first? I deferred my fee to pay the vendors. I have a parachute I could pull because Alec breached his contract, but I've seen a cut [of the film] and it's a good movie. I hang in on a movie that goes from $13.5 million to a $28-million budget and he can't roll with the punches when an investor pulls out?

Baldwin saw things very differently. He had budgeted tightly, indeed had asked for cuts in all departments in order to control the outlay – and only Corinne Mann refused to play ball. As a fifty-fifty producing partner,

Baldwin contended, his means were limited, and so he owed nothing to Mann. As for Cutting Edge's budget management claim, Baldwin insisted the problem started with his friend, Anthony Hopkins. Hopkins wasn't to blame, but Baldwin insisted he had been quite ready to make the film 'with an actor of lesser juice', but had been outvoted by Glasser, who was obviously in thrall of the great Hopkins. '[Glasser's legal action] is a smokescreen to cover his own inadequacies and potential fraud,' Baldwin said. 'Glasser was the one who said, let's storm the castle and give Tony the money. We didn't demand he find the extra $6 million. We're suing because they completely defrauded us, told us they had the money to finish the film when they knew before they started they didn't have it. They hoped they could raise it and when they couldn't, they thought we wouldn't notice.'

Hopkins hardly noticed the unfolding crisis because, with the absorption of his new resolve, by summer he was already shooting another Hollywood thriller, the Bruckheimer-Shumacher cop story, *Bad Company*. If ever his most loyal fan base – the purists who'd loved him in British theatre and the Merchant Ivorys – was tested, it was tested now. Since *Hannibal*, the gilded mantle of true superstardom, with all its accoutrements and excesses, had been bestowed. Apart from presidential visits, during *Hannibal* sets were routinely closed and a 1,000-yard cordon thrown round the star. In Virginia, just before the wrap of the film, residents petitioned against the restrictions. After *Hannibal* opened to superlative box-office returns – $58 million in the first week, going on to a projected gross of $350 million – the mould of stardom set even more. In Queens, New Jersey and downtown Manhattan, the locations for *Bad Company*, unprecedented fanfare followed every unit move and, though Hopkins' co-star was the fast-talking *Saturday Night Live* teen favourite Chris Rock, no one was in any doubt of Hopkins' dominance. Lee Gregg, a freelance journalist, summed up the change: 'You don't even bother approaching the [film publicist] for interviews, because you get the potted party line: *I'm just an actor, the business isn't my concern, I just learn my lines* . . . Baloney is the privilege that comes with superstardom.'

The risk inherent in taking on the notoriously cartoon-inflected Bruckheimer, was, of course, the risk of self-parody. All great actors milking the Hollywood circus walk this line and few, certainly not Olivier, nor Burton, survive unscathed. Early on, when WENN first announced *Bad Company* (then titled *Black Sheep*), the signs were bad. The proposed film was reported as 'a horror spoof'. It wasn't; but its flashy blaze would take it close to the edge. The story concept itself was Bruckheimer's: 'I had it for years. It was essentially a play of opposites, but also a story with inbuilt comedy, where a guy is forced to "become" his own twin brother, who couldn't be more unlike him.' Bruckheimer employed Joel Schumacher, whose work ranged from *Car Wash* to *Tigerland*, by way of two *Batman*s, and together they opted for Hopkins, the fastest-rising top-ten box-office draw. 'I was offered it and I read some of the script and I thought, yes, I know this Rock guy, I've seen him on television,' said Hopkins. 'I like action movies. I like Schwarzenegger and all that. People assume I'm very cerebral and reflective, but I like to have fun.'

It could have been fun, but a minor element of the storyline reared its head in the most unfortunate way. The plot had Hopkins as Gaylord Oakes, a CIA operative who is forced to replace his Harvard-educated partner, killed during a key nuclear arms purchase, with the agent's goofy twin brother. The plot centres on the terrorists' attempts to compromise Jake, played by Rock, but the overlying story which shadows the action is the threat of a nuclear terrorist attack on New York City. *Variety* reported a character in the original script threatening to 'turn Wall Street into a piece of charcoal'.

The film was in post-production when the 11 September terrorist attacks occurred. Immediately, Disney announced a postponement of release until June of the following year. Minor cuts were made, but for once serendipity failed Hopkins. By the time the film was in circulation, the pall of 9/11 had seeped into every facet of American life and culture. The cavalier and summery New York depicted in *Bad Company* no longer existed. And the very word 'terrorist' connoted a despicable reality that changed the everyday existence of all Americans. Hopkins, like everyone else, was stunned by the attacks: in Toronto to promote *Hearts in Atlantis* at the time, he phoned Jenni for the first time in months and reevaluated his life; in the circumstances, the failure of *Bad Company* seemed less than important.

The dimension of the film's failure, though, was salutary. *Hannibal*, despite its excellent financial performance, had been judged merely visceral, and a considerably lesser work than *Silence of the Lambs*. *Bad Company* by comparison was buried under bad reviews. For the *New York Times* it bore 'the whiff of something gone stale'; the *Toronto Star*, always a Hopkins fan, decried 'all concept and no content, overly art-directed and artlessly rendered, brilliantly cast and terribly performed . . . the kind of movie that might make you angry if it wasn't so deeply inconsequential.' Worst of all came from the *Boston Globe*'s Sam Allis who blamed Hopkins first and foremost: 'We assume he had a bad run in the market or a costly divorce, because there is no earthly reason other than money why this distinguished actor would stoop so low.'

It seemed, globally, a time to rethink. When he called Jenni on 11 September, she later told Quentin Falk, she was very surprised. They had been talking about divorce but, all of a sudden, he wanted to put it on hold. Weeks later, he called to say the reprieve wouldn't work, that they must proceed with the formal split. Jenni was unready for it, believing divorce was unnecessary, but her affection for him was such that she complied with his plan and negotiated the settlement, rubber-stamped in July 2002, which gave her an income, and the house in Kensington. Hopkins had already begun to date a new lady, a small-time South American antiques dealer called Stella Arroyave, whom he'd met while shopping for furniture for the house in Malibu. 'When I saw him go Hollywood,' said David Scase, 'I thought, well, that is what I call a three-act life. But certain people have that extra something. You always wonder about the possibilities of the fourth act . . .'

Chapter 19

ACTION MAN

Simple remedy as it seems, the union with Stella Arroyave stemmed the recurrent tendency to crash and burn. Suddenly, on the LA party circuit he was subdued, so relaxed in fact that the past could be countenanced for once not defensively, but productively.

A few years before he'd been asking interviewers not to pester him with questions about alcoholism: 'That was 25 years ago, it's dead and buried.' Now he was defying the nay sayers who insisted his dual citizenship insulted Wales by redoubling his support for old friends. Already, he had given $1 million to the Snowdonia Appeal. To this was added another $1 million for the Anthony Hopkins Foundation, a sponsorship programme for theatrical students, and $300,000 to the Welsh College of Music and Drama. Now, hearing about the renovation problems of the 112-year-old Palace Theatre in Swansea, a venue he'd briefly appeared at forty years before, he pledged more support. 'There was a reluctance to let go of the theatre,' David Hare opined, 'because it defined that sense of liberty he cherished.' During 2001, a friend's approach about the voluntary Ruskin School of Acting, a small-time operation based in a disused hangar at Santa Monica Airport, elicited all out support. Throughout the following year, without payment, Hopkins provided his tutorial services once a week. 'I asked him how I could pay him back,' said school founder John Ruskin, 'and he said, "You've already given me a cup of coffee . . ." '

The tranquillity was genuine. In between coaching a student production of Strindberg's *Miss Julie*, optimism brimmed: 'I don't want to use that word "important" or talk about "giving back",' he told a visiting writer. 'That's too Mother Teresa, but being here is pleasant and it's touching. My tiny little mission in life is to say to them, "There's no mystery to acting", and the great pleasure is seeing them open up.' Underlying this calm was a new refinement of his pragmatic philosophy. Film, he concluded, he preferred to theatre. But neither could shake his world. At the time, *Bad Company* was on release, and dying on its feet. But he would not be depressed by it. It was, after all, just a film and he had found the best way to weather disappointment. 'No, I'm not passionate about anything anymore,' he said. 'I used to be fascinated by the process of acting, but as time goes by I can't take it seriously. I just learn the lines, show up and do it, that's all. They pay me well, I don't need to work again.'

The implicit, stubborn contradiction – loving and hating all at once – remained, but part of the new calmness was about letting it all hang out. To live in fear, he once told James Cellan Jones, would be no life at all. 'My life these days is much more fun because I have surrendered to it,' he told the *Calgary Sun*. 'The older I get, the more I've let go of cares, worries and expectations. It has helped me get in touch with the most important and potent parts of my life.'

The regular AA meetings, still faithfully attended, benefited from this new relaxation. Openly, long before the media stories of his relationship with Arroyave started in the summer of 2002, he was confessing her crucial presence in his life. Without guilt or embarrassment he permitted the public release of a taped session at AA – at $5 per copy, to benefit the organisation – in which he listed his priorities. His alcoholism, he said, was 'an amazing experience', which affected every day of his life. His great concern was for his mother's well-being. Now 88, she had recently undergone repeated invasive surgeries to relieve 'a circulatory problem' at St John's in Santa Monica, but was recovering. Elsewhere, he emphasised his new way of maintaining balance:

> Nothing is important [but] my mother is important. I enjoy taking care of her and I phone her and make sure she's OK. She loves to go out and party and it's a lot of fun making sure she's OK. Sometimes you're [sic] in rush hour, driving like a maniac, and you stop by a cemetery in a traffic jam and you notice that everyone's *very quiet*. I am just lucky to be above ground instead of underneath it. To hell with the traffic jam, you think, it's really nice to be alive. That's important . . . to have a garden, to grow flowers or walk on the beach or feed the birds. I'm going home to play the piano this afternoon.

Forty-six-year-old Arroyave, a raven-haired, naturally buoyant woman with no connections and no particular interest in showbusiness, took her fiancé's lead and dodged the media, steeling herself instead to weather the gossip mill, which ranged, in the British and American tabloids, from accusations of recent insolvency to a fraud lawsuit by a French business-man. Though she dined with Hopkins' agent and friends, all of whom joyfully approved, Arroyave was socially more or less invisible, concentrating her energies on redecorating the Malibu property around the elegant Bosendorfer piano, centrepiece of the living room and of Hopkins' evening meditations, and on accompanying him on his still-beloved, long, desert drives. 'At last,' Hopkins told a friend, 'I have someone who loves to drive just as much as I do.'

Working the Lecter franchise was the big outstanding issue. De Laurentiis had made it clear that yet another film – and maybe more – would follow the lucrative *Hannibal*. Obviously waiting for Tom Harris to generate new material was a hopeless endeavour: *Red Dragon*, overworked or not, would fit the bill.

From Hopkins' point of view, affectionate commitment to De Laurentiis, who always treated him with immense professional respect, kept him in the picture, but there were serious second thoughts this time round. 'I needed to be convinced,' he later said: Ted Tally's participation became the great persuader. Tally's literary sensibilities matched Hopkins'. For Tally, understatement was the order of the day. On *Bad Company*, for instance, Hopkins had complained to Schumacher about the verbosity of the script. 'I got to New York [to start filming] and I said to Joel, "You have to cut some lines. It's too many words. You don't need to explain it all."' Mamet and Zaillian, if they had any weakness, had the same prolix tendencies. Tally was content with suggestion and keen to renew Lecter because, 'There was a trilogy, and I said, yes, let's finish it with this great actor.'

Discharging Harris' trilogy became the be-all *raison* for resuming Lecter. As ever, Hopkins stepped back from the politics of mounting the production, but was approving of De Laurentiis' savvy instincts. Scott's *Hannibal* had been most criticised for its gore; this time De Laurentiis was happy to concede to Universal's suggestion to employ director Brett Ratner, spawn of the MTV generation, whose hundred or so music videos, for the likes of Mariah Carey and Madonna, had led to a handful of lightning-fast witty actioners, most recently the colossal successes for Jackie Chan, *Rush Hour 1* and *2*. Hopkins hesitated when he heard of Ratner's multi-take reputation, but met him in New York and liked his humour and youth (he was just 32). Finally, the decision to jump came with a simple question from Ratner: How did Hopkins *want* to play this new Lecter? Here, Hopkins was clear-visioned. *Red Dragon*, precursor of *Silence* as it was, did not feature Clarice at all, instead it concerned Will Graham, the obsessive FBI agent whose hunt for a different serial killer, the Tooth Fairy, launched the 'cannibal' series. Graham was a sideline player in *Silence*, as Lecter was in *Red Dragon*. But the success of *Silence* had prompted a total reevaluation of *Red Dragon*, with a reissue of the original novel, to which a 'linking' prelude by Harris was added. Tally, De Laurentiis and Universal bridged the gaps further, exaggerating Lecter's role in *Red Dragon* and remoulding to set up retroactively the tone of relationships established on screen by *Silence*.

In the original book, Graham, who has been responsible for Lecter's incarceration, uses him as a guide to get inside the mind of the Tooth Fairy. In this, Hopkins saw, was his 'doorway in' to the reworked character. Anger, Hopkins judged, was the key. 'Because Will Graham puts Lecter inside for life,' Hopkins told Ratner, 'he's pretty angry. I want to capitalise on that. I want to play him in a blindly quiet rage. If I ever get out, I will destroy Graham. I want that to be the ticking time bomb that runs under the Graham–Tooth Fairy story, because it then sets up everything.'

Ratner's genius was the opposite of Scott's. Neither a stylist nor a masterful director of actors, he was gifted in isolating the unique strengths of his fellow workers. With Mariah Carey the grandstanding was embraced, with Jackie Chan the Keatonesque acrobatics, with Hopkins, unquestionably, the furious restraint. Working numerous variations on Michael Mann's *Manhunter*, Ratner's film postulated a tense triangle between Graham, the Tooth Fairy and Lecter, building to the name-check introduction of Clarice Starling and setting the scene in terms of temporal chronology for *Silence*. Elements were taken from Harris' new prelude of the reissued *Red Dragon*, and from the film *Manhunter* (where Brian Cox played Lecter), and, as with *Hannibal*, Harris' finale was altered entirely. Hopkins loved all this chess-playing, and was stimulated, too, by his new co-stars, Ed Norton (as Graham) and Ralph Fiennes (as the Tooth Fairy). So stimulated, in fact, that he was prepared – almost – to put up with Ratner's unshaken multi-takes style of direction. Almost. Hopkins recalled:

> One day we were doing the fight scene with Edward Norton where I stab at him, and we had done that, maybe, eight or ten times. I went back to look at it on the monitor, and this was early in the film. I hadn't done the cell scenes. It was late at night and I thought, 'Well, this is going on and on and on.' And I asked Brett, 'Well, what do you *want*?' And he said, 'I want more.' And then he asked me, 'Well, how do I compare to Marty Best?' And I said, 'Well, you're close, I'll give you that. You're getting close. You and Kubrick. You're close,' I said, 'and don't push it.' And I meant it. But that's the only little skirmish we had, sort of a little jab at him. But he did it for a reason, he trained at NYU film school, and he's one of those directors who can *see* what he wants. He wants to see what he wants to see!

ANTHONY HOPKINS

What Ratner wanted to see was the anger, and by a process of attrition, he got it. Hopkins recalled:

> There was a later scene, in which I was kind of disappointed. It just somehow didn't work, and it was a scene where Ed – Graham – says to me, 'You have one disadvantage.' 'What's that?' Lecter says. 'You're insane.' And it was early in the story, and it had troubled me. I wasn't losing sleep over it, but there was something weak about it. It was my first scene in the cell and I just thought there was something too loose or too light in it. And I don't like asking for retakes, but it troubled me to the point where I said, 'You know that scene we did?' and Brett said yeh. I said, 'Well, I wonder if we could do that again.' Ed wasn't around but he said that I could just play to a cross on the lens. He asked me how I wanted to do it. A few days before he'd asked me to whisper obscenities to Ed off-camera. And he wanted the reverse now, but Ed was in New York. So we tried it with Brett, and it was getting me angry. I told him that this was too much, that it was really going beyond the script, that it was unnecessary, and he said, 'OK good, *do it now*, and *action!*' And I was still – *grrrrrr* – and I looked into the camera . . . and I got it. Brett said, 'Yes, yes, that's it!' Ed wasn't there, but I felt that if I could get through the glass, I'd rip his face off . . .

Miles from *Hannibal*'s explicit violence, *Red Dragon* surpassed itself by tapping into Hopkins' personal reality, and the actor's quiet intellectualisation of Hannibal Lecter. Ratner was effusive with praise – 'He just gets it, he knows how to be threatening, and how to be seductive' – but it was apparent that Hopkins had done his homework:

> What I find attractive about Lecter, and I don't mean this in any sort of self-gratifying way, obviously, is that this guy is a killer, that he's not a hero, he's a monster, but there's a great depth to him, especially at the end. I realise that's the way Tom Harris has created this character, and of course Ted Tally has reinterpreted some of it – especially that last speech where he says, 'We live in strange times.' Lecter, you see, has a

great perception of the world. I asked Jonathan Demme some years ago why he wanted me to play this character and he asked, 'Well, don't you want to play him?' He said he'd seen me in *The Elephant Man* playing the doctor, and I thought at first, 'There's no connection.' But there was. Demme saw Lecter as a great humanitarian, trapped inside this monstrous mind – and *that* is a tragedy, because he is a brilliant man, and had he been released from this insanity, he would have been a great benefactor, but he's caught in this nightmare of his own making. And he understands psychology, understands Will Graham. I met a man recently who explained he can 'get inside' people. He's a psychologist and he can open you up and he can get into you and sort you out very quickly, within, I'd say, three minutes. And that's a gift, and I think that that is the gift Lecter has.

The conclusion of *Red Dragon* marked the emphatic closing of a chapter in his life. Already, De Laurentiis was explaining his plan for the extended franchise – 'Hannibal 4', announced in 2003, would be called *The Lecter Variation*, 'a three-generation exploration of the development of a serial killer, from childhood, through teenager to old man', apparently schemed outside Tom Harris' *oeuvre*, though, hopefully, with his and Tally's input. Hopkins' affection for Dino and Martha De Laurentiis remained, there was acknowledged gratification that the esteemed American Film Institute's poll of the screen's best villains ranked him first, facing down Gregory Peck's Atticus Fink (from *To Kill a Mockingbird*) as the best hero, but there was no longer any desire to 'do the same thing over and over. It's done, it's past . . . I don't dwell on things.'

The abrupt switch down after *Red Dragon*, friends believed, was the ultimate expression of the actor's intelligence. In the early nineties, Hollywood veteran James Coburn, another big admirer of Hopkins' 'specialness', mused on the questionable nature of stardom. Coburn had broken through in *The Magnificent Seven* but had felt himself – and his close friend Steve McQueen – 'sidetracked' by stardom 'because it is seductive, ego-flattering, financially wonderful . . . and finally soul-destroying.' Hopkins had dabbled with a kind of distorted self-parody in *Bad Company*, but, according to Coburn, there was a dangerous step beyond:

> Steve felt it. You do one or two strong, popular roles. Then they throw the bucks at you. So you do them, or variations of them, again. Then they throw huge bucks . . . because they want the *sure thing*. Hollywood is a market economy, nothing else. They talk about creativity, but it's all lies. Hopkins is on the brink now. Richard Burton was there, and then he went over the edge. And before he knew it, he was playing . . . *Richard Burton*. That is the biggest burden of 'the big hit' – you stop being an actor and start playing 'yourself'. You become a celebrity, and cease being an actor. At the end, Steve wanted to return to Ibsen, and thankfully he did [in *The Enemy of the People* in 1978]. No one who is a true artist – *a true actor* – will be content to die a celebrity.

'There was a time,' said Hopkins in 2000, 'when I took every role they threw at me, because I didn't want to fail, I didn't want to have to hightail it back to London begging for jobs.' That time was over. Around the agentry circuit the word went out, as early as mid-production on *Red Dragon*, that Hopkins wanted no more garbage. 'I knew him as a restless soul,' said one former CAA agent, 'and I heard the word. Five years before, you'd offer him the new Bruce Willis. You didn't want to be doing that now.'

Of the filtered list of films on offer from CAA's Nicita, Hopkins selected the most intellectually illustrious in direct counterweight to the inevitability of another worldwide Lecter success. Director Robert Benton's adaptation of Philip Roth's acute social essay, *The Human Stain*, displayed the smart casting skills that won him an Academy Award for *Kramer vs Kramer*. Dustin Hoffman, many remembered, was famously going through an anguished divorce when Benton cast him in a story that anatomised divorce; Hopkins, at 66, was madly in love with Arroyave, more than twenty years his junior, when Benton offered the role of Coleman Silk, the old academic who falls in love with Faunia Farley, a woman in her thirties. Hopkins, of course, acknowledged nothing of this. For him, the choice of Benton's film was down to pedigree: he admired Benton and Roth, and appreciated the skills of the co-stars, Nicole Kidman (playing Faunia), Gary Sinise and Ed Harris. Plus he liked the themes of the film which, like Roth's novel, chose the reference time frame of the summer of 1998, when the world's rapacious curiosity was focused on the Clinton–Lewinsky–Tripp–Starr scandals, to explore the secret life of a fading old professor who is called to reevaluate his entire existence through a succession of serendipitous encounters. 'It is a story which is non "PC",' said Hopkins, referring to the racist probings of the story which parallel the issues of ageism in sexuality. 'I hate "PC", absolutely loathe it.'

For *Red Dragon*, Hopkins had again worked hard with a trainer, lifting weights (a new intermittent pastime), jogging, suffering a low-carb diet. Facing the prospect of the first sexually intimate scenes since *Magic*, the fitness factor again obligated him to two months of the treadmill. But the visual difference between *Red Dragon* – in which he wore his hair long, slicked in a ponytail and dyed at the top – and *The Human Stain*, spoke volumes about his undiminished ambition. His performances, when judged side by side as works discharged within months of each other, answered anyone harbouring doubts about his art.

For Benton's film, Hopkins was required to project a benevolence and vulnerability unlike anything he'd attempted. The arc of the story is a long one, following Silk (by circuitous route of immaculate flashbacks in which Wentworth Miller plays the younger version) from a stressful childhood, through his joyful tenure as an arts professor at a New England College, through the school scandal in which he is accused of using a racist epithet, through the sudden death of his wife, through the affair with Faunia, through his strange friendship with reclusive author Nathan Zuckerman, through lawsuits and a final, conclusive personal disaster.

Throughout, Benton observed, Hopkins portrayed not the familiar restraint of his British romances, but delicate, heart-rending passion. Thrilled with the daily yield from Hopkins – who had always been his one and only casting choice for Silk – Benton said, 'There are actors who take you to the character . . . and then there are some who take you beyond, into the place where reality happens. Tony is one of those actors.'

Shot at evocatively autumnal locations in Quebec (including McGill University campus in Montreal) and Massachusetts (including Williams College), the film utilised every aspect of cinema to state its case, which was less about late life sexuality than American bigotry. Silk's secret, we learn, is that his bloodline is not Caucasian, but black: he is sacked from his university post for using the word 'spook', but cannot bring himself to confess his true identity to anyone, except Zuckerman and, finally, Faunia. Roth's novel, which Hopkins read and loved, was acerbic social indictment; Benton's film was different: 'I'm a gentler voice,' said the director, 'and I see this principally as a human tragedy.' Indeed, the scene that won Benton, who had penned all but two of his ten films (since starting as a writer on *Bonnie and Clyde* in 1967), was not polemical speech, but a moment where Silk, hiding out in the woods to narrate his life story to Zuckerman, dances with the writer. 'That's why I did it. There are scenes that are incredibly delicate, where none of it depends on the words. There are scenes where the most interesting thing going back and forth between the actors is *inside*, interior – the words are there, but it's not about the words. The words are the least of the scenes . . .'

To exploit the poetic metaphors – autumnal opportunity, denial begets pain – Benton and his cinematographer Jean-Yves Escoffier experimented with a new intermediate digital mastering process that allowed film stock to be processed, heightened or muted beyond the capabilities of conventional colour timing. 'I told Jean-Yves I wanted the film to look like a handwritten postcard sent to a friend, that intimate and personal,' said Benton. 'The idea was for the images to be beautiful, but not pretty. I did not want primary colours. I wanted contrast between winter and spring, where winter is bleak and spring is bright and vivid. And I wanted the dramatic scenes at night to be dark and confrontational.'

The resultant tweaking lent an extraordinary picturesque poignancy – all the more eye-catching because, texturally, it had never been seen in a film before – but Benton was in no doubt that the technology, great as it was, was only secondary to the performances. At the start, said Benton,

Hopkins had worried that perhaps he couldn't play the part, and asked did he need special make-up or dark contact lenses to match Wentworth Miller's. 'I told him no. I knew he could do this on performance alone. It was a case of, take me as I am.' Benton had previously directed Nicole Kidman – whom he and his wife viewed as 'another daughter' – in *Billy Bathgate*. With her fuller maturity, he believed she was the only match for Hopkins. 'This was finally an actors' movie. Those actors owned it.'

And Hopkins, surely, was never more fully stretched nor at ease in the depiction – for once – not of evil or madness but of common humanity. 'I was never comfortable [acting intimately] with women,' he'd said. 'Maybe if I looked like Brad Pitt . . .?' Coleman Silk pitched him in at the deep end, where all existential questions are at least ameliorated by human intimacy. 'Action is the enemy of thought,' says Faunia, urging Hopkins' emotionally stranded Silk to surrender and win. 'Who said that?' asks Silk breathlessly, and the wide-eyed wonderment as he concedes, following to the bedroom to find her naked and awaiting him, becomes a moment of transcendent, self-defining acting – a moment of true autobiography, perhaps? – to match the Tahitian tribal scenes of *The Bounty* that Lindsay Anderson so admired.

It was hard to imagine Hopkins turning back on himself after a noble elevation like *The Human Stain*. What, after all, was there to gain? Money? Money was no longer an issue. He had money aplenty to look out for Muriel whom he knew was fading fast, and Jenni in London, and Stella. Simple arithmetic shows his earnings from the mid-nineties totalled in excess of $40 million; to that would be added the generous percentage points in the Lecter films, all of which cumulatively had earned over half a billion dollars.

What was on the cards was a little personal pampering. He had laboured for forty years to achieve the security – and the fantasy – of an acting career and an American identity. He finally had the chance to stop and smell the roses. 'I once confronted him,' said his old friend Alan Dobie, 'about age. I said, "What about those December days when you've done it all, and built the nest egg and bought the cottage with the asters and roses? Then what will you want?" "To act," is what he answered. "Oh," I said, "to run away from yourself?" "No," he said. "To find myself."'

Some of the most blisteringly real lines spoken by Hopkins on celluloid come in the middle of *The Human Stain*. He has danced with Zuckerman to Fred Astaire's 'Cheek to Cheek' and is unloading himself, revealing the extraordinary changes wrought by his intimacy with a sensitive and sexually uninhibited woman. 'When this stuff comes back so late in life, completely unexpected, completely unwanted, it comes back with such force. And there's nothing you can do about it . . .'

Alan Dobie would be forgiven for thinking Coleman Silk was a moment when Hopkins found himself. Just days after completing the film, on 1 March – St David's Day – Hopkins married Stella Arroyave in a private ceremony in the hillside garden of his Malibu home. The house was festooned with daffodils, and among those attending were Steven Spielberg, Catherine Zeta-Jones, John and Alice Cleese and Nicole Kidman. As a special treat for Muriel, a twinkling Hollywood golden boy from her era – Mickey Rooney – was also present. The *New York Daily News* was among the first to report the happy day. Oblivious to the irony of its own editorial posture, the *News* reported Hopkins saying America was now, emphatically, his home 'because the Americans treat me so much better than the Brits'. 'British news coverage of the wedding might only bolster his bad feelings,' said the shame-faced *News*, before going on to quote Jimmy Esebeg, who allegedly sued Arroyave in 1994 over a bad business deal: 'I'm surprised she's with Anthony Hopkins. I'd like to warn him.'

Hopkins met this calumny with the response it deserved: a witty and expressive silence. By now he knew the game.

Even with the best intentions, working from the best discerning artistic instincts with no compromise in his heart, the muddy mire of showbiz was ready to swallow him up. During the summer of 2003, he chose two important films by directorial heavyweights – John Madden's *Proof* and Oliver Stone's *Alexander* – and temporarily lost all forward momentum. Madden's film, particularly, was the stuff of substance, a worthy successor to *The Human Stain*. It began life in 2000 as a play by the thirty-year-old, Chicagoan David Auburn, staged at Broadway's Walter Kerr Theatre, and running for 916 performances with actress Mary-Louise Parker and director Daniel Sullivan both winning Tonys and Auburn winning a Pulitzer. Transferred to London in 2002, *Proof* became a kind of intense return-to-theatre workshop for the partnership of John Madden and Gwyneth Paltrow, whom Madden had directed so winningly in *Shakespeare in Love*. Madden had not worked in theatre since the mid-eighties; Paltrow's last theatre work was a brief run of *As You Like It* at Williamstown, Massachusetts, in 1999. At the tiny Donmar Warehouse, over four sell-out weeks in May and June, Paltrow had exceed all expectations. 'Not unlike Mary-Louise Parker on Broadway,' wrote the *Guardian*'s Michael Billington, 'Paltrow makes Auburn's play look substantially better than it is.' Charles Spencer in the *Telegraph* also endorsed Paltrow, but cited *Proof* as 'powerfully affecting'.

Auburn's story had some common links with Roth's *Human Stain*. A triangular tale of family relationships, it revolved around Catherine, a woman who has sacrificed her education and social life to tend to her dying father, a maths genius who has mentally disintegrated. The play skips from her relationship with the old man to the aftermath of his passing, as she struggles to cope with assumptions of her own madness, while all the time jousting with her stable, lightweight sister Claire and Hal, the student who wishes to trawl through her father's papers. At the Donmar, Ronald Pickup, Hopkins' old RADA mate, played the role of the father and the attention garnered had the *British Theatre Guide* describing 'Donmar Madness', a repeat of the 24-hour queuing binges that had accompanied Nicole Kidman's visit four years before in David Hare's *The Blue Room*. The follow-up film was a given. 'I had originally been offered it as a movie,' said Madden. 'But Gwyneth and I had been talking about doing something in theatre since *Shakespeare in Love* which, after all, was a love letter to theatre in general. So this progression seemed right.'

Early in 2003, Miramax announced the project and Madden announced his cast: of the stage originals, only Paltrow was booked for the film adaptation (written by Rebecca Miller, playwright Arthur's daughter), with Hope Davis (from *Hearts in Atlantis*) and Jake Gyllenhaal filling out the roles of Claire and Hal. Madden had been pleased with Pickup's work on the London stage, but knew a big-name star was needed for Miramax: Hopkins became his first choice, and signed on in September, just weeks before shooting.

For a variety of reasons, not least of which was Hopkins' hardened standoff approach to the media, *Proof* always lacked what the industry calls a marketing profile. Much of this honourably reflected the earnestness of the project and its principals, but it augured bad for the finished work. For Auburn, the project was a very personal work. He had studied for his Bachelor's degree at the University of Chicago, and based his central character on 'a dotty chemistry professor' he knew. The setting of the play is the rear porch of an off-campus house that becomes Catherine's mausoleum. In an early draft, Auburn tried to generalise the locale, but felt the truth of the work must be 'grounded'. Consequently, the setting was changed to the Hyde Park district, just off the university's campus, and the ground rules were set for accuracy. Initially, the University of Chicago resisted hosting the production, but Auburn's Pulitzer and the reputation of Madden opened the doors. After weeks of searches, a seedy-looking house with the right porch was found on 48th street, north of the campus, and new scenes were styled to make use of Rockefeller Chapel, and Eckhart Hall and the Divinity School.

Hopkins' role in the film was interwoven, like the Coleman Silk role, though less pervasive. Only 20 per cent of the film was shot in Chicago; the rest was on various stages at Elstree in Britain. It was Hopkins' first film work on home soil in almost ten years and, if anything, the homecoming was even more low key than might have been expected. No friends from the past were called, no interviews were granted. The best the tabloids could scoop was a catering story leaking from the Hertfordshire location, where Paltrow allegedly was instructing her driver to conduct a daily round trip to the London home she shared with her husband, Coldplay's lead singer Chris Martin, to collect macrobiotic lunches at a cost of $370 (approximately £200) a day.

The portentous silence, unfortunately, endured. Finished shortly before Christmas, *Proof* was originally announced for release in the summer of 2004, then delayed till October to ensure better chances of Academy Awards attention, according to Miramax. A further post-ponement until December, then yet another until an unspecified date 'later in 2005', stirred not gossips but industry investigative journalists. What emerged, it seemed, was a film caught in the internal power squabblings of the mighty Disney corporation.

Hart-Sharp Productions, the company that had produced and financed the development of *Proof*, washed its hands of responsibility, announcing, 'Our side of the project is completed, so it's totally up to Miramax now. The film is out of our hands.' Elsewhere, the leading industry magazines proposed the real reason for delay. The embattled Michael Eisner, Disney's chief, had 'put a clampdown on Miramax's budget', while shaky negotiations were under way to determine Miramax's fate after the existing contract with Miramax founders Bob and Harvey Weinstein terminated in September 2005. Disney already had Scorcese's *The Aviator* and the elegant Johnny Depp vehicle, *Finding Neverland*, in prime position for the next Oscars and, in the words of a Miramax spokesman, 'There [was] simply no marketing budget available.'

Paltrow was livid, said the trade press, because her recent *Sky Captain and the World of Tomorrow* had 'tanked' at the box office and *Proof* was her best awards shot since *Shakespeare in Love*. The delays incurred caused other embarrassments: a January cover story for *Vogue*, immaculately negotiated to maximise the film's profile, would also have to be cancelled.

Hopkins kept mum. In December he was at Shepperton studios, joining Oliver Stone 'as a favour', to contribute to Stone's $190-million, mega-epic, *Alexander*, a project that had been floating around him in different formats for two years. After *Hannibal*, De Laurentiis had told Hopkins of his plans to mount a lavish bio-pic called *Alexander the Great*, starring Leonardo DiCaprio as the Macedonian conqueror and financed by Universal and Dreamworks. The project started well, with Ridley Scott expressing interest and De Laurentiis carving a script draft that had

Hopkins as Aristotle. But De Laurentiis was sidetracked with the Lecter films, allowing Stone to bring his fifteen-year project to fruition with substantial German and French government co-production funding to beef up Warners' commitment. 'I heard that Baz Luhrmann had taken on [the De Laurentiis] film,' said Stone, 'and that galvanised me. I'm sure he'll do something original and astonishing with Leo – and I only hope I can live up to the legend of Alexander myself.'

The task ahead of Stone was momentous. Few productions had ever been mounted on this scale and, from the earliest, voices of concern were expressed among French and German backers. Designer Jean Roelfs identified the challenge, and the inherent problem: 'We needed to find locations to stand in for Macedonia, Persia, Bactria, Sogdiana, the Hindu Kush and India. With landscapes, you have to be very specific, otherwise they all blend together.' Producer Jon Kilik said, 'We had to consolidate to make the film possible. We could not actually go through dozens of countries and thousands of miles, as Alexander did.

Apart from the Himalayas, Morocco and Thailand, major set building took place at Pinewood and Shepperton, where the Library of Alexandria, housing 25,000 scrolls, would be home to Ptolemy, Alexander's last surviving general, and the narrator of the story. 'We knew we had taken on something extraordinary,' said Stone at the start. 'The real challenge for everyone was balancing the elements.'

For *Alexander*, Stone had first chosen Liam Neeson, but Neeson decided he needed to spend more time with his family and turned the project down. In his place came a relative newcomer, the Irish actor and natural Richard Harris successor, Colin Farrell. Angelina Jolie was cast as Olympias, Alexander's mother, and Hopkins as Ptolemy. Almost immediately there were doubts raised. Farrell was inexperienced and bore a strong Irish accent; Jolie, at 28, was just a year older than Farrell. And Hopkins, who would only work five days at Shepperton, was in the uncomfortable position of carrying much of the story. As Ptolemy, he was the history-lesson device, appearing (in younger guise) in the very opening scene, which is Alexander's death scene, then, as the story flashes forward to the Alexandrian Library, lecturing the young scribes – and the audience

– on the details of the political ancient world. Stone admitted early on that the specific burden on Hopkins was 'hard on him', but the greater difficulty was the unwieldy production – and Stone's dogged adherence to conspiracy theories in a script (written with Christopher Kyle), which one *New York Times* wag summed up as 'all about Alexander running away from his mother'. Worse, the storyline took an aspect of Alexandrian history – his alleged homosexuality – and laid emphasis on it. One line of Ptolemy's concerning the great conqueror's fixation with his gay boyhood friend Hephaistion (played by Jared Leto) – 'It was said that Alexander was never defeated, except by Hephaistion's thighs' – became the film's soft target, and instigated an avalanche of criticism about Stone's propensity for controversial revisionism at any price.

In the film, Darius of Persia is Alexander's great enemy. But by the time Stone was previewing early cuts of the films, scheduled for release worldwide early in November 2004, the eunuch Bagoas, Alexander's male fling, was the real villain. In late summer, MSNBC announced that Warners had pushed back the release date, demanding 'cuts in the homosexual love scenes'. At the same time, a group of influential Greek lawyers led by Yannis Varnakos threatened to sue Warners and Stone. 'We are not saying we are against gays,' said Varnakos. 'But this is pure fiction. We cannot come out and say that the former US President John F Kennedy was a shooting guard for the Los Angeles Lakers basketball team, so Warners cannot come out and say Alexander was gay.' Colin Farrell's response, true to form, was verbally dexterous: 'It's not a fucking gay film. It's not a fucking straight film. It's just a fucking story.'

As it turned out, neither the lawsuit nor the alleged threatened cuts went ahead, but it hardly mattered. *Alexander* staggered all the way – from the first content controversies to the incident in Bangkok where, three days before filming ended, Farrell fell down a stairway after a boozy party and broke an ankle and a wrist, forcing Stone to muster fill-in shots. Stone attempted to contain his fury: 'Colin came very close. He gambled. We made it.' But *Alexander* didn't make it. Finally released in America at Thanksgiving, it took just $8.2 million in its opening weekend, trailing average fare like *National Treasure* and *Christmas with the Kranks*. Seven weeks later, it premiered in England with Stone and Farrell, but not Hopkins, in attendance, and rated a poor second to a low-budget Michael Keaton thriller, *White Noise*.

On both sides of the Atlantic, reviews concurred. All *Alexander* had really achieved was a KO to De Laurentiis' competing film, which was dropped, then reactivated, then dropped again. *Alexander* failed on the most basic level: as entertainment. The *New York Daily News* said it all. Writer Jack Mathews concluded that it was now understood how Alexander conquered most of the known world by the age of 25: 'He may have bored everyone into submission. I would have surrendered in the first of the film's nearly three long hours.' Stone defended till the end, blaming 'raging fundamentalism' in the era of Bush gung-ho politics on the death of his film. 'From day one, audiences didn't show up. They didn't even read the reviews in the South[ern states] because the media was using the words *Alex is Gay*. As a result you can bet that they thought, "We're not going to see a film about a military leader that has got something wrong with him."'

The extent of Hopkins' disappointment was unknown: he gave no promotional interviews, taking cover and comfort, as usual, in the workload. This time it was an invitation from old working partner Roger Donaldson, to lead the cast of *The World's Fastest Indian*, a quirky film shooting in New Zealand and in Utah, in terrain familiar from Cimino's *Desperate Hours*, from October. In support of Robert Benton's film the previous year, he'd conceded to a trip to Venice for an out-of-competition festival screening, but he felt no obligation to sell his wares any more: 'It's funny. When you've done a film, it's over. I guess my main attitude now is detachment. I'm a bit shy of the showbiz side of it. I'm not a party animal.' The glumness, friends believed, was exacerbated by the death that summer of Muriel, at St John's, the Santa Monica medical centre that had cared for her during her visits throughout the nineties, and had become a haven in her last days. 'Theoretically she died of old age,' said one colleague. 'But that's not strictly true, because she was ageless. Tony depended on her for his fighting spirit. She may once have battled with him, but that only served him. He adored her. The medical centre even acknowledged it, giving him a special honorary evening. His last great gift to her was the wedding [to Arroyave]. Her gift to him was that spirit of tenacity that more and more defined his career.'

In that spirit, the negatives had to be countered: *Alexander* was a major flop, *Proof* was in limbo, *The Devil and Daniel Webster* was in limbo (though a *Variety* report said a new cut of the film had won an award at an unspecified Naples festival, and had been taken up by Tricor Entertainment, who had a 'first look' distribution option with Universal). Lecter apart, the only rounded significant work since *Titus* was *The Human Stain*, a critical success which grossed only $5.3 million and disappeared in a flash. There were other, fatter cheques on offer for projects set to balance the box-office scales but instinct, art and stubbornness pushed him to Donaldson, a relative outsider.

The 'Fastest Indian' of the title intrigued Hopkins. The Indian he quickly learnt was not an ethnic reference, but a motorcycle. With the submitted script came a copy of a documentary Donaldson had made in 1973. A lifelong biker enthusiast who had started in his pre-teens in the late fifties in his native Australia, Donaldson became enamoured of the story of Burt Munro from the day he met him. Donaldson had emigrated to New Zealand at 19, and followed the legendary exploits of the self-taught Southland mechanical maestro who'd set himself the task of building and racing the fastest ever two-wheeled machine. From 1920 until the early seventies, Munro worked from his shed at Invercargill, remodelling his modest bike – a 1920s model Indian Scout capable of speeds of around 60 mph – and turning it into the wonder machine. Hard labour and risk ruled his life, and he routinely worked eighteen-hour days, developing his own lubrication systems, flywheels, cylinder barrels and cogwheels from Caterpillar tractor axles. The unique streamlining he perfected was inspired by watching goldfish in Invercargill's Queen's Park ponds, and he tested it relentlessly, rejecting all failure. The speed testing grounds of Utah's Bonneville Salt Flats – where Craig Breedlove became internationally famous for his four-wheel speed records – obsessed Munro, and over fifteen years he made fourteen pilgrimages, frequently crashing.

In his writings, Munro recorded 250 serious engine blow ups, eight concussions, seven broken bones, a haemorrhage of the brain and 5 minor heart attacks – but he refused to let go of his dream. He was 62 when he first won the land speed trials on the Bonneville Flats, but he kept competing, finally reaching a new world record of 183.586 mph in 1967. Donaldson found Munro deeply inspiring 'because of what he symbolised, which was the most amazing courage and determination and startling originality'. Gary Hannam, the film partner Donaldson schemed with to turn the 1970s documentary into a feature film, agreed: 'Burt had a great philosophy of life. One of his sayings was: "If you don't go when you want to go, when you go, you'll find you're gone." That captures his determination.'

Hopkins joined the production, working out of Salt Lake City offices, in October, and found himself happier than he'd been in years. Once again the concentric circles of destiny were calling the shots. He had argued with Donaldson twenty years before – but profitably. Then, he'd called The Bounty 'not at all a bad experience'. Donaldson turned out to be one of the few whose multi-take perfectionism paid off. Recently he'd seen The Bounty on television – 'though I never watch my movies apart from the premieres' – and liked it. Many others, like Lindsay Anderson, saw it as his finest hour. So it was good to be going back, stretching again. It was also good to be distancing himself from Britain and its ambiguities. And good to be hunkering down in T-shirt and Levis with bikers, grease-guns and machines, living the kind of youthful liberal defiance that had been missing from his own confused teens. More than anything, there was the joy of immersing himself in Munro's doctrine: 'He was all about tenacity. It's a beautiful, uplifting story because it is about the power of the human spirit. I'm enjoying myself like I've never enjoyed myself. Hopefully, Munro will motivate others to set goals and achieve them.'

The Munro spirit made its personal mark. After Titus he had been close to stopping. Now he was speeding up. With Stella by his side, anything seemed possible. She was with him in Tooele County, Utah in October, fostering stray cats (he had a soft spot for those most single-minded and independent of pets), side-saddling out to the desert, dining with him all hours in roadside diners. She was with him on New Zealand's Oreti beach, the world's most southernmost, as he aped Munro, railing against the dying of the light in November. And she was with him again in the spring of 2005, in Louisiana, when he joined new director Steve Zaillian's *All the King's Men* playing the judge opposite Sean Penn's corrupt Southern politico Willie Stark, in yet another classic remake.

In March, at the end of the Zaillian shoot, Sean Penn professed himself exhausted, and in need of a two-year break. His career had spiralled upwards since the inertia of the nineties, and he was routinely appearing in two films in different corners of the world every year. The same could be said for Hopkins – though he was in no mood for a sabbatical. 'He continually gives you a sense of the search for new boundaries,' Roger Donaldson said of him, and there was no diminution of appetites.

Early in 2005, new projects were raining down like confetti. Adrian Noble's *Papa*, based on the memoirs of journalist Denne Bart Petitclerc, might afford him the chance to portray the dying Ernest Hemingway in a $35-million film scheduled for shooting in late spring in Queensland. *Harry and the Butler*, announced as the directorial debut of billionaire Steve Bing, looked suspect (Bing's major contribution to films so far being the $80-million investment in Spielberg's animated *Polar Express*), though the participation of Morgan Freeman, an actor of equal status, improved the prognosis. And, with a little nudging from CAA, Paula Wagner persuaded him to commit to a reprise performance alongside Tom Cruise in *Mission Impossible 3*, another Barnum work horse best excusable for its diversionary theraputic value.

'I've done ten years of action films,' Hopkins said during *The World's Fastest Indian*. 'Now is the time to be more thoughtful.' In this mood, after months of negotiations, he turned away from Noble's Hemingway film. Perhaps, friends contend, he'd had enough of playing madness. Whichever way, the measured decision-making proved he was walking the walk. If, as Philip Roth wrote in *The Human Stain*, action is the enemy of thought, the inversion doesn't hold true. 'Anthony Hopkins taught me more about discernment than anyone I've ever known,' said Alan Dobie.

'I once thought acting was about learning lines. I learned with Anthony that it is about choices. In acting styles, he preferred Olivier to Brando but, in the end, he preferred Spencer Tracy to all of them. "You don't need tricks to do it," he'd say. "You need to know who these characters you're portraying are, and make the decisions they'd make."'

Once, Anthony Hopkins told writer Colin Wills, 'I was standing on the brink of hell . . . I was driving over the canyons, blacking out, not knowing where I was going. In the mornings I would wonder, *did I kill somebody?* and would check the front of the car.' That was the seventies, in the fugue, in the laboratory of Lecter, when the mysteries of his very existence as much as his insanity addled him. He was older now, and experienced. He had seen the sun rise and set on so many schemes – countless films, countless business deals and, not least, on his own dream to escape himself. He had won America, and the Olympian view and the triumph, finally, was in seeing himself in all the chaos of continual contradictions. There were many regrets too unbearable to share – the loss of Abigail, the squandered friendships, the drunken wasted times. But maybe, as Eliot said, the sanctity was simply in the doing. Maybe, for him as for everyone, it is the trying that counts. Moral rectitude notwithstanding, maybe, finally, Hannibal Lecter is of small consequence. He is a characterisation of human pathology understood, essayed, and dismissed. It is the moving on that counts, the equilibrium of the good work ethic. Maybe Old Dick, the Fabian patriarch, would have been most proud of that.

SOURCES AND BIBLIOGRAPHY

The substantial direct quotations from Anthony Hopkins used throughout the text are from interviews conducted by Tony Crawley, some previously unpublished, dated 1968, 1979 and 1984.

Otherwise Hopkins has been quoted from a vast array of articles in the following journals spanning forty years, from 1965 to 2005: *Cinema Papers, Country Living*, the *Daily Express*, the *Daily Mail*, the *Daily Telegraph*, the *Evening News*, the *Evening Standard, Films and Filming, Films Illustrated, Film Review*, the *Guardian*, the *Hollywood Reporter*, the *Independent*, the *Los Angeles Times*, the *New York Times*, the *Observer*, the *People, Photoplay, Premiere, Radio Times, Screen International, Shivers*, the *South Wales Evening Post, Starfix* (Paris), the *Sun*, the *Sunday Express*, the *Sunday Times, Time Out, The Times, Today, Vanity Fair, Variety*, the *Washington Post* and the *Western Mail*.

Reviews and commentaries were quoted from *Films and Filming, Films Illustrated*, the *Hollywood Reporter*, the *Monthly Film Bulletin*, the *New York Times, Playboy, Premiere, Punch, Rolling Stone, Sight and Sound, Time, The Times* and *Variety*.

I wish to express my indebtedness to the many journalists and diarists who have graciously given me access to files, and permission to quote from their features or interviews.

The following books were consulted:

Abuse of Power by Stanley Cutler, Free Press, London, 1997

The Actors' Director: Richard Attenborough Behind the Camera by Andy Duggan, Mainstream, London, 1995

Adventures in the Screen Trade by William Goldman, Warner, New York, 1983

Agee on Film by James Agee, McDowell, Obolensky, 1958

American Cinema/American Culture by John Belton, McGraw Hill Humanities, New York, 2004

American Cinema and Hollywood: Critical Approaches by Richard Dyer, E. Ann Kaplan, Paul Willemen, John Hill and Pamela Church Gibson, Oxford University Press, Oxford, 2000

An Actor and His Time by John Gielgud, Sidgwick & Jackson, London, 1979

Anthony Hopkins: Too Good to Waste by Quentin Falk, Columbus Books, 1989; Virgin Books Ltd, London, 2004

August/Uncle Vanya by Anton Chekhov and Julian Mitchell, Amber Lane Press, Oxford, 1994

Behind the Scenes: Theatre and Film Interviews from the Trans-Atlantic Review ed by Joseph McCrindle, Pitman, Harlow, 1971

Blind Ambition by John Dean, Simon and Schuster, London, 1976

Brando by Charles Higham, New American Library, New York, 1987

The Bright Lights: A Theatre Life by Marian Seldes, Houghton Mifflin, Boston, 1987

British Television Drama edited by George W. Brandt, Cambridge University Press, Cambridge, 1981

A Cinema of Loneliness: Penn, Stone, Kubrick, Scorcese, Spielberg and Altman by Robert Phillip Kolker, rev. ed, Oxford Unviersity Press, Oxford, 2000 [Note: Earlier editions include study of Coppola's work, excised in favour of Stone.]

The Cinema of Oliver Stone by Norman Kagan, Continuum International, New York, 2001

The Complete Dictionary of Shakespeare Quotations compiled by D. C.

Browning, New Orchard, London, 1961 & 1986

The Complete Directory of Prime Time Network TV Shows, 1946–present, Ballantine, New York, 1988

Curtains by Kenneth Tynan, Atheneum, London, 1961

The Death of Satan: How Americans Have Lost the sense of Evil by Andrew Delbanco, Noonday Press, 1996

Early Stages by John Gielgud, Macmillan, London, 1939

The Ends of Power by H. R. Haldeman and Jospeh Dimona, Dell, New York, 1978

Equus by Peter Shaffer, Penguin, London, 1984

A Film Hamlet edited by Brenda Cross, Saturn Press, 1948

The Films of Merchant Ivory by Robert Emmet Long, Harry N. Abrams, New York, 1997

Focus on Shakespearian Films ed by Charles W. Eckert, Prentice-Hall, London, 1972

Freedom from the Bottle by Liz Cutland, Gateway, New York, 1990

The Great Movie Stars: the International Years by David Shipman, Angus & Robertson, London, 1973

Halliwell's Filmgoer's Companion by Leslie Halliwell, Grafton, London, 1988

Halliwell's Television Companion by Leslie Halliwell, Granada, London, 1984

Hannibal by Thomas Harris, Delacorte, New York, 1999

The Hannibal Files by Daniel O'Brien and Adrian Rigelsford, Reynolds & Hearn, Richmond, 2001

He That Plays the King by Kenneth Tynan, Longmans, Green & Co, London, 1950

Hearts in Atlantis by Stephen King, Pocket Books, New York, 2000

The History of Port Talbot by Sally Roberts Jones, Goldleaf, 1991

A History of Tai Bach to 1872 by The Reverend Richard Morgan, Port Talbot Historical Society, reissued 1987

Hollywood vs America by Michael Medved, HarperCollins, London, 1993

Hooked by Pauline Kael, Marion Boyars, New York, 1989

Horror Man: The Life of Boris Karloff by Peter Underwood, Leslie Frewin, 1972

The Human Stain by Philip Roth, Houghton Mifflin, Boston, 2000

James Ivory in Conversation by Robert Emmet Long, University of California Press, 2005

John Gielgud directs Richard Burton in Hamlet by Richard Sterne, Heinemann, London, 1968

Laurence Olivier by Donald Spoto, Harper Collins, London, 1989

The Making of the National Theatre by Geoffrey Whiteworth, Faber & Faber, London, 1951

The Making of the President by Theodore H. White, Atheneum, New York, 1960

Mean Tears by Peter Gill, Oberon Books, London, 1987

Millennium Movies: End of the World Cinema by Kim Newman, Titan Books, London, 1999

Movie-Made America: A Cultural History of American Movies by Robert Skylar, revised ed, Vintage, London, 1994

My Father Laurence Olivier by Tarquin Olivier, Headline, London, 1992

Nixon: An Oliver Stone Film ed by Eric Hamburg and Oliver Stone, Hyperion, New York, 1995

Nixon at the Movies by Mark Feeney, University of Chicago Press, Chicago, 2004

Olivier at Work: The National Years: An Illustrated Memoir by Joan Plowright, Richard Olivier and Lyn Haill, Theatre Arts, 1990

The Oliviers by Felix Barker, Hamish Hamilton, London, 1953

Picasso: Creator and Destroyer by Arianna Stassinopoulos Huffington, Simon & Schuster, New York, 1988

Picasso: The Real Family Story by Olivier Widmaier Picasso, Prestel, 2004

Playing with Fire by Julie Taymor, Harry N. Abrams, New York, 1999

The Premiere Movie Guide ed by Howard Karren, HarperCollins, London, 1991

President Nixon: Alone in the White House by Richard Reeves, Simon & Schuster, London 2002

The Ragman's Son by Kirk Douglas, Simon & Schuster, London, 1988

Ralph Richardson by Garry O'Connor, Hodder & Stoughton, London, 1982

The Real Nixon: An Intimate Biography by Bella Kornitzer, Rand McNally, Chicago, 1960

Red Dragon by Thomas Harris, Dutton, New York, 2000

Reel Power by Mark Latwak, Sidgwick & Jackson, London, 1987

Rich by Melvyn Bragg, Hodder & Stoughton, 1988

Richard Burton by Paul Ferris, Weidenfeld & Nicolson, London, 1981

Richard Burton by David Jenkins, Century, London, 1993

Richard Burton, My Brother by Graham Jenkins, Michael Joseph, London, 1988

RN: The Memoirs of Richard Nixon by Richard M. Nixon, Simon & Schuster, London, 1990

Robert Wise on his Films: From Editing Room to Director's Chair by Sergio Leemann, Silman-James, 1995

Shakespeare and the Film by Roger Manvell, Dent, London, 1971

Shakespeare on the Stage by Robert Speaight, Collins, London, 1973

The Silence of the Lambs by Thomas Harris, St Martin's Press, New York, reprint ed, 1999

Spencer Tracy by Larry Swindell, W. H. Allen, London, 1970

Stage People by Roger Lewis, Weidenfeld & Nicolson, London, 1989

Steven Spielberg by John Baxter, HarperCollins, London, 1996

Steven Spielberg: Interviews (*Conversations With Filmmakers* Series) ed by Lester D. Friedman and Brent Notbohm, University Press of Mississippi, 2000

Stone: A Biography of Oliver Stone by James Riordan, Aurum Press, London, 1996

Study Guide for American Cinema by E. Sikov, McGraw-Hill, London, 1993

Subsequent Performances by Jonathan Miller, Faber & Faber, London, 1986

Thank You for Having Me by C. A. Lejeune, Hutchinson, London, 1964

Theatre Guide by Trevor R. Griffiths and Carole Woods, Bloomsbury, London, 1988

Titus: The Illustrated Screenplay by Julie Taymor, Newmarket Press, 2000

Tracy and Hepburn by Garson Kanin, Angus & Robertson, London, 1971

Transactions of the Port Talbot Historical Society, 1963 to date, Port Talbot Historical Society, 1989

Tyrone Guthrie on Acting by Tyrone Guthrie, Studio Vista, 1971

Variety Obituaries, 1905–1986 (12 vols), Garland, New York, 1988–89

Welsh National Heroes by Alun Roberts, Y Lolfa, Talybont, 2002

Who's Who in Shakespeare by Peter Quennell and Hamish Johnson, Chancellor, 1973

Wide-Eyed in Babylon by Ray Milland, The Bodley Head, London, 1974

I acknowledge with gratitude the following who gave permission to quote extracts from the works mentioned: Faber & Faber, for T. S. Eliot's *Collected Poems, 1909–1962* and *The Waste Land*; David Higham Associates, for Graham Greene's *The Power and the Glory*, Copyright © 1940 Verdant S.A.; Scribner's, New York, for F. Scott Fitzgerald's *The Great Gatsby*; Virgin Publishing for Quentin Falk's *Anthony Hopkins: Too Good To Waste*. Thanks also to Sandra Sljivic, Kate Lyall Grant and Sally Holloway.

THE PLAYS

Note: *The listings are for Hopkins' major theatrical work and do not include his touring plays in Wales with Raymond Edwards' group or otherwise, nor his repertory work in Manchester, Nottingham, RADA, Leicester, Liverpool and Hornchurch, Essex.*

Julius Caesar at the Royal Court (1964)
Producer: Lindsay Anderson   Written by: William Shakespeare
As Metellus Cimber.

A Flea in Her Ear at the National/Old Vic (1966)
Producer: Jacques Charon   Written by: Georges Feydeau
As Etienne Plucheux.

Juno and the Paycock at the National/Old Vic (1966)
Producer: Laurence Olivier   Written by: Sean O'Casey
As an Irregular Mobiliser.

A Provincial Life at the Royal Court (1966)
Producer: Peter Gill   Written by: Anton Chekhov, adapted
                          by Gill

As Boris Ivanov Blagovo.

Dance of Death at the National/Old Vic (1967)
Producer: Laurence Olivier   Written by: August Strindberg
As Captain Edgar.

The Three Sisters at the National/Old Vic (1967)
Producer: Glen Byam Shaw   Written by: Anton Chekhov
As Andrei.

As You Like It at the National/Old Vic (1967)
Producer: Clifford Williams   Written by: William Shakespeare.
As Audrey.

Hamlet at the Roundhouse (1968)
Producer: Tony Richardson   Written by William Shakespeare
As Claudius.

The Architect and the Emperor of Assyria at the National/Old Vic (1971)
Producer: Victor Garcia   Written by: Fernando Arrabal
As the Emperor.

A Woman Killed with Kindness at the National/Old Vic (1971)
Producer: John Dexter   Written by: Thomas Heywood
As Master John Frankford.

Coriolanus at the National/Old Vic (1971)
Producer: Manfred Wedwerth   Written by: William Shakespeare
As Coriolanus.

The Taming of the Shrew at the Chichester Festival Theatre (1972)
Producer: Jonathan Miller   Written by: William Shakespeare
As Petruchio.

Macbeth at the National/Old Vic (1972)
Producer: Michael Blakemore   Written by: William Shakespeare
As Macbeth.

Equus at the National/Plymouth (New York) (1974)
Producer: John Dexter   Written by: Peter Shaffer
As Dr Martin Dysart.

Equus at the Huntington Hartford (Los Angeles) (1977)
Producer: Anthony Hopkins   Written by: Peter Shaffer
As Dr Martin Dysart.

The Tempest at the Center Theatre Group/Mark Taper Forum (Los Angeles) (1979)
Producer: John Hirsch   Written by: William Shakespeare
As Prospero.

The Arcata Promise at the California Center for Performing Arts (Los Angeles) (1981)
Producer: Anthony Hopkins   Written by: David Mercer
As Theo Gunge.

Old Times at the Roundabout Theatre Company (New York) (1984)
Producer: Kenneth Frankel   Written by: Harold Pinter
As Deeley.

The Lonely Road at the Triumph Apollo/Old Vic (1985)
Producer: Christopher Fettes   Written by: Arthur Schnitzler
As Julian Fichtner.

Pravda at the National (1985)
Producer: David Hare   Written by: David Hare, Howard Brenton
As Lambert Le Roux.

King Lear at the National (1986)
Producer: David Hare   Written by: William Shakespeare
As Lear.

Antony and Cleopatra at the National (1987)
Producer: Peter Hall   Written by: William Shakespeare
As Antony

M. Butterfly at the Company London Ltd/Shaftesbury (1989)
Producer: John Dexter   Written by: David Henry Hwang
As Rene Gallimard.

August at Theatre Clwyd (1994)
Producer: Anthony Hopkins.   Written by: Julian Mitchell, from a
                                translation of Chekhov's *Uncle Vanya*
                                by Tania Alexander
As Ieuan Davies.

THE FILMS

Note: The titles listed below do not include Hopkins' participation in the drama shorts *Changes*, directed by Drew Henley and written by James Scott (c. 1956), and *The White Bus*, directed by Lindsay Anderson and written by Shelagh Delaney (1958).

A. H. denotes Anthony Hopkins and the role he played follows in brackets.

The Lion in Winter (Avco-Embassy, Great Britain, 1968)
Director: Anthony Harvey. Executive Producer: Joseph E. Levine. Producer: Martin Poll. Screenplay: James Goldman, based on his own play. With: Peter O'Toole, Katharine Hepburn, Jane Merrow, John Castle, Nigel Terry, A. H. (Prince Richard), Timothy Dalton, Nigel Stock, O. Z. Whitehead, Kenneth Ives, Kenneth Griffith, Henry Woolf, Karol Hagar and Mark Griffith.

The Looking Glass War (Columbia, Great Britain, 1969)
Director: Frank R. Pierson. Executive Producer: M. J. Frankovich. Producer: John Box. Screenplay: Frank R. Pierson, based on the novel by John le Carré. With: Christopher Jones, Ralph Richardson, Pia Degermark, Paul Rogers, A. H. (John Avery), Susan George and Ray McAnally.

Hamlet (Columbia/Woodfall, Great Britain, 1969)
Director: Tony Richardson. Producers: Leslie Linder and Martin Ransohoff. Screenplay: Tony Richardson's adaptation of the play by William Shakespeare. With: Nicol Williamson, Judy Parfitt, A. H. (Claudius), Marianne Faithfull, Mark Dignam, Gordon Jackson, Michael Pennington, Ben Aris, Clive Graham, Richard Everett and Roger Livesey.

When Eight Bells Toll (Rank, Great Britain, 1971)
Director: Etienne Périer. Producer: Elliott Kastner. Screenplay: Alistair MacLean, based on his own novel. With: A. H. (Philip Calvert), Robert Morley, Nathalie Delon, Jack Hawkins, Corin Redgrave, Derek Bond, Ferdy Mayne, Maurice Roeves, Leon Collins, Wendy Allnutt, Peter Arne, Oliver MacGreevy, Jon Croft, Tom Chatto, Charlie Stewart, Edward Burnham and Del Henney.

Young Winston (Columbia/Open Road, Great Britain, 1972)
Director: Richard Attenborough. Producer: Carl Foreman. Screenplay: Carl Foreman, based on the book *My Early Days* by Winston S. Churchill. With: Simon Ward, Anne Bancroft, Ian Holm, Jack Hawkins, Edward Woodward, A. H. (David Lloyd George), John Mills, Peter Cellier, Ronald Hines, Dino Shafeek, Raymond Huntley, Russell Lewis, Pat Heywood, Laurence Naismith, Willoughby Gray and Robert Hardy.

A Doll's House (MGM-EMI/Freeward, Great Britain, 1973)
Director: Patrick Garland. Producer: Hillard Elkins. Screenplay: Christopher Hampton, based on Ibsen's play. With: Claire Bloom, A. H. (Torvald), Ralph Richardson, Denholm Elliott, Anna Massey, Edith Evans and Helen Blatch.

The Girl from Petrovka (Universal, USA, 1974)
Director: Robert Ellis Miller. Producers: Richard D. Zanuck and David Brown. Screenplay: Allan Scott and Chris Bryant, based on the book by George Feifer. With: Goldie Hawn, Hal Holbrook, A. H. (Kostya),

Gregoire Aslan, Anton Dolin, Bruno Wintzell, Zoran Andric and Hanna Hertelendy.

Juggernaut (United Artists, USA, 1974)
Director: Richard Lester. Executive Producer: David V. Picker. Producer: Richard De Koker (Richard Alan Simmons). Screenplay: Richard De Koker. With: Richard Harris, Omar Sharif, David Hemmings, A. H. (Supt John McCleod), Ian Holm, Shirley Knight, Roy Kinnear, Roshan Seth, Cyril Cusack, Freddie Jones, Kristine Howarth, Clifton James, Mark Burns, Gareth Thomas, Andrew Bradford, Richard Moore and Jack Watson.

All Creatures Great and Small (EMI, Great Britain, 1974)
Director: Claude Whatham. Executive Producer: Ronald Gilbert. Producers: David Susskind and Duane Bogie. Screenplay: Hugh Whitemore, based on the books *If Only They Could Talk* and *It Shouldn't Happen to a Vet* by James Herriot. With: A. H. (Siegfried Farnon), Simon Ward, Lisa Harrow, Brian Stirner, Freddie Jones, T. P. McKenna, Brenda Bruce, John Collin, Christine Buckley, Jane Collins, Fred Feast, Glynne Geldart, Harold Goodwin and Doreen Mantle.

A Bridge Too Far (United Artists, Great Britain, 1977)
Director: Richard Attenborough. Producers: Joseph E. Levine and Richard P. Levine. Co-Producer: Michael Stanley-Evans. Screenplay: William Goldman, based on the book by Cornelius Ryan. With: Dirk Bogarde, James Caan, Michael Caine, Sean Connery, Edward Fox, Elliott Gould, Gene Hackman, A. H. (Lt-Col John Frost), Hardy Kruger, Laurence Olivier, Ryan O'Neal, Robert Redford, Maximilian Schell, Liv Ullmann, Arthur Hill, Wolfgang Preiss, Siem Vroom, Marlies Van Alcmaer, Eric Van't Wout, Mary Smithuysen, Hans Croiset, Nicholas Campbell, Christopher Good, Keith Drinkel, Peter Faber, Hans von Borsody, Josephine Peeper, Paul Maxwell, Walter Kohut, Hartmut Becker, Frank Grimes, Jeremy Kemp, Donald Pickering, Donald Douglas, Peter Settelen, Stephen Moore, Michael Byrne, Paul Copley,

Gerald Sim, Harry Ditson, Erik Chitty, Brian Hawksley, Colin Farrell, Norman Gregory, Alun Armstrong, Anthony Milner, Barry McCarthy, Lex Van Delden, Michael Wolf, Sean Mathias, Tim Beekman, Edward Seckerson, Tom Van Beek, Bertus Botterman, Henny Alma, Ray Jewers, Geoffrey Hinsliff and Fred Williams.

Audrey Rose (United Artists, USA, 1977)
Director: Robert Wise. Producers: Joe Wizan and Frank De Felitta.
Screenplay: Frank De Felitta, based on his own novel. With: Marsha Mason, A. H. (Elliot Hooper), John Beck, Susan Swift, Norman Lloyd, John Hillerman, Robert Walden, Aly Wassil, Mary Jackson, Richard Lawson, Tony Brande, Elizabeth Farley and Ruth Manning.

International Velvet (CIC/MGM, Great Britain, 1978)
Director: Bryan Forbes. Producer: Bryan Forbes. Screenplay: Bryan Forbes, suggested by the novel *National Velvet* by Enid Bagnold. With: Tatum O'Neal, Christopher Plummer, A. H. (Capt. Johnny Johnson), Nanette Newman, Peter Barkworth, Dinsdale Landen, Sarah Bullen, Jeffrey Byron, Richard Warwick, Daniel Abineri, Jason White, Martin Neil, Douglas Reith, Dennis Blanch, Norman Woodland and James Smilie.

Magic (Twentieth Century-Fox, USA, 1978)
Director: Richard Attenborough. Executive Producer: C. O. Erickson. Producers: Joseph E. Levine and Richard P. Levine. Screenplay: William Goldman, based on his novel. With: A. H. (Corky Withers), Ann-Margret, Burgess Meredith, Ed Lauter, E. J. Andre, Jerry Houser, David Ogden Stiers, Lillian Randolph, Joe Lowry, Beverly Sanders, I. W. Klein, Stephen Hart, Patrick McCullough, Bob Hackman, Mary Munday, Scott Garrett, Brad Beesley and Michael Harte.

The Elephant Man (Columbia-EMI-Warner, USA, 1980)
Director: David Lynch. Executive Producer: Stuart Cornfield. Producer: Jonathan Sanger. Screenplay: Christopher De Vore and Eric Bergren and

David Lynch, based on *The Elephant Man and Other Reminiscences* by Sir Frederick Treves and *The Elephant Man: A Study in Human Dignity* by Ashley Montagu. With: A. H. (Frederick Treves), John Hurt, Anne Bancroft, John Gielgud, Wendy Hiller, Freddie Jones, Michael Elphick, Hannah Gordon, Helen Ryan, John Standing, Dexter Fletcher, Lesley Dunlop and Phoebe Nicholls.

A Change of Seasons (Columbia-EMI-Warner, USA, 1980)
Director: Richard Lang. Executive Producer: Richard R. St Johns. Producer: Martin Ransohoff. Screenplay: Erich Segal, Ronni Kern and Fred Segal, from a story by Erich Segal and Martin Ransohoff. With: A. H. (Adam Evans), Shirley MacLaine, Bo Derek, Michael Brandon, Mary Beth Hurt, Ed Winter, Paul Regina and K. Callan.

The Bounty (Columbia-EMI-Warner, Great Britain, 1984)
Director: Roger Donaldson. Producer: Bernard Williams. Screenplay: Roger Bolt, based on the book *Captain Bligh and Mr Christian* by Richard Hough. With: A. H. (Bligh), Mel Gibson, Laurence Olivier, Edward Fox, Daniel Day-Lewis, Bernard Hill, Philip Davis, Liam Neeson, Wi Kuki Kaa, Tevaite Vernette, Philip Martin Brown, Simon Chandler, Malcolm Terris, Simon Adams, John Sessions, Andrew Wilde, Neil Morrissey, Richard Graham, Dexter Fletcher, Pete Lee-Wilson, Jon Gadsby, Brendan Conroy, Barry Dransfield, Steve Fletcher, Jack May, Mary Kauila, Sharon Bower and Tavana.

The Good Father (Mainline/Film Four, Great Britain, 1986)
Director: Mike Newell. Producer: Ann Scott. Screenplay: Christopher Hampton, based on the novel by Peter Prince. With: A. H. (Bill Hooper), Jim Broadbent, Harriet Walter, Frances Viner, Simon Callow, Miriam Margolyes, Joanne Whalley, Michael Byrne, Jennie Stoller, Johanna Kirby, Stephen Fry, Clifford Rose, Harry Grubb, Tom Jamieson and Chris Bradshaw.

84 Charing Cross Road (Columbia-EMI-Warner, Great Britain, 1986)
Director: David Jones. Producer: Geoffrey Helman. Screenplay: Hugh
Whitemore, based on *Q's Legacy* by Helene Hanff. With: Anne Bancroft,
A. H. (Frank Doel), Judi Dench, Maurice Denham, Eleanor David,
Wendy Morgan, Ian McNeice, Jean De Bear, J. Smith-Cameron, Tom
Isbell, Anne Dyson and Connie Booth.

The Dawning (Enterprize, Great Britain, 1988)
Director: Robert Knights. Executive Producer: Graham Benson.
Producer: Sarah Lawson. Screenplay: Moira Williams, based on *The Old
Jest* by Jennifer Johnston. With: A. H. (Major Angus 'Cassius' Barry),
Rebecca Pidgeon, Jean Simmons, Trevor Howard, Tara MacGowran,
Hugh Grant, Ronnie Masterson, John Rogan, Joan O'Hara, Charmian
May, Ann Way, Mark O'Regan, Brendan Laird, Adrian Dunbar and
Geoffrey Greenhill.

A Chorus of Disapproval (Hobo/Curzon, Great Britain, 1989)
Director: Michael Winner. Executive Producer: Elliott Kastner and
Andre Blay. Producer: Michael Winner. Screenplay: Alan Ayckbourn
and Michael Winner, from the play by Alan Ayckbourn. With: A. H.
(Dafydd Ap Llewellyn), Jeremy Irons, Prunella Scales, Jenny Seagrove,
Gareth Hunt, Richard Briers, Barbara Ferris, Patsy Kensit, Lionel
Jeffries and Sylvia Sims.

Desperate Hours (Twentieth Century-Fox, USA, 1991)
Director: Michael Cimino. Producers: Dino De Laurentiis and Michael
Cimino. Screenplay: Lawrence Conner, Mark Rosenthal and Joseph
Hayes, based on the stage play by Joseph Hayes. With: Mickey Rourke,
A. H. (Tim Cornell), Mimi Rogers, Lindsay Crouse, Kelly Lynch, Elias
Koteas, Shawnee Smith, Danny Gerald, Gerry Bamman and Matt
McGrath.

The Silence of the Lambs (Orion, USA, 1991)
Director: Jonathan Demme, Executive Producer: Gary Goetzman.
Producers: Edward Saxon, Kenneth Utt, and Ron Bozman. Screenplay:
Ted Tally, based on the novel by Thomas Harris. With: A. H. (Hannibal
Lecter), Jodie Foster, Scott Glenn, Ted Levine, Anthony Heald,
Lawrence A. Bonney, Kasi Lemmons, Lawrence T. Wrentz, Frankie
Faison, Don Brockett, Frank Seals Jr, Stuart Rudin, Masha
Skorobogatov, Jeffrie Lane, Leib Lensky, Red Schwartz, Jim Roche,
Brooke Smith, James B. Howard, Bill Miller, Chuck Aber, Gene Borkan,
Pat McNamara, Tracey Walter, Kenneth Utt, Dan Butler and Paul
Lazar.

Spotswood (Meridian, Australia, 1991)
Director: Mark Joffe. Producers: Timothy White and Richard Brennan.
Screenplay: Max Dann and Andrew Knight. With: A. H. (Errol Wallace),
Angela Punch McGregor, Alwyn Kurtz, Bruno Lawrence, John Walton,
Rebecca Rigg, Toni Collette, Russell Crowe, Dan Wyllie and John Flaus.

Freejack (Warner Brothers/Morgan Creek, USA, 1992)
Director: Geoff Murphy. Executive Producers: James G. Robinson,
David Nicksay and Gary Barber. Producers: Ronald Shusett and Stuart
Oken. Screenplay: Steven Pressfield, Ronald Shusett and Dan Gilroy;
story by Steven Pressfield and Ronald Shusett, based on the novel
Immortality Inc by Robert Sheckley. With: Emilio Estevez, A. H.
(McCandless), Mick Jagger, Rene Russo, Jonathan Banks, David
Johansen and Amanda Plummer.

Howards End (Mayfair Entertainment, Great Britain, 1992)
Director: James Ivory. Executive Producer: Paul Bradley. Producer:
Ismail Merchant. Screenplay: Ruth Prawer Jhabvala, based on the novel
by E. M. Forster. With: A. H. (Henry Wilcox), Vanessa Redgrave,
Helena Bonham Carter, Emma Thompson, James Wilby, Samuel West,
Prunella Scales, Joseph Bennett, Adrian Ross Magenty and Jo Kendall.

Dracula (Columbia/Zoetrope-Osiris, USA, 1992)
Director: Francis Ford Coppola. Executive Producers: Michael Apted and Robert O'Connor. Producers: Francis Ford Coppola, Fred Fuchs and Charles Mulvehill. Screenplay: James V. Hart. With: Gary Oldman, A. H. (Van Helsing), Winona Ryder, Richard E. Grant, Keanu Reeves, Sadie Frost, Cary Elwes, Bill Campbell, Tom Waits, Monica Bellucci, Michaela Bercu, Florina Kendrick, Jay Robinson, I. M. Hobson, Laurie Franks, Maud Winchester, Octavian Cadia, Robert Getz, Dagmar Stanec, Eniko Oss, Nancy Linehan Charles and Tatiana von Furstenberg.

Chaplin (Carolco, USA, 1993)
Director: Richard Attenborough. Producers: Richard Attenborough and Mario Kassar. Screenplay: William Boyd, William Goldman and Bryan Forbes, based on *My Autobiography* by Charles Chaplin and *Chaplin: His Life and Art* by David Robinson. With: Robert Downey Jr, Geraldine Chaplin, Paul Rhys, Dan Aykroyd, Marisa Tomei, Penelope Ann Miller, Kevin Kline, Diane Lane, Kevin Dunn, Nancy Travis, Moira Kelly, John Thaw and A. H. (George Hayden/Narrator).

The Innocent (World Films, Great Britain, 1993)
Director: John Schlesinger. Producers: Norma Heyman, Chris Sievernich and Wieland Schulz-Kiel. Screenplay: Ian McEwan, based on his novel. With: A. H. (Glass), Isabella Rossellini and Campbell Scott.

The Trial (BBC Films, Great Britain, 1993)
Director: David Jones. Executive Producers: Kobi Jaeger and Renate Compostella and Mark Shivas. Producer: Louis Marks. Screenplay: Harold Pinter, based on the novel by Franz Kafka. With: A. H. (The Priest), Kyle MacLachlan, Jason Robards, Juliet Stevenson, Polly Walker and Alfred Molina.

Shadowlands (Savoy/Spelling/Price Entertainment, Great Britain, 1993)
Director: Richard Attenborough. Executive Producer: Terrence A.

Clegg. Producers: Richard Attenborough and Brian Eastman. Screenplay: William Nicholson, from his own play. With: A. H. (C. S. Lewis), Debra Winger, Edward Hardwicke, Michael Denison, John Wood, Joseph Mazzello, Andrew Hawkins, James Frain, Peter Firth, Matthew Delamere, Gerald Sim, Julian Firth, Karen Lewis and Robert Flemyng.

The Remains of the Day (Columbia, Great Britain, 1993)
Director: James Ivory. Executive Producers: Mike Nuhob, John Calley and Harold Pinter. Producer: Ismail Merchant. Screenplay: Ruth Prawer Jhabvala, from the novel by Kazuo Ishiguro. With: A. H. (Stevens), Emma Thompson, James Fox, Christopher Reeve, Peter Vaughan and Hugh Grant.

The Road to Welville (Beacon, Great Britain, 1995)
Director: Alan Parker. Producers: Alan Parker and Robert F. Colesberry. Screenplay: Alan Parker, from a novel by T. Coraghessan Boyle. With: A. H. (Kellogg), Bridget Fonda, Matthew Broderick, John Cusack, Dana Carvey, Michael Lerner, Colm Meaney, Lara Flynn Boyle, Traci Lind and Jacob Reynolds.

Legends of the Fall (Columbia TriStar, USA, 1995)
Director: Edward Zwick. Producers: Edward Zwick, Bill Witliff and Marshall Herskovitz. Screenplay: Susan Shilliday and Bill Witliff, from the novel by Jim Harrison. With: Brad Pitt, A. H. (Col William Ludlow), Aidan Quinn, Julia Ormond and Henry Thomas.

August (Granada/Majestic Distribution, Great Britain, 1995)
Director: Anthony Hopkins. Producers: June Wyndham Davies and Pippa Cross. Screenplay: Julian Mitchell. With: A. H. (Ieuan Davies), Kate Burton, Leslie Phillips, Gawn Grainger, Rhain Morgan and Hugh Lloyd.

Nixon (Illusion-Cinergi, USA, 1996)
Director: Oliver Stone. Producers: Clayton Townsend, Oliver Stone and Andrew G. Vajna. Screenplay: Stephen J Rivele, Christopher Wilkinson and Oliver Stone. With: A. H. (Richard Nixon), Joan Allen, Powers Booth, Ed Harris and James Woods.

Surviving Picasso (Warners, USA, 1996)
Director: James Ivory. Producers: Ismail Merchant and David L. Wolper. Screenplay: Ruth Prawer Jhabvala, based on *Picasso: Creator and Destroyer* by Arianna Stassinopoulos Huffington. With: A. H. (Picasso), Natascha McElhone, Julianne Moore, Joss Ackland and Peter Eyre.

The Edge (Twentieth Century-Fox, USA, 1997)
Director: Le Tamahori. Producer: Art Linson. Screenplay: David Mamet. With: A. H. (Charles Morse), Alec Baldwin, Elle Macpherson, Harold Perrineau and L. Q. Jones.

Amistad (UIP/Dreamworks-HBO, USA, 1998)
Director: Steven Spielberg. Producers: Steven Spielberg, Debbie Allen and Colin Wilson. Screenplay: David Franzoni. With: Morgan Freeman, Nigel Hawthorne, Djimon Hounsou, Matthew McConaughey and A. H. (John Quincy Adams)

The Mask of Zorro (TriStar/Amblin-Zorro, USA, 1998)
Director: Martin Campbell. Producers: Doug Claybourne and David Foster. Screenplay: John Eskow, Terry Rossio and Randall Johnson. With: A. H. (Zorro), Antonio Banderas, Catherine Zeta-Jones, Stuart Wilson and Matt Letscher.

Meet Joe Black (UIP/City Lights, USA, 1998)
Director: Martin Brest. Producer: Martin Brest. Screenplay: Ron Osborn, Jeff Reno, Kevin Wade and Bo Goldman. Based on works by Maxwell Anderson and Gladys Lehman. With: Brad Pitt, A. H. (William Parrish), Claire Forlani, Jake Weber and Marcia Gay Harden.

Instinct (Buena Vista/Touchstone-Spyglass, USA, 1999)
Director: Jon Turteltaub. Producers: Michael Taylor and Barbara Boyle. Screenplay: Gerald DiPego, based on the novel *Ishmael* by Daniel Quinn. With: A. H. (Ethan Powell), Cuba Gooding Jr, Donald Sutherland, Maura Tierney and George Dzundza.

Titus (Buena Vista/Clear Blue Sky, USA, 1999)
Director: Julie Taymor. Producers: Conchita Airoldi and Julie Taymor. Screenplay: Julie Taymor, based on William Shakespeare's *Titus Andronicus*. With A. H. (Titus), Jessica Lange, Alan Cumming, Harry Lennix, Laura Fraser and Colm Feore.

Mission Impossible 2 (UIP/Paramount, USA, 2000)
Director: John Woo. Producers: Terence Clegg, Tom Cruise and Paula Wagner. Screenplay: Robert Towne. With: Tom Cruise, Ving Rhames, Dougray Scott, Thandie Newton and A. H. (Chief of IMF).

The Grinch (UIP/Imagine, USA, 2000)
Director: Ron Howard. Producers: Ron Howard and Brian Grazer. Screenplay: Jeffrey Price and Peter S. Seaman, based on *How the Grinch Stole Christmas* by Dr Seuss. With: Jim Carrey (the Grinch), Jeffrey Tambor, Christine Baranski, Taylor Momsen and A. H. (Narrator).

Hannibal (UIP/De Laurentiis-Scott Free, USA, 2001)
Director: Ridley Scott. Producers: Ridley Scott, Dino De Laurentiis, Martha De Laurentiis. Screenplay: David Mamet and Steve Zaillian, based on the novel by Thomas Harris. With: A. H. (Hannibal Lecter), Julianne Moore, Ray Liotta, Gary Oldman and Giancarlo Giannini.

Hearts in Atlantis (Warner/Castle Rock, USA, 2002)
Director: Scott Hicks. Producer: Kerry Heysen. Screenplay: William Goldman, based on the short story by Stephen King. With: A. H. (Ted Brautigan), Anton Yelchin, Hope Davis, Mika Boorem and David Morse.

The Devil and Daniel Webster (*Unreleased, USA, 2001/2)
Director: Alec Baldwin. Producers: Alec Baldwin, Jonathan Cornick, David Glasserm and Adam Stone. Screenplay: Pete Dexter, Bill Condon and Nancy Cassara, from the story by Stephen Vincent Benet, and the play *Scratch* by Archibald MacLeish. With: A. H. (Daniel Webster), Alec Baldwin, Jennifer Love Hewitt, Dan Aykroyd and Kim Cattrall.

Bad Company (Buena Vista/Touchstone-Jerry Bruckheimer, USA, 2002)
Director: Joel Schumacher. Producers: Jerry Bruckheimer and Mike Stenson. Screenplay: Jason Richman and Michael Browning. With: A. H. (Gaylord Oakes), Chris Rock, Gabriel Macht, Peter Stormare and Matthew Marsh.

Red Dragon (UIP/De Laurentiis-MGM-Mikona, USA, 2002)
Director: Brett Ratner. Producers: Dino De Laurentiis and Martha De Laurentiis. Screenplay: Ted Tally, based on the novel by Thomas Harris. With: A. H. (Hannibal Lecter), Edward Norton, Ralph Fiennes, Emily Watson and Harvey Keitel.

The Human Stain (Buena Vista/Miramax-Lakeshore-Stone Village, USA, 2003)
Director: Robert Benton. Producers: Gary Lucchesi, Tom Rosenberg and Scott Steindorff. Screenplay: Nicholas Meyer, based on the novel by Philip Roth. With: A. H. (Coleman Silk), Nicole Kidman, Ed Harris, Gary Sinese and Wentworth Miller.

Alexander (Warner/Intermedia-Pacifica, USA, 2004)
Director: Oliver Stone. Producers: Moritz Borman, Jon Kilik, Thomas Schuhly and Iain Smith and Oliver Stone. Screenplay: Christopher Kyle and Oliver Stone. With: Colin Farrell, Val Kilmer, Angelina Jolie, A. H. (Ptolemy), Jared Leto and Rosario Dawson.

Proof (Miramax/Hart-Sharp, USA, 2005)
Director: John Madden. Producers: John Hart, Jeff Sharp and Robert

Kessell. Screenplay: David Auburn and Rebecca Miller, from Auburn's play. With: Gwyneth Paltrow, A. H. (Robert), Hope Davis and Jake Gyllenhaal.

The World's Fastest Indian (Three Dogs and a Pony/WFI/, OLC Rights, USA, 2005)
Director: Roger Donaldson. Producers: Gary Hannam, David Gribble. Screenplay: Roger Donaldson. With: A. H. (Burt Munro), Bruce Greenwood, Diane Ladd, Lana Antonova, Juliana Bellinger, Chris Bruno, Jessica Cauffiel and Max Payne

All the King's Men (AKM-Sony Pictures Entertainment, USA, 2005)
Director: Steve Zaillian. Producers: Mike Medavoy, Arnold Messer, Pawel Edelman. Screenplay: Steve Zaillian, based on the novel by Robert Penn Warren. With: Sean Penn, James Gandolfini, Jude Law, A. H. (Judge Irwin), Mark Ruffalo, Kate Winslet, Glenn Morshower, Arden James, Bruce Heinrich, Kathy Baker and Patricia Clarkson.

TELEVISION PERFORMANCES

A. H. dentoes Anthony Hopkins

The Three Sisters BBC, 1969. Producer-director: Cedric Messina. Screenplay: Anton Chekhov (adapted by Moura Budberg). Cast: Janet Suzman (Masha), Michele Dotrice (Irina), Eileen Atkins (Olga), A. H. (Andrei), Michael Bryant (Vershinin), Joss Ackland (Chebutikin).

Danton BBC, 1970. Producer: Mark Shivas. Director: John Davies. Screenplay: Arden Winch. Cast: A. H. (Danton), Alan Dobie (Robespierre), Tenniel Evans (General Westermann), Terry Scully (Fabre D'Eglantine), David Andrews (St Just).

The Great Inimitable Mr Dickens BBC, 1970. Producer-director: Ned Sherrin. Screenplay: Ned Sherrin, Caryl Brahms. Cast: A. H. (Dickens), Sybil Thorndike, Freddie Jones, Arthur Lowe, Patrick Cargill, Jenny Agutter.

Hearts and Flowers BBC, 1970. Producer: Irene Shubik. Director: Christopher Morahan. Screenplay: Peter Nichols. Cast: A. H. (Bob), Donald Churchill, Priscilla Morgan, Colin Cunningham, Constance Chapman.

Uncle Vanya BBC, 1970. Producer: Cedric Messina. Director: Christopher Morahan. Screenplay: Anton Chekhov. Cast: Freddie Jones (Vanya), A. H. (Astrov), Ann Bell (Elena), Roland Culver (Serenriakov).

Decision to Burn Yorkshire TV, 1971. Producer: Peter Willes. Director: Marc Miller. Screenplay: Kevin Laffan. Cast: Helen Cherry, Gerald Sim, A. H., Patricia Brake, John Welsh.

Poet Game BBC, 1972. Producer: Mark Shivas. Director: Silvio Narizzano. Screenplay: Anthony Terpiloff. Cast: A. H. (Hugh Saunders), Billie Whitelaw (Jeanne Saunders), Susan Clark (Diana Howard), Cyril Cusack (Dr Saunders).

War and Peace BBC, 1972. Producer: David Conroy. Director: John Davies. Screenplay: Jack Pulman, from Tolstoy's novel. Cast: Morag Hood (Natasha), Alan Dobie (Prince Andrei), A. H. (Pierre Bezuhov), David Swift (Napoleon), Faith Brook (Countess Rostova), Frank Middlemass (Marshal Kutuzov), Rupert Davies (Count Rostov), Neil Stacy.

The Edwardians (Lloyd George) BBC, 1972. Producer: Mark Shivas. Director: John Davies. Screenplay: Keith Dewhurst. Cast: A. H. (Lloyd George), Annette Crosbie (Mrs Lloyd George), Joanna David, Thorley Walters.

QB VII Columbia TV, 1974. Producer: Douglas Kramer. Director: Tom Gries. Screenplay: Edward Anhalt, from Leon Uris' novel. Cast: Ben Gazzara (Cady), A. H. (Kelno), Juliet Mills (Samantha), Lee Remick (Lady Margaret), Leslie Caron (Lady Kelno), Edith Evans (Dr Parmentier), John Gielgud (Clinton-Meek), Jack Hawkins (Hon. Mr Justice Gilray).

The Childhood Friend BBC, 1974. Producer: Graeme Macdonald. Director: Mick Newell. Screenplay: Piers Paul Read. Cast: A. H.

(Alexander Tashkov), Susan Fleetwood (Janet Morton), George Pravda (Nikolay Tashkov), Alison Key (Alison Tashkov).

Find Me BBC, 1974. Director: Don Taylor. Screenplay: David Mercer. Cast: A. H. (Marek), Sheila Allen (Olivia), David Collings (Stanton), Charlotte Cornwell (Catherine), Stephen Moore (TV Producer).

Possessions Granada, 1974. Producer: James Brabazon. Director: John Irvin. Screenplay: George Ewart Evans (adapted by Elaine Morgan). Cast: A. H. (Dando), Rhoda Lewis (Caffie), Christopher Jones (Tom), Terry Lock (Willie), David Holland (Gomer).

The Arcata Promise Yorkshire TV, 1974. Director: David Cunliffe. Screenplay: David Mercer. Cast: A. H. (Theo Gunge), Kate Nelligan (Laura), John Fraser (Tony).

Dark Victory NBC/Universal, 1976. Producer: Jules Irving. Director: Robert Butler. Screenplay: M. Charles Cohen. Cast: Elizabeth Montgomery, A. H. (Michael), Michele Lee, Herbert Berghof, Michael Lerner, Vic Tayback.

The Lindbergh Kidnapping Case NBC/Columbia, 1976. Producer: Leonard Horn. Director: Buzz Kulik. Screenplay: J. P. Miller. Cast: Cliff De Young (Lindbergh), A. H. (Bruno Hauptmann), Sian Barbara Allen (Ann Morrow Lindbergh), Joseph Cotton (Dr John F. Condon), Walter Pidgeon (Judge Trenchard), David Spielberg (David Wilentz).

Victory at Entebbe ABC/David Wolper, 1976. Producer: Robert Guenette. Director: Marvin J. Chomsky. Screenplay: Ernest Kinoy. Cast: A. H. (Rabin), Burt Lancaster (Peres), Julius Harris (Idi Amin), Elizabeth Taylor (Edra Vilnovsky), Richard Dreyfuss (Col. Netanyahu), Kirk Douglas (Hershel Vilnovsky), Helmut Berger (German Hijacker).

Kean BBC, 1978. Producer: David Jones. Director: James Cellan Jones. Screenplay: Jean-Paul Sartre. Cast: A. H. (Kean), Robert Stephens (Prince of Wales), Sara Kestelman (Elena, Countess of Koefeld), Julian Fellowes (Lord Neville), Cherie Lunghi (Anna Danby).

Mayflower: The Pilgrims' Adventure CBS, 1980. Producer: Linda Yellen. Director: George Shaefer. Screenplay: James Lee Barrett. Cast: A. H. (Capt. Jones), Richard Crenna (Rev. William Brewster), Jenny Agutter (Priscilla), David Dukes (Miles Standish), Michael Beck (John Alden).

The Bunker CBS/Time-Life/SFP/Antenne 2, 1980. Producer-director: George Shaefer. Screenplay: John Gay. Cast: A. H. (Hitler), Richard Jordan (Speer), Cliff Gorman (Goebbels), Piper Laurie (Magda Goebbels), Susie Blakely (Eva Braun), Michel Lonsdale (Bormann), Martin Jarvis (Hentschel), Michael Kitchen (Misch).

Peter and Paul MCA, 1981. Producer: Stan Hough. Director: Robert Day. Screenplay: Christopher Knopf. Cast: Robert Foxworth (Peter the Fisherman), A. H. (Paul of Tarsus), Raymond Burr (Herod Agrippa), Eddie Albert (Festus), Jean Peters (Priscilla), Julian Fellowes (Nero), Herbert Lom (Barnabas).

Othello BBC, 1981. Producer: Cedric Messina. Director: Jonathan Miller. Screenplay: Shakespeare. Cast: A. H. (Othello), Bob Hoskins (Iago), Penelope Wilton (Desdemona), Rosemary Leach (Emilia), David Yelland (Cassio), Anthony Pedley (Roderigo), Geoffrey Chater (Brabantio).

Little Eyolf BBC, 1982. Producer; Louis Marks. Director: Michael Darlow. Screenplay: Henrik Ibsen (trans. Michael Meyer). Cast: Diana Rigg (Rita Allmers), A. H. (Alfred Allmers), Peggy Ashcroft (the Rat Wife), Emma Piper (Asta), Charles Dance (Borghejm), Timothy Stark (Eyolf).

The Hunchback of Notre Dame CBS/Columbia, 1982. Producer: Norman Rosemont. Director: Michael Tuchner. Screenplay: John Gay, from Victor Hugo's novel. Cast: A. H. (Quasimodo), Lesley-Anne Down (Esmerelda), John Gielgud (Charmolue), Robert Powell (Phoebus), David Suchet (Trouillefou), Derek Jacobi (Dom Claude Frollo).

A Married Man LWT for C4, 1983. Producer: John Davies. Director: Charles Jarrott. Screenplay: Derek Marlowe, from Piers Paul Read's novel. Cast: A. H. (John Strickland), Ciaran Madden (Clare), Lise Hilboldt (Paula), Tracey Childs (Jilly Mascall), John Le Mesurier (Eustace Clough).

Strangers and Brothers BBC, 1984. Producer: Philip Hinchcliffe.
Director: Ronald Wilson. Screenplay: Julian Bond (from the novels by C. P. Snow). Cast: A. H. (Roger Quaife), Shaughan Seymour (Lewis Eliot), Cherie Lunghi (Margaret Eliot), Edward Hardwicke (Sir Hector Rose), John Normington (Monty Cave).

Arch of Triumph CBS/HTV, 1985. Producer: John Newland, Mort Abrahamson, Peter Graham Scott. Director: Waris Hussein. Screenplay: Charles Israel. Cast: A. H. (Dr Ravic), Lesley-Anne Down (Joan), Donald Pleasence (Haake), Frank Finlay (Boris), Richard Pasco (Veber), Joyce Blair (Rolande).

Mussolini: The Decline and the Fall of II Duce (a.k.a. *Mussolini and I*) HBO/RAI/Antenne 2/Beta, 1985. Producer: Mario Gallo. Director: Alberto Negrin. Screenplay: Nicola Badalucco. Cast: Susan Sarandon (Edda), A. H. (Count Ciano), Bob Hoskins (Mussolini), Annie Girardot, Barbara De Rossi.

Hollywood Wives ABC/Warner's, 1985. Producer: Aaron Spelling.
Director: Robert Day. Screenplay: Robert L. McCullough, from Jackie Collins' novel. Cast: Candice Bergen (Elaine Conti), Angie Dickinson (Sadie La Salle), A. H. (Neil Gray), Stefanie Powers (Montana Gray),

Joanna Cassidy (Maralee), Rod Steiger (Oliver Easterne), Steve Forrest (Ross Conti), Suzanne Somers (Gina Germaine).

Guilty Conscience CBS, 1985. Producer: Robert Papazian, Richard Levinson, William Link. Director: David Greene. Screenplay: Levinson, Link. Cast: A. H. (Arthur Jamison), Blythe Danner (Louise Jamison), Swoosie Kurtz (Jackie Wills), Wiley Harker (Older Man), Ruth Manning (Older Woman).

Blunt BBC, 1985. Producer: Martin Thompson. Director: John Glenister. Screenplay: Robin Chapman. Cast: A. H. (Guy Burgess), Ian Richardson (Anthony Blunt), Michael Williams (Goronwy Rees), Rosie Kerslake (Margie Rees), Geoffrey Chater (Guy Liddell).

Across the Lake BBC/Challenger, 1988. Producer: Innes Lloyd. Director: Tony Maylam. Screenplay: Roger Milner. Cast: A. H. (Donald Campbell), Ewan Hooper (Leo Villa), Angela Richards (Tonia Bern), Phyllis Calvert (Lady Campbell), Julia Watson (Sarah Williamson), Rosemary Leach (Connie Robinson), Peter Harlowe (Benson), Dexter Fletcher (Jimmy).

The Tenth Man CBS /Norman Rosemont-William Self, 1989. Producers: David Rosemont, William Hill. Director: Jack Gold. Screenplay: Lee Langley, from Graham Greene's novella. Cast: A. H. (Chavel), Kristin Scott Thomas (Therese), Derek Jacobi (the Imposter), Cyril Cusack (the Priest), Brenda Bruce (Therese's Mother), Timothy Watson (the Victim).

Heartland BBC Wales, 1989. Producer: Christine Benson. Director: Kevin Billington. Screenplay: Steve Gough. Cast: A. H. (Jack), Lynn Farleigh (Rachel), Mark Lewis Jones (Ieuan), Martin Glyn Murray (Glyn).

Great Expectations Disney/HTV-Primetime, 1989. Producer: Greg

Smith. Director: Kevin Connor. Screenplay: John Goldsmith, from Dickens' novel. Cast: Jean Simmons (Miss Havisham), A. H. (Magwitch), Anthony Calf (Pip), Ray McAnally (Jaggers), Kim Thomson (Estella), Johy Rhys Davies (Joe Gargery).

One Man's War HBO/TVS/Skreba Films, 1990. Producer: Ann Skinner. Director: Sergio Toledo. Screenplay: Mike Carter and Sergio Toledo. Cast: A. H. (Joel), Norma Aleandro (Nidia), Fernanda Torres (Dolly), Leonardo Garcia (Joelito), Reuben Blades (Perrone).

To Be the Best RPTA-Primetime/Robert Bradford-Gemmy Productions, 1991. Producer: Aida Young. Director: Tony Wharmby. Screenplay: Elliot Baker, based on the novel by Barbara Taylor Bradford. Cast: Lindsay Wagner (Paula O'Neill), A. H. (Jack Figg), Christopher Cazenove (Jonathan Ainsley), Stephanie Beacham (Arabell Sutton).

Selected Exits BBC Wales, 1993. Producer: Geraint Morris. Director: Tristram Powell. Screenplay: Alan Plater, based on Gwyn Thomas' autobiography. Cast: A. H. (Thomas), Abigail Harrison (Nana), Bernard Lloyd (Walt), Richard Lynch (Walt as a boy), Sue Roderick (Lyn), Robert Pugh (Gwyn's father).

INDEX